The Big Book
of Italian American
Culture

The Big Book of Italian American Culture

Edited by
Lawrence DiStasi

Formerly Titled *Dream Streets*

HarperPerennial
A Division of HarperCollins*Publishers*

THE BIG BOOK OF ITALIAN AMERICAN CULTURE. Copyright © 1989, 1990 by Lawrence DiStasi. All rights reserved. Printed in the United States of America. No part of this book may be used or reproduced in any manner whatsoever without written permission except in the case of brief quotations embodied in critical articles and reviews. For information address HarperCollins Publishers, 10 East 53rd Street, New York, NY 10022.

First HarperPerennial edition published 1990.

Editor: Lawrence DiStasi

Project Director: Bob Callahan

Art Direction and Design: John Sullivan, Dennis Gallagher/*Visual Strategies*, San Francisco

Production Management: Rugh Hagopian, Kina Sullivan

Research Editors: Rhona Klein, Judith Dunham, Susan Lombardo

Copy & Line Editors: Judith Dunham, Deborah Bruce, Karen K. Johnson

Permissions Editor: Mia DiStasi

Pages 249-251 constitute an extension of this copyright page.

The Library of Congress has catalogued the hardcover edition as follows:
   [1st ed]
Dream streets : the big book of Italian-American culture / [edited by]
   Lawrence DiStasi.
      p.   cm.
   ISBN 0-06-016030-6
   1. Italian Americans. I. DiStasi, Lawrence. 1937–
E184.I8D73   1989   89-46580
973′.0451—dc20

ISBN 0-06-091680-x (pbk.)
90 91 92 93 94 MPC 10 9 8 7 6 5 4 3 2 1

Contents

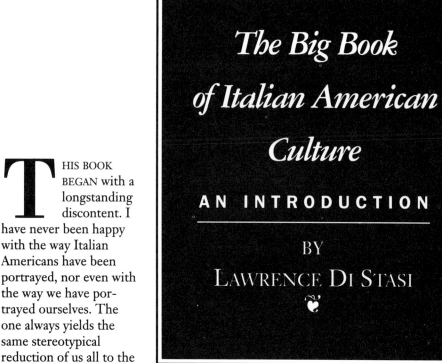

The Big Book of Italian American Culture

AN INTRODUCTION

BY
LAWRENCE DI STASI

THIS BOOK BEGAN with a longstanding discontent. I have never been happy with the way Italian Americans have been portrayed, nor even with the way we have portrayed ourselves. The one always yields the same stereotypical reduction of us all to the Italian trilogy: passion, pasta, and power. The other always yields the same anti-stereotypical reaction: the 'look-we-got-judges (or stockbrokers, surgeons, senators)-too' shuffle.

Both perspectives belittle. And that's why *Dream Streets* struck me as a fruitful title. The ideas dancing around and between those two polar words seemed to me capable of broadening, even popularizing the field on which Italian American culture can be played.

Consider the word "Dream". Of course it evokes the American Dream — basically the dream of material success. But in the case of Italians coming to America I think it points to something more, that something which John Dos Passos, in his eulogy for Carlo Tresca, put this way:

"A certain explosive and direct logic was inborn in the peoples of Latin speech, and they had never lost their early Christian faith in the millennium."

Faith in the millennium. Paradise on earth. A single human family. These mythic yearnings have never quite subsided on the Italian peninsula, and something like them, I think, was rekindled in those who took the awful step of leaving their home villages to come to America. Were it otherwise, were New York not, even as late as the 1930s, the mythic capital of the world to Italian peasants, many would not have come.

And "Streets." Aside from suggesting the bitter irony in the Italian immigrant's having to dig the very streets he expected to find paved with gold, the word recalls something even more central to Italian America. Urbanity. Urbanity not by chance, but by choice.

For though it is true that some Italian immigrants settled in farm areas, the overwhelming majority made straight for the big cities: New York, Boston, Philadelphia, Chicago. There they had relatives and there they could bask in the dense familiarity that reminded them of Italy — that urban Italy where for generations, even farm workers lived clustered in hill towns and walked daily to outlying fields to work. To live isolated on an individual plot of land, one had to be odd, or crazy, or one of the gentry — which to the peasants came to the same thing.

Urban dreamers, then. These are the people who people this book. Heroes who dream the millennial dream, but one tempered by several millennia of city dwelling.

That qualifier, I think, makes a big difference.

For if the American dream in its anglicized, protestant playing out tends to result in isolates, in heroes who move through institutions to win as much privacy as they can, then the same dream among Italian Americans tends toward something other. Something that does not undervalue its need for the other. That is to say, Italian American heroics — and that is what this book is about — tends towards individuals alright, as heroics must. But, within the Italian American community, this process tends towards some intensified, some "citified" form of individuality that seeks to turn *itself* into an "institution."

The concept of the individual as institution is William Irwin Thompson's, and in his essay on the subject Thompson uses Paolo Soleri, our opening hero, as his type case: the Catholic individual as institution.

THIS IS THE kind of person who may seem antisocial, even anarchic. He shuns institutions such as the uni-

2

versity or the corporation or the government, mistrusts them as impersonal, soul-devouring. Instead, where he can he creates his own institution—in Soleri's case, the Cosanti Foundation — out of the authority — *not* the power, which is institutional — of his own unique vision. This distinction between power and authority is crucial.

Here, for example, is Soleri on the difference: "You don't understand. I have no *power* over my students. They are free to come and go. I have only *authority*. If they come to me because of my authority, and then do not respect that authority, they have no reason for coming to study and work with me." Artists and visionaries always invoke such authority.

More concretely, Soleri as arcologist designs his structures to oppose, even de-structure all the trappings and effects of institutional power in America — automobiles, suburban sprawl, the cult of the unbridled individual which masks a deadly conformity. He sees the human future in cities — fantastic mega-cities which, through an astonishing implosion, crowd millions together into compressed space, thus leaving large natural areas open for everyone to enjoy. Soleri insists that such urban crowding, when it is intelligently designed, is "theological" rather than "pathological". By this he means that it responds to some divine order of evolution, rather than to the path of least resistance and most profit that characterizes consumerism and suburbia.

However right or wrong Paolo Soleri may prove architecturally, his vision of utopia in the city (where the American mythos usually sees only corruption) suggests something of that quality I have always missed in the standard Italian American portrait. The one I usually see as a naive, almost utopian faith in the American Dream.

This missing quality might better be understood as anti-institutionalism.

It's a big word; an ungainly word that, reduced to its simplest terms, might be taken to mean simply that the Italian in America spurns all but the one institution he has always been able to rely on: the family.

But I think it means more than that. I think it opens up the possibility that Italian Americans and their heroes may in fact be cut in the Soleri manner. This would mean that not only do they tend to act counter to institutions, but that at the same time, they tend toward weaving institutions around themselves, indeed, toward becoming institutions in themselves.

DiMaggio, for instance, with a batting stride like no one else's, becomes baseball personified;

as Sinatra, with a singing style like no one else's, becomes The Voice;

as Atlas becomes the perfect body;

and Bufano the archetypal sculptor,

and Toscanini the pure conductor,
Caruso the essence of opera,
Capra the filmer of the Dream,
Rodia the fantasy builder,
Valentino the idol, La Guardia the mayor, Vanzetti the anarchist, Durante the nose, Giannini the bank . . .

The roster, extendable, contains an amazing number of names which, by themselves alone, signify. And what they signify are those who create not so much institutions to exceed or supercede them, but rather intensely personal constructs to be consumed when the fire and authority of their own unique gift is itself consumed.

YET IN THE end all such theories must yield to the real concern of this book: people; those luminous or lucky or loony characters who, taken together, begin to form a people's map of Italian America. In this regard, I should also admit that I would like to have created a book of little heroes — those *gente di nessuno* whom Alessandro Manzoni tried to raise to the main stage of history. Alas, it was not possible. For in order to celebrate "nobody's people," one would have to find them first, and then write about them oneself, as they are seldom chronicled. This time, at least, there was not time.

THERE ARE SOME people I would like to single out for thanks. My father, for one, who gave me his name and his sense of the worth of being Italian that eventually led here. And Bob Callahan, without whose example and invitation to do so, I would doubtless never have thought to involve myself with such a book. And researcher Rhona Klein, without whose expertise in navigating library corners this book would still be looking for itself. And art directors Dennis Gallagher and John Sullivan, whose graphic touch gives to words a visual life they never knew they had. And editor and researcher Judith Dunham, whose informed prodding and encouragement helped refine nearly every page. And Craig Nelson, for knowing when, and when not to insert an editorial hand. And Augusto Troiani, whose personal materials about many characters herein helped rescue them from certain oblivion. And Andy Canepa's Italian Collection, Susan Lombardo's photo research, the production expertise of Kina Sullivan and Ruth Hagopian, and all the others I have no room to mention but whose contributions I have not forgotten.

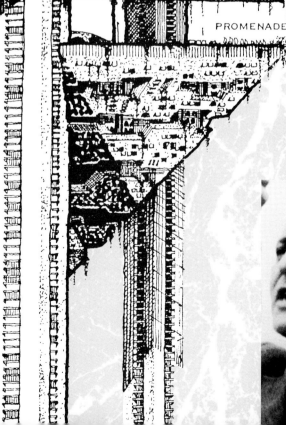

DENTIAL

PROMENADE

Cities on the Hill

THE ABBOT OF ARCOSANTI

by J. Tevere McFadyen

Although conjoined here, Christopher Columbus and Paolo Soleri are the alpha and the omega of Italian America, utopian dreamers both. Columbus, the alpha dreamer, dreamed himself West into lands of "natural Christians" so paradisal that on his third voyage he convinced himself (and tried to convince his world) that he had found the actual earthly paradise. Soleri is the omega dreamer, singing the ghost dance for the West's pathological suburban sprawl, dreaming the implosion and recivilizing of humans into new mega-cities where alone, according to him, humanity can evolve into totally free — which is for Soleri totally urban — beings.

▲ Paolo Soleri talks about arcology at Arcosanti.

AT THE CORNER of Scottsdale and Doubletree, in Scottsdale, Arizona, a small wooden sign says: Soleri. The sign points down a wide lane lined with imposing suburban homes, directing the devoted and the merely curious to a compound of low-slung, earth-colored buildings scarcely visible from the street.

The Soleri buildings are unlike anything else on Doubletree Road. They are cells enlarged on a microscope, a loosely connected chain of playful organic shapes, at once awkward and graceful. Dug into the earth to avoid the southwestern sun, full of unexpected passages and courtyards, they seem — in Frank Lloyd Wright's phrase — not to be on the land, but of it.

This place is Cosanti, an Italian coinage for "before things," and it attracts visitors because it contains the home and offices and much of the completed work of the Italian-born arcologist Paolo Soleri.

Soleri is probably the only contemporary architect better known for what he hasn't built than for what he has.

In thirty years of practice, only five of Soleri's projects have gone into construction. Of these the most important by far is still in its infancy. This project is Arcosanti, an experimental megastructure for five thousand in hesitant progress in the barren mesa country of central Arizona. Soleri contends that, by compressing the built environment into a single, highly efficient structure surrounded by open country, his future city will attempt to marry the cultural excitement of urban areas to the beauty of nature. For this Soleri has coined the term *arcology*, a synthesis of architecture and ecology applied to the creation of what he calls "the City in the Image of Man."

Scottsdale, where the architect has lived and worked for twenty-five years, is a

sprawling suburb — the antithesis of arcology. This is an irony not lost on Paolo Soleri, who sees suburbia as the symptom of a culture drowning in excess. Paradoxically, he first came to the United States as an apprentice to Frank Lloyd Wright, perhaps the epitome of the American suburban aesthetic. He then developed a design called Mesa City, a theoretical design for a community of two million. It was the first of the imaginary cities for which Soleri has become famous, and it led him to his principal thesis:

Suburban division, though perceived as liberating, actually enslaves people by depriving them of either the dynamism of an urban scene or the real complexity of nature.

In 1970 Soleri purchased 860 acres of high range seventy-five miles northwest of Phoenix, and there began Arcosanti, the first arcology.

"I call it an urban laboratory, because I want to distinguish it from an experiment," he cautions. "The experiment will be the end of the line. At the present time, we are building the laboratory in which we will conduct the experiment someday off in the future."

With less than 2 percent of the city completed, the end of the line at Arcosanti is a long way off; yet, over the past ten years, Soleri and his dedicated, if mostly transient and untrained, crew have confounded skeptics. Slowly, Arcosanti is coming to life in the deserts of the American Southwest. Not in the most efficient manner; not, perhaps, at a rate that will guarantee construction of the twenty-five-story main building within Soleri's lifetime; yet, incrementally, the arcologist's dream is becoming a reality.

Arcosanti is unsettling. The buildings are without precedent. They are also eerily beautiful. From across the mesa it is impossible to determine whether the tiny figures scrambling through the scaffolding are building a new civilization or excavating the remains of another, long lost and buried.

In fact Arcosanti is something of both. There is a pervasive sense that Arcosanti exists at the narrowing of the hourglass, in a sort of ebb tide between past and future.

When Soleri's first arcological sketches appeared, they were inevitably likened to fantastic space colonies. What the critics overlooked was the fact that these sketches were also incredibly reminiscent of the hill

PARK

RESIDENTIAL

PROM

MINNESOTA MORNING ODE

for Giordano Bruno

The City of the Sun is coming! I hear it! I smell it!
here, where they have made even the earth a jailer
where not even the shadows of animals sneak over the
    land
where children are injured & taught to apologize for
    their scars
the City of the Sun cannot be far now —

(that's what you said then, brother, waiting in prison
eight years to be burned, to find the sun at last
on the Campo dei Fiori — FIELD OF FLOWERS —
    yes)
how could it be far?
isn't evil at its peak?
(you asked 300 years ago) has not
the descent into matter reached a nadir? & here
5000 miles later, Northern Minnesota
a forest once, now wasteland
where they mow grass, rake leaves:

I vomit lies like the rest, not knowing
whom to trust, here where betrayal is taught as virtue
I weep alone for the words I would like to say
& silently put the faces of the old gods
into the hands of the children; hope they recognize them
here in this Christian place, where Christ the Magus
& Christ the Healer are both forgotten, where the veil
of the temple is rent, but no resurrection follows. . . .

THE CITY OF THE SUN comes soon, cannot be far
yes, you are right — what's a millennium
or two to us, brother? The gods can wait
they are strong, they rise — the golden tower
flashing the light of planets, the speaking statues
that guard its four gates, the holy wind
that carries the spirit of heaven down thru the stars

it is here! it is here!
I will build it
on this spot. I will build it at Attica
& Wounded Knee
on the Campo dei Fiori, at the Vatican:
the strong, bright light of flesh which is the link
the laughter, which transmutes

— DIANE DI PRIMA
Minnesota Home School
Sauk Centre

towns in Soleri's native Italy. There's also a strong temptation to compare the construction of Arcosanti with that of the great cathedrals — a comparison Soleri helps to invite with his theological reference. To Soleri, the city is more than mere habitat: it is a vital step, a necessary instrument in the spiritual evolution of life on Earth.

But Arcosanti has no Medicis, no great Land Lords, no Papal Coffers to serve as a building fund. The construction, at a cost of some $2 million to date, has been financed mostly from Soleri's pocket. Soleri, however, is not a wealthy man. A sizable chunk of his construction budget has been paid by student tuition. In five-week shifts from March through November, the students themselves are the body of the project's work force.

Soleri and Arcosanti are caught now at the tight waist of the hourglass, beset with opportunity from the burgeoning interest in urban problems, but harried by it too. If the project isn't pushed rapidly forward, it may not be fully built in time to prove itself. On the other hand, if Soleri moves too quickly he may undermine the real point of his work by completing a design which has not fully evolved.

For some reason none of this seems especially important at Arcosanti on an autumn afternoon when the late sun is still warm and work has ceased for the day. At dusk this is a stunning place. The rusts and umbers of the land contrast with the darkening blue sky, and the stream, lit by the last shafts of sun, reflects the whole scene virtually without distortion.

"I think that somehow we have to come up with something that gives us answers," he says with a certain urgency, "maybe not true answers, but at least hypothetical propositions that might eventually lead to true answers."

After a long moment Soleri speaks again. "I think we have time," he says, "though that doesn't mean we should relax. Yes, we have time," he grins. "I'm not an apocalyptic person." ❧

EARTHLY PARADISE

1498: SANTO DOMINGO

In the evening, beside the Ozama River, Christopher Columbus writes a letter. His body creaks with rheumatism, but his heart jumps for joy. The discoverer explains to Their Catholic Majesties *that which is plainly evident:*

Earthly Paradise is on the nipple of a woman's breast.

He realized it two months ago, when his caravels entered the Gulf of Paria. *There ships start rising gently toward the sky. . . .*Navigating upstream to where the air has no weight, Columbus has reached the farthest limit of the Orient. *In these, the world's most beautiful lands,* the men show cleverness, ingenuity, and valor, and the extremely beautiful women wear only their long hair and necklaces of many pearls wound around their bodies. The water, sweet and clear, awakens thirst. Winter does not punish nor summer burn, and the breeze caresses what it touches. The trees offer fresh shade and, within arm's reach, fruits of great delectability that arouse hunger.

But beyond *this greenness and this loveliness* no ship can go. This is the frontier of the Orient. Here waters, lands, and islands end. Very high and far away, the Tree of Life spreads its enormous crown and the source of the four sacred rivers bubbles up. One of them is the Orinoco, *which I doubt if such a great and deep river is known in the world.*

The world is not round. The world is a woman's tit. The nipple begins in the Gulf of Paria and rises to a point very close to the heavens. The tip, where the juices of Paradise flow, will never be reached by any man.

THE LANGUAGE OF PARADISE

The Guaraos, who live in the suburbs of the Earthly Paradise, call the rainbow *snake of necklaces* and the firmament overhead *sea*. Lightning is *glow of the rain*. One's friend, *my other heart*. The soul, *sun of the breast*. The owl, *lord of the dark night*. A walking cane is a *permanent grandson;* and for I forgive, they say *I forget*.

— Eduardo Galeano

FASANELLA REMEMBERS MARCANTONIO

by Patrick Watson

THIS IS RALPH FASANELLA talking.

"The point I'm trying to make is, great human leaders have this compassion for men. But strong guys like Rockefeller and these head men! And a lot of movement people — worried about causes, not worried about people. You've got to have that feeling. It's a kind of artistry. . . ."

In 1949 Ralph Fasanella discovered a leader who had that "artistry." The effect upon him was instant and electric. He gave his heart and energy to this politician, and on his death five years later felt heartbroken and deserted. The man was Vito Marcantonio, friend and protégé of Fiorello La Guardia. Marcantonio followed in La Guardia's footsteps, until, as the "Little Flower" became more conservative, Marcantonio moved further Left, finally heading the American Labor Party.

". . . AN UNBELIEVABLE MAN, Marc. When this man spoke at a rally, you should have had him taped. This man was a Beethoven when he spoke. Music! He'd have hundreds of people having orgasm; he could rip right into your belly. Kind of guy you run into once in a lifetime. He'd get you at a goddam meeting and spin you around in a way that when you walked out you went through the wringer.

"Like the painting I made of the church. Real symphony from Beethoven. Bring you right around. He had the turmoil and the anguish of the people. And he also had the intellectual depth. Tremendous intellect, but you'd never know it the way he spoke. 'Hey you! Come over here! Hey you! What number you takin'?' He knew everybody. Even the gangsters.

"When he died there were a couple of his pallbearers there, his bodyguards. Tough ghee turns to me and he says, 'You killed him!' And I says, 'You know it's not me!' Says, 'Yeah, I know it's not you personally, Ralph — but some of those other stupid Red bastards with their mechanistic approach to politics.' "

MARCANTONIO WAS A man of the Left, but was constantly at war with the doctrinaire people of the ALP. For Fasanella that was an additional source of appeal,

Vito Marcantonio was unique in American politics. An idealist who fought for such causes as Fair Labor Laws, Open Housing Laws, and repeal of the poll tax, he was also a formidable tactician who won support in his 20th Congressional District from such an unlikely coalition of Communists, Democrats, Republicans, and anarchists that he was amiably referred to as "the honorable Fritto Misto." Yet no matter how distant the cause he was fighting, he always spent Sunday afternoons in his East Harlem office — said to resemble nothing so much as a hospital clinic overflowing with neighborhood devotees seeking, and usually getting, his help.

▲
**Vito Marcantonio
in his East Harlem
congressional
district.**

11

matching as it did his own thinking. He had been at odds with the Left all the time he had been part of it. He had been opposed to the ALP merging with the CIO instead of remaining an independent force. In his view it had been the merger with the CIO, and the subsequent struggles, that had split the CIO and led to the destruction of the American Left. It had enabled the conservative faction of the CIO to gain strength and isolate the Left. Then it sat back and allowed the fear of Communism and the witch-hunting movement, in which anyone who admitted to being a Socialist was labeled Red, to have its own momentum. The present so-called Left is not authentic, says Fasanella.

"It's made up by the bourgeoisie. Has nothing to do with the real Left. The Left we came through was in the shops, in the streets, in the battle. Three, four, five million people. This was Marcantonio's Left. The Left now is made up of displaced middle-class people. They mean well but they don't represent the people. They represent their class. I'm not opposed to this but you don't get the guy in the shop this way, you don't stir him up.

"But let me go ahead with Marcantonio. His relationship with the ghees was unbelievable. All the gangsters in Harlem — and I'm talking about big guys, you know, big top guys — had tremendous respect for Marc. You know why? Integrity. He did battle for the people in the streets. He understood their crime, their aches and pains. They admired him because he was a bright guy. For the first time some fucking Italian could express politics. And these guys were sharp guys. These gangsters weren't stupid, you know. They knew politics. You don't get there if you don't have any idea how to beat the ball game. They liked Marc because you couldn't buy him. They all spoke of him as an honest man, and yet they were the biggest crooks you ever met in America!

"Well, I worked with Marc. We lost the campaign. He ran again as a congressman and they gave him the business, what do you call it? Gerrymandered Harlem all the way down, so he couldn't make it. I used to go along and watch him talk to ten, twelve people up in Harlem, on the side streets, ten Italian people. And Marc would get up on the corner and say, well, he'd talk about the Italians defending the rights of the Puerto Ricans and the Blacks. And he lost more votes every time he talked. Always took a principled position no matter where he was. I found out later his people used to say to him, 'Don't be so heavy on principle — don't you want to win the election?' Marc would say, not in so many words, he'd say, 'Go to hell!' And he always stated his position. Beautiful how he did it. He'd say how he remembers when his family came over and they were called guineas and greaseballs and all that shit, and he says, 'I don't like the words *spik* and *nigger* because my people took the same kind of beating and I don't buy that stuff.'

"Anyway, Marc lost the campaign, and I decided to move into his area and work with him. This was my type of politician. I had an identity with him — I'm an Italian. And I had tremendous admiration for his . . . tremendous historian, by the way, knew American history better than any guy. Unbelievable fucking guy! And I had no roots and I figured I'd go with Marc and anyway he died.

"Died of a heart attack in front of City Hall, fifty, fifty-four. I forget. Young man. A little younger than I am. And Jesus Christ he died . . . [he was] about the third person I ever cried for. A tremendous Wail for this man. Images that came into my mind. And I didn't know him all that well, either. But I was affected by him. Jesus Christ!" ❧

Mazzei in America

IN 1773, THE Virginia merchant Thomas Adams was giving an Italian friend a tour of the Virginia countryside, hoping to convince him to bring his ideas on agriculture to the colonies. They stopped to spend the night at the estate of one of Adams's friends.

The young master of the estate, Thomas Jefferson, was fascinated by the Italian. Lost in their discussion, they wandered the grounds for hours, and when they returned Adams said to Jefferson, "Well, I see that I've lost him to you."

It was true. The Italian had decided to buy land adjacent to Jefferson's, to which Jefferson added two thousand additional acres of his own, thereby acquiring both a new neighbor and a compatriot. And that is how

Philip Mazzei, farmer, businessman and pamphleteer, came to live in America.

It's easy to understand what made Mazzei so appealing to Jefferson. Thirteen years Jefferson's senior, Mazzei was well educated and widely traveled, an urbane and endlessly interesting sophisticate whose accomplishments did not stop him from leaving his business as a wine merchant in London to try his hand at agriculture in the Virginia countryside.

By contrast, Jefferson was barely out of his twenties, his personal experience confined to the vicinity where he had been born. Too, Mazzei was an Italian, and Jefferson was intrigued by Italian culture. He had taught himself Italian, and when Mazzei brought workmen from Italy to build his new home — to be called "Colle" or "hill" — Jefferson was able to converse with them in a proper Tuscan dialect.

Jefferson spent endless hours with his new neighbor, learning much about the arts and agriculture. In his own garden at Monticello, he identified vegetables with small signs written in Italian. The two carried on cross-pollination and transplantation experiments with orchard and vineyard cuttings from abroad. Like many other prominent Virginians, including George Washinton, Jefferson joined the new agricultural company which Mazzei formed in 1774.

Mazzei's influence was equally great in philosophy and politics. One of his many pamphlets, printed in the *Virginia Gazette* in 1776, contained an idea which every American schoolchild learns almost as soon as he learns his own name. It was the concept of political equality. In *A Nation of Immigrants*, John F. Kennedy wrote that Jefferson's "great doctrine that 'All men are created equal' was paraphrased from the writings of Philip Mazzei."

Mazzei had put it thus: "Tutti gli uomini sono per natura egualmente liberi e independenti — all men are by nature equally free and independent."

DURING THE NEXT several years, Mazzei neglected his agricultural interests to work for the Revolution: he wrote pamphlets, traveled to Paris to raise money, returned in 1783 to found a Constitutional Society, and in 1785 left Virginia for good. But he never stopped promoting the American cause. As he said in a letter on his departure: "America is my Jupiter; Virginia my Venus."

By the time his friend Jefferson became president, Mazzei was in retirement at Pisa, writing his memoirs, and working in his garden. During these final years, this Italian immigrant whose words are embodied in the Declaration of Independence, was known to his neighbors and friends by the simple nickname which might just have been his favorite.

They called him *Pippo l'ortolano:* Phil the gardener.
— *Charles Guzzetta*

ANDREA SBARBARO'S VISION

by Lawrence DiStasi

Andrea Sbarbaro, founder of the Italian Swiss Colony.

ANDREA SBARBARO SEEMS to have been a man of vision almost from childhood. Living with his mother and his nine brothers and sisters in New York City, he began to create his first empire at age seven peddling toys on the ferryboats to Brooklyn. As if that weren't enough, he also practiced his English on the ferry, during lulls between the crowds.

After following his brother to San Francisco in 1852, Andrea wasted little time "getting ahead." In dramatically short order, he took over his brother's commission business and began to teach English at his own night school. He also opened a bank and pioneered in building-and-loan societies for his fellow Italians.

Sbarbaro also proposed to the mayor of San Francisco that the city should build huge reservoirs atop the hills. Seawater pumped into the reservoirs — Sbarbaro suggested — would serve as a cheap source of water for fire fighting, for flushing the sewers, and even, if brought into houses, for bathing.

"Mr. Sbarbaro is very enthusiastic in improving and beautifying our city," San Francisco Mayor James Phelan is quoted as responding, "but he reminds me of the man who longed for a Utopia. This man had put it into his head that he wanted to build a perfect city, and the result was that he eventually got his head chopped off."

Had Sbarbaro's idea been implemented, it is worth noting, it might have saved San Francisco from the devastating fires that followed the Great Earthquake of 1906.

Sadly, particularly for an early group of Italian workers, this was not the only time that Andrea Sbarbaro's vision was ignored.

Andrea Sbarbaro and A. P. Giannini were both driven toward New World wealth. Yet each in his own way incorporated the visionary spirit into that drive. Giannini, welcoming bootblacks and farmers as well as businessmen into his bank, and then into his pioneering branch offices, changed the stuffy face of American banking forever. Sbarbaro, influenced by the cooperative philosophy of Robert Owen, applied it first to building and loan societies and then to his wine-making ventures. Their vision helped give California Italians access to capital and opportunity that they lacked virtually everywhere else in America.

Early in 1881, Sbarbaro read a report on prospects for wine growing in California. The report suggested that with grapes selling for $30 a ton, a typical acre of land held the promise of a $130 return. It seemed the perfect opportunity both for investment and for a cooperative venture for the Italian *contadini* in San Francisco, many of whom regularly besieged Sbarbaro's office looking for work. Sbarbaro's readings in John Ruskin and in Robert Owen, as well as his experience in building-and-loan societies had convinced him of the value of cooperative ventures.

Sbarbaro immediately set out to get investors and to find a suitable site. The investors agreed to his plan, creating five thousand shares at a par value of sixty dollars each for each new shareholder. Sbarbaro and his original group of investors controlled most of the shares, but a large percentage was reserved for common vineyard workers. Upon joining the project, each worker was to subscribe to at least five shares, for which one dollar per share would be withheld from his monthly wages.

At first the scheme seemed to work perfectly. Working capital was quickly made available, and Sbarbaro soon found a site — the old Truett Ranch, in Sonoma County north of San Francisco, which, at that time, was still supporting two Englishmen and five hundred sheep. Sbarbaro bought the ranch and began to make preparations for planting grapes.

Sbarbaro screened his future workers carefully, selecting his colony largely from those workers who had immigrated to California from the wine-growing regions of Italy. Sbarbaro explained his plan. "I told them," he would later write, "that their wages would

Giannini

PEOPLE NEVER TIRE of asking A. P. Giannini how he managed to take the little Bank of Italy that he started in 1904 in premises formerly occupied by a waterfront saloon in San Francisco, and run it up to a string of five hundred banking offices now owned by his Bank of America.

"Well," he answers, "we were new to the game when we started out; we did unusual things."

A. P., ignorant of banking, and with the air of the produce-market man he had been when he made his first fortune by the age of thirty, went bustling about Market Street and all the waterside district hounding his old business friends into opening desposit accounts. After hours, his three clerks also fanned out into the Italian-populated North Beach district, actually soliciting deposits, which was considered "unethical" in those days. A. P. himself hit the highroad up the Sacramento Valley, looked up all the farmers who used to sell him grapes and scallions, and inveigled them into taking their gold out of their chimneys and entrusting it to him. If he found those farmers busily plowing their fields, he would follow them about, nimbly hopping over the clods of earth while, in his rapid, if broken Italian, he expounded on the beauties of a savings account at 3$\frac{1}{2}$ or even 4 percent. And he even sold shares of his bank's stock in small lots to humble immigrants or tillers of the field.

"They used to say I was undignified," A. P. recalls of his competitors. "Old fogies! I say, if you want something, you may as well go after it."

Giannini is remembered to this day for his "going after it" during the great San Francisco earthquake of 1906.

On the day of the earthquake, after removing his own resources from the city, A. P. hurried back into San Francisco, to find most of the downtown buildings leveled, and the fire spreading.

That day, while conventional bankers considered imposing a six-month moratorium on future loans, Giannini had a desk set out on the pier in his old commission-house district, which was all in ruins. A clerk was accepting deposits and making loans for the bank's customers. A cardboard sign on a stick showed the Bank of Italy was open for business.

Many Californians recall how Giannini "first made a hit and was much talked about" after the earthquake and fire of 1906. He had quickly calculated that this catastrophe would be followed by a period of strenuous rebuilding, amounting to a boom in trade.

In no small part because of Giannini's commitment of resources, San Francisco surprised the world by the speed of her reconstruction. And the devastated North Beach quarter, largely Italian in population, was the first to rise from the ashes. Hundreds of its residents received building loans from Giannini's Bank of Italy, and always remembered that.

"The time to go ahead in business," Giannini philosophizes, "is when the other fellows aren't doing much."

By bringing banking to the people — first through his personal approach, and then through his pioneering system of branch banking — he did just that.

— *Matthew Josephson*

be from thirty to forty dollars a month, with good food, wine at their meals, which was a necessity to them, and comfortable houses to sleep in. But in order to inspire an interest in the work and desiring that the Colony should be strictly cooperative, I explained that each laborer must subscribe to at least five shares of stock. In fact, our bylaws provided expressly that all permanent laborers on the grounds must be members and that preferences would be shown to Italian and Swiss laborers who were either American citizens or had declared their intentions to become such."

To a man, the workers balked. They would work, they said, but they wanted cash, not shares. Sbarbaro was stunned. He tried again and again to explain the idea of cooperation and the advantages of ownership. It was no use. "The Cavaliere Andrea," Dr. Paolo DeVecchi said, "pleaded until he was hoarse. But no, the men at Asti were deaf to logic and oratory. Not one single share in the Colony would they buy."

Sbarbaro could do nothing but accept their decision. He and his investors pledged the remaining funds needed and hired the workers strictly for wages. Then, after weathering a plunge in wine prices, and a wine price war that nearly bankrupted them, the colony at Asti began to prosper. Neat homes were built for the workers, and then schools, a church, an electric plant, and telephone lines. Sbarbaro himself had a Roman villa built, at which he entertained lavishly. He brought in then-exotic plants and trees, among them lemons, oranges, pomegranates, chestnuts, and olives.

When, in 1911 at the International Fair in Turin, the Grand Prix was given to the Italian Swiss Colony Champagne, Sbarbaro's triumph was complete. It was the highest award yet given for an American champagne. It made all the more vivid Sbarbaro's comment on the "error of judgment" of the original workers: "Any laborer who would have taken twenty-five shares out then, which they all could have done, would today be receiving sixty dollars in monthly dividends — enough to make him modestly independent for life."

The final irony is that seventy-five years later, Andrea Sbarbaro's original plan for his colony would come to fruition: in 1959, a cooperative of thirteen hundred growers assumed complete ownership of the original Italian Swiss Colony Wine Co. to become the largest producer and merchant of wine in the world.

Perhaps it takes a generation or two before the average man can see a Utopia in seawater, an empire in a sheep ranch. ❧

16

THE END OF THE LINE

by Rob Haeseler

One worked as a tile setter and laborer. The other worked digging the New York subways. Yet Simon Rodia, with his Watts Towers, and Baldasare Forestiere, with his Fresno caverns, have given more eloquent voice to the dream life seething within all migrants than libraries of writings by psychologists or critics. Rodia, like some Sumerian potentate, drove his vision skyward. Forestiere, like the tomb builders of Malta, dove earthward. As to what each thought he was doing for so many isolated years, perhaps Rodia's words express that best: "A man has to be good good or bad bad to be remembered."

SAM RODIA LIES in a Martinez, California convalescent home patiently awaiting immortality.

In the morning the sun shines in his window and he can look out and see the sky and a fringe of green shrubbery in the small courtyard. The nurses come and go, straightening his pillows, cranking up the bed, checking the thin white belt that holds him to it.

The belt is a precautionary measure, they say lightly. Sam has a tendency to crawl out of bed and wander off. He tells them he has to go home to wash a window or take the coffeepot off the stove.

Occasionally there is a visitor — a favorite niece, a fellow sculptor who has seen his work and wants to meet him, a devoted patron who steals an hour from the workaday world of clocks and calendars and appointments, sometimes a reporter, and always the doctor who takes his pulse, listens to his flagging heart, then goes away.

IN 1954 SAM Rodia left his home in Watts, a suburb of Los Angeles, and said he was going away to die. Since 1921 he had struggled with a monumental obsession. From broken bottles, twisted scraps of steel, seashells and tons of cement he fashioned a world of dreamlike mosaic spires known today as the Watts Towers.

Reference to the towers may not be found in many guidebooks. Only recently have they come into the public ken by virtue of several articles published about them in national magazines. And of their creator, next to nothing is known.

The most recent edition of the *Columbia Encyclopedia* offers a passing reference: "Rodilla, Simon (1879 —) American architect and sculptor."

The old man in the Alhambra Convalescent Hospital prefers the simplified name of Sam Rodia. He is at once a figure of sad senility and abiding, awesome strength.

"You see this, boy," he says, tugging at the loose restraining belt with his shiny, veined hand. "How the hell you gonna sleep when you got that thing on? You need a knife for this." And then he makes you jerk the belt with him and scowls. "Go on, pull!" he orders, and the bed fairly shakes to pieces.

◄

Simon Rodia's incomparable Watts Towers.

17

He is a thin man with a sparrowlike frame, filmy brown eyes and drawn cheeks and lips. He is nearly toothless and half deaf, but he is very much alive.

His curious predilection for geographical names is evident when he speaks of his railroad days, and he rarely refers to a city without linking it to its proper state. "We start railroads in west of Berkeley and we go to Cheyenne, Wyoming, Chicago, Illinois, Denver, Colorado."

IN THE EARLY 1920s Rodia settled in Watts and began working on the towers. For the most part, the task of constructing them was painful — something perhaps he would rather forget. Neighbors called him crazy. Children tormented him by throwing rocks. But slowly and steadily the towers went up, unshaken even by the Long Beach earthquake of 1933.

"I work three, four, five hours in a night. One take three years, 'nother five years, 'nother ten years, 'nother fifteen years . . . I build something we never had before."

He had. Constructed of cement reinforced with steel rods and wire mesh, the three main towers soar to a height of nearly one hundred feet. Surrounding them is a magic garden of smaller towers, inverted cones, fountains, pavilions, spires, arches, labyrinths, love seats, and a ship Rodia once identified as the Ship of Marco Polo. The whole is decorated with a multicolored mosaic of found objects and incised decorations. There are impressions of Rodia's tools, his hands, horseshoes, corncobs, and his initials with the date a given section was completed. He also incised the title words *Nuestro Pueblo* — "Our Town" in the Spanish of his Watts neighbors. When asked once what he meant by this, he said, "Lotsa things, lotsa things."

Then in 1954 he signed his property over to a neighbor and vanished. The towers fell victim to malicious mischief. The grounds became a dumping place for the neighborhood's refuse. The small house he had built and carefully studded with bright tiles burned to the ground.

For all anyone knew, Sam Rodia was dead. Neighbors furnished the precise name of cemeteries where he was buried to persons inquiring about his whereabouts. The city of Los Angeles condemned the towers as unsafe and ordered their destruction. A small group of art-conscious citizens acquired the property and began a historic legal battle with the city to preserve them.

At a cost of several thousand dollars, paid from the pockets of concerned patrons, the towers were subjected to an elaborate stress test comparable to a·seventy mph gale. Although neither nuts nor bolts nor welding had been used in their construction, the towers withstood the force, and the city was obliged to leave them standing.

Now the Watts Towers are an art monument, open to the general public.

ABOUT FOUR YEARS ago Sam Rodia was discovered living by himself in a shoe-box room in downtown Martinez. For half a century his relatives had lived in the city, and he had paid them frequent visits.

Those who sought him out found him evasive, hardly willing to discuss the towers, totally reluctant to return to them. There is a story that two of the patrons had to chase him along the street to get a few words. When asked why he wouldn't talk about the towers, he supposedly replied: "If your mother dies and you loved her very much you don't talk about her."

Until a severe heart attack a year ago, he continued to refuse assistance and lived the life of a recluse, divorced from a world that troubled him with incessant questions to which he knows few, if any, of the answers.

When asked what he is by profession, he says "tile setter." If he has ever entertained notions of himself as a sculptor or architect, he has long since repressed them. If he has ever thought of himself as a genius, he has not talked about it.

His talk is often rambling, sometimes incoherent and unintelligible, except to the nurses who know him well. He gestures with the shiny hands, scooping the air and cutting imaginary curves. On one of his "good days," he can get up and walk around. On a "bad day" he stays in bed and rests.

Generally, he does not like to talk about the towers. Often he avoids the subject by launching a discursive monologue — sometimes on the history of houses, tracing the structure from its mud-hut origins to the present day in a few tangled sentences. When shown a magazine picture of the towers, he pokes it with a finger and then turns the page and scans the color advertisements: "Yeah, thats-a United States," he says.

When you say: "Are these your towers, Sam?" he pokes at them again and mutters,

"Yeah, I never forget them. . .ten hours a day with pick and shovel, five hours at night. I built them. You never find one justa like it."

He tells how he worked on the railroads for thirty-seven years, coming home at night to work on the towers. On Sundays he walked along the beach picking up shells to add to the mosaics. He built the towers and tiled fountains and gazebos entirely from found materials. And most significant, he did it all alone.

Just when Rodia came to the United States from his small Italian town in the province of Avellino is somewhat of a mystery. In the course of twenty minutes he is apt to say that he was eighteen when he left, or eleven or nine. Persons who have studied his life seem to think he was about fourteen. For some years he

▲

Simon Rodia and the towers he worked on
every day for over 30 years.

19

worked as an itinerant laborer and railroad watchman.

It is hardly fair to expect a plausible reply (should one exist) to the question of why he built the towers. Variously he has said he began to build them when he stopped drinking or, as he has told the nurses, because he wanted to leave his mark on the world. Patrons who have delved into his life have unearthed nothing but contradictions — attributable in part, no doubt, to his increasing senility.

When the question is put to him, a certain weariness clouds his eyes and his brow wrinkles as if he might be thinking: *Don't ask me again. How am I to know? I have spent my whole life wondering the same thing.* Then with a slight peevishness he answers: "Why I build it, I can't tell you. Why a man make the pants? Why a man make the shoes?"

Rodia's eighty-year-old brother-in-law, Samuel Calicura of Martinez, whom he has not seen since an argument they had five years ago, offers few clues to the artist's true nature.

At his Mellus Street home, Calicura possesses several of Rodia's works which were built some twenty-five years ago while Rodia was in Martinez on a visit. They are large outdoor flower vessels of unique cement and mosaic composition, and despite any indifference it is evident that Calicura is proud of them. He calls Rodia "a hard workin' man," but the vessels "those things."

"Any man with common sense can make those things," Calicura says.

In a roundabout way Rodia has said that he got the ideas for his works largely from books and museums. He has mentioned Alexander the Great, Julius Caesar, Amerigo Vespucci and Buffalo Bill as his heroes. When he last spoke of what had motivated him, he said, "I want to do something. I read something — what they doing in Boston, Massachusetts, Philadelphia, Pennsylvania — all over . . . I said, 'My God, I'm-a gonna do something . . .'"

His narrative dwindled off into incoherence: "Sunday I go no pants on pick up one shell — no shell no water no water no shell . . ."

A nurse brought his lunch in and set it down in front of him. He excused himself and ate with relish. ❧

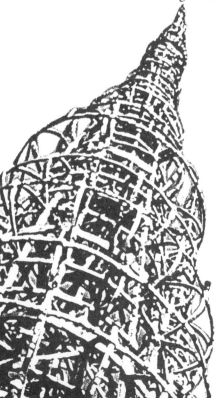

Sam (his real name was Sabato, but in 1939 an interviewer called him "Simon" and Rodia never bothered to correct it) Rodia died ten days after the above article was written. It was June 1965, he was ninety years old, and though he may not have known the extent of it, Rodia had certainly "done something." Besides building, unaided and untutored, his unique monument, Rodia, by deserting his work in 1954, set in motion an avalanche of controversies which has never slowed. All center on the problem of how best to preserve the towers — by now so famous as a signature of Los Angeles that some call them the city's Parthenon.

The first problem was how to save the towers from destruction by the city government. That solved by the famous stress test, it was necessary to restore the damage caused by both weather and vandals. The original Committee for Simon Rodia's Towers soon saw that this was too large a project for a private group and deeded the property to the city of Los Angeles. The city promised it would have the work done, but soon a controversy over the quality of the restoration resulted in a lawsuit that took seven years to settle. Meantime the state intervened, took title to the monument in return for $1.2 million in restoration funds, and then leased the whole thing back to the city to maintain. The state's repair work was finished in 1985, but the city's was just beginning. The city settled the lawsuit for a promise to spend $800,000 on the towers, legal fees, and a $50,000 donation to the new Watts Towers Community and Conservation Trust. The latter group was to raise private funds to care for the towers and create a community center.

Yet at last report, the restoration work is far from finished and the towers continue to decay in ways impossible to anticipate. Community groups have settled into what appears to be permanent bickering over how best to spend funds — those who want to concentrate on the towers argue with those who insist that the surrounding community needs funds for its own well-being.

The result is that Sam Rodia's Towers have been covered with scaffolding for most of the last decade. A fence keeps the public out. Only school groups and people who attend the annual music festivals are permitted to peek inside. All anyone else can see are the tops of the towers.

And so, in a way he never suspected, Sam Rodia still lives. For it has become as difficult to pry information from his towers in order to care for them as it was to pry information from Rodia himself about why he built them. Both live, crusty and unyielding, in the silence that is art.

— Ed.

THE HUMAN MOLE

AN ITALIAN IMMIGRANT spent forty years living a molelike existence beneath the city of Fresno in California's San Joaquin Valley. With pick and shovel, Baldasare Forestiere created a ten-acre subterranean maze of curving passageways, rooms, courtyards, patios, and grottoes, beneath the surface of his property.

"During his lifetime he was ridiculed and called the Human Mole," recalls Baldasare's nephew, Ricardo Forestiere, forty-six, a Fresno school teacher. "His family tried to get him to stop his digging. And when he died, they wanted no part of his caverns."

The family, Ricardo said, wanted to destroy the tunnels and more than one hundred underground rooms that had been created. "Uncle Baldasare and his underground diggings were an embarrassment to them."

Forestiere, who died in 1946 at the age of sixty-seven, left no will. But he left a fortune in real estate, including more than one thousand choice acres of rich California farmland.

Forestiere migrated to America from Messina, Sicily, in 1902 when he was twenty-three. He worked in the subways and tunnels of New York before moving to Fresno. He began building his own tunnels in 1906.

First he dug living quarters, then a room where he made wine and a vault where he aged cheese and cured meats.

He built a chapel, then grottoes, then a whole series of tunnels and rooms. One room is a gigantic auditorium, one hundred feet long, fifty feet wide with a twenty-five-foot ceiling.

In the ceilings of his rooms he dug skylights out of the hard bedrock for ventilation. He fashioned glass lids to keep out the rain. He planted orange, tangerine, lemon, and lime trees in his underground courtyards. The trees flourish to this day, producing fruit each season, their branches reaching to the surface out of deep holes.

Forestiere's graceful symmetric arches and curved passageways were reinforced with tons of bricks, built in three levels at some places and as deep as twenty-five feet.

"I remember when I was much younger and Uncle Baldasare was still alive, my father would worry about him after not seeing him for several days," Forestiere's nephew said. "Dad and I would go into my uncle's underground maze and start looking for him. It was easy to get lost. We would look with a lantern. Father would holler out his name — 'Balde, Balde.'

" 'Hey, over here,' Uncle Baldasare would shout back. And we would find him busy at work late at night."

For five years after Forestiere died, his estate was in litigation and the underground diggings were unattended.

"There were many stories all over Fresno that my uncle had buried a fortune in money somewhere in the tunnels or in one of the rooms," said Ricardo.

"To this day people claim they have it on good authority my uncle buried anywhere from $100,000 to $500,000 in cash somewhere down here underground."

— *Charles Hillinger*

Cornucopia

Life on a Mushroom Farm

by Tullio Francesco DeSantis

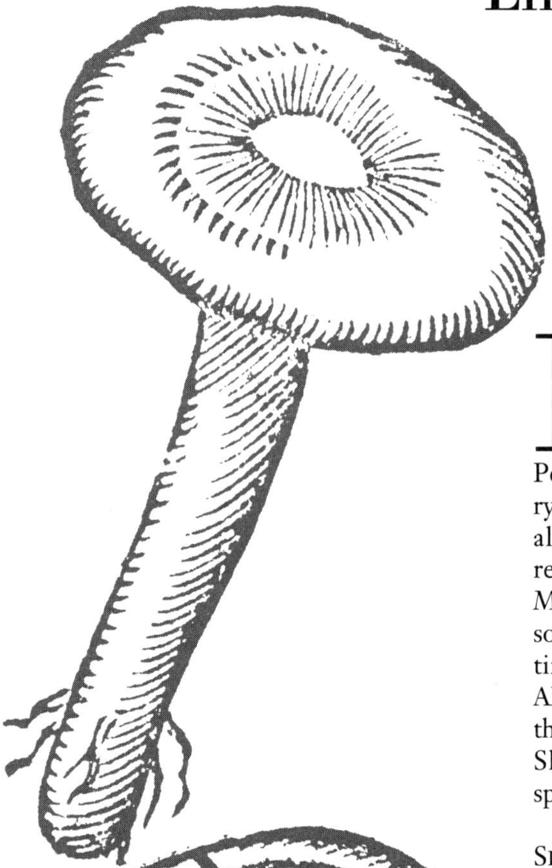

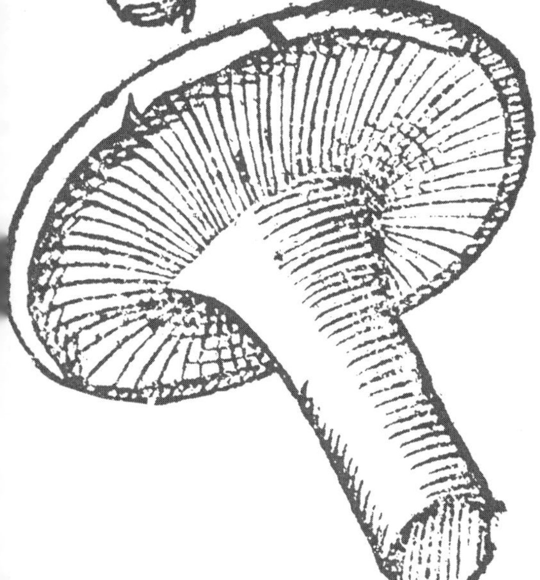

BETWEEN WARS, FRANCESCO DeSantis leaves Maria, his wife, and first son, Giuseppe, in Ascoli. He intends to secure work in America and his emigration ends near Reading, Pennsylvania. Immediately he goes to work: as a quarryman, railroad trackman, and later — when owners allow the hiring of Italians — a steel worker. He returns to Italia, then returns to America, followed by Maria, Giuseppe (soon to be called Joseph), and new son, Leo. All have life in the new land. Francesco continues loving Maria and soon son, Ezio, daughters Alvia and Ida come to him. Maria tosses a knife out of the house when thunder and lightning are in the sky. She is superstitious and does not believe in outer space. She believes only what she knows . . .

SINCE HE IS already poor, Francesco DeSantis is not depressed by the Depression. Defiantly, he throws his last three cents into a field of tall grass. He rolls boulders, builds WPA walls on Skyline Drive, and buys the big white house on the first hill above the railroad bridge in Temple. Eventually, he buys the field of tall grass containing his pennies...

FOR AN UNKNOWN reason, he decides to grow mushrooms and shares this idea with his friends who share it with his enemies. Carpenters, builders, workers, people of the soil, they erect giant structures with borrowed tools and hopes of future harvests. Bare chested, with red and blue kerchiefs tightly wrapped above the eyes, they fork hundreds of steamy tons of hot manure into tiered canyons. Sweated and fog shrouded, families and friends fill the shelf-beds, periodically running out into cooler air to draw clear breath. Then the heavy doors are shut and sealed with mud. The ooze is packed into cracks while the manure burns with inner life. Teeming swarms of microbes and bacteria digest and metabolize, seething for a half month or more, curing the sour mass into a musty sweetness. Impregnated with spawn, covered with topsoil, soaked with misty spray again and

Hunting wild mushrooms always associates with finding buried treasure: suddenly, where there has been nothing, they arise. Although the cultivation of mushrooms on the DeSantis farm involves a huge output of work, the critical moment of the "flush" carries that same feeling of sudden wealth. It is the mystery that drives most farmers, a metaphor for that not-insignificant minority of Italians who were able to find their America on the land.

▶
Francesco DeSantis, a few years after his arrival in Reading, Pennsylvania

24

and Maria go to college, while I, firstborn of a new generation, bounce beside Francesco in his Chevrolet panel truck delivering hand-picked baskets of brilliant white mushrooms to market, endlessly checking operations on his several farms, buying tools, visiting and organizing an extended family of friends and growers. In memory I continue to ride with him as, today, his heirs — sons, relatives, new immigrants, strangers — run their farms by calendar, clock, calculator, computer . . .

I HAVE LIVED thousands of days with mushrooms, sensing their slow meandering of invisible mycelia penetrating tons of compost; later, seeing colonized spawn forming millions of primordial foci upon damp peat moss; nurturing their development into white pinpoints of succulent flesh; and finally witnessing the urgent surge of growth in which each crop springs forth. I remember prodding heaps of loamy night-chilled topsoil, caked mud clinging to shoe soles, sun-baked insights, nocturnal scenery, cinder-block farmhouses on windswept hillsides, hand-built worlds of endless scent, sounds of wet soles on cypress scaffolds, whirling blades in whirring fans, turmoil of steam-drenched atmospheres, black manure stacked up to dripping ceilings above cavernous interiors, yellow incandescences illuminating bright mycelial masses of respiring fungus, damp white nightfruit. Mushroom universe — rooms black as moonless nights, heat filled with rolling steam, or chilled damp with flowing air, dream worlds, alien and all-enveloping where white caps pierce the dark like points of secret consciousness. The ancient plants create, contain, and release a billion spores, each one a messenger of evolution . . .

WHEN THE MUSHROOM grower leaves the farm, he can not shelve the smell. His hat, kerchief, pants, shirt, and shoes retain it. Standing in line at American Bank, the blind identify him before he speaks. As farmers do he bets his life, counting on the crop to redeem his risk . . . The cultivation of mushrooms is a complex man/plant symbiosis combining physical force, mental acuity, experience, perception, intellect, instinct. The farmer of mushrooms creates and maintains, under wildly varying meteorological conditions, a stable, yet flexible artificial ecosystem, a micro-world adapted to the life forms it perpetuates. Anticipating the momentary requirements of this sometimes inscrutable, intermittently invisible crop and its interdependence with its environment is the constant and total preoccupation of the grower. Because it is nature, he survives, or else, because it is nature, he does not. Finally, things continue because it is now. Things die for the same reason . . .

again, finally night-wind chilled to the temperature of cool caves, the chalky tissue yields harvest after harvest of fruit since the spawn does not die of old age . . .

NOT MAGICALLY, FIFTY lean workingyears later the mushroom farms sprout Francesco & Maria, Inc., core stockholders of a group of local growers canning and distributing more than two million pounds of mushrooms per annum, immigrant dream success story . . .

AFTER WORLD WAr II, all the children of Francesco

TIME SHIFTS AS it is this century and there are new

25

THE SUMMER KITCHEN

IN JUNE WHEN the Brooklyn garden
boiled with blossom,
when leaflets of basil lined the paths
and new green fruitless fingers of vine
climbed the airy arbor roof,

my Sicilian aunts withdrew
to the summer kitchen,
the white bare secret room
at the bottom of the house.
Outside, in the upper world,

sun blistered the bricks of the tiny
imitation Taormina terrace where fierce
socialisti uncles
chainsmoked Camels and plotted politics;
nieces and nephews tusseled

among thorny bloodcolored
American roses;
a pimply concrete
birdbath-fountain dribbled ineffectual
water warm as olive oil.

Cool and below it all,
my aunts labored among great cauldrons
in the spicy air
of the summer kitchen: in one kettle
tomatoes bloomed into sauce;

in another, ivory *pasta*
leaped and swam;
on the clean white table
at the center of the room
heads of lettuce flung themselves open,

and black-green poles of zucchini
fell into slices of yellow
like fairytale money.

Skidding around the white
sink in one corner

the trout that Uncle Christopher brought back
from the Adirondacks gave up
the glitter of its fins
to the glitter of *Zia* Francesca's
powerful knife.

Every August day *Zia* Petrina
rose at four to tend the morning:
smoky Greek chignon
drawn sleek,
she stood at the sink.

Her quick shears
flashed in the silence,
separating day from night, trunk
from branch, leaf
from shadow.

As the damp
New World sunrays struggled to rise
past sooty housetops,
she'd look suddenly up
with eyes black as grapes

that fattened in the arbor:
through one dirt-streaked window
high above her
she could see the ledge of soil
where her pansies and geraniums anchored.

Higher still,
in tangles of heat
my uncles' simmering garden grew,
like green steam swelling from the cool
root of her kitchen.

— *Sandra Gilbert*

farms and new farmers, new ways of farming and making money. But the human being is more than this. Francesco DeSantis has a life spanning time on Earth from horse cart to Lunar lander — the only moment in history this occurs. During World War I he dodges bombs and bullets. He never realizes Il Duce is not a great man. He mistrusts the Catholic Church, yet he builds St. Anthony's for his community in America and does not attend Mass. His brother is an anarchist; never comes to America; so Francesco returns periodically to argue over disputed family property. He eats spaghetti, drinks vermouth, smokes some cigars. He is born in 1901. He does die in 1984. What he lives in his life can be lived by a man so he does live it. We live, remember, and do what we can do now. We can not do what he did. We continue and die, as he died. But the spawn does not die. Mushrooms, like us, are instantaneous, fruit of eternal trees. ❧

A VISIT TO TONTITOWN

by John L. Mathews

It was a constant question in the minds of urban social workers: Why didn't a population with generations of expertise in farming move to agricultural areas? In most cases the answer was simple: no money to buy land. But through the unremitting efforts of Father Bandini in Tontitown and Secchi DeCasale in Vineland , Italians not only kept themselves "down on the farm," but kept themselves together too. Even after seeing Broadway.

TONTITOWN LIES IN the uplands of the Ozarks, in that section of the Southwest which seems to the eastern visitor the very essence of all that is wonderful in farm country. This is the land of the big red apple, the glowing peach, vineyards that bear with extravagant abundance. And in the very heart of it all, where Arkansas merges into Oklahoma, Tontitown lies at a prairie crossroads.

Though it is too new to be mapped, the Arkansas farmers know where it is, and the railroad men too; for, in recent years, more prosperity has come through this little community than through any other region in the state.

This is true because of the spirit of the men and women who have created Tontitown . . . of Father Bandini, first, who gave up his scholarly career to devote his life to proving the value of the Italian in America, and to teaching the reality of America to his people . . and also to the Italians of Tontitown themselves — men and women who have entered with irrepressible good will into a demonstration of the truth of Pietro Bandini's faith.

The story of Tontitown began with the search of Austin Corbin, philanthropist and millionaire, for an alternative to New York's congested slums. He bought a big plantation, Sunnyside, beside the Mississippi River in Arkansas, and persuaded a large number of Italian families to go down there to grow cotton.

The experiment was at the start a ghastly tragedy.

Sent into a hot and sickly climate to work under masters accustomed to driving slaves, and placed in the heart of swampy country swarming with malarial mosquitoes, the Italians were soon

◄
Father Bandini, looking rather pleased with himself and his venture at Tontitown

overwhelmed with a plague that threatened to develop into a panic.

It is a far cry from this suffering colony in the swamps to Garibaldi and the Young Italy movement; yet it was the spirit of Garibaldi in a young priest which came to their rescue. Too young to join his brother in Garibaldi's struggle, Pietro Bandini was not too young to be roused by the liberating spirit of the times. After college he began to study the problem of the migration of Italians to America. So brilliant were his writings on this subject that, in 1896, his government sent him to America. The colony at Sunnyside had his interest from the start, and when he heard of the trouble the Italians were in he hastened to their aid.

Arriving in Arkansas, Father Bandini confronted a terrible situation. Of 100 families, 125 members had died of malaria in a year. Some families had been entirely wiped out. In others young children were left orphaned. And the Italians, angered and embittered by the treatment they had received, and weary of the attempt to grow a cotton crop which they neither liked nor understood, were beginning a mass exodus.

Bandini had to work quickly. Assembling the survivors, he told them that he would go out and find them a new home. On the prairie west of Springdale he found an old farm about to be abandoned. The farm's white clay soil had been ploughed through several profitless years by an American who had received a turnover of only two to three dollars a year per acre. He had given up, and was ready to sell.

Bandini opened the negotiations. Yet the farmer, realizing that he had these new Italian immigrants upon the hip, raised his price from eight dollars to fifteen dollars an acre. With no choice, Bandini paid it. Collectively, the Italians took the land on mortgages, and divided it up, ten acres to a family, buying other tracts alongside to accommodate the surplus.

The men went out into the mines of the Ozarks for the winter to earn money for the next mortgage payment, and the women and boys built pole cabins on the land and settled down to the worst winter the Ozarks had known in years.

Even today they will not tell the story of that first winter. A thousand rabbits, caught in traps set about the land, furnished the only meat for the community. The men at the mines worked steadily, and in the spring came home with their second payment. Then began the real work of establishing the community.

The Italians began to set out vines, planning the vineyards for future extensions. They planted strawberries and fruit trees and vegetables, and from dawn till dark they broke in the new land. From Italy they secured shoots of the Italian willow, with which to tie their vines, and beside each vineyard planted a tree of it. The American willow when tied will break, but the Italian, which will neither rust a vine like wire nor sicken it like hemp, can be tied many times without cracking.

IN THIS NEW colony, Bandini quickly established himself as the master. "He rules us," one of the colony told me later, "with a velvet glove, through which we can barely feel the iron fingers."

Father Bandini had determined that this should be an American village. He adopted the name of Tontitown because Henry de Tonti was the first Italian ever to explore Arkansas. And yet, all the while, the Americans nearby sought means to harass the newcomers and drive them away. A rough element from the adjacent Indian Territory repeatedly raided their settlement. One evening, Father Bandini confonted them. "We are all Americans here," he said, "and I give you notice that we shall exercise the American right of self-defense. There are few men among us who have not served in the Italian army. We are familiar with our guns. I am hereafter the colonel of our regiment, and I assure you that night and day a sentinel shall patrol our streets. Any person coming among us and manifesting malice will be shot."

The Americans muttered and threatened, but there was peace in Tontitown thereafter.

Slowly, prosperity came with close tillage. The immigrants soon began to build their own houses — neat cottages, each with its own rose garden, flowerbeds, and on either side, orchards and vineyards. As the settlement grew, apple and peach trees came into bearing and added to the wealth of the community. Then the grape vines, planted each year an acre at a time, began to bear and the grapes to be turned into wine. Before the colony was six years old there were single acres producing as much as $300 a year in cash return.

The railroad people soon learned that the immense shipments of fruit from Springdale came largely from the little village out west of town. American fruit farmers from two counties away came to see and learn how such crops were grown on that formerly barren soil.

All this was the work of Bandini.

IT WAS IN June 1906 that I left the train at Springdale and drove out to see the village, then seven years old. We halted at Bandini's residence, and the priest came forth to greet us. He took us from farm to farm, introducing us to the vine-tenders, questioning them for their memories of Sunnyside, asking them to tell their own story of the prosperity at Tontitown.

After dinner we talked with the Father. In the shade of the church, rifle in hand, he answered our

SECCHI DeCASALE AND THE ITALIANS OF VINELAND

IN ITS 1911 report, the U.S. Senate Immigration Commission called Vineland, New Jersey, "the first Italian agricultural colony in the United States," and gave the honor of its founding to Signor Secchi DeCasale. For this and other activities, DeCasale was knighted and called Chevalier DeCasale.

DeCasale wasn't a farmer, though, but a newspaperman — the editor and founder of New York's first Italian American newspaper, *L'Eco d'Italia*. Nor did he live at Vineland — which was founded by Charles K. Landis in 1863 — but in Elizabeth, New Jersey.

It was in his newspaper that Signor DeCasale tirelessly promoted the settling of Vineland. On the front page of the March 6, 1875, issue of *L'Eco d'Italia*, appears the following:

The project which the editor of this newspaper began about two years ago to have Italians settle in the pleasant and healthful area of Vineland, which is located in the central part of the state of New Jersey . . . . has been a complete success. About 250 of our hardworking and industrious compatriots bought land there which they allocated to fruit-growing and truck-gardening, in addition to raising grains. Most of them have built homes there with the intention of settling.

To confirm what we have stated many times about the advantages Vineland offers farmers, we print a letter sent to us by Mr. G. B. Baretta, who nine years ago left his position as a singing teacher, and moved to Vineland.

Baretta's letter goes on to extol the

virtues of Vineland, not only for grape growing, but for garnering a profit from reselling land. He compares its climate with central Italy's and concludes that "nothing your reporter states has been exaggerated."

Aside from the exaggerations in detail — Vineland was situated in southern, not central, New Jersey, with a climate hardly that of Italy's — the article did point to a basic truth. Italians were

indeed successful in Vineland. In his journals, Landis repeatedly lauds the virtues of the Italian settlers with statements like, "What would I do without the Italians? They buy to stay. They make homes not alone for themselves but for every member of their families."

As to DeCasale's prominence, that appears to have been a sometime thing. On August 8, 1878, Landis writes: "At five o'clock came the Chev. Secchi

deCasali to select a town lot in pay for advertising, which advertising has not done one particle of good . . . such was the prejudice of Italians against him that he did nothing and it stopped the movement."

But two days later, we find Landis touring Vineland with "Mr Secchi," who now "appears to be a real friend to the Italians here, and to Vineland." By late August, Landis is staying overnight with DeCasale in Elizabeth, New Jersey, and enjoying his family, a relationship that seems to continue until DeCasale's death in 1885.

The curious thing is that Landis's ambiguity toward his Italian promoter seems to be reflected in a second area — that of the Italians and wine.

We have a place whose very name, Vineland, evokes the grape. We have a population who had wine making in their veins. Yet how to square this with Vineland's role as a center for the Temperance Movement — the birthplace of Dr. Welch's grape juice, which Welch first used in his church as a substitute for alcoholic altar wine?

Or that Landis himself, at first enthusiastic about Italian wine making ("I have had an idea that encouragement of pure native wines would remedy drinking, and do away with the habit of drinking whiskey"), was by 1880 having second thoughts: "I begin to doubt about the good that wine is to do as a temperance."

Off again, on again: that may be the best we can say. And that however they bridged the gulf between them, the Italians and Vineland, like Secchi DeCasale and John K. Landis, seem to have been a match "made in heaven." Or someplace else.

— *Lawrence DiStasi*

questions about his life and career while occasionally taking potshots at the woodpeckers eating holes in his newly built church steeple.

Did he not feel isolated, we wondered?

"Not at all," said Bandini. "This is so big, this little place; it does not seem to me as though I had left a larger for a lesser career."

FATHER PIETRO BANDINI remained in Tontitown, and was the first to be buried in its cemetery. The town he founded did not go untroubled after him. But Tontitown prevailed, and still produces the bulk of the grapes grown in the southwestern Arkansas area. ❧

ROOTED IN THE EARTH

by Angelo Pellegrini

LEONARDO IS ONE of the most noble among the surviving south Europeans who came to America at the end of the last century. He came, as did many others, to work rather than to exploit; to find the means of subsistence rather than to accumulate wealth. He fled from penury and unrewarded effort to realize, in a new environment, his dignity as a human being. He found much more than he had dared to hope for.

When he arrived in the West, in 1903, he went immediately to work as a common laborer with a street and road construction gang. For the spade of the Italian peasant he substituted the shovel of the American worker — a much lighter implement.

After several years of labor, during which he learned the half-dozen words necessary to one who wields the pick and shovel, he made the appropriate response to the American environment: he got big ideas. Having decided to improve his lot, he chose a means that betrayed an unconsciously perverse respect for the "ladder of success" myth. For work *above* he substituted work *below* the surface of the earth. He passed from grading roadbeds to digging sewer ditches.

That was forty-five years ago, and although he is still in the sewer ditch, he has literally come up. Today, with one of his sons, he has a well-established and profitable sewer contracting business. He has put two sons through college — one of them through the Harvard medical school. But he himself, at sixty-five, with two other men, still works eight hours a day with pick, shovel, and steel bar, doing all the digging that cannot be done by mechanical means. Mike, who put the idea into his head, is one of his employees.

They argue interminably about issues totally undefined. Frequently they quarrel

For most Italians in America, the ancient call of the land was appeased by working a patch of garden, often planted beside a gnarled, bad-tempered grape arbor. For Angelo Pellegrini, this "grubbing in the soil" is what truly humanizes a person and, in Jeffersonian terms, restores the natural balance between ditch-digger, college professor, and president of the republic as well.

with verbal vehemence about the best means for laying out a simple job; but completely undriven by any master, they work like men. Day in and day out, without either straining or sacrificing verbal combats, they produce easily the work of four men picked at random on any construction gang.

THESE TWO MEN, each on his way to seventy, at an age when most academics are retired for reasons of general debility, are doing the heaviest work in the category of common labor. During the spring and summer each goes home at the end of the day's labor to cultivate an acre of land — his garden.

Neither does it because of necessity. The produce is consumed by the family and distributed generously to friends.

While I worked with them, I wanted to know why they worked so hard; why they were so gay; why they gardened on such a large scale.

I think I have discovered the reasons. Their behavior is partly habitual. These men were born to the soil and came from a long line of beasts of burden. They know intimately the earth on which they tread. Though they grumble about the hard work, they accept it with a kind of reluctant acquiescence in fate.

"Siamo nati asini e bisogna lavorare."

"We were born mules and we must therefore labor."

They scorn machinery and take pride in the work of their hands: the appropriate fall in the sewer ditch, the permanence of the pipe they have laid in it, the feeling they have that once a job is done, it is done for eternity. If ever they retire, it will be to a larger plot of earth than the paltry acre they are now gardening for fun.

I noticed, also, that each took pride in the quality of his produce, in coaxing it out of the earth before the normal season, and in making the soil yield what no one had been able to extract from it before. When the peppers were in season each boasted about the quality of his own; and he whom an unfortunate yield obliged to defend an indifferent crop summoned such sophistry to the task as would have done credit to any medieval philosopher.

Every summer is a contest, never defined as such but nonetheless real, to see who can bring forth the first tomatoes, the

first Windsor beans, the first peas. No one ever wins, because no one will ever concede the victory. No matter who brings the first tomatoes and the first bag of beans, the other will insist that they are either hothouse produce or that they come from the Imperial Valley. The insistence is always in such verbal violence that among Americans it would certainly be a prelude to blows. With them it leads to ultimate laughter.

But above all else, they take great delight in eating what they produce in their gardens. While they argue about anything under the sun, and even about some things above the sun, they can never find reason to quarrel about this: that you can't beat what you grow in your own garden.

Every day during the season, each brought bags of tomatoes and ate them as one eats apples. For dessert they would eat in common several pounds of peas or Windsor beans. And always, of course, quantities of radishes, green onions, and peppers so hot that they would blister the lips of any ordinary mortal.

Leonardo is as fine a man as I have ever known. His faults are as the unpolished surface of a precious stone. He is in no way unique among his kind except in this: that his lithe, muscular body, topped with a heavy head of gray hair, is young in appearance as well as in endurance. And that he is interested in ideas. In politics and economics he has read rather widely.

As I see him sweating in the sewer ditch or turning the sod to make a bed for his hot peppers, powerful and confident in every movement, I cannot resist wondering with grave misgivings what he might be like today had he gone to college and become — what?

For obvious reasons, we cannot all seek the cool and invigorating atmosphere of the metropolitan sewer in order to grow old as gracefully as Leonardo. But most of us can approximate the same results by doing our own gardening. Golf, certainly, is a dubious substitute, since the course ends at the clubhouse, where there are beer, cocktails, and other temptations. By all means, let us play the game and enjoy it.

But for keeping trim and close to the pulse of life, there is no better recreation than grubbing in the soil. ❧

THE KUBLAI KHAN OF KERN COUNTY

by E.D. Fortuna

SEVENTY-TWO-YEAR-OLD Joseph DiGiorgio, the largest grape, plum, and pear grower in the world, the largest citrus producer in Florida, is also, as would not seem too surprising, the most influential fruit auctioneer in the U.S. DiGiorgio has risen from lemon packer on his father's Sicilian farm to chief owner and boss of corporate enterprises carried on the books at about $21 million but hardly to be duplicated in 1946 at less than $80 million.

In late May of this year, Mr. and Mrs. DiGiorgio left their New York apartment on Central Park South, took the Twentieth Century to Chicago, boarded the Santa Fe's Chief, and beat the railroad strike into Barstow, California. From there the DiGiorgio's chauffeur drove them west through the Mojave Desert.

Mr. DiGiorgio, between studious plunges into the racing charts, noticed that the spring flowers had already withered from the face of the wasteland. Seventy-five miles west of Barstow his car climbed the Tehachapi mountain range, which joins the Coast Range with the Sierra Nevada. On its farther side, DiGiorgio had his car stopped. He was at the southern tip of the San Joaquin Valley, which is also the southernmost extension of the Central Valley's long domain. Below him was his own land, lying at the foot of hills tawny and napped as a lion's paws.

Looking down on DiGiorgio Farms, the heart of his nationwide ownership of about twenty-six thousand acres, he saw a rectangle of green six miles long and three miles wide. On its eastern and southern sides it was bordered chiefly by the same sort of sagebrush-covered semidesert from which he had wrested the fruit land itself. On its other sides it was hemmed in by the ranches of growers who had followed him into the neighborhood. The whole perimeter of his land was marked by a row of tamarisk, slightly darker green than the leaves of his vines and plum trees. A pale green strip in the north was his asparagus, which he knew was now being left uncut and ferny after a profitable growing season.

Nearer, at DiGiorgio's left, lay the small town of Arvin. Not so far beyond Arvin, and within his ranch's limits, DiGiorgio spied the monolithic concrete of his new winery. At this point in the road DiGiorgio expressed the same sentiment to many friends: "All this I create myself. Before I drill the wells, all was desert like you see close here."

The eighteen square miles that DiGiorgio has girdled round with tamarisk is now known as DiGiorgio, California. Not far from the company office and the post office stands DiGiorgio's house. It looks more or less like the other low and simple clapboard houses in which his head men live, but its interior has a graciousness that belies its plain facade.

In a dining house to the rear, the DiGiorgios sat down that evening to a dinner of steak — from the same beef cattle DiGiorgio slaughters in his own stockyard to provide daily meat for all his ranch help — some eight hundred hands year-round. Among the guests were two DiGiorgio nephews also named Joseph. One was Joseph Salvatore DiGiorgio, vice chairman of the DiGiorgio Fruit Corp. and heir apparent to the throne. To distinguish him from all other Joes, greater or lesser, he is known as J. S. Another was Joseph Arthur DiGiorgio, who is in general charge of all the company's California farming operations. He is J. A.

California farming, like its landscape, runs to extremes. Joseph DiGiorgio created DiGiorgio Farms — at his death in 1951 the world's largest producer of fresh fruit, the apex of corporate farming and all it signifies, both good and bad, to agriculture. John Brucato created the San Francisco Farmer's Market — a cooperative venture designed to frustrate the monopoly of large farms like DiGiorgio's. It remains to be seen whose vision will ultimately prevail.

A bust of DiGiorgio has been erected in the town of Arvin by grateful citizens. It immortalizes him as an Italian American serious thinker, thus tending to fix in bronze the notion that his rise has been from bandana neckcloth to stuffed shirt. This is not the fact. At seventy-two, DiGiorgio is still the personal melting pot of more bubbling forces than even his picturesque speech can evoke. He knows well that as Toscanini is to the baton, Giannini to credit, Obici to peanuts, and La Guardia to the five-cent fare, so is DiGiorgio to grapes, plums, and pears.

CEFALU IS A small town on the north coast of Sicily, about forty miles east of Palermo. One evening in Cefalu, fifty-eight years ago, a boy known as Peppino packed his clothes to enter a local seminary. But Peppino heard on the same evening that one of his gang had been beaten up by another young mob of fighting Cefalutani. He organized a counter-attack. It succeeded in breaking a few noses. It also convinced the head of the seminary that young DiGiorgio was not going his way. Instead of taking the sandals, Peppino DiGiorgio sailed a few months later to New York with a small consignment of his family's lemon crop.

As early as 1918 DiGiorgio had established himself in all the kinds of enterprises with which he is now associated. In 1904 he founded the Baltimore Fruit Exchange, cornerstone of the present auction business. In the off-seasons he had twenty-nine banana freighters operating between Europe and the Caribbean, bucking the giant United Fruit Co. He went into the shipping and commission business on a transcontinental scale with his purchase of the Earl Fruit Co., an old California shipper, in 1910.

It was through the Earl Fruit Co. that DiGiorgio had learned about California and California growing. When in 1919, DiGiorgio observed with increasing distrust the high prices of fruit and fruit lands, he began to consider the possibility that the Earl's loans to growers might be overextended. DiGiorgio gradually drew in the company's line of crop credits. With the ready cash that resulted from leaving an inflated situation at the right time, he visited California on a land-buying venture of his own. He bought 5,845 acres at Delano. Within a year he had

also acquired a box factory in Oregon. It was the beginning of what is now known as California agribusiness.

"After we get the land," DiGiorgio says of California desert farming, "fruit is nothing but water, and labor, and more labor and freight."

IT IS THIS simple and direct intelligence that DiGiorgio's nephews, now in charge of most of his operations, salute as their ideal. His roots, far into the soil, have defied the years as his grapevines have defied the phylloxera.

"If an insect try to eat his way through this root," he says, meaning, presumably, both the vegetal and the corporate root, "he take a hundred years."

Just before the war, Joseph DiGiorgio visited his old roots in Cefalu. An old priest in the seminary he had once thought of attending began to muse over the possibility that the fruit man might have taken the rosary instead of the corporate ledger.

"I tell you one thing right away," said DiGiorgio. "If I'd been gone in then, I would be Pope or there'd be a new Church." ❧

▲
Joseph Di Giorgio (second from left) by 1925 had begun to acquire what would eventually become 26,000 acres of the most productive farmland in the world.

THE FATHER OF FARMER'S MARKET

▲
John Brucato, left, celebrates the founding of the Farmer's Market with some good luck garlic.

JOHN BRUCATO, THE man who founded San Francisco's Farmer's Market, has no trouble remembering the battles or the blows.

"I was accused of being a Communist," he said. "One guy even called me a lousy Sicilian Communist — for selling directly to the people."

He smiled at the recollections. "I was in more damn political fights at the beginning," he said. "But I was fighting for a cause, and I had the people with me. Now, well, if I have any enemies left, I love 'em."

It is fair to say that at a healthy and mostly unscarred seventy-five, John Brucato has outlasted a majority of old foes — and old friends, too.

BRUCATO HAS A lifetime of Bay Area business and public service behind him, but his role in the Farmer's Market is the one history will remember most.

Shift, if you will, back to 1943, a plenty tough time rather than a time of plenty in the United States. John Brucato was named to head the Victory Garden Council, which helped San Franciscans grow food in more than seventy thousand backyard and community plots.

And he noticed something. "Food prices were beginning to skyrocket in the city," he said. "Pears selling for twenty-three cents a pound at local stores. Apples were out of sight. But at the same time, fruit was drop-

ping on the ground in the Sonoma and San Jose areas. You couldn't give it away."

So John Brucato came up with an idea. "Why not get the farmers to come to town with their produce and sell it direct?"

With the help of area newspapers, Brucato found a lot at Market Street and Duboce Avenue in San Francisco. The first Farmer's Market was born.

"We thought we'd operate maybe two weeks," he said, "just to take care of the glut."

For a while, even that modest goal seemed overoptimistic.

"We expected 60 to 70 trucks the first day," Brucato said. "Only 6 came in. They were scared off by wholesale produce merchants and retail grocers. But three days later, on a Saturday, 128 trucks came in and all hell broke loose. We really discovered how much produce wasn't being marketed."

That was in August. By September, Brucato was feeling a pinch. He had a ranch in Sebastopol to run, along with a winery he operated in San Francisco with brothers Frank and Pete.

"I announced the market was going to close on September 15," he said, "and was swamped with protests. The decision was finally made that it might be the best thing to have the city take it over."

IN 1944, THE City and County of San Francisco assumed management of the market and Brucato became chairman of its Citizens Advisory Board, a position he's never relinquished. And a position that still is seldom tranquil, because agribusiness and some retailers mistrust the market's direct-to-consumer concept, and politicians periodically want to change it.

But the small farmers who come to the market's current site at 100 Alemany Boulevard every Tuesday through Saturday from forty-one California counties to sell everything from almonds to zucchinis to weeds for decorative rather than digestive purposes don't. And neither do the shoppers.

— *Dwight Chapin*

THE FISH KING

by Pauline Jacobson

PALADINI, THE FISH King, is reckoned the second wealthiest Italian on the West Coast.

He began life as a soldier in Garibaldi's army. The son of a stage driver from Ancona, Italy, he ran away to join the red shirts. After several battles, he received his honorable discharge and returned home.

But his father's calling and his home town failed to satisfy him after his experiences in the war. Grown restive, he decided to follow the more adventuresome calling of the sea. For five or six years he followed the sea as a common sailor on ships plying the Italian coast. Then one day he met with an engagement on a ship sailing for America around Cape Horn.

The ship anchored in the port of San Francisco. Achille Paladini came ashore with ten dollars in his pockets, all he possessed.

The city seized his fancy.

"I meet some friends," related Paladini. "They tell me money is to be made in the fish business. So I stay. I buy fish on Fisherman's Wharf. I work to buy and catch fish on the Sacramento River."

PALADINI DID NOT believe in insurance. The earthquake and fire of 1906 found him broke, the wealth of a hardworking lifetime swept away in a night. He had fourteen pieces of property burnt to the ground with not a cent's worth of insurance to cover the loss. His one night's sleep in his home in Filbert Street had cost him $35,000. He had bought the house the day before the earth opened.

Several days after the earthquake his friends discovered him in great distress bemoaning over and over again: "My horses, oh, my poor horses!"

"But Paladini," he was challenged, in an attempt to

When he died in 1921, Achille Paladini was already a legend of the West Coast fishery. He had pioneered in the use of powerboats over the early sail rigs, of steam-powered deep-sea trawlers, and of modern refrigeration in his warehouses. But most of his renown came from his reputation as the original "deep pockets." Because he always dealt in cash, he had special pockets made for his trousers that extended to his knees. They could, and apparently did, accommodate as much cash as he needed to transact the day's business.

assuage his sense of loss, "what of your wife and children?"

"My wife and children are well, and in Oakland. But my poor horses! They are cold. They are out in the park without shelter."

Paladini is a mark for dumb animals. In the days of his vigor, *the* sight of the fish district was the dogs nibbling at Paladini's heels, rubbing against him, running between his short, powerful bowlegs.

Today, several chickens have a royal habitat in a corner of his main fish market in Clay Street. When Paladini had become sick, a friend in the country had sent the chickens to him for his table. But Paladini would not consent to their slaughter. They remain a bit of barnyard color in the midst of tons of fish.

But of all the world's dumb animals, the horse is Paladini's favorite. His greatest recreation and delight, in the spare moments of his eighteen-hour days of toil, was the exercising of his racehorses in the park.

After the earthquake, he could not rest until he had found workmen to build a new shelter for his horses. The workmen were not moving fast enough. Paladini implored them to speed it up. Finally a workman spoke up and said if they could have beer they could work faster. You could not find beer in San Francisco in the days after the earthquake. The lid was on. And so, by the next morning Paladini had cut a deal in Oakland. His workmen received a fresh keg in time for lunch.

Paladini turned to the subject of his own earthquake losses only when the new shelter for his horses was completed. He summoned his sons. His one overwhelming ambition in life had been to build up the business for his sons. He called them now together and said: "We will start all over again."

▲

**Achille Paladini in his salad days as
one of the shrewdest fish dealers on
the Pacific Coast.**

The common sailor turned fish king then built a second fortune on the ruins of his first: three new fish markets in San Francisco, one in Oakland, one in Monterey, with buyers all up and down the coast, and salesmen ranging as far east as Utah.

PALADINI IS NOW seventy-eight years old. He has had a stroke. His sons sent him to the country to recuperate. He remained three days. The fish market was his life; to remove him from it was to kill him outright.

He sits, clad in working clothes of rough serge, a flannel shirt, an old black felt hat, on a little side bench at the wide open gateway of the market teeming with activity. Afternoons, a young worker upends a box, sits, and reads to him from an Italian newspaper. Then Paladini watches the work once again.

"I was once full of the pepper," said Paladini, turning on me his haunting smile.

"Paladini," said I, "I understand you are the second richest Italian on the coast."

"My God!" he exclaimed.

It was like the bellow of some wounded animal.

"My God! I sit here, I sit here all day. I have the stroke. I am sick in the head. I am sick in the leg. I can not walk much. The automobile take me down in the morning; the automobile take me home seven o'clock.

"Forty years I am in this business and I am never sick, I never miss the day, seventeen, eighteen hours and I never feel it. Forty years I am close to the water and I work, work, work . . ."

He lapsed to chewing the end of his unlit cigar.

"Paladini" said I, pointing across the street. "You had your first little stand there, your son tells me, and now you own the building."

But he was not to be aroused.

His wealth had been in his work. In his stroke he had met his first defeat. He would give all his fortune to be able to stand with the lowest paid of his employees, apron strung about his hip, knife in hand, behind the block. ଈ

36

FRANK POMILIA:
STILL HOOKED ON FISHING.

DAY AFTER DAY, Frank Pomilia subjects himself to nature's whim, hoping the winds will be gentle, the seas charitable, and he will be allowed to make his living as he has for almost half a century.

As always, he leaves his wife, Giovanna, and his Corte Madera home at an infant hour, bound for Fisherman's Wharf and the mounds of frozen squid and fish carcasses he'll use as bait.

Nature is gracious today.

The defiant gusts and fourteen-foot swells that kept him ashore all week have waned.

Pomilia's weathered hands steer his thirty-six-foot trawler *Josephine* out of Berth 92 and into the fog-veiled Bay. Three hours later, at about 6 a.m., Pomilia finds his "spot" about fourteen miles southwest of Point Bonita.

There, punctuated by fitful tugs at hundred-pound crab traps, ropes, and buoys, the grueling workday really begins.

Pomilia holds the course as his longtime fishing partner, Roger Firenzi, baits the hooks and throws the half-dozen wire mesh traps into the ocean. Their gloved hands rummage through the catch, tossing starfish, octopi, and squid back into the water. She-crabs, undersized males, and the paprika "reds" go, too.

The ritual goes on. One trap over the side, another aboard. Some catches yield only two, maybe three salable crabs. But by day's end, the pair boasts a six-hundred-pound haul at $2.55 per pound.

"Not so bad," says Firenzi.

POMILIA SAYS FISHING is his lot, his legacy. Like his father Francesco, who immigrated to San Francisco in the late 1800s, and the long line of Pomilia men that began in the Mediterranean port town of Sciacca in western Sicily, he'll die a fisherman.

"Quit? Me? Not as long as there's a crab or salmon around," he says. "Where am I going to go? What do I do now?"

At fifty-eight, Pomilia is a chunk of a man, a five-foot nine-inch, two-hundred-pounder with dirt-brown eyes, graying brown hair and a belly that's earned him the nickname Bubbles.

Pomilia wraps his earliest memories of Fisherman's Wharf in poignant and loving recollections of his father. The wharf was a fascinating place then, he says, with "a lot of fish people together, all Italians, like a family. The old-timers used to stretch their nets out on the sidewalk, and the tourists took about a thousand pictures a day of those guys. They didn't come here to see the street artists or the guys selling pizza. Hell, they could be in Arizona someplace and see that."

Today the number of independent fishermen has gone from hundreds to a handful. Still, Pomilia stays, remembering a time when Genoese and Sicilian fishermen like his father were king.

"I remember him in his one-cylinder," he says. "He'd leave at twelve in the morning to go crab fishing. Everything was by hand then. All he had was a compass and a pocket watch.

"And they used nets," he adds, pointing to a hydraulic pulley that yanks his traps to the ocean surface. "They didn't have any equipment like this. And when crab season opened, you couldn't walk [on the wharf], people couldn't wait to buy them."

Pomilia often skipped school to go to the dock and "fool around on the boat." At eighteen, he got his own. With a loan from his mother, he bought the trawler three years later for $8,500 and gave it his mother's name — *Josephine.* Today the boat would cost $90,000, Pomilia figures.

"Crab used to bring five cents a pound," Pomilia recalls. "Today, we're getting $2.50, but we're getting one-fifth of what we used to get. We used to fish for sardines. There were thousands and thousands around. Now, you can't find one. Everything is depleted."

FOR A MOMENT, Frank Pomilia envisions himself at the end of a long line of fishermen that began countless generations ago in Sciacca. Then, he thinks of his grandson, seven-year-old Vito Pomilia. Just days away from his first Holy Communion, Vito wants to be a fisherman, too.

"He likes it now because it's exciting," Pomilia muses. "He helps bait the hooks and cleans them. But in ten, fifteen years from now, it'll probably be all factory ships.

"I would like to see him go to school. I don't want him to be a knucklehead like me.

"Vito should be a dentist or something. Fishing . . . sit's just not the same."

— *Howard Taylor, Jr.*

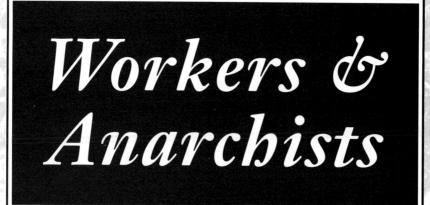

Workers & Anarchists

CARLO TRESCA: TROUBLEMAKER

by Max Eastman

He was loved — his celebrated love affair with revolutionist Elizabeth Gurley Flynn made them a leftist Gable-Lombard. He was hated — his editorial attacks on both the Communists and the Fascists provoked constant threats. And on January 11, 1943, Carlo Tresca was shot down outside his office on Fifth Avenue in New York. The murder, still officially unsolved, evoked grief and outrage and countless eulogies for the man John Dos Passos termed a "guerrilla leader" in the war for the rights of the working man.

CARLO TRESCA IS the despair of all those young men whose idea of success and glory is to get arrested and sent to jail in the cause of the working class.

Tresca holds the international all-time record in this field. He has been arrested thirty-six times. He has been tried by jury seven times. The crimes charged against him run all the way from shouting "Viva Socialismo" in a cop's face to first-degree murder, taking in on the way blasphemy, slander, libel, disturbing the peace, sedition, disorderly conduct, criminal obscenity, conspiracy, unlawful assemblage, and incitement to riot.

He has had his throat cut by a hired assassin, been bombed, been kidnapped by Fascisti, been shot at four times, been marked for death by the agents of Mussolini, and snatched from death's jaws by the magic power of the Black Hand. He was arrested seven times during the great Paterson silk strike, held in thirty-thousand-dollar bail, and tried by jury three times. He has cost the state as much money in legal prosecution as the most desperate criminal.

And he is, I believe, since Eugene Debs died, the most universally esteemed and respected man in the revolutionary movement.

TRESCA CALLS HIMSELF a syndicalist, and stands closer to the Industrial Workers of the World than the political parties, Socialist or Communist. But he is not an organization man. You can't label him. You can't classify him — not even as an anarchist.

He began his career in southern Italy by organizing a branch of the Socialist Party in his home town of Sulmona, and planting a little revolutionary paper called *I Germi (The Seeds)*. As he was the scion of one of the big landlord families — Don Carlo to the peasants even while they marched behind him under the red flag — his seed made a loud noise and grew like a green bay tree.

At the age of twenty-two, he was secretary of the Italian Railroad Workers' Union and one of the best-loved undesirable citizens in that part of Europe. When he was indicted for libeling his father's friend, the political boss of Sulmona, the Socialist Party sent two lawyers to defend him. He was so sure these great men would get him off that he went across the square to a cafe to celebrate while the jury was out, only to find himself sentenced to a year and six months in prison. Released pending an appeal, he forgot — believe it or not — he *forgot* to file his appeal! That lapse of memory caused his rather hasty departure for America.

Tresca stopped off in Geneva on his way to America, and met a local Socialist celebrity who had just made a sensation by challenging God to strike him dead on the platform, an old gag which offended Tresca's sense of fair fighting. Why challenge an unarmed enemy to strike you dead?

Tresca argued all night with this ultra-revolutionary comrade, the gist of his argument being, "Don't mount the barricades till you build them." They parted cool, and the local celebrity's last words were: "Well Comrade Tresca, I hope America will make you over into a real revolutionist."

Tresca's last words were: "I hope, Comrade Mussolini, that you'll quit posing and learn how to fight."

TRESCA DID NOT know too much about the fight himself when he sailed. He knew that he was with the steerage against the first and

second class. He was with the proletariat in a fight to abolish classes. But he still thought the Socialist Party was the proletariat. He edited the official organ of the Italian Socialist Federation for three years, and only in 1907 resigned and quit the party, and went out to the Pennsylvania coal fields to start a purely industrial movement of his own. Syndicalism, he calls this. A better name would be guerrilla fighting.

When Tresca enters a district where a strike is in progress, he is generally alluded to by the newspapers and the powers trying to hold the lid down as "Tresca, the troublemaker." This is a base slander. Tresca never makes trouble. He merely goes where it is, cultivates it, cherishes its fine points, props up the weak ends, nurtures and nurses it along, so that from being a little, mean, and measly trouble, it becomes a fine, big, tumultuous catastrophe approaching the proportions of a national crisis.

That is what he did in Paterson, Lawrence, Pittsburgh, Westmoreland, Mesabi Range, Calumet, the great hotel workers' strike of 1913, and many other less-memorable battlefields. There is hardly a major industrial conflict in the last twenty years of our history in which Carlo Tresca has not joined the vanguard and stood in the front line under fire.

THERE IS SOMETHING peculiarly Italian in the position occupied by Carlo Tresca. He is not the head of a political party or any formal league or union, but an individual revolutionary chief, with his own personal following, devoted and ready to die for him. Enrico Malatesta, the famous Italian anarchist, was such a chief. So in a way is Mussolini. The big black felt hat that Tresca wears — a five-and-a-half-gallon hat, to be accurate — is an essential accessory to this role. Absolute personal courage is another essential.

During the great strike of the iron miners in the Mesabi Range, Tresca was ordered

41

out of the town of Grand Rapids by the sheriff and the district attorney on pain of imprisonment. He took his departure in an automobile driven by a friend, and they were followed into the next county by five automobiles filled with plainclothesmen and armed deputy sheriffs. As they approached the next town, they saw that the main street was lined from one end to the other with deputy sheriffs, strikebreakers, and irate citizens armed with rifles and revolvers.

"It looks like a lynching party," his friend said.

"If so, the sooner it is over, the better," Tresca answered. "Stop the car and I'll walk. You drive on ahead slowly, and don't mind what happens to me. Take care of yourself."

He walked slowly, and with formidable dignity in that big black hat, through a block and a half of these armed enemies, who shouted their taunts at him but stood still in their tracks. His followers, the Italian miners, were in the background, and they shouted, too: "Bravo, Tresca! Coraggio!"

STILL, TRESCA HAS his weakness, his one unforgivable sin. When he stands up at the bar of Heaven, a critical question is going to be asked: "Why did you not study the English language?"

In Italy, Carlo Tresca was on his way to being one of the great leaders of the revolutionary left of the Socialist Party. He was one of the best editors they ever had.

If Tresca had learned English, he would have been one of the biggest men in the history of American labor.

As it is, Tresca's high point was his victory in the New York civil war between Fascists and anti-Fascists. Congress had to appoint a committee to investigate Hitler's propaganda in the United States. Congress once thought of investigating Mussolini's propaganda, but Tresca saved them the trouble.

"We don't argue with the Fascists," he says. "When they offer to debate, we say we'll debate when our brothers in Italy have a free press and the right to speak and meet in the streets. Until then, we do our arguing with guns. You Americans think this is very Latin and very far away. You fool yourselves. Fascism is already here in embryo, and it can't be stopped except with out-and-out war. Either they get the drop on you, or you get it on them. And if they get it, you can wait for the Resurrection."

That is Carlo Tresca's contribution to the chief political problem of our time. It is the contribution of a born fighter, a man to whom fighting is like food and drink, the necessary satisfaction of an instinct.

My own purpose, with this word *instinct*, is to get into a fight with the Freudians. They have a neatly cut-and-dried explanation of all agitators. Agitators are in revolt against the "father-image." And moreover, Tresca fits into their picture perfectly. Did he have a tyrannical father and a gentle mother? Of course he had.

Plenty of other boys, however, are smart and bad and have austere fathers and gentle mothers. Few of them abandon their class privileges and consecrate their lives to fighting the battles of labor against capital, of man against God, of the revolutionary trade union against the state. Few of them develop a propensity for getting loved, shot at, and arrested which puts them in a class with the most famous bandits of history.

I do not say that the father complex is irrelevant; I say it is inadequate. To explain a healthy and clear-thinking man like Carlo Tresca, you've got to explain something besides a child.

As Carluccio himself puts it: "When you have the fighting spirit and the will and power to fight, you must have an enemy, you must have a cause to fight for. I was brought up, or brought myself up, on the tradition of Garibaldi. I grew up in the love of war, and war to me meant war for liberty. I don't call anything else war."

YES, IT TAKES the instinctive love of the fight to explain a life like Tresca's. It takes adrenalin. A man has got to thrive on fighting to live such a life. I can fight when I have to, but it always makes me sick.

It makes Tresca sick not to fight. He is a little sick now from this cause, a little flabby. He has licked the Fascists to a standstill, the Church is on the run, and there's no place for a strictly amateur champion in the revolutionary labor movement, as at presently constituted in America.

For at present, most camps and factions think Tresca is a little irrelevant to the revolutionary movement. They all value his judgment. They all cultivate his friendship. But there's no definite thing for him to do. Revolution is getting to be an organized, large-scale, systematic disciplinary enterprise, like war, or hog butchering. It's the age of the "professional revolutionist," to quote a phrase coined by Lenin.

And although Carlo Tresca comes far closer to what Lenin meant by that phrase than some of the bureaucratic party politicians who now wear it as a title, still Tresca remains an amateur, an artist — an "irreconcilable," as he calls himself.

And by that he means, I think, that the fight is for liberty, and there'll be no victory if you tramp liberty to death in the fight. ❧

THE KING OF LITTLE ITALY

by Lawrence DiStasi

HAD ONE OF the thousands of workers Jim March recruited written a description of the famous padrone, it might have resembled this early sketch of his boss by Cesidio Simboli :

"OUR BOSS WAS a man 'round forty, of medium height, with broad herculean shoulders. His large, apish head, resting upon a solid, bull-like neck, gleamed from a pair of eyes that recalled those of the screech owl. His whole appearance was calculated to inspire more dread than respect; a man, once you made his acquaintance, whom you would walk a mile to avoid. But he was not without graces. He spoke a beautiful, flowing southern Italian dialect, howbeit interlarded with many checked and maimed English words. Under excitement he accompanied almost every word with a gesture and won his audience with a torrent of phrases that flowed from his massy lips like a stream of hot lava.

"I shall never forget him. The impression he made upon me in Mulberry Street that day will never be effaced. He was recruiting recently arrived immigrants for the building of a railroad and was telling us that the country to which he was going to take us, together with the job, the wages, and the board, was the best in the world.

" 'Taliani,' he went on to say, 'why do you doubt me? We are going to a country abounding in fruit trees, flowers, and grass. It is rich in water and game. The surrounding scenery rivals that of Italy itself. The work is easy, the pay good, the board the best to be had, the housing conditions wholesome and comfortable, if not luxurious. What more do you want? Now, how many of you wish to go?'

"As he finished, all hands went up and a joyous murmur broke from the crowd. Most of us had landed at Ellis Island but a few weeks earlier eager to work and anxious to redeem our fortunes. Who could wish a better luck? No wonder we all clustered around him

Most Italians who migrated to America for work came as single males. Unschooled in either customs or language, they were easy prey for padrones like Jim March — who made a fortune mediating (or is pandering the better word?) between management and labor. On the other side was Pascal D'Angelo, who worked as a pick and shovel man even after he became a published poet. His excerpt here begins with his helplessness at being left stranded and unpaid in West Virginia after a contractor went bankrupt.

ENGLISH LESSONS

THAT NIGHT I lingered a long time outside the shanty, thinking. And darkness made the vast solitudes of heaven populous with stars.

At first my mind was turbulent.

And I thought to myself, "Why, I am nothing more than a dog. A dog. But a dog is silent and slinks away when whipped, while I am filled with the urge to cry out, to cry out disconnected words, expressions of pain — anything — to cry out!"

I looked around. I felt a kinship with the beautiful earth. She was like some lovely hard-hearted lady in velvets and gaudy silks — one whom we could gaze at in admiration, but never dare approach.

For a long time I paced the soft green in front of our shanty. Then I entered. The men inside were grumbling mournfully to one another, barely visible in the gloom. I had resigned myself to my fate. I was a poor laborer — a dago, a wop or some such creature in the eyes of America. Well, what could I do? Nothing.

STRANGE TO SAY, I had become lighthearted

like flies, desirous to touch his hand and invoke upon him a thousand blessings. Very few, indeed, realize what a staggering thing it is to land in a new world, whose magnitude, differences of customs, law and language are enough to give one the vertigo. And the fact that nearly all of us came without money and without a friend raised a man like our padrone to the level of a patron saint."

THOUGH HE WAS never canonized, Jim March did get so far as to be labeled "a picaresque hero," "the Mayor of Lafayette Street," and doubtless many other less-printable epithets in his long career. He numbered among his friends not only the local bigwigs among New York Republicans, but the president of the United States himself, Teddy Roosevelt.

None of this could have been predicted when there arrived from Lucania in 1873, a penniless thirteen-year-old named Antonio Michelino Maggio. With no trade and no prospects, Maggio's first earnings came as an itinerant harp player in the small towns outside New York City. When he got to Lowville, New York, the young minstrel tired of wandering and took his first job, distributing milk early mornings in return for room and board. This left his days free for schooling, first at public schools, then at Lowville Academy.

That Maggio was already moving fast is clear, because it was at this time that friends unable to pronounce his real name took to calling him Jim March. The name stuck and was later legalized by the courts.

By 1880 Maggio, now March, had returned to New York City and joined the Erie Railroad. Unskilled to begin with, March didn't take long to make use of his by now Americanized talents — his tongue was as nimble as his feet. The opportunity came in the form of a railroad strike. Because he could speak English to management and Italian to the workers, March was chosen to settle the dispute. He succeeded in short order, and with such satisfaction to both sides that he was rewarded with a purse of $7,670, raised jointly by the railroad company *and* the workers.

That money was all he needed. He entered the padrone business — the railroad called it "labor agent" — recruiting Italian workers for the Erie Railroad's projects all over the state.

The padrone of that time has been called many things — sharper, shylock, flesh merchant, thief. As important as any label, however, is the fact that he served a critical need. He brought workers ignorant of all aspects of the labor market to employers eager to hire them. Along the way he provided lodgings, food, banking services, and even personal counsel. Called boss or even King, the padrone combined the func-

after my return. Foremen would shout at me, and I laughed as soon as their backs were turned. I didn't care. I had resigned myself to the gradual eking out of my life. Work and food.

Up on Hudson Heights, on top of the Palisades, was a boardinghouse kept by a paisana. And there I would spend the evenings, joking and fooling. I walked up and down with a broad smile on my face. And it was just by accident, and from this same sense of joking, that my life took an upward turn.

First of all, a crowd of Mexican laborers were brought up from the south to work with us in the yard. There was one, a wiry young man, who had been with Villa and had been taken prisoner by the Americans. Besides Spanish he could speak a strange Indian language that sounded very queer to me. That winter he and another old man came to live in our box car, and our quarters, already crowded, became packed.

I began to learn some Spanish from these two Mexicans. The younger one received a Spanish weekly from some town in Texas. To my amusement he would sit hours at a time reading it. Little by little I became interested in the paper, and tried to pick out words that were like Italian. I had gotten to think of a newspaper as something to start a fire with or to wrap objects in.

But now I began to read again — very little at first, I must confess. Somehow I found English more to my liking than Spanish. And about once a week I even bought an English newspaper to look at. There was very little in them that I could understand, even though I spent many a puzzled hour trying to decipher the strange words. When I did learn a word and had discovered its meaning, I would write it in big letters on the moldy walls of the box car. And soon I had my first lesson in English all around me.

One day a friend of mine who was a bartender in one of the many saloons that lined River Road took me to an Italian vaudeville show in a theater on the Bowery in New York. Included in the program was a short farce. I heard it and decided to myself that I could do better.

I went home and tried to write something after work. I began it in Italian, but unable to manage the language, on a sudden thought I decided to attempt it in English. After a few Sundays of hard work I had about three closely written pages of the most impossible English one could imagine. In triumph, I showed it to a couple of brakemen. They laughed long and loud. There was some doubt whether it was the jokes or the manhandled English which caused their hilarity. However, I gave myself the benefit of the doubt, and agreed with myself that I could write English.

— *Pascal D'Angelo*

tions of employer, middleman, worker's agent, contractor, and eventually political leader as well.

Clearly the opportunities for chicanery were enormous. Many took full advantage of them. Jim March evidently took his share. One occasion when he did has passed into padrone folklore.

The Erie Railroad had made him an overseer in 1885. Not long after, the railroad handed him a rush order for one thousand laborers for construction work in upstate New York. March wasted no time. He hustled down to Mulberry Bend Park—the gathering place of Lower East Side Italians—and without sparing the flourishes began his pitch for workers. Like some pick-and-shovel Garibaldi, he had his "thousand" in short order.

He also had his pockets wide open. From each man he collected not only the usual "bossatura" or commission, but also five dollars for transportation to the job, and an extra three dollars for lumber to build shacks in which to live while on the job. His claim was that the fees were required by the railroad — but it was an open secret in the community that since the railroad gave free transportation and shelter with the job, March himself had pocketed the eight thousand dollars he collected.

Nor was this all. March had already obtained sole commissary rights for the thousand workers while on the road, so that in the end most of their earnings wound up in the padrone's deep pockets as usual.

It wasn't long before Jim March became a King of Little Italy. He invested in several choice pieces of real estate. He became a trustee of the Italian Savings Bank. He became a power in the political life of his community, organizing the first Republican Club with Italian American membership in his Sixth District. Now that he could deliver votes as well as bodies, Jim March became visible to the outside politicians as well. In 1897, his friend and then-governor Theodore Roosevelt appointed him port warden of the port of New York. The perfect position for an old padrone, it was a post ripe with potential for patronage, and graft.

March lived magnificently until he died in 1910. A dazzling and envied figure in the downtown night spots, he was known, admired, and, if not loved, at least so influential in his world that in the election for Republican Presidential Elector in 1904, he received 859,553 votes — 250,000 more than his Democratic rival. It was the largest number garnered in that election by any elector in the entire country.

The old padrone had definitely "made America." ❧

THE LIGHT OF INSURRECTION

My Dear Mrs. Glendower Evans:

Thanks to you from the bottom of my heart for your confidence in my innocence; I am so. I did not spittel a drop of blood, or steal a cent in all my life. A little knowledge of the past; a sorrowful experience of the life itself had gave to me some ideas very different from those of many other umane beings. But I wish to convince my fellowmen that only with virtue and honesty is possible for us to find a little happiness in the world.

I preached: I worked. I wished with all my faculties that the social wealth would belong to every umane creatures, so well as it was the fruit of the work of all. But this do not mean robbery for a insurrection.

The insurrection, the great movements of the soul, do not need dollars. It need love, light, spirit of sacrifice, ideas, conscience, instincts.

It need more conscience, more hope and more goodness.

And all this blessed things can be seeded, awoked, growed up in the heart of man in many ways, but not by robbery and murder for robbery.

I like you to know that I think of Italy, so speaking. From the universal family, turning to this humble son, I will say that, as far as my needs, wish and aspirations call, I do not need to become a bandit.

I like the teaching of Tolstoi, Saint Francesco, and Dante.

I like the example of Cincinati and Garibaldi.

The epicurean joi do not like to me. A little roof, a field, a few books and food is all what I need. I do not care for money, for leisure, for mondane ambition. And honest, even in this world of lambs and wolves I can have those things. My father has many field, houses, garden. He deal in wine and fruits and granaries. He wrote to me many times to come back home, and be a business man. Well, this supposed murderer had answered to him that my conscience do not permit to me to be a business man and I will gain my bread by work his field.

And more: The clearness of mind, the peace of the conscience, the determination and force of will, the intelligence, all, all what make the man feeling to be a part of the life, force and intelligence of the universe, will be brake by a crime. I know that, I see that, I tell that to everybody: Do not violate the law of nature, if you do not want to be a miserable. I remember: it was a night without moon, but starry. I sit alone in the darkness, I was sorry, very sorry. With the face in my hands I began to look at the stars. I feel that my soul want goes away from my body, and I have had to make an effort to keep it in my chest. So, I am the son of Nature, and I am so rich that I do not need any money. And for this they say I am a murderer and condemned me to death.

Death? It is nothing.

Abbominium is cruel thing.

Now you advise me to study. Yes, it would be a good thing. But I do not know enough this language to be able to make any study through it. I will like to read Longfellow's,

◀ Bartolomeo Vanzetti, center with mustache, just before being sentenced to die with Nicola Sacco.

Paine's, Franklin's and Jefferson's works, but I cannot. I would like to study mathematics, physics, history and science, but I have not a sufficient elementary school to begin such studies, especially the two first and I cannot study without work, hard physical work, sunshine and winds; free, blessing wind. There is no flame without the atmospheric gasses; and no light of genius in any soul without they communion with Mother Nature.

I hope to see you very soon; I will tell you more in the matter. I will write something, a meditation perhaps and name it: Waiting for the Hanger. I have lost the confidence in the justice of man. I mean in what is called so;

not of course, of that sentiment which lay in the heart of man, and that no infernal force will be strong enough to soffocate it. Your assistance and the assistance of so many good men and women, had made my cross much more light. I will not forget it.

Bartolomeo Vanzetti
July 22, 1921
Charlestown Prison

47

PORTRAIT OF A BOARDINGHOUSE WOMAN

by Angelo Pellegrini

BEFORE SHE PUT the sea bass in the oven, Rosa Mondavi let me look at it. It was a three-pound cut placed in the center of a large baking dish. "There are parsley and marjoram and garlic and lemon juice, salt and pepper. It will bake about two and a half hours at 450, reduced to 400 the last hour. When it begins to brown, I will add a cup of white wine — we usually use our own Riesling. You will like it." She lowered her eyelids and smiled.

"I am sure I shall. In the kitchen you are superb, signora. Why don't you write a cookbook?"

"Eh, write, write. It is easy to say. But I never went to school."

"Not even the first grade?"

"Not even one day. The signora for whom I worked taught me to read and write a little. But at eighteen I married Cesare and went to Minnesota, where I kept boarders and cooked and washed and scrubbed floors. And here I am."

So Rosa Mondavi had kept boarders too. While still a young mother with four children, she had fed and housed and kept clean immigrant laborers. I could easily imagine the rest. I had heard it from dozens of other immigrant mothers. I myself had grown up with a dozen boarders in our home.

THE ITALIAN IMMIGRANT boardinghouse is a neglected bit of Americana. As an institution it had a relatively short life — about a quarter of a century; but in its time it was as indigenous to, and as authentically of, America as were the saloon and the brothel of the frontier West. The saloon and brothel thrived where

▲
Rosa Mondavi: the keeper of a neglected bit of Americana

The struggle of women who worked outside the home to better their lot — as illustrated by Angela Bambace in the garment industry — is by now familiar. Not so well known is the struggle of Italian American women who worked inside *the home, maintaining that institution indispensable to migrant males, the boardinghouse. Rosa Mondavi was one of those women, and her story reveals a kind of backstage heroism seldom publicized.*

there were men who needed liquor and women; the boardinghouse thrived where there were men who needed women to cook and wash for them.

From 1900 to 1905, approximately three million Italians came to America, the great majority men without women. In response to this wave, beginning around 1900 and continuing for about twenty years, nearly every Italian family in America offered room and board.

The burdens imposed on the women of these boardinghouses were of course enormous. Without the aid of automatic appliances of any kind, the woman cooked and washed for an average of eight men in addition to her own family. She baked bread, made lunches, scrubbed floors. Her work day began at five in the morning and ended at eleven at night.

Why did she wash for the men? Why didn't she insist that they have their laundry done elsewhere? Why accede to their demands: Tony did not like fish; Mike never ate pork; Joe could not abide lamb; Pasquale did not care for spaghetti; nine different meals each evening; why? The answer is in the word tradition. A creature of Old World culture, the immigrant mother who took boarders assumed the responsibilities of their mothers, especially when the men were young. It was a sacred duty.

And there were other burdens, in the long run more destructive to body and spirit than the physical. These immigrant men were men without women. As a class they were rough, crude, simple, without formal education, men of strong passions and weak inhibitions, hard workers. It was inevitable, however, that

ANGELA BAMBACE
OF THE ILGWU

NOTHING IS MORE mystifying — and at the same time more natural — than the way in which the influence of a parent bears fruit in a child. This is the case with Angela Bambace.

She could have followed in her father's stuttering footsteps — he had worked as a fisherman with a fleet in Brazil until ill health forced him back to Italy, then to America for a time, then back to Italy, and finally to East Harlem where his wife had to support the family trimming plumes for ladies' hats. She could have supported her own husband — the man her father had picked for her — in the same way. Angela Bambace did not. She seems to have taken her cue from that plume-trimming mother.

At eighteen, she began to work in a shirtwaist factory, and was soon busy organizing the women workers for the International Ladies' Garment Workers Union. Her mother, Giuseppina, not only allowed Angela to do this hazardous work (manufacturers routinely hired toughs to harass union organizers); she often accompanied her on her rounds, brandishing that ancient weapon of all Italian mothers — the rolling pin.

Angela's sister, Maria, also an organizer and later the wife of Industrial Workers of the World activist Antonio Capraro, recalls one such occasion. It involved an enforcer called Gagliano. "When my mother heard that a young Jewish woman had been beaten up, she went to him and said, 'Do you know what happened today in the shop?' Mr. Gagliano replied, 'What happened? Your daughters weren't hurt, were they?' He had respect for her, and her daughters were not to be harmed according to him. My mother said, 'Not my daughters, but another mother's daughter was. So what difference does that make?'

"Gagliano called off his boys. Even though he was considered a racketeer, he behaved in a considerate manner towards my mother."

IT IS NOWHERE recorded that Angela Bambace carried a rolling pin while organizing. And yet it — or something like it — gave her the kind of courage and fire to successfully compete in an area previously reserved almost exclusively for men.

In the 1919 garment workers' strikes in Harlem, for instance, regarding a truculent worker Bambace is reported to have advised her sister, "Don't talk to her, punch her in the nose."

In the bitter strikes in New York and New Jersey of 1932 and 1933, she was often on the other end, once being pushed down an entire flight of stairs by an irate employer, several times landing in jail. She seemed to thrive on the excitement.

This is not to say that her attitude and tactics remained static. She was by turns a Communist, an anarchist supporter of Sacco and Vanzetti, a housewife, the companion of Italian anarchist and writer Luigi Quintilliano, an organizer in Baltimore of the first garment workers' local composed entirely of women, a New Deal supporter, and vice president of the ILGWU's executive board. In 1962 she was named by President Kennedy to his Commission on the Status of Women.

Her best days, perhaps, were spent in Maryland. In Baltimore, first, then in the small towns of Maryland where unions were not only rare, but virtually unheard of, especially when promoted by a New Yorker who was also an Italian, Angela continued to organize. A woman unable to drive, she was driven to her appointments by a black man with whom she would eat lunch in the park rather than leave him outside the white-only restaurants which refused him service. Angela Bambace became something of a folk legend in Maryland.

In Maryland, she also organized a group of women cloak-makers into Local 227, the first local composed entirely of women. In 1936, the local won its first victory after a walkout, winning recognition from a large, nonunion firm. Further victories came in long bitter strikes against the American Raincoat Company and then against the Roberts Dress Company of Baltimore, where Bambace introduced the "big city" tactic of the "sit-down" strike.

So successful was she that she became the first Italian woman to penetrate the male-dominated leadership of her union. In 1942, she was named manager of the newly created Maryland-Virginia District, a post from which she helped establish an outpatient clinical service for union members. In 1956 she was elected vice president of the ILGWU's General Executive Board, the first non-Jewish woman to be elected to that post. Only in 1972 did Angela Bambace retire from the ILGWU to devote herself to more general social causes. And only in 1975 did she succumb to the cancer she had been resisting for several years.

— *Laura Segretti*

◀ **Angela Bamace: union organizer for ladies garment workers**

there should be among them a grossly offensive few: men whose speech was vile, men who did not hesitate to spit on the floor, men who were obsessively preoccupied with sex, whose curses were usually sexual imprecations, bluntly and openly expressed.

"If I could but once spread the thighs of the blonde who works at the grocery store . . . Last night I dreamed that I had driven it deep into . . ."

"Driven what? You haven't enough to fill a thimble."

In such an environment thousands of immigrant mothers, helpless and traditionally subservient, wept and suffered in silence. But there were mothers of extraordinary mettle, of courage and uncompromising principles. They kept boarders, but on their own terms. Rosa Mondavi was such a woman.

When she came to America in 1908, Mondavi was a young bride of eighteen. Before her nineteenth birthday, in a mining camp in Minnesota, she was cooking and washing for sixteen men. In fourteen years she never had less than fifteen men in her home. Without hired help, she cooked, washed, and scrubbed for them. When they were ill she was their nurse and mother. In America, the land of plenty, where the men worked ten long perilous hours in the mine, she catered to their gastronomic whims. Her day began at four-thirty in the morning and ended at eleven-thirty in the evening. Every evening when the dishes were done, she packed the men's lunches. During the bitter cold weather she brought hot food to her men in the mine — on her own initiative. A woman must protect her man; and while the men were in her home and they behaved, they were all her men.

At thirty-one, when Rosa Mondavi abandoned the boardinghouse, her achievement had been considerable. She had been a mother to men without women. She had helped her husband to establish a home for four children. She had launched with him a creative partnership. And she had finally earned the right to devote all of her remaining time to the care of her family. A right that most women claim as a matter of privilege, Rose Mondavi had had to earn with fourteen years of hard labor. ❧

James Petrillo would take on anyone — if it meant a better deal for his musicians. But his main adversary was the machine that makes music — records, movies, television. As he said, "What did the movies do to musicians? Overnight, put twenty-two thousand musicians out of theaters." He was fighting a rearguard action, and he knew it, but he won most battles in this war, the most famous being his twenty-seven-month strike to force record companies to pay musicians royalties. When he died in 1984, an era in American labor ended.

THE UNPREDICTABLE PETRILLO

by Jack Gould

AS THE UNION pooh-bah of musicland, James C. Petrillo is a man of provocative, if peculiar, distinction. A scratch of his pen on the bottom of a one-paragraph letter usually has reverberations from the recesses of Tin Pan Alley to the halls of Congress. Instinctively thereafter legal minions between Hollywood and Radio City forgather to calculate what his deed will cost and to ask if it has been done ever before. It seldom has.

Yet in personal life Mr. Petrillo is out of Hamlet by Falstaff, alternately brooding over his controversial state and indulging in histrionic highjinks of gusty humor. Czar of the world of melody by consent of 225,000 instrumentalists in the United States and Canada, he has shown no qualms when called on the carpet by the Army and the Navy and the president of the United States. But his fear of stray germs is so great that in meeting a stranger he declines to shake hands and insists on hooking little fingers fraternity style.

Though his own musical career has consisted of brief exposure to a cornet, Jimmy gives the economic downbeat for Toscanini and Spike Jones and everyone between. His role as president of the American Federation of Musicians is to make sure there is always a financial obbligato to the tune, be it Beethoven or bebop. The musicologist may be concerned whether the instrumentalist has talents; Petrillo wants to know if he has groceries.

Controversial as his economic theories may be, it is Mr. Petrillo's methods which are primarily responsible for his national renown. His principal technique is to reverse labor's usual practice in negotiations. Rather than first deciding what he wants and then mobilizing his union's strength to win it, he often first stops all work and then decides what it is he wants.

More than a year ago he issued a ukase forbidding

musicians to work for television under any circumstances, blithely explaining: "We want to see where it's going first." Television leaders, wondering how video could go anywhere if everybody decided it should not be allowed to start, say that not even in the electronic era is it possible to have a cake before it is baked.

IF THERE ARE often two sides to the issues and methods which Mr. Petrillo has brought to the fore, there are many more to the enigmatic personality of the man himself. It is a personality which once prompted a radio official to make this cryptic quip: "You've got to know the guy to like him, but once you know him you've really got to watch out."

Mr. Petrillo was born fifty-five years ago, the son of Italian immigrants. His mother had a particular fondness for the name Caesar and named him James Caesar Petrillo, and his brother, now a Chicago orchestra leader, Caesar James Petrillo. Jimmy blew his first feeble toots on a horn at the age of eight and received encouragement in this pursuit at Hull House from Jane Addams, of whom he always speaks with deep respect. He went to school for nine years, in which time he was graduated from the fourth grade. He likes to recall that he was good at least at arithmetic. In the tradition, too, he was a newsboy. At eighteen he was a member of a band which did odd assignments at funerals, picnics, and weddings.

Mr. Petrillo's career as a union leader began in 1915, when he was president of a Chicago organization known as the American Musicians Union. Failing reelection three years later, he transferred his allegiance to the Chicago local of the American Federation of Musicians and has headed it since 1923.

Petrillo was elected to the presidency of the American Federation of Musicians, now the seventh largest international union in the AFL in 1940, when he succeeded Joseph N. Weber. Under the constitution and bylaws of the federation, Mr. Petrillo enjoys virtually absolute powers. That fact, coupled with his deeds and his middle name, finally has enabled him to edge out John L. Lewis in the affection of newspaper cartoonists. The walls of his offices in both New York and Chicago are covered with drawings depicting him as "a dictator" and "a czar."

When asked bluntly about being "a czar," Jimmy replies in the form of an analogy involving either David Sarnoff, chairman of the board of the Radio Corporation of America, or Nicholas M. Schenck, head of Loew's Inc., the two men with whom he makes his most important contracts.

"That fellow Zharnoff, do they call him a czar?" Jimmy asks, pronouncing the name with an Italian accent. "He can fire two thousand men down at his plant in Camden because he thinks it is the thing to do for his company and his stockholders, and nobody says nothin'. Do they call him a 'czar'? Naw, he's head of the company and he's put in there to run it. Well, it's the same thing with the federation. When you've got a lot of people somebody's got to have the power to act or you'd never get anything done. The union convention chose me just like the stockholders okayed Zharnoff."

In his dual capacity as president of the national federation and of the Chicago local, Mr. Petrillo receives an attractive annual salary, plus generous expenses, and he lives up to his means. When in New York he stops at the Waldorf Astoria and eats frequently at Luchow's. He goes to concerts and Broadway shows with some frequency, and his taste leans to the popular side, his last visit to the theater having been to see *High Button Shoes* rather than *Allegro*.

JIMMY'S MANY AND diverse acts have been approved thus far repeatedly at union conventions. Whoever tries to harness Jimmy Petrillo is not likely to find it an easy task, as one of the more sardonic of film producers once testified. After several days of negotiations, the producer was asked if he was making progress with the union leader. "That bird knows more tunes than a musician," he replied.

THE REAL ANTONINI

So MUCH HAS been written and spoken about Luigi Antonini in praise and disparagement; he has been so thoroughly lauded and so abused and reviled that there would seem to be no reason for this essay. But since very few, if any, people know the real Antonini — or dare describe him as he is frankly — and since I believe I know him as well as any other person, and maybe better, I venture to come out with these few opinions.

I have known Antonini for about thirty years, during which I have been his close friend, coworker and fellow fighter, a sort of foster brother, in fact everything that goes with reciprocal devotion, attachment and profound affection, except as an advisor and councillor — not because I have not tried, but because no one can advise a precipitous mountain torrent to go any other way but its bed and course.

Born in Vallata Irpina on September 11, 1883, the son of a teacher-poet with Garibaldian and Mazzinian ideals, Antonini came to America after serving in the Italian Army. He became a presser but, according to his "Mastro," was never meant to be a good one. After editing *L'Operaia*, he organized and became General Secretary of Local 89, a post he has retained to this day.

He is first and above all a full-blooded human being, a lover of humanity and a consecrated warrior for all its causes, a bullheaded, uncompromising fighter for individual rights and universal emancipation.

He is now about sixty-one years old. He stands close to six feet, a bit bent by the weight of not unkindly years, full-maned, smooth-shaven but by a silly shadow of a black mustache now growing gray, rather somewhat shambling in his military gait.

He wears a large Stetson hat and a flowing black Windsor tie, which I suspect he originally copied from me — if so, this is his only imitation — and he carries a cane, not because he is halting and not as the baton of a field marshal, but because he must keep one of his hands bothered as the other flails the air while he is in motion.

He has no children, a source of chagrin but not of distress for both him and his Jennie, as they compensate, if they do not sublimate it altogether, by their love for all children who flock over to them with reciprocated freedom.

He also loves, next to human beings, all kind of animals; in his small home he keeps a sizable aviary stocked with all sorts of obtainable birds including a tame bluejay partial to provolone, a small kennel of gift dogs generally very large, a dwarf Sardinian donkey christened Vitemma, a mangy fangless old she-wolf named Benita, and a spayed striped hyena which answers to the sweet name of Adolfina.

I don't know when Luigi goes to bed, maybe he never does, for he works with the ants in the day and the owls at night; but I know that he rises every morning at five, and after bathing and a substantial breakfast he visits and feeds his dogs and his birds and then proceeds to his office, which he reaches more often than not before any of his large staff arrives, whereupon he begins to bawl out everybody and anybody and continues to bellow and boom stentoriously for the rest of the day.

— *Arturo Giovannitti*

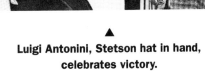

▲
Luigi Antonini, Stetson hat in hand, celebrates victory.

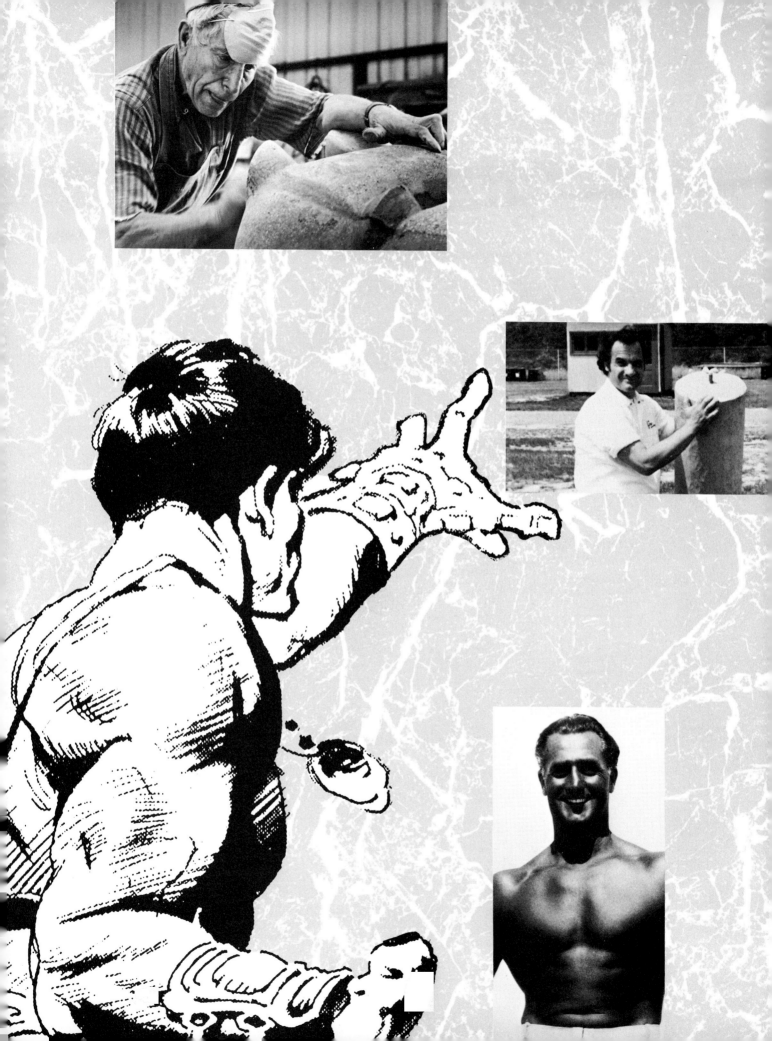

The People's Eye

THE COLOR OF HUMANITY

by Patrick Watson

IN 1972 WHEN I met him, Ralph Fasanella was still wiping windshields and pumping gas at his brother Nick's gas station underneath the Cross-Bronx Expressway. This work had been a major part of his livelihood for nearly thirty years. Just turned fifty-eight, he was perfectly prepared to keep on working as long as his health held out, should that prove necessary or desirable. "After all," he said, "I need my daily aggravation."

A short, stocky, comfortably rumpled guy in a work shirt and gas station hat, usually needing a shave, usually drinking coffee, usually smoking a Camel cigarette, Fasanella calls you "old man" if you're getting along all right, and "guy" when he's feeling affectionate.

RALPH FASANELLA TURNED to painting at the age of thirty, he will tell you, because he felt he was losing his roots. Despite the growing success of the labor movement, and his own success as an organizer for the United Electrical Workers of the CIO, he had become restless, with a sense of imprisonment in the work he was doing. He felt no growth in himself and resented being crowded by the developing character of the unions, their increasing rigidity and apparent movement away from what he would call the "wail of the working man."

And so he began to look backward to his own childhood, to the agony of his father the iceman and his mother the buttonhole-maker. The environment of vitality and exhaustion, of intensely close, comforting family in the midst of dark and noisy Greenwich Village tenements, had been the nourishing ground out of which his politics and his anger had grown, and he could feel it no longer.

All he could feel was restless and tense — his fingers hurt and he didn't know what to do about it. So he began to paint. He began with the streets. Sullivan Street in Greenwich Village where he grew up, the real root, the lost root, the first significant way station on the search for America.

Untrained, virtually unknown until 1972, Ralph Fasanella comes as close to being a "natural" as any artist can. Art began for him when his fingers hurt and he didn't know what to do about it. Thinking it was arthritis, he tried rubbing his fingers on paper not only to ease the pain but "to make the paper talk." That was in 1944, and since then he has been talking on canvas as he talks in person — a mile a minute. As an expression of Italian American life in New York, his work is invaluable.

▲
"McCarthy Era — Gray Day" oil on canvas, 1963.

56

They played on the roof, Ralph and Bobby and Jim and Tony. The kids who didn't go to school if they could help it, the kids who ran across the rooftops, jumping across the chasms, building to building. Sometimes a boy would miss, and just go down, five, six, seven stories to the pavement. That was that.

Ralph painted Sullivan Street from memory. He might have gone around the corner and found it in 1945 or 1946 not all that much changed from the twenties, but he was determined to see it with the eyes of his boyhood. Here were the rooftops that had been his backyard. Next door was a little pizza place, said to be the first pizzeria in America.

The building is gone now, no plaque to honor the first pizza in America, but there is a plaque next door, because in that house, the one with the For Sale sign on it in the painting, Fiorello La Guardia was born in 1882. La Guardia became mayor of New York in 1934 and is one of the few Italian Americans, according to Fasanella, that you can really feel proud of.

"You see, we don't have too many, not in a political sense. Besides La Guardia, there was Marcantonio, who died young, and that's about it. We have our daily stars, our Joe DiMaggios, the current guys that go with the newspaper headlines.

"But for a working guy to grab a bit of knowledge

in this society, it's a rough ball game. If you've got anything on the ball you end up as a little-time gangster, a racketeer.

"I'm talking about 1922, 1923 now. I was eight, nine years old. You saw, you knew nothing. You kept quiet. And some of the guys that came from this era became the Big Ghees, I use the word *ghee*, you understand, gangster, the Big Ghee. Very important word with the Italians, derives from the Italian. He's a big shot, a man who knows how to maneuver. Now they use the word *Mafia*, but that's all garbage."

Fasanella cherishes his Italian origins — more accurately his Italian American origins. When I told him that the third biggest group in Canada, my own homeland, was Italian, and that the city of Toronto had a quarter of a million Italians, and a little Italy, he paused in wistfulness a moment and wondered if he should move up there where a different kind of start could be made, where Italians could "grab" something back they had tragically let go in America.

"We got caught in the money culture. We became Americanized and we forgot our own ways."

A PAINTING: *Pie-in-the-sky.*

The foreground wall of the right-hand building is open, so you can see the rooms within. And to balance the interior of the rooms, the left-hand building has been ironically painted with a whiskey advertisement.

"I used to go down Houston Street and they had all these assholes coming down and giving you beautiful ads in the street. The question of ads in this country has always been preying on the people with illusions. Give them the lollipop dream. Now listen. Through advertising and affluence we get to the place where we can now paint houses pink, yellow, anything we want, right? In these old tenement houses — dark, frightening buildings by the way — the problem was always, how do you bring in some light? Then I find people, with any color they want, they're painting dark inside. My sister, over on Mott Street, another guy painted a dark ceiling, another guy cocoa walls.

"What *is* all this shit?"

Man's Dream. The pie-in-the-sky.

A suburban house, detached, with a fireplace and brightly painted walls and garden space around it. And on the other side of the church spire, there is the other part of the dream — the swings, the playground, the outdoor private swimming pool, all the *House and Garden* desiderata of the advertising age.

"All that shit! It's death . . . I've got a painting to do . . . too many to do."

Why was the dream of the suburban house a dream of death?

"Well, we have to live together, you know. People live with people, and grow with people. We all dreamed about the house in the country years ago, we talked about a porch, we talked about a backyard, we talked about people, we got together.

"But then what happened, when the dream came true? He gets the house in the country, gets the fucking pool table, the television set, got all the things. The kid next door, he has all the other things, all the same things, and suddenly they're all by themselves. That's no good.

"Life is together. Fighting together, playing stickball together. Games are made — you need the other guy to play with. Can't play by yourself. Can't be a so-quiet sensitive fellow in the room, jerking off by yourself."

Fasanella lets out a sigh, and walks around the room a bit, sipping coffee.

"The color — I keep going back to the Church. I think these ghees took the beautiful colors out of the church and made nightclubs and whorehouses out of them. So you get your purples and your blues. Go down there and begin to find out why these guys pick these colors out. You see, they took their background, stained glass, and brought it into their nightclubs.

"The Negro did it more natural, more a wailing blue. The Italian blue to me has more of an emotional hardness inside — it's been Americanized. Look at Puzo's book, *The Godfather*, talking about the guy who shoots people. He's talking an American product — cold, you know. You're killing and you don't think of it as killing. That's cold. They've glorified this whole shit, made a big something out of nothing. A monumental book about the Mafia? I'll tell you something. To me, in my mind, it's a monumental joke. Clever. These writers, they are sharp cookies. But they have missed most of the meaningful stories about Italians.

"My old man who got up every morning to bust his chops at his job, and cursed and swore — he was so bitter! That's a different color entirely. *That's* humanity!"

That's Ralph Fasanella. ❧

THE RETURN OF HERCULES

by Charles Gaines

He numbered among his pupils Joe DiMaggio and Gandhi. The ad promoting his method of bodybuilding may be the best-known few cartoon panels in history. At the least it started what could be the most popular art form of all — making one's own body into the ideal artifact Charles Atlas first envisioned and embodied and tirelessly promoted. Curiously, another Brooklyn native, Frank Frazetta, took the ideal into hyperspace with his fantastic illustrations.

All I want is to build a perfect race, a country of perfect human masterpieces.

— Charles Atlas

HIS REAL NAME was Angelo Siciliano. He was born on October 30, 1893, near the town of Acri, in Calabria. When he was ten, his parents separated, and his mother took him off to America, settling with one of Angelo's uncles in one of the tough waterfront sections of Brooklyn. He was pale, thin, weak, and just off the boat. He was an easy target for local thugs.

A pathetic picture of him at fifteen reveals a true ninety-seven-pound weakling. In that year, 1908, he left school and began a ten-hour-a-day job making women's pocketbooks. On Halloween night on his way home from work, he was attacked by a neighborhood bully who beat him with a stocking filled with ashes.

"It seemed like he was beating the brains out of me," Charles Atlas remembered later. "I must have lay there in the gutter for an hour resting up. When I got home, my uncle said, 'What's the idea of getting in fights?' and he gave me another beating. I went to my room and cried myself to sleep. But before I fell asleep, I swore an oath to my God that I would never allow any man on this earth to hurt me again."

There would be one additional beating. Although the event would later be given such resonance by the advertisement featuring it that it seems now to have occurred at the very dawn of American history, the continuing transformation of young Angelo Siciliano into Charles Atlas occurred the following year on the beach at Coney Island. In the ad — one of the most successful in the history of advertising — the incident was depicted in a comic strip called "The Insult that Made a Man out of Mac."

Listen to Charles Atlas, at the age of seventy-six, recalling what actually happened on that now immortal day: "I went out to Coney Island, and I had a pretty girl with me. We were sitting on the sand. A big, husky lifeguard kicked sand in my face. I couldn't do anything, and the girl felt funny. I told her that some day if I meet this guy, I would lick him."

The girl, we learn, did not wait around. Neither

did Angelo. He was finding his secret — Dynamic Tension — at the zoo.

"I was standing in front of a lion's cage at a local zoo, and an old gentleman was lying there asleep. All of a sudden he got up and gives a stretch. Well, he stretched himself all over — you know how they do — and the muscles ran around like rabbits under a rug. I says to myself, 'Does this old gentleman have any barbells, any exercisers? No, sir. Then what's he been doing?' And it came over me. I said to myself: 'He's been pitting one muscle against another!' "

It is fundamental isometrics. Young Angelo Siciliano had found what he was looking for.

The man's a legend, like the Lone Ranger.

— Howie Poret

IT COULD BE convincingly argued that in a long, dramatically lucky life, the luckiest thing that ever happened to Charles Atlas was meeting Charles Roman. In 1928, Roman was twenty-one and a new employee of the Landsman Advertising Agency — the agency which handled the fading Charles Atlas account. Roman was given that account. Four months after they met, Atlas offered him half his business in exchange for Roman's management. Roman accepted and one of the most successful partnerships in the history of marketing was launched.

It was a perfect coalition. Atlas was the idealist with the goods — his body a piece of sculpture, his head full of visions of a physically perfect race of Americans. Roman was the realist, the packager and dispenser of the ideals, enjoying Rolls-Royce convertibles and boats for his labor.

By the 1950s, under Roman's management, Atlas had nearly a million pupils all over the world. By then the Atlas course had been translated into seven languages and braille. Mail came from Africa, India, the Philippines, Australia, everywhere — at the rate of two truckloads a day. Atlas's figure was appearing in ads in more than four hundred comic books and magazines from Iceland to New Zealand.

One ad, from an *Argosy* magazine, even made its way into a Bantu village in Africa — where a Dr. Goldberg reported having seen it set up over a candle in a niche of the wall of a mud hut, as homage to the white god it represented.

We are created in God's image, and God doesn't want to be a weakling.

— Charles Atlas

HIS DAYS BEGAN before seven with a cup of warm water and lemon juice and twenty-five minutes of his exercises done naked before a mirror.

Then he would shower and breakfast on bananas and grapefruit juice. At his office on Twenty-third Street shortly after noon, he would lunch on figs and prunes. His work in the afternoon consisted of reading and answering his mail, and receiving visitors who came from all over the world, often to find out if there really was a flesh-and-blood Charles Atlas.

Three afternoons a week he would go to the New York Athletic Club to run a few miles or swim, do handstands, box or bowl, play handball or badminton. Then back in Brooklyn, he would eat a broiled steak with fresh fruit and vegetables for dinner, listen to a little Rossini or Verdi, do twenty-five more minutes of Dynamic Tension, and go to sleep. With very little variation, Charles Atlas lived practically every day of his life in this way. Apparently he loved every minute of it.

He loved his life because he believed in it, and himself, with religious intensity. Like other men who have undergone the enormous labor of re-creating themselves out of whole cloth, Atlas imposed an almost monastic strictness on himself which defined his re-creation, and articulated its significance. It also made him into the truest sort of zealot.

"Rich men call me up," he said during the Depression. "They say, 'Charlie, I've lost half a million dollars. I've got to sell my house. I'm going to blow my brains out.' I say, 'You ought to stick your head under water for that statement. Get to exercising. Forget it. Burn your bonds. Tear up your stocks. Give away your property. Get on a healthy basis. My God, man, it's the body that counts. The hell with your possessions.' We are created in God's image and God doesn't want to be a weakling. Jesus held a tree on his shoulders. Sure, he dropped it a couple of times, but nevertheless, he carried it."

Musing once on the collective significance of his following, Atlas said: "If just ten thousand of my best pupils could march down Fifth Avenue in their leopard skins — just ten thousand — why, it would bring back the age of Hercules."

Charles Atlas died of a heart attack two days before Christmas, on December 23, 1972. ✦

A CONAN GROWS IN BROOKLYN

His autobiography is entitled *Frank Frazetta, the Living Legend.*
It is no fantasy. He may be the most important and influential artist ever to work in the fantasy–science fiction genre. Collectors buy paperbacks just for his covers. Book companies buy Frazetta paintings and then have authors write novels to go with the art. His posters, published by his own poster company, have long been cult favorites. He has illustrated record jackets, movie posters, and fantasy films. Ballantine's series, *The Fantastic Art of Frank Frazetta,* cannot be kept in libraries, so numerous are those willing to steal to get his work.

THE LEGEND GOES back to Brooklyn where Frazetta was born in 1928. He began to draw before he was three years old, and studied at the Brooklyn Academy of Fine Arts with classic artist Michael Falanga for eight years. He also played baseball whenever he could (and still does), and had trouble defending his artistic leanings with Brooklyn toughs. Says Michael Gross, Frazetta's former editor at *National Lampoon:* "Frank couldn't face the tough Brooklyn street fighters he grew up with, until one day he took on the biggest bully in the neighborhood and beat him; then he became the meanest kid on the block."

He also became, during his last two years in high school, fill-in artist for science-fiction cartoonist John Giunta.

A period of struggle followed: drawing for several comic houses, landing his own strip, "Johnny Comet," which failed in a year, and working for nine years with Al Capp on "Li'l Abner."

The break came when Canaveral Books asked him to illustrate several Edgar Rice Burroughs reprints, including the *Tarzan* stories. This was followed by cover illustrations of Burroughs's work for Ace Books. And then the leap into his true genre — a series of covers for the *Conan the Barbarian* stories by Robert E. Howard.

Here Frazetta hit his stride with his heroically muscled men and erotically muscled women cavorting in simian- and saurian-filled dreamscapes. The covers became collectors' items. Dealers clamored for the originals.

"How marvelous," says Ian Ballantine. "Here is a man who was never

romanced by the art critics or the big art dealers but was simply seen by the public — and now his work is being eaten alive."

It might be said that Frazetta had circumvented the world of art and gone straight to the collective unconscious of his time. But Frazetta would probably reject such terms. For Frank Frazetta, the feeling has always been for real bodies and real people.

"I'm very physical minded." he told an interviewer. "Brain, fine, but this body is put here for use. If anybody could jump around like my heroes, it's me. Not many artists are physical types. I've been jumped on by twenty guys in a movie theater and got out alive. In Brooklyn, I *knew* Conan. Conan looked like guys I knew back in Brooklyn."

— *Lawrence DiStasi*

Jimmy Grucci with "Fat Man II."

EULOGY FOR JIMMY GRUCCI

by George Plimpton

JIMMY GRUCCI WAS an honored member of a remarkable profession — craftsmen whose artistic function is momentarily to change the face of the heavens themselves, to make the night sky more beautiful than it is, and in the process give delight and wonder to countless hundreds of thousands.

It can surely be said that Jimmy Grucci designed, and prepared, and fired firework shows that were witnessed by more people in his lifetime than any contemporary artist I can think of — including the great concert virtuosi, even the most fashionable of pop stars. Over a million people watch the annual "Venetian Night" show along the Chicago waterfront; over two million watched the "Brooklyn Bridge Centennial" this past May; "Fireworks Night" at Shea Stadium has invariably filled every seat. Countless millions watched this last Inauguration's fireworks on television.

And Jimmy Grucci, of course, has been an integral part in making Fireworks by Grucci responsible for these beautiful and mammoth displays. One of them, designed by him, won his family the championship of the world in Monte Carlo.

But I don't think these honors and renown — the fact that Grucci has become a household word — mattered to him as much as the simple and wonderful art of fireworks themselves. Of his family Jimmy was the one involved to the point truly of passion. He worked in the fireworks assembly area for as many as ten hours a day, six days a week. He loved making shells. He turned and admired a fireworks shell in his hand as a collector might relish a statue of jade. His favorite was the split comet — perhaps the most famous American shell ever made — in the sky, tendrils of gold that split at their ends, and then once again, until the entire night sky seems like a latticework.

What joy fireworks gave him — to take an inanimate

The Grucci family of Bellport, Long Island, was at the top of the fireworks world in 1981. Started by Felix Grucci, an immigrant from Bari, their firm had won first place in the World Fireworks Competition of 1979 in Monaco, and had fired the largest firework in history, Fat Man II, in Florida in 1977. Then, on a Saturday in November of 1983, an explosion rocked their fireworks factory. Jimmy Grucci and his cousin Donna were killed in the blast. At the funeral, George Plimpton delivered the following eulogy.

object, a canister, a thing of chemicals and minerals, and, like a magician, an alchemist at his astonishing best, illuminate the skies with his performance — and what joy he gave us with them!

His recreation after dinner was to relax and sit and watch tapes of his favorite Grucci fireworks shows on the great curved extrasized television screen at the foot of his bed. What woke him in the morning — and I might add everyone else in the Grucci household — was an alarm-clock system rigged to that same TV screen. At the wake-up hour it burst on and showed the climactic moment of the Tchaikovsky *1812 Overture* as played by Arthur Fiedler and the Boston Pops — the fireworks booming and echoing over the Esplanade. There was no yawning and stretching in the Grucci household, his brother, Felix, once told me. At the first sound of that alarm system, everyone was up!

There is a famous early nineteenth-century essay by William Hazlitt about the death of a great athlete of his time, John Cavanagh, in which Hazlitt says that when a person dies who does any one thing better than anyone else in the world, it leaves a gap in society. But fireworks is an ongoing and perpetuating art that will continue to have its great craftsmen. Jimmy is one of a great tradition. He is one with Claude Ruggieri, Martin Beckman, Peter the Great, Vigarini, Brock — artists all. His family will continue in that tradition. They will not allow a gap to be left in our society.

In the ancient Greek scheme of things, mortals were penalized by the gods when they went beyond the bounds and became godlike themselves. In those times, the people would have said about the terrible tragedy of last week that the gods were taking exception, vengeance, because Jimmy Grucci was doing better with the heavens than they could ever dream of. ❧

BUFANO'S PEACE

by Randolph Falk

ALTHOUGH THE EXACT year of Beniamino Bufano's birth is obscure, it is known he was born in San Fele, Italy (near Rome), the youngest of sixteen children. Shortly after his third birthday, his family immigrated to New York. There he studied with several sculptors, including Paul Manship and John Fraser, before coming to California in 1915. (While serving his apprenticeship with Fraser, he claimed to have made the mold for the buffalo on the buffalo nickel and to have been the model for the Indian on the reverse.)

Benny was, by choice, a man of few words. "Talk is cheap. It's action that counts," he often said. "I'm not interested in what a person says but what he does."

In many ways this attitude was a convenience for him. It prevented him from having to answer what he considered "foolish questions," and from having to reveal himself or justify his art. Too many questions made him nervous. His quiet manner added greatly to his mysteriousness. People who knew him for twenty or thirty years are often at a loss to describe him.

People interfered with his work and he ignored them as much as he could. His family was no exception. He denied ever having been married and denied the existence of his two children.

One morning while he finished some work in his studio, he told me someone would be arriving soon, and asked if I would join them for lunch. Within minutes, an attractive woman arrived and the three of us walked a few yards to a café adjoining his studio. Benny made no introduction, and conversation was awkward. Only after he left the table (to complain to the waitress for buttering his toast) did I learn the woman was his daughter. He never revealed her identity to me.

SCULPTURES WERE BUFANO'S "money" and he bartered with the doctor, the dentist, and the lawyer. Beyond these essential services, his needs were extremely simple. They consisted of a place to work, a place to sleep, and just enough food to keep him alive — none of which cost him a cent. His studio rent was paid by a friend, his room at the Press Club was free, and he ate at several restaurants "on the house."

Nevertheless, he despised waste. Once, while driving past an orchard, he saw hundreds of apples rotting on the ground. He asked me to stop, jumped out of the car, and gathered as many apples as he could. Along with bread, which he dried to preserve, this was his lunch for the next several weeks.

His dress was usually shabby. On many occasions, I saw him brush the dust off his work clothes with a shoe brush, file his fingernails with a metal file from his workbench, then set off for an appointment.

He did have a few suits made in exchange for some sculptures, but on the rare occasions he wore one, his appearance was not significantly improved — especially if, in an attempt to look a few years younger, he applied shoe polish to his hair.

AS WITH HIS life, he wanted his creations to last forever. And he wanted them to be seen. He said that people kept stealing his smaller sculptures so he decided to make them so large that "no one could possibly carry them away."

This created different problems. Five years after completion, his monument to peace at Timber Cove Inn remained

Although he did everything with flair — which caused some to condemn him as a publicity hound — Beniamino Bufano kept the details of his life religiously simple. There was his art, and there was his work for peace, and there was being human. As he wrote in stone:

My mother said son
To be a member of
The fanely of man
Is being god.

unassembled on a bluff overlooking the Pacific Ocean. The problem was how to raise the huge head and hand atop the seventy-foot body.

During the fall of 1969, a rigging company managed to get a truck and long boom up the narrow highway to do the job. Benny was at his studio in Italy, but a number of his fans, myself included, were there. Benny had often talked about completing the statue — that it symbolized the unity of all nations and was to look out over the ocean as a gesture of peace. However, when the head was lowered into position over a previously welded framework, it didn't fit — not if it was to face the ocean. A decision was made to change the framework and the head and hand were placed.

When Bufano returned from Italy a few weeks later, I anxiously told him about the "surprise." The next day as we drove up the coast, I mentioned the difficulty we had had, and of the necessary changes.

"If that head is on backwards," he said, "I'm going to blow the son-of-a-bitch up! How could you put it on backwards? It would only fit one way!"

When we arrived, Benny looked up and, not being able to see the top (his eyesight was failing), asked me to show him which direction the head was facing. I managed to point a shaky arm toward the ocean. Swinging his arm wildly over his head, he yelled, "You idiot! Look around! The water is everywhere! Only the seals can see the face the way it is now! And the feet! How can the toes point one direction and the face another?"

After an hour or so, Benny calmed down. He finally decided he would add another face of mosaic tiles to the back of the existing head. Today, the statue stands looking in two directions — across the ocean as a symbol of peace, and, as Benny put it, "toward the highway so people can see the damn thing!"

A Lost Art

IT'S THOSE HANDS of Raymond Bocci you notice first.

Big, rock-raw and gnarled, the color of Wisconsin Colonial Rose granite, with a light coating of white dust etched permanently into the cracked nails and crevices around his fingers.

They are the "before" hands of the perfect hand lotion ad, the mitts of a millionaire stone-carver.

For all but a very few of his seventy-four years, Bocci has been wrestling with granite, hefting and measuring it, learning its subtle complexities, cutting and chipping, shaping and carving and smoothing it.

Following the 900-year-old tradition of his Italian family, Raymond Bocci has spent a lifetime in the tombstone game and a steady vocation it's been.

"I don't have to ever worry about this business going to pot," he said in his soft Italian accent. "There's always going to be cemeteries, no question about it."

With his brother Joe, who is two years older, Bocci runs L. Bocci and Sons Monuments Co., in Colma, the largest granite tombstone company in Northern California and possibly the oldest. The business was founded around the turn of the century by the brothers' father, Leopoldo, who died in 1944, and the Bocci clan has evolved into a formidable Colma dynasty.

Like other traditions, the centuries-old art of carving tombstones is dying out, so to speak, and only a few old-timers like Bocci, who learned his somewhat arcane craft the old way, are still around.

The business, notes Bocci, isn't what it used to be.

The advent of mausoleums, those chilly safe-deposit boxes for the dead, in recent years has cut down the demand for grave markers. Also, more and more

cemeteries are imposing tougher restrictions on the type of stones they allow. Many are now requiring flat, boringly uniform markers that can be driven over easily by lawn mowers.

"That's what's making it a lost art," said Bocci, who has a piercing gaze behind dust-spattered spectacles, a bristly white mustache and curly, snowy hair under an old blue cap.

Though slight of build, Bocci is in enviable physical condition. He runs, he hunts; he is definitely not a very convincing endorsement for his own product. And he scoffs at the possibility of his own retirement anytime in the near future.

"What would be the point of that? A man has to work, or his mind gives up and dies. Work is the greatest gift God ever gave to human beings. I'll come to work as long as I can walk to get here. I've got no regrets. A man can be

anything he sets his mind to be, so I didn't have to do this. But I'd do it all over again."

IT SEEMED AN inevitable question: Has Bocci picked out a tombstone for himself?

He frowned at the suggestion. He discourages customers from buying their own gravestones.

"I don't believe in pre-need. The time to buy one is after the person dies. And you should wait until two or three months after the funeral so you have a clear mind," he recommends.

"It's the last thing you can do for a loved one," he said brightly. "You can look at it and remember the happy times you had with them. But remember, the dead don't suffer. Only the ones who are living suffer.

"You do it to soothe yourself."

— Rick Dower

"I'M NOT A religious man in the orthodox sense," Bufano once said. "Why hell, there's as much corruption in the Vatican as there is in our society . . . the whole world is my temple and I treat everything with great respect . . . I even try not to walk too hard on the floorboards of my studio."

Although Benny claimed he was "not a religious man," there are significant indications to the contrary. His creation of a bronze relief dramatically illustrates his identification with Christ. He made a life-size crucifixion with the index finger of the right hand missing — the same finger Benny cut off his own hand, either intentionally to protest war, or accidentally, years before. In its place protrudes a single flower.

And in Benny's studio, on the very day of his death, I found a new sketch for a mosaic of himself with Pope John. A tear suspends delicately beneath the pope's eye. The theme, as always, was peace:

"My sculptures are meant to speak of peace and the dignity of man. If they in any way help bring an end to folly or place a cobblestone in the road to peace, I shall have done my part." ❧

MANTEO'S MARIONETTES

by Mark Singer

RENTS BEING WHAT they are, about a hundred and fifty of New York's most promising actors have ended up living together in a shed on Stillwell Avenue, in Coney Island. In fairness to all underemployed actors around town, it should be pointed out that the members of the Coney Island clique are, technically speaking, marionettes. In fairness to these particular marionettes, however, it should be pointed out that they are rare ones.

Onstage they orate in an Italian idiom that is virtually extinct; they dress in silk and satin; they wear armor made from discarded hubcaps and electric toasters; and each of them can incarnate twenty or thirty different personalities. The room that these puppets inhabit — the work premises of a seventy-year-old electrician named Miguel (Mike) Manteo — brims with dramatic possibilities. When spurred on by Manteo, the puppets tend to fight among themselves until mechanical failure intrudes. At rest, they are regal.

Three generations of Manteos have owned the puppet troupe, which is called Papa Manteo's Life-Sized Marionettes. Before Mike Manteo inherited the brood, they belonged to his father, Agrippino, the eponymous Papa. Before that, many were the property of Papa's papa, also named Agrippino. Around 1900, after both of his parents had died, Papa moved from Catania, Sicily, to Argentina, taking with him a few puppets that he had salvaged from his father's collection. During the next few years, he added creations of his own, improving the breed considerably in the process. When he returned to Argentina after World War I, he trundled along about fifty more marionettes, all of which he brought with him when he and his family immigrated to the United States in 1919. Their arrival in America made Papa Manteo one of this country's few practitioners of the Sicilian art of *opera dei pupi*.

For a prosperous stretch during the twenties and thirties, Papa Manteo and his family of two hundred

Miguel Manteo is the latest in a long line of classic Sicilian puppeteers. His greatness lies at least partly in his will to preserve an art form and a linguistic lineage that without him would be broken. Romano Gabriel is sui generis. His art has no roots, and may have no successors. It erupts out of what can only be the singular necessity of his time, place, and person. Yet both artists articulate a vision that speaks directly, without mediation, to people.

Mike Manteo mugs with one of his lifesized marionettes.

▼

puppets occupied a series of small theaters in Little Italy, Brooklyn, and Newark. Each evening — every single evening — the Manteos staged episodes from *Orlando Furioso*, the chivalric epic written by Lodovico Ariosto, the Italian poet. To sit through the entire *Orlando* cycle — a peripatetic series of royal encounters, battle scenes, incidents of sorcery, slayings of dragons and winnings of the hands of maidens — a theatergoer had to attend the performances every night for thirteen months.

Not long after World War II, Papa Manteo died, and Mike, the eldest child, assumed the stewardship of the family puppets. By that time a variety of circumstances had forced Papa Manteo's troop into semi-retirement, where they have remained. This means that today, unless the Manteos are hired to perform, the only way a New Yorker with a hunger for *opera dei pupi* can satisfy that appetite is to travel to Sicily. And even then, a true aficionado will be disappointed. The purists of this school argue that Papa Manteo imparted to his children a rare and subtle command of *il dolce idioma*, a style of theatrical Italian that is central to bona fide *opera dei pupi*. Ironically, the argument goes, what is offered in Sicily today, mainly for the benefit of tourists, is a bastardization of the form that Mike Manteo has preserved. In this sense, a friend has explained to me, he is a "linguistic island." He has, by the way, never seen Sicily.

WITHOUT THE *ORLANDO* saga, Papa Manteo's Life-Sized Marionettes wouldn't have much to say, but without Papa's interpolations of Ariosto, they would merely be wooden poets.

Both Papa and his father, Agrippino, went to great trouble to rephrase Ariosto in the vernacular and to transcribe the results into notebooks. Papa Manteo's notebooks, two hundred in all, rest on a small shelf in the office, and they provide the source material for Mike's staging of *Orlando*. Each day, in gratitude to Ariosto, Manteo reads a few pages of unadulterated *Orlando* in the *antico* Italian.

"People think during the performances that I'm reading directly from a script," he said. "Actually, I only begin with a little speech from the manuscript, and then I — let's say I improvise. It's all in my head — somewhere. Backstage, though, I'm asking Ida, 'What's next, Ida? What happens next?' She says, 'So-and-so and so so so,' and I keep going. It's 90 percent ad-lib, with some occasional passages of poetry. You know, every now and then you need some poetry."

TO STAGE *ORLANDO*, Mike Manteo needs the assistance of at least four marionette manipulators on the bridge, all of whom must have strong shoulder and back muscles. The puppets, which are made of wood, various metals, and cloth, weigh from 40 to 140 pounds each, and are controlled from above with two iron rods and a thick string. A heavy rod connected to the puppet's head makes it possible for him to walk, fight, nod, swivel when he speaks, and suffer decapitation when a mortal sword blow arrives. A thinner rod attaches to the right hand — in the case of a knight or an enemy warrior, this is the sword-bearing hand — and the thick string manipulates the left, or shield-bearing, arm. Ariosto's women squabble often, but rarely with weapons. This leaves them free to talk with their hands, which, thanks to the crew on the bridge, they do fluently.

One day I rode the B train to Coney Island to see how Manteo and his leading players were getting along.

It turned out that, despite a few bumps and dents, they were getting along well. The same could not be said for Fanfilo and Califo, a couple of pagan comrades, who had sustained breastplate-piercing sword blows.

"It's no problem," Manteo said a few minutes after greeting me. He waved a small hammer in the air. "I just take off the armor and hammer it down and solder it. This was my father's hammer — over seventy years old. Every now and then, I change the handle."

The worktable that Manteo uses in removing his marionettes from the disabled list held more hammers, several chisels, two vises, a polishing wheel, and a lead block for pounding metal into different shapes. There were puppet heads dangling from the ceiling, and along one side of the room hung rows of armored, off-duty marionettes — a silent audience. The room was littered with scraps of metal — sheets of tin that Manteo buys in bulk, and the stainless steel carcasses of electric toasters that he finds on the street. He held up a hemispherical piece of silvery armor.

"This is the knee protector for a puppet I'm repairing. It used to be part of somebody's rotisserie."

At the worktable, Manteo paused to give advice to his grandson Michael, seventeen years old, who was busy building a small marionette, a scaled-down version of the almost life-sized stage marionettes. "When I was little, I used to come here to visit my grandfather, and I could wear this armor. I was just the right size," said Michael. "Now I'm learning how to make it."

NEAR THE SPOT where a puppet named Ruggiero hangs, there is an inscription in black ink on a door: "Che è L'avvenire di Questi Marionetti? Buono? Beh! Speriamo nel futuro."

"I wrote that," Manteo said, "and it translates to mean, 'What is the future of these marionettes? Good? Well! Let us hope for the future.'" ᴥ

ROMANO GABRIEL'S WOODEN GARDEN

IT TOOK ROMANO GABRIEL, a carpenter and gardener, nearly three decades to make the hundreds of brilliant and arresting objects with which he filled the front yard of his home at 1415 Pine Street in Eureka, California.

Gabriel fashioned his brightly painted trees and flowers out of vegetable crates, adding droll faces and figures to create a fantasy that dazzles and delights like the finale of an old-fashioned Fourth of July fireworks display — pinwheels fixed but appearing to spin in a triumphant, breathtaking outburst.

The variety of forms is dazzling: a carousel with giraffes, zebra, dog and horse surmounted by a lemon tree, the awkward lemons dangling from thick wires; a tree hung with salamis for all, eyed fearfully or hungrily by a piglet; an opera house; a sporting event, probably basketball; and the pope either accepting money or distributing the host.

Unlike much other "naive" art, the Wooden Garden was not made from found objects or arranged in patterns; nor was it a structure intended for real or imagined use. It was, rather, a seeming jumble of objects, taller in back, smaller in front, set up in the approximately thirty-by-sixty-foot yard, behind the picket fence, and intended to be seen by passersby.

Some of the figures are commentaries on contemporary people or events, political or religious. Some are even caricatures. Some of the pieces are animated by motors.

"I just wanted to make something different," Gabriel has told author Jan Wampler. "I just made up pictures out of wood. I used to be a gardener here in Eureka. But Eureka is a bad place for flowers — the salty air and no sun. So I just make this garden."

Since flowers flourish in Eureka, this may be the disarming comment of an artist who is impatient with the inquiring critic.

We do know that Gabriel, working in the small shed in his yard, liked to peek out, unobserved, to watch the people who stopped by to look at his garden.

Gabriel used a handsaw to cut out his objects, and later a circular saw. His equipment was repaired by a friend in town, but after the last repairs, ten years before his death, the artist simply quit working. He never returned to his work. He was ill for six years before he died in 1977, at about age ninety.

Ironically, on the day of his death, a letter arrived from the California State Arts Council informing Gabriel that his garden had been designated an official example of "folk art."

— *Patricia Elsen*

An Empire of Food

THE FACE THAT MADE SPAGHETTI FAMOUS

by Lawrence DiStasi

THE FACE SMILES with geniality and good health. White hair and a trim white mustache, capped by the crisp, white chef's hat and scarf, complete the grandfatherly look of a culinary Santa Claus.

This is Chef Boy-Ar-Dee, the face that defined Italian food for millions of Americans in the days before pasta became chic.

His real name was Hector Boiardi, and his story begins with his brother Paul. Working as a hotel waiter in 1910 in Italy, Paul Boiardi was one morning told by a guest: "You know your job, my boy."

"Thank you, signor. Soon I hope to go to Berlin. I have a friend at the Hotel Adlon."

"Why not America?" asked the guest.

"America, signor — ah, that is a distant dream. I have no friends there."

"You have now," said the gentleman, giving the waiter a card. "Come to see me if you go there."

The card read: "Enrico Caruso."

A year later, Paul Boiardi had a job as a waiter at the Knickerbocker Hotel, whose manager was a friend of Caruso. Other jobs followed until in 1917 Paul became a waiter at the Plaza Hotel; when the Persian Room opened there in 1934, he became maître d'hôtel.

Meantime, younger brother Hector was apprenticing in his native Piacenza to be a chef. When he turned seventeen, Paul sent for him and got him a job at the Plaza. Another brother, Mario, soon followed.

Hector's skill in the kitchen soon had him on the move: he worked at Rector's, Claridge's, the Ritz Carlton, and then at the Hotel Greenbrier in West Virginia where he directed the catering at President Woodrow Wilson's marriage reception. Next came an offer to

Italians in America have always been distinguished by their foods. Philip Mazzei was encouraged to come to America to introduce the exotic plants of Italy to the New World. Then nativists used the eating habits of Italians to denigrate the entire culture as "spaghetti benders." The schizophrenia was compounded when American housewives fed Chef Boy-Ar-Dee's canned spaghetti as "fun food" to their children, while nutritionists frowned. Now we have come full circle: Balducci's capitalizes on a pasta craze that sees Italian cuisine as not only chic but the ultimate in health.

move farther west: only twenty-four years old, he took charge of a staff of forty cooks in the kitchens of the new Hotel Winton in Cleveland, Ohio.

Unlike his brother Paul, Hector didn't take to working for wages; he had a yen to go into business for himself. So in 1924, he opened his own restaurant, Il Giardino d'Italia, in Cleveland. The restaurant was an instant success, not least because of Hector's special spaghetti and tomato sauce. Patrons began asking for take-out portions. The demand became so great that Hector found a distributor, and soon had a packaged food business, the Chef Boiardi Food Products Company.

IN A TINY loft near the restaurant, Hector began — preparing the tomato sauce in a three-gallon vat and packaging it along with dry spaghetti and his special grated cheese. By the late 1930s America's hunger for Italian foods had propelled Hector through four processing plants and into a search for still more space somewhere closer to tomato growers. It had also led him to change the name of his product to CHEF BOY-AR-DEE because even his salesmen had difficulty pronouncing all the vowels in his real name.

Hector found his new place in the central Pennsylvania farmland around Milton. As luck would have it, an abandoned silk mill was up for sale, and Hector and his associates bought it. The interior of the mill was transformed, local growers given contracts for one thousand acres of tomatoes, and the huge operation begun.

Meantime, brother Paul at the Plaza had another momentous encounter. Among his regular customers were Mr. and Mrs. John Hartford of the great Atlantic and Pacific Tea Company, the A&P chain, with thousands of stores nationwide. Looking over the menu of delicacies one night, Hartford allowed that what he truly hungered for was a dish of real Italian spaghetti.

"I'll make you some," said Paul, "from my brother's recipe."

After Hartford raved about the sauce, Paul told him about Hector's business, and his difficulties in cracking the chain-store market. It was then that John Hartford said, "I'll see that the products get into all A&P Stores." It was no idle boast. Before long, A&P shoppers around the country were buying Chef Boy-Ar-Dee products by the millions, and Paul had quit the Plaza and joined the corporation as vice president.

CRITICAL AS THE A&P connection was, it may have been World War II that lifted Hector Boiardi and his spaghetti company into the exalted pantheon of promethean food purveyors.

The American army, like all armies, traveled on its stomach. It needed food, packaged food, food that could be backpacked by the individual soldier. To meet this demand, Chef Boy-Ar-Dee put its facilities in the service of the U.S. government. The Milton, Pennsylvania, plant became a major supplier of rations for the U.S. forces and its allies.

Hector Boiardi said that now began one of his greatest challenges as a chef: to convert carload upon carload of ham and eggs into field rations that would be palatable for our troops. The nub of it was in the synthesis, via packaging, of taste and convenience.

Apparently he met the challenge. On June 14, 1943, in a ceremony broadcast across the nation, the Army Quartermaster Corps presented Hector Boiardi with the coveted "E" pennant for the excellence of his wartime products.

The troops were fed, and the war was won. Perhaps more important, convenience foods had been introduced to an enormous population. The name Chef Boy-Ar-Dee would become a household word.

It was not long after this that Hector Boiardi sold his Chef Boy-Ar-Dee company to American Home Foods, a leading food processor. It was 1946, the postwar boom was on, and consumers hungered for convenience as never before. American Home Foods expanded the Milton plant, and added research, administration and training facilities.

Yet though he sold out his control, Boiardi continued his association with American Home Foods as a consultant for thirty-three years, and as an adviser after that.

HECTOR BOIARDI DIED in Parma, Ohio in 1985; he was eighty-seven years old. As far as is known, Andy Warhol never painted a can of his Spaghetti-O's. Maybe he should have. On it he might have portrayed not only the face that made spaghetti famous, but the fundamental Americanism Chef Boiardi coined when he changed his product name to BOY-AR-DEE: "Everyone is proud of his own family name," he said, "but sacrifices are necessary for progress." ❧

73

BALDUCCI'S THEATER OF FOOD

"EVEN WHEN WE became a specialty store, my father-in-law refused to close the fruit stand," Nina Balducci remembered, "because he felt that without fruit and vegetables outside, people wouldn't want to come in."

That invitation to come in, to taste and smell and touch the foods on display, is really the seed of the current success of Balducci's. Started in 1947 as a tiny fruit and vegetable stand situated on Greenwich Avenue in New York's Greenwich Village, it has become the busiest and highest-grossing specialty food store in the country, perhaps the world.

Nina Balducci, wife of original founder Andrew Balducci, who with his father, Louis, opened the original fruit stand in 1947, has no doubt about the whys of this astonishing growth.

"Freshness and quality of the product," she says. One walk through the store at Sixth Avenue and Ninth Street confirms this. The fruits and vegetables are prime, some imported from as far away as New Zealand. The fresh fish and meats are kept in a special display case designed and patented by Andy Balducci himself. Cheeses from Italy, France and elsewhere are kept outside, so quickly do they turn over. As to the delicate ones — the fresh mozzarella and the mascarpones — the Balducci's make their own, fresh daily. It is impossible to keep enough in stock.

As Andy Balducci said in an interview recently about a chef who refused to believe that Balducci's mascarpone was anything other than whipped cream: "He was used to serving imported mascarpone that was at least a week old. He had never eaten it when it was freshly made and didn't know how delicious a cheese it can be."

Then there's that "invitation to touch."

When, in 1972, the Balducci's were forced to move their operation from the original "shack," as Nina called it,

Andrew Balducci designed the new space with this in mind. "He low-keyed the design," she said, "because he wanted food to be the show. Everything else recedes into the background."

Balducci's is nothing if not that — a food show. Whole rounds of Reggiano Parmigiano are piled center stage. Cheeses and breads and tortas and foccaccias tumble down invitingly. Salamis and hams and whole prosciuttos hang from the ceilings, talking to trays of over 150 prepared foods to go, gesturing a bit condescendingly to radicchios and melons in the "mother department." The lighting is dim, filtered through the stained glass of Tiffany lamps, flattering to customers and eggplants alike.

"Every day it's like a Broadway production," Nina said. "Which is exactly how it's approached. Every department — fish, vegetables, prepared foods, cheeses, breads and pastries, coffees, all of them — sets up a new show every day."

The customer is invited in with open arms. "Every department each day has samplings. You can literally eat your way through the store. Customers while shopping are always nibbling, drinking sample coffee."

For those with Italian food addictions, it is a delirious, even dangerous place to browse.

Compared with this, the mail order end of Balducci's would seem one-dimensional. But under Nina Balducci's direction, it has become something of a sensation. Begun in 1981 as a single-sheet flyer to regular customers, it today reaches out in full color to half a million food lovers nationwide. A wholesale distributing operation and a new set of offices with full baking facilities in Long Island City complete the operation.

All this from a tiny, twenty-four-hour fruit stand. In describing this transformation, Andy Balducci once said: "Before we had the melon; now we've got the prosciutto to go with it." And a whole opera besides.

— *Lawrence DiStasi*

THE REAL MR. PEANUT

by Dominick Lamonica

Spaghetti is one thing. But an Italian hand behind one of the central icons of American junk food? Preposterous as it may seem, it's true: Amedeo Obici invented Mr. Peanut for an ad campaign. He also made Planter's Peanuts one of the most dominant food operations in the nation. Domenico Ghirardelli did the same in California with chocolate. Perhaps in some confectioner's heaven, they are now united, busy inventing the ultimate candy bar.

IN RECOUNTING THE lives of successful, self-made millionaires, Americans love to point to the example of Frank W. Woolworth, who built his fortune on the thin American dime. But consider the case of Amedeo Obici, who based his fortune on the lowly nickel.

When he arrived in this country at the age of twelve, a nickel constituted just about all of Amedeo Obici's working capital. Yet, by 1930, the Planters Nut and Chocolate Company, of which Obici became president and general manager, was doing more than $12 million in business annually.

The fundamental idea by which Obici has been guided is extremely simple. People think much less of spending twenty nickels, proportionately, than they do of spending a single dollar. The young immigrant noticed this immediately after his arrival in the United States, the country where, as his mother had told him back at Aderzo, everybody must make much money. Why seek dollars, which were so guarded, Obici wondered, when nickels were so plentiful? They were so plentiful, in fact, that, at fifty-two, Amedeo Obici became one of the wealthiest Italians in America.

At Scranton, Pennsylvania, his uncle, who had sent for him, put him to work on his fruit stand, and sent him to school the following week. Obici was not built for the schoolroom. "The books" he says, "meant nothing to me. All I could understand was arithmetic."

Obici's education took different forms. After working at Pittston and Wilkes-Barre for fruit stands and cigar-makers, he got a job in a popular cafe, whose owner, Billy McLaughlin, "taught me about Shakespeare and helped me to learn English. The patrons (doctors, lawyers, city officials, and businessmen), discussed everything under the sun, and I listened. I learned much about life there."

Obici was seventeen when McLaughlin died, and for a while he worked for a rival firm. But working for someone else, after having worked for McLaughlin, was not to his liking. Obici had made and saved enough money to bring his mother and two sisters to America in 1896. In 1897 he decided to go into business for himself.

Obici rented sidewalk space in front of a store, obtained enough lumber to build on credit, and in the same way managed to win over wholesale fruit dealers. "But for my peanut roaster I had to pay cash," he adds.

That humble little peanut roaster was the precursor of what became one of the great corporations of the United States, with four huge factories at Suffolk, Virginia, Wilkes-Barre, Pennsylvania, San Francisco and Toronto, over two thousand employees, and an authorized capital of five million preferred stock and ten million common stock.

But that $4.50 roaster demanded constant attention, lest the peanuts be scorched.

"One day I got hold of an old electric fan motor and rigged up a set of pulleys. I put that fan motor to work turning my peanut roaster. So far as I know, it was the first electrically operated one in the world.

"Then over my stand I put a sign, 'Obici, the Peanut Specialist.' People came from miles around to buy my peanuts."

THAT WAS THE beginning. Soon he was packing five-cent bags of shelled peanuts for the trade. This he stimulated by placing in the packages coupons bearing the letters of his name, one letter per package, giving dollar watches to those who spelled out his name with coupons. "I gave away some twenty thousand watches in two years," he admits.

The peanut specialist was also experimenting with salted peanuts and peanut candy bars. With business now expanding, he was determined to make a national market for his product. Obtaining as a partner M. M. Peruzzi, sales manager for one of the biggest Scranton wholesale confectionary jobbers, the Planters Peanut Company of Wilkes-Barre was incorporated in 1906, with $20,000 capital stock paid in, two small store buildings, and about fifteen employees.

A little showmanship occasionally does no harm, Obici had also discovered. When he was able to purchase his first carload of peanuts, he unloaded the whole car in wagons with a Peanut Specialist sign in gilt letters, and paraded them through the streets of Wilkes-Barre. Fewer people now were skeptical of the idea of selling salted peanuts in five-cent bags. Fewer people, too, were saying that Obici and Peruzzi had "gone nutty with peanuts."

In time it became necessary to look to their sources of supply. "I think it was intuition," says Obici, reminiscing, "that brought me to Suffolk, Virginia, in 1913 with $25,000, all that Planters Peanut Company could venture at the time, to establish a peanut-cleaning business. The plan was to buy the nuts direct from the Virginia planters and clean them ourselves. But our venture in Suffolk grew into the manufacture of the finished product itself there."

THERE IS NOT a man, woman or child in this country today who is not familiar with the jaunty, monocled and top-hatted figure of Mr. Peanut. Obici found him by asking schoolchildren to suggest a character symbolizing his peanut business. To the winning drawing of a peanut pod with legs and a head, Obici himself added the top hat, cane and spats. Thus the lowly peanut took on swank. He appeared in the company's first national advertising campaign, launched with a series of full page ads in the *Saturday Evening Post* and other publications in 1917. During the many years that have passed since Mr. Peanut's formal debut, he has made himself an internationally known character.

Since 1928 the growth of the company has been prodigious, for besides producing the enormous tonnage needed to supply its salted peanut, peanut butter, and candy departments, large volumes of raw peanuts,

▲
Amedeo Obici started in business as the "Peanut Specialist."

A HOUSE MADE OF CHOCOLATE

SOMETIMES WHEN THE wind is right, the rich odor of chocolate drifts out over North Beach from the brick factory on North Point Street, just across the way and up the hill from Aquatic Park. The delicious smell reminds local residents of one of San Francisco's oldest industries — the D. Ghirardelli Company, which identifies itself modestly but with pride as "Manufacturers of Chocolate Since 1852."

The Ghirardelli story actually begins in 1848 when the legendary astronomer James Lick brought ashore with him six hundred pounds of chocolate manufactured by his friend, the Lima confectioner, Domenico Ghirardelli.

By odd accident, these two men, who were to become so closely identified with San Francisco, had set up business establishments side by side, on the same Peruvian street — Lick, the Pennsylvania piano-maker, and Ghirardelli, the young confectioner from Rapallo, Italy. When the news of the gold discovery reached Lima, Ghirardelli followed Lick to the shores of San Francisco.

After giving up on his search for the Mother Lode, the new immigrant ran a grocery store at the shore end of the Broadway wharf, grubstaked miners, and opened what the newspapers called a "French soda fountain" in nearby Stockton. A series of fires destroyed his first few stores, but, on July 18, 1852, the readers of the daily Alta California newspaper encountered the following advertisement: "Messers. Ghirardely & Girard — Candy and Syrup Manufactory — Confectionery — This new store, situated at the corner of Kearny and Washington streets, is the only depot of the best French and American candy . . ."

Other products listed in the ad were ground coffee, jujube paste, guimauve paste, French bonbons, fruits, syrups and pastries.

Then in 1867, quite by accident, Ghirardelli discovered "Broma," the early name for ground chocolate. It was his real "mother lode," for from sales of 570 pounds the first year, it grew to tens of thousands and then several million pounds annually.

Early in his California career, Ghirardelli must have resigned himself to the fact that only by a miracle was anybody going to get his name right. He is variously listed in directories and newspaper accounts as Ghirardely, Glirardel, Girandello, Ghiarardeli, Geradilli, and once, by some genius of inaccuracy, as Gheardly. The firm has endeavored to cope with all this — at least to the extent of correct pronunciation — through its famous trademark, the brightly plumaged parrot and the words, "Say Gear-ar-delly," which is a phonetic spelling of the name.

Domenico Ghirardelli, the patriarch and founder of this business, died in his native Rapallo in 1894, leaving six sons and daughters. The business he started so modestly more than a century ago now converts tons of Brazilian and Central American cocoa beans into millions of pounds of ground, cake and sweet chocolate every year. Some of the current plant employees are the direct descendants of some of the men and women who worked for Ghirardelli as far back as the 1860s. Ghirardelli's legacy is an enduring institution belonging now not only to his family and San Francisco but to visiting tourists from around the world.

— Robert O'Brien

◄ **Domenico Ghirardelli: patriarch and founder of Ghirardelli Chocolate**

shelled and unshelled, are sold to jobbing and manufacturing interests throughout the United States. It is the largest concern of its kind in the world and dominates the American market. The total American production of peanuts for 1930 was about 4 million bags, of which 90 percent passed through the hands of Mr. Obici's Planters Nut and Chocolate Company.

A far cry from the days of Obici, the Peanut Specialist, with his humble $4.50 peanut roaster. ❧

THE TRANSFIGURATION

SCENE EIGHT

Lights up on Benno and the Girl. Near her is a small night table with stained and sticky looking bottles and jars on it.

When the light hits her she sprays a large amount of very smelly hair spray on her hair, then teases her hair violently. Then she smears an enormous amount of purple lipstick on sensuously puffed-out lips. During this she sings a very ugly rock tune and occasionally does a dance step to it.

GIRL: Last night I spilled spaghetti all over me. The sauce went over my white blouse and my blue dress; and it was thick sauce with peppers and bits of meat in it. It was a big mess. And Donny, my cousin, wiped it off. He's spiffy. Twenty and in the Navy. He took his napkin, it had red stains from his mouth on it, and wiped my blouse off. Wiped and wiped, not too hard but strong. Then he took another napkin, my brother's, and wiped my dress off. Wiped and wiped, makin' a small circle in my lap. Donny has big hands, a lotta hair on them around the knuckles and the veins is very thick. His fingers is thick, too, and the middle one is long and heavy. I dream about Donny's hand makin' circles in my lap.

(Freezes in place. The light on her dims.)

BENNO: Benno grew up thinking that talent and sensitivity were things people took seriously. At least that important people took seriously — artists, for instance, and teachers. Benno grew up hoping that looks and sex didn't matter. That paintings would satisfy any longing he'd ever have. And when that longing got too strong, a quick pulling with the palm would be enough. Benno was wrong. Benno has been heard to say that nothing matters save the taste of his own flesh. But since then, time has passed. For your benefit he has conjured up scenes better not remembered. And Benno realizes that he was guilty of over-simplification. There are things that matter: looks matter, sex matters. These are all that matter. Benno feels that those who deny this are participating in a huge joke. Benno has learned his lesson. Paintings, you see, aren't enough. When loneliness and emptiness and longing congeal like a jelly nothing assuages the ache. Nothing, nothing, nothing. It was the end of spring, the traditional season of youth, renewal and young love. Benno returned to his old neighborhood, having celebrated his twentieth birthday. He found the poorest street in his old neighborhood, Fitzgerald Street by name. And he rented a room on the third floor of a row house on Fitzgerald Street. Benno nailed shut all the windows in that room, even though it was summer. Something about imbibing his own smell. Benno is not as isolated as you might think. He hears the horrible street noises. He hears the monster children screaming. He even allows himself to have his shade up one-half hour a day. Today at 1 p.m., Benno had his shade up. He stared out his nailed window, stared through the caked dirt that streaks the window's glass. He saw a wild circle flashing red across the street. He stared at that circle and was tempted to . . . never mind. He was tempted and stared and was tempted some more. And then he saw the agent of that circle. It was a little girl. A beautiful little girl. Oh yes, Benno knows beauty. He knows if he tells you. Once when he saw something beautiful, it would flash across his eyes like a hot knife and he would peer, eyes stuck there until they ached. Once, he tells you, no longer. For beauty has lost his power over me, it has lost its power, no more beauty, no more longing to grasp it within me and smother it with my bulk, please God, no more beauty.

(He is almost weeping. He eats passionately and slowly pulls himself together.)

OF BENNO BLIMPIE

GIRL: When Donny finished wiping me off, I smiled up at him and his eyes, they're black, got very big. When Ma wasn't looking, I let my fingers take a walk along his thigh. I saw the big bump in the middle of his thigh get bigger. Then, when Ma was clearin' the table, I spilled the plate of meatballs all over me. While she was in the kitchen, Donny licked them off with his tongue. Ma caught him and gave him hell. Pop laughed. Donny ran into the bathroom and puked all over, like a sissy. I changed my mind about Donny. I think Donny is a jerk-off.

(Lights out on Girl.)

BENNO: Benno has decided: He will no longer lift the shade, he will no longer look out into the street. Benno stayed in this tiny room. He left every two days to buy food. Otherwise he never went out. Except in cases of emergency such as when the ice cream truck came along. He did nothing. He ate continually from when he awoke until he fell asleep. He did nothing save remember. When I become so fat I cannot get into his clothes and can barely move, I will nail the door shut. I will put his eyes out with a long nail and I will bite at himself until he dies. In the middle of this filthy hole on the third floor of a row house in the poorest side of the street of my old neighborhood there will I be: A mountain of flesh. There are rats in this room. I see them slithering along the sides of the wall. They will eat me. These rats will find Benno beautiful. They will long for him. He will be a sexual object to them. They will make the devouring of Benno's body an erotic act. They will gnaw hollows into his face, into his belly. And in those hollows, they will fornicate. Then, they will perish. The instant before he is ready to die, Benno will swallow a huge draught of poison. These rats in eating Benno will be eating poisoned meat. The poison will cause a fearful splitting of stomachs, vital rat organs will swell up and burst even while the rats are making love. Even while they are eating. Posthumously, Benno will have been loved.

— *Albert Innaurato*

79

LITTLE BIG MAN

by Ellen Wojahn

Like countless Italian Americans before him, Jeno Paulucci started in business by selling produce. Fast Jeno didn't (or couldn't) stop there though. He went on to found several fast-food companies that made fortunes, a magazine, Attenzione, *which failed, and a city of the future,* Heathrow, *in Florida, which is struggling. He has been called everything from an exploiter to a visionary — the price, perhaps, of moving, and talking, very fast.*

IF YOU WERE to capture Jeno Paulucci's life in a photograph, the image would be mostly blurred. Over the years, Paulucci has been photographed most often in a variety of business poses: the Duluth vegetable peddler who turned a field of bean sprouts into Chun King Foods before selling it all to R. J. Reynolds Industries Inc. for $60 million; the king of frozen pizza who got an offer of about $200 million from archrival Pillsbury Co. that he couldn't refuse; the developer of Heathrow, a 3,500-acre planned community for the rich located north of Orlando. Not content to hang it up yet, he has recently launched Pizza Kwik, a chain of pizza-delivery shops that he is now taking national.

Along the way there have been shots of Paulucci even more flattering: handing out pizzas to the unemployed on a subzero New Year's Eve in his native Hibbing, Minnesota; hawking moccasins for a struggling Indian tribe to a Sears Roebuck & Co. buyer in Chicago; lobbying for the rights of the homeless with Ralph Nader in Washington, D.C.; launching a statewide aid program for the hungry in St. Paul.

Jeno Paulucci is the very picture of a mover and shaker, a man who inspires admiration, envy, maybe even a touch of resentment. There is an obsessive quality to Paulucci's brand of social responsibility — one no doubt deeply rooted in his family experience. His father, Ettore, was an immigrant miner too sickly to be more than sporadically employed in one of the open-pit mines that were once the mainstay of the hardscrabble economy of Minnesota's Iron Range.

The family lived in a house they had built on a foundation of railroad ties, and heated with stray pieces of tar block and coal. Jeno remembers a childhood spent mostly by himself: the Scandinavian mothers of his childhood pals, he remembers, forbade them to play with "the dago, the wop."

The desire of a poor kid who made good to give something back, the need for the outcast to be at last accepted and praised — these are the underlying motivations. You see them both in Paulucci's determination to settle up accounts with Duluth, the city he has long loved and twice forsaken.

First it was Chun King, closed in 1974 by the tobaccomen of R. J. Reynolds. The loss was seven hundred jobs, most of which Paulucci had filled with the disabled and the down-and-out. Eight years later it was Jeno's Inc. — the city's largest manufacturing employer, with twelve hundred jobs — that left. Its reluctant owner explained that the company was forced to move by prohibitively high freight costs that made it unprofitable to make frozen pizzas in the frozen environs of Minnesota. With unemployment in Duluth then running around 20 percent, Paulucci came under attack.

"I pledge that I will some way, somehow, bring new business to Duluth," replied an embattled Paulucci in a full-page ad, promising to replace every one of the lost jobs.

Little did most Duluthians realize that Paulucci's promise would become an unofficial oath of office. Though he now spends most of each year more than a thousand miles to the south, Paulucci remains close enough to Duluth's civic affairs to be considered its other mayor and director of economic development.

Single out any major civic or economic project in this city of eighty-five thousand, and if Jeno Paulucci didn't have something to do with making it happen, it's because he judged it either a sure thing or a worthless cause. He is the one-man ad hoc committee that makes others superfluous.

When the city council balked at funding a feasibility study to support its bid as the home of the state's new convention center, it was Paulucci who came up with the money — a third from his own pocket. A bureaucratic logjam standing in the way of a proposal to build a six-hundred-job paper mill also loosened under Paulucci's pressure. He has even talked of mooring an old ocean liner on Lake Superior to lure tourists to Duluth's shores.

Getting new jobs and businesses back into the old Jeno's pizza factory on Lake Avenue South, however, is Paulucci's top priority. Need space for your company? Jeno will give it to you rent-free until the business is in the black. Need financing? You might try the local bank Paulucci owns. Meanwhile, Salomon Brothers, Inc., on retainer from Paulucci, is keeping an eye out for companies spun off in Wall Street's merger mania that might be acquired and moved to Duluth.

Still, the big green question mark on the sign outside the old Jeno's factory reminds Duluth residents that five years of moving and shaking on the part of their First Citizen has yet to make them whole. There's an ad agency and a fishing-tackle company; a garment manufacturer and an electronics company; and Joanna's Food down in the basement, the new maker of the dry-mix pizzas that Paulucci used to sell as a sideline to his frozen pies. All together, these firms have generated only about 120 jobs. Nobody, least of all Paulucci, would consider this anything but a good start. It's a little like building a company, he says. Revitalizing a city takes luck, faith, and a lot of patience.

Patience is not one of Jeno Paulucci's virtues. Fishing, he'll give any lake five minutes to yield up a satisfying catch, or he's off in his seaplane for another lake and another try.

Then there was the time Paulucci tried to beat the crowd out of a hockey game at the Duluth Civic Center he helped to build, only to find his illegally parked Wagoneer blocked by buses. The bus drivers, intent on a game of cards, suggested that he wait until the hockey match was over.

"Do you know who I am?" the angry Paulucci is said to have roared.

To which one bus driver reportedly replied, "Hey, fellas, we got a guy here who doesn't know who he is."

YET PAULUCCI KNOWS very well who he is. He's gotten by in life on a powerful instinct for what sells and how to sell it. These days he spends much of his time selling himself. Jeno sees it in grander terms: "I'm telling the story of America. But I'm also selling a product and using the power and influence of the media to deliver a message."

The message?

"Dammit, we are our brother's keeper. We've got a responsibility and we've got to live up to it." ❧

▲
Jeno Paulucci: a mover and shaker with a strong sense of social responsibility

An Aria, a Game of Cards, and an Espresso

New York City in the Gay Nineties had almost everything: vaudeville, opera, thriving businesses, a cosmopolitan population, and numerous gin mills, honky-tonks and clubs. What it lacked, at least for Italians, was a place where an opera singer, after a night of Verdi or Puccini, could relax, play a Neapolitan card game called *scopa* and drink a few cups of espresso.

It was to remedy this situation that, in 1892, Antonio Ferrara, opera impresario and showman, united with his friend Enrico Scoppa to open a cafe called Caffè A. Ferrara. Located in the heart of Little Italy on Grand Street, it had an Old World atmosphere that quickly made it the meeting place and unofficial headquarters for musicians, opera singers, newspapermen, and visiting statesmen from Italy.

Caruso thought the coffee marvelous, but especially loved the *sfogliatelle* that reminded him of Naples. The impresario of the Met, Giulio Gatti-Casazza, and the founder of the Italian language daily, *Il Progresso*, Carlo Barsotti, were also regulars.

As the first and for many years the only *pasticceria* in the United States, Ferrara's cafe had institutional status almost from the start. It was not only Italian Americans living in New York who made it their favorite cafe, it was those who had moved outward to Brooklyn, Connecticut, Philadelphia, Boston, and beyond who made the trip back to Grand Street a virtual pilgrimage.

A trip to New York without a stop at Ferrara's to emerge with a huge, warm box filled with rum babas, *cannoli, sfogliatelle* and a dozen varieties of nut-filled cookies was simply no trip at all. New York's Little Italys were the source of American Italianismo, and Antonio Ferrara had captured in his cafe the taste and the smell of that source — a shrine redolent of the finest creams in perfect combinations of lemon and almond and orange and chocolate.

After World War I, a nephew of Antonio Ferrara named Peter Lepore left his village of Avellino and stowed away on a ship bound for New York. Before too long, Peter Lepore had married the daughter of Ferrara's partner, Enrico Scoppa, and succeeded to the business.

Lepore was to spend the rest of his life at Ferrara's, living with his family in an apartment above the cafe for many years. In fact, the Lepore family can be said to have never left. As Peter's son Alfred Lepore, now president of Ferrara Foods & Confections, said recently: "We constantly joke that I'm right back in my bedroom, because my office now is where my bedroom was when I was a child."

Ironically, the Depression added to the quality and the dominance of the Ferrara pastries. In order to make sure that there was very little waste, the Lepore's began to bake two, three and sometimes four times a day in small batches. Because of the frequency of baking, Ferrara's reputation for freshness and quality increased. Hard times had been a blessing in disguise.

Today, in addition to its cafe trade, Ferrara's packages and ships its own brands of coffee, petite rum babas, and hundreds of other Italian delicacies to wholesalers, department stores, and chain stores coast to coast. But it is still, to thousands of second-, third-, and even fourth-generation Italian Americans, the shrine — the necessary stop at Christmas, Easter, or the Festival of San Gennaro for a supply of not only taste but the indispensable ingredients of sweet memory.

— *Anthony Telesino*

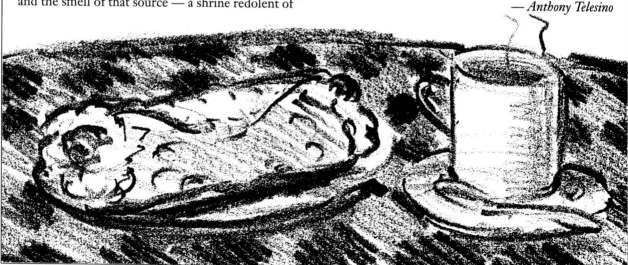

GALLO CRUSHES THE COMPETITION

by Jaclyn Fierman

Not surprisingly, Italian Americans have been associated with wine in America for centuries. Philip Mazzei brought the first cuttings over in the 1770s, but the vines were trampled by Hessian troops during the Revolution. Secondo Guasti built the world's largest vineyard in Southern California. And a little farther north, Ernest and Julio Gallo have battled their way to the top of the wine industry's volume charts, and seek to top the quality lists as well. To the side, quieter in the swells of his valley, smiles August Sebastiani among the peacocks.

WHEN IT COMES to business, the brothers Ernest and Julio Gallo brook neither waste nor weakness. Age may be weakening their hearing and sight, but Ernest, seventy-seven, and Julio, seventy-six, have not lost their desperate will to dominate. Nor their unerring ability to do so. Though their illustrious careers are drawing to a close during the toughest time for U.S. wine-makers since Prohibition, their corporate offspring continues to thrive.

What is the Gallo secret?

"A constant striving for perfection in every aspect of our business," says Ernest. That may sound self-serving, but it is in large part true. Plainly put, Ernest and Julio are better at the nuts and bolts of the wine business than anyone else in the world.

IT WAS NOT always so, for the Gallos learned early how bitter the wine business can be. They got their first taste as young boys, toiling in their father Joseph's Modesto vineyard in their spare time. After Julio finished high school and Ernest graduated from Modesto Junior College, they worked full-time for their father. "He believed in hard work and no play," says Julio. "None at all."

An immigrant from the Piedmont region in northwest Italy, the Gallo's father Joseph was a small-time grape grower and shipper. Prohibition did not put him out of work: the government permitted wine for medicinal and religious use. But the Depression took a tragic toll. The Gallo business went under, and in the spring of 1933 Joseph shot his wife and reportedly chased Ernest and Julio across his fields waving a shotgun. After they escaped, Joseph killed himself. Ernest is reminded of the tragedy daily: his childhood residence is on the road from the winery to his present home.

Prohibition ended the same year that their parents died, and the Gallos, then in their early twenties, decided to switch from growing grapes to producing wine. Problem was, they had no idea how to make the stuff. They found instructions in two thin pamphlets in the Modesto Public Library and, with $5,900.23 to their names, burst out of the post-Prohibition gate with six hundred other newly formed wineries. "My confidence," recalls Ernest, "was unlimited."

Finding customers was the next hurdle, and Ernest was born with an instinct for that. A Chicago distributor wrote to newly licensed California wineries, inviting them to send him samples. Ernest went the extra mile. He boarded a plane for Chicago, met the man at his office, and sold him six thousand gallons at fifty cents a gallon. Ernest continued east and sold the rest of the first year's production for a profit of $34,000. The Gallos initially sold wine in bulk to bottlers, but in 1938, they started doing their own bottling under the Gallo label, a far more profitable venture. Sales grew unabated for years.

The Gallos had their first phenomenal success with a high-alcohol, lemon-flavored beverage they began selling in the late 1950s. A radio jingle sent the stuff to the top of the charts on skid rows across the country: "What's the word? Thunderbird. How's it sold? Good and cold. What's the jive? Bird's alive. What's the price? Thirty twice."

But Thunderbird also left Gallo with a gutter image it has been hard pressed to shake.

Each in his own way, the Gallos are fighting to change that image. Julio, the wine-maker, may be more easygoing than Ernest, but he is no pushover when it comes to getting what he wants from growers. Says George Frank, Gallo's former East Coast executive: "He works with grapes as if he's pursuing the Holy Grail."

With the help of graduates from California's top enology schools, Julio has experimented with hundreds of varieties over the years. Gallo was among the first producers to store wine in stainless steel containers instead of the usual redwood casks that can breed bad-tasting bacteria. Like giant thermos bottles, tanks at Gallo's three crushers and at the Modesto headquarters protect 300 million gallons of wine from the searing heat. Passersby could easily mistake the Modesto plant for an oil refinery.

The refinery image is a sore point with Julio. "It never was my ambition to run the biggest winery in the world," he says. "It doesn't impress me at all." Gallo offers no tours to the public. Rather, Julio prefers to sweep the visitor underground to see his new oak aging cellar. Gallo dug the crypt in deference to those who prefer their wine aged and dated.

But changing Gallo's image is really an above-ground proposition, and it is Ernest who is throwing more than $40 million into advertising this year to get the quality message to consumers. A new television campaign could be powerful enough to finally overcome the Thunderbird association.

In his business office is a framed *New Yorker* cartoon that tells the tale: it shows two couples drinking wine in a restaurant. The caption reads:

"Surprisingly good, isn't it. It's Gallo. Mort and I simply got tired of being snobs."

AS TO THE future, Julio has begun to pass the scepter: His son Robert, fifty-two, and son-in-law, James Coleman, fifty, oversee much of the day-to-day production.

But Ernest refuses to give anyone an aerial view of his part of the kingdom. Both sons, David, forty-seven, and Joseph, forty-five, work on his side of the business, but neither is heir apparent. Both lack their father's drive and authority. But if Ernest's sons are less prepared than they should be, the problem may have more to do with his management style than with their deficiencies.

Critical and intimidating, Ernest cannot bear to relinquish control. The deep-rooted need to hold on is understandable: in his world, events can get so wildly out of control that they produce the tragedies of his youth.

Call his style shortsighted, even paranoid. Rest assured, though, that Ernest has figured out how to sell Gallo products from the grave. He probably is well along on a manual outlining every conceivable war that could break out in the wine world and ten steps to win each one. ✒

THE PEACOCK IN THE GROVE

AUGUST SEBASTIANI HEADS the famous Sebastiani Vineyards forty-five miles north of San Francisco in Sonoma. This particular day the rains have come and gone, turning the lawn in the town plaza a brilliant green. By noon, sunlight is pouring through the windows of the stone mansion where August and his wife, Sylvia, live and entertain lavishly, often with unbuttoned ease. Cresting the hill, their spacious home overlooks vineyards and a deep blue reservoir upon which some of August's beloved birds — swans, geese, and ducks — float serenely, untroubled by the affairs of the larger world outside.

Farther down the hill — perhaps two hundred yards away — are the Sebastiani wine cellars and tasting room. And across the street is a refurbished house accommodating a small secretarial staff and modest, even plain offices.

Earlier in the morning, photographer Randolph Falk and I had met August at his desk and chatted with him about his memories, including those of A. P. Giannini, until at some unmarked point in our conversation he'd decided we comprised a companionable trio and invited us to come home with him in his pickup truck for lunch.

As August pours the wine, he speaks of his father, Samuele, a poor Italian immigrant from the Tuscany region of Italy who first made a living in this country by working in the fields and hauling cobblestones from the nearby quarries in Sonoma to pave the streets of San Francisco. With the money he saved, he went into wine making.

"From the time my father bought one old five-hundred-gallon redwood vat and a wheezy handpress for crushing grapes, he banked with Giannini. Later, in the twenties, I remember going with my dad to see Giannini about a loan. Neither of them ever bothered with paper when they did business. That wasn't their style. They were men of their word. They'd just shake hands — and that was it."

AUGUST IS CUT from the same mold — a multimil-

▲
August Sebastiani, complete with 'stripees,' inspects the vineyards.

lionaire without airs. From my quick survey of his living room I see no priceless paintings or antique jeweled boxes on the Chippendale table. How, I wonder aloud, does he spend his fortunes? "Well," says August, "I may end up having to get my overalls custom-made. They're getting harder to find in the stores. But my real luxury is birds. I'm the original hippie environmentalist."

We are standing with him under the gigantic oak tree in his backyard and gawking at the four or five peacocks resting gracefully in the branches. In the gentle breeze their unbelievable tails — as iridescent as the Spanish matador's suit of lights — are moving lightly to-and-fro in the dying sunlight.

The truth — though August is not the one to tell us — is that he is an internationally recognized bird-watcher and ornithologist. In his aviary are over a thousand specimens of rare birds.

"Doves," he explains, "are what got me started. I was fascinated by them as a child. I never tired of listening to their haunting sound, their soft cooing — in the early hours of dawn.

"Do you know what I especially like to do? On a hot summer night I like to put organ music on the stereo and go out in the moonlight and take a swim in my pool. As I float along on my back, I can look up and see the stars and the outline of my peacocks against the sky as they rest in the branches of my oak tree."

— *Marion Rosetta*

The Musical Theater

THE REMINISCENCES OF
ROSA PONSELLE

by James A. Drake

If opera, as some have said, was the cinema of the nineteenth century, then Adelina Patti was the Grace Kelly of her time. Traveling in her own railroad car, living in a castle, and commanding movie star fees, she was the last of the great divas. Rosa Ponselle, having come to opera from vaudeville, had strong links to the popular arts. Perhaps more importantly, she proved once and for all that American soil had no deleterious effects on the Italian voice.

ON A RECENT visit to her villa outside Baltimore, I invited the great diva, Rosa Ponselle, to sort out the "facts" of her career. Forty years after her last stage appearance, the legend of that career — beginning with her emergence from the vaudeville circuit onto the stage of the Metropolitan Opera in November 1918 — remains firmly ingrained in the minds of opera enthusiasts.

"It's true that I started out as a silent-movie pianist," she began, "but like everything else in my career I didn't seek it out myself. My sister, Carmela, who had all the drive and ambition I lacked, took me to the manager of the Bristol movie house in Meriden, Connecticut, because she was convinced that I was old enough to start earning my keep.

"As for my vaudeville career, that too was something that I merely happened to fall into. By 1915 my sister was a huge success in vaudeville, and at the time 'sister acts' were being booked by all the big managers. Gene Hughes, Carmela's manager, asked her out of curiosity whether she knew of someone who could sing and would pose as her sister. She told him that she had a real-life sister who could sing well.

"We made our vaudeville debut in the Bronx, and made our way to Brighton Beach and finally to the Riverside Theater; eventually, we played the Palace, which was the high point of any vaudeville career in those days.

"In terms of my getting to the Metropolitan, though, it was the Riverside Theater that proved important, because it was there that Romano Romani, who later became my coach, heard Carmela and me and was very impressed with both of us. I

first met Caruso during that audition. He had come to hear these singing sisters that Romani had been filling his ears about. When he entered the room, he walked diagonally across and spoke to me as if I were one of his own. We took to each other from the moment we met, and as he was kidding me I could see him sizing me up, thinking to himself, 'Now here's a brash, outspoken little urchin whom I might want to sing with, if she's as good as she's cracked up to be.'

"After he heard me he told me confidently that I had everything I needed in the throat and in the heart, and that what remained was for me to get what I needed musically in my head. Then he told me flatly, 'You'll sing with me.'

"That next fall I made my debut opposite him in *Forza del Destino*, and it seemed just that — the force of destiny.

"As for my debut, it is true that I had never sung on an operatic stage before I was engaged by the Metropolitan. But I want to point out that I was already a vaudeville headliner by the time I auditioned for the Met, and so I was accustomed to singing to very large audiences. You must remember that vaudeville and grand opera were no strangers to each other then. A great many established singers made vaudeville appearances in those days.

"Still, even though I was used to singing fairly demanding music as a vaudevillian, I wasn't totally ready for the pressures of the Met. Even though it makes for a good story, I didn't faint at any rehearsals, however. The truth is that I was extremely confident, right through the general rehearsal."

Ponselle later found out that Giulio Gatti-Casazza had carried on a continuous argument with Caruso over the wisdom of letting her debut in a new production without trying her elsewhere. "If she succeeds," Gatti confessed to Caruso, "American singers will have the doors opened to them. If she fails, I will be on the first boat back to Italy and New York will never see my face again."

Ponselle did succeed, though not without scars. Between the general rehearsal and the day of her debut, the Italian tenor Giulio Crimi made his Met debut and received negative reviews.

"Unfortunately for me, my secretary happened to give me copies of the papers, and when I read what the critics did to an already well-established singer, I panicked. I was in such bad shape by the time I got to the opera house that I couldn't even manage my own makeup — I'd been given all kinds of sedatives and hardly knew where I was.

"To make matters worse, the manager insisted that I vocalize in my dressing room. That's when I really panicked — my voice sounded horrid, and I was sure I'd lost it. Later I realized that I'd been vocalizing in a room that had massive drapes, carpeting, and every other kind of sound-absorbing thing you could imagine."

Though she lived through her debut, it colored every other opening night of Ponselle's career. "I was always nervous no matter how many times I sang a role. I took some comfort in knowing that Caruso, even though world famous, became nervous before every performance."

But what of Caruso, and of the other legendary singers of her day?

"Among tenors, there are two classes. In the first there is but one: Caruso. He had the most beautiful, the most awesome tenor voice in my recollection. All the tenors who succeeded him are in the second category and I wouldn't presume to try to rank them."

ONE QUESTION ABOUT Ponselle's Met career remains open: her abrupt retirement in 1937.

Even today, she will only say, "People who know me will tell you that I am a victim of the emotions, and when I left it was for emotional rather than vocal reasons."

Her few professional regrets center around her commercial recordings. Nonetheless, whatever their technical limitations, her early records are in a class of their own. So was her musicianship, for both in the opera house and in the recording studio, Ponselle chose her own tempos, and no conductor objected.

Tullio Serafin pronounced her one of the greatest musicians he had ever encountered. Toscanini several times described her musicianship to the late Bruno Zirato as being *per Dio*, a gift of God.

If Ponselle does harbor any regrets, it is that she never sang with Toscanini. "Each season he would send Zirato or another emissary to approach me about singing under him, and I'd admit that I was too terrified to work under him. He knew how uneasy I was, and he never pressed me by asking directly."

Opera fans can only imagine the results had he done so. ❧

THE QUEEN OF SONG

IN MADRID ON the night of February 8, 1843, an Italian soprano sang the title role in the opera *Norma* and in the early hours of the next morning gave birth to her seventh child. That child was Adelina Patti.

Today, Adelina Patti is an almost legendary figure, one of the greatest singers of all time, who ranks as the "Queen of Song" because no one can think of a higher or better title to give her. Unsurpassed in coloratura vocal gymnastics, she was capable of the heavier demands of such operas as *Aïda*, but ballads were her favorites. "Comin' Through the Rye," "Annie Laurie," and "Home Sweet Home" when sung by Patti were unforgettable.

When Adelina was two, the Patti family came to America and settled on Tenth Street in New York. It was a time when Italian opera had just begun to flourish in American cities. Adelina made her first public appearance at the age of seven when her father and mother were singing at Tripler Hall in New York. She followed her mother's cadenzas with ease. She had had almost no vocal instruction — she scarcely needed it, having been born virtually on stage — and was hailed as a prodigy. She toured with her family until she "retired" at the age of sixteen to study.

Her actual operatic debut took place in the old Academy of Music on Fourteenth Street in 1859. She played the role of Lucia in *Lucia di Lamermoor*, and it was a sensational success, followed by other delirious appearances around the country.

With Patti, something different had come to opera: a petite, beautiful woman with a glorious voice. Prima donnas of the day were big women, full-bosomed types, who labored as they sang and acted, and it was believed that their heftiness lent power to their voices. The diminutive Patti disproved this notion. Her audience fell in love with her ease of song — "One should sing like a bird," she said. "Suppose a lark should stop to think what kind of method he used!" — her stage presence, and her youthful self-assurance.

FOR THE NEXT quarter century Patti sang in England in summer; in winter in Paris, St. Petersburg, Berlin, Vienna, Madrid, and Brussels. She also made numbers of triumphal tours of the United States where her business acumen — she never sang until she had her fee in hand — was legendary.

Patti's business rule was simple: "My price, no questions, no arguments." She had no arguments, she lost no money, she always got her price, and when traveling in her opulent private railroad car, said to be worth upwards of $60,000, her price was $5,000 a night plus expenses, which, with her entourage, were considerable.

When she sang *Semiramide* in Washington during her American tour of 1882–83, it was calculated that Patti received more for singing this one opera than Rossini was paid for composing it. When it was pointed out to her that she was paid more for her work than the president of the United States received for his, she replied, "Then ask the president to sing for you."

— *Georges Lewys*

THE DREAMBOY

by Louise Continelli

DREAMBOY MICHAEL BENNETT never dreamed he'd grow to be the hottest ticket on Broadway. Nor could his fervid imagination prepare him for his ending. Death from AIDS.

Yet if immortality is luminescence, and if it can be gained by touching lives and lighting them up with laughter, then Michael Bennett's star blazes brightly in the other Great White Way.

Here, then, is another piece conceived, choreographed, and directed by Michael Bennett.

ACT 1

From the beginning, recalls his mother, Helen DiFiglia, Michael "determined the way we were going to live. More so than we determined his life, he set the pace, and we just went along with it."

Michael Bennett DiFiglia was a World War II baby and a child of Buffalo's 1950s.

"My husband was in the Navy and didn't see Michael a lot the first few years. When he saw Michael's talent, he was just awed."

Home movies taken when Michael was four years old attest to the "singular sensation," as the rickety frames flash his young form tapping and spinning at one of his first public performances.

Bennett discovered early that dancing is like life: All the important moves come from the hips up. Though his footwork was applauded by dance-jaded agents, he wanted most to become a choreographer, to control the dancers. And control he did, both on stage and off. Dancers, agents, critics, and lawyers were under his spell.

"His father took him on the Comet at Crystal Beach when he was a little boy," Mrs. DiFiglia remembers. "People asked, isn't he afraid? He couldn't wait to get back on.

"He was not afraid of anything, including death. I often had this feeling that, because he was so different and so magical, maybe he would not live to a ripe old age.

"In a lot of ways, he was like a little boy who never grew up. When he came back to Buffalo, he wanted to go on the roller coaster. He did, and he loved it.

"I always thought the character of Peter Pan was fabulous," Bennett once admitted. "I grew up playing 'let's pretend.'"

No stage mother, Mrs. DiFiglia hoped her son would grow out of his obsessions with the theater. But the kid seemed born to dance. "I held him back," she says. But it was like trying to hold on to a live wire.

ACT 2

Manhattan: The most intoxicating city in the world seduced eighteen-year-old Michael Bennett when he flew in from Buffalo. The city glimmered like an impossible jewel, but Bennett's lust for success sharpened his talents to an edge as fine as a lapidary chisel.

Bennett developed a friendship with another dancer, Bob Avian, and together they shared flights of fancy and flights of a fourth-floor walk-up. He had his first slice of the Big Apple.

"Did they like me? Did they applaud?" he would ask, coming off the stage. He didn't see the audience. "I'm in another world," he'd explain.

In the 1960s shimmy show *Hullabaloo*, he shared some step secrets with another dancer, Donna McKechnie. "Even then he was giving me his best stuff," says a still-incredulous McKechnie, who later played Cassie in *A Chorus Line*. "He taught me what taking risks was."

With a musical heritage and a sense of theater second to none, Italian Americans might have been expected to dominate musical theater. That had not been the case — until Michael Bennett came along. In a very few years, he began to influence the Broadway musical in a way that would surely have grown. When his life came to a sudden end, it was as if a light had gone out on the Great White Way.

▲
Michael Bennett wanted *A Chorus Line* to run forever.

Big risks thrilled Bennett, a guy who wasn't scared in an industry based on fear.

"Everything in the theater is fear — total, abject, perishing, gut-wrenching fear," says gossip columnist Liz Smith, a pal of Bennett's. "The horror of forgetting your lines. The dread of not finding a prop. And the real fear you might find yourself naked out on stage.

"Michael would have made a winning general. I could see him shaping up the logistics — and the look — of World War III."

The child of the theater soon began to collect Tony Awards like chestnuts.

Bennett's *Chorus Line* gypsies whirled into American folklore. At thirty-two, Michael Bennett had it made. Applause and kudos rose as abundantly as bubbles from a bottle of Dom Perignon. Manhattan was his crowning jewel. Earning $100,000 a week, the cabdriver's son bought a white Rolls-Royce. He also bought a mansion with a pool in East Hampton, his "starter home" worth $6 million.

"He went kind of crazy," Mrs. DiFiglia says. "But it didn't last. He realized it was superficial."

Another smash hit, *Dreamgirls*, followed *A Chorus Line*, with Bennett as director-choreographer-producer.

Michael Bennett's vision was turning dreams to reality; his intensity was turning reality to perfection. On opening night the only question was, "What are you going to do next?"

"For years he wanted a theater," Mrs. DiFiglia says, "and he finally built a theater in his building, a beautiful theater and a restaurant also. Michael told me he intended to run *A Chorus Line* forever at his theater at 890 Broadway. Unfortunately, that was not to be."

ACT 3

"It's just chest pain," Michael said of reports of his illness in early 1986. "I've been working hard, and now I'm going to rest."

Just as night follows day, so does terrible realization follow the most ambitious denials.

Michael had contracted acquired immune deficiency syndrome. The news echoed through the media like the howl of a specter in a haunted house.

He sold the East Hampton house. He moved to Tucson, Arizona, for treatment, and bought a home that faced spectacular Southwest scenery.

"For two years he went through a lot of pain, tests, different drugs, experimental treatment, chemotherapy," Mrs. DiFiglia says.

He could control everything but a virus.

Friends had died of AIDS; the disease had already killed hundreds who worked in theater. But Bennett was not promiscuous. "He was bisexual. He did not go to bars and pick up men," Mrs. DiFiglia says. "But whatever your sexual preference, you are not a terrible person. It's a virus. The myth is you're a bum if you get AIDS. He was not."

He cut down to eight cigarettes a day, and drank cranberry juice instead of coffee. Once strong enough to dance around the world, Bennett became so weak and emaciated that he could no longer walk.

While Michael was in Arizona, *Dreamgirls* reopened on Broadway.

"Michael couldn't be at the reopening, so he decided to have his own celebration," his lawyer, John Breglio, says. "He threw an enormous party at his home. This time there were no stars, no celebrities. Michael sent invitations to everyone who cared for him in the Tucson hospital — every nurse, doctor, intern, and orderly.

"No show runs forever," he said.

Four days later, Bennett slipped into a coma. He died — as he had been born — on a Thursday morning. ❧

THE POLITICAL OPERA OF GIAN CARLO MENOTTI

POLITICAL OPERA HAS a distinguished history. There's the servant rebelling against the master in *The Marriage of Figaro*, political oppression in Verdi's operas (though the censors did their best to control it), and the ferocious social commentary of the Brecht-Weill works like *The Threepenny Opera* and *The Rise and Fall of the City of Mahogany*. Gian Carlo Menotti's *Tamu-Tamu* is in such a tradition.

Menotti wrote *Tamu-Tamu* (Indonesian for "The Guests") in 1973. The Vietnam War was on, and the atrocities of My Lai and the bombing of Cambodia were in the newspapers and on TV. Menotti was asked by a group of anthropologists to compose an opera for the Ninth International Congress of Anthropological and Ethnological Sciences that would reflect its theme of "Man, One Species, Many Cultures."

"They wanted me to write a big pageant, about how all races are getting together and so on," Menotti says. "Well, I don't believe that they are. So I had dinner with Margaret Mead and Sol Tax and the rest of the committee, and told them that there's no use writing a pageant exulting something that doesn't really exist. It would be better to teach people to be aware of what our neighbors go through, and make them realize how indifferent we really are to the human condition."

The composer, who also writes his own librettos, came up with a story of an American couple who see a newspaper photo of a family of Indonesian refugees being chased by soldiers, and then suddenly find this same family, bleeding and terrified, on their doorstep. The Americans sing in English; the Indonesians in Indonesian, without subtitles. The audience is supposed to be in the same situation as the American characters: unable to understand what the foreigners are saying. Just as they are all beginning to understand each other, two soldiers burst in and massacre the family.

Menotti says that the work was inspired by the famous news photograph of the Vietnamese girl, ablaze with napalm, screaming and running toward the camera.

Menotti had written political operas before. *The Consul*, premiered in 1950, is a Kafkaesque tale about political outcasts in a totalitarian state who seek asylum in a foreign consulate and are destroyed by its bureaucracy. "*The Consul* has been done in Russia, Turkey, and Poland," says Menotti. "It's extraordinary. Everybody thinks it is about some other nation or some other people — never about themselves."

Audiences today tend to think of opera as being about something that happened long ago; many were appalled by the up-to-the-minute references to homosexuality and the petty family fights in Leonard Bernstein's *A Quiet Place* several years ago. Still, the best opera has that universality to which Menotti aspires, so that we can still love *Figaro* even though the class struggle at its center no longer means anything specific to us. With Vietnam an increasingly distant reality, *Tamu-Tamu* will now stand on its own.

— *Heidi Waleson*

Menotti's *Amahl and the Night Visitors* was the first opera created expressly for television. ▶

LORENZO DAPONTE IN NEW YORK

by Lawrence DiStasi

IN DESCRIBING THE death of Mozart, musicologist Henry Krehbiel noted again the now-famous irony that for the world's greatest composer, buried as a pauper, there exists no grave, no headstone, no remains.

"That was in 1791 in Vienna," Krehbiel continues. "Almost half a century later, Lorenzo DaPonte, the Italian poet who had been Mozart's friend and collaborator with him on three operas — *Le Nozze di Figaro*, *Don Giovanni*, and *Così fan Tutte* — died in New York.

"DaPonte had lived in the New World a full generation — more than one-third of a marvelously checkered life, the term of which embraced the birth and death of Mozart, Beethoven, Schubert, Byron, Scott, and Napoléon Bonaparte, and the entire creative career of Haydn.

"Before coming to America, DaPonte had been *improvvisatore*, professor of rhetoric, and politician in his native land; poet to the Imperial Theatre and Latin secretary to the Emperor in Austria; Italian teacher, operatic poet, litterateur, and bookseller in England; and then tradesman, teacher, opera manager, and bookseller in the United States.

"DaPonte had enjoyed the friendship of some of the great ones of the Old World, and some of the noble ones of the New. In New York he came nearer to finding a home than anywhere in Europe. And yet, much like his colleague, Mozart, the exact location of his grave is also unknown."

IT ALL SEEMS too ironic, too fictional. No marked grave for the composer of *Don Giovanni* in the Old World. And no marked grave for the librettist — and probably the model as well — of *Don Giovanni* in the New.

Yet in a remarkable life in America, Lorenzo DaPonte did enjoy some meetings with remarkable men. In a New York

◀ **Mozart used a DaPonte libretto for three operas: *Don Giovanni*, *Le Nozze di Figaro*, and *Così fan Tutte*.**

◄

**Lorenzo DaPonte:
poet, professor,
politician, librettist,
tradesman, and
rogue**

bookstore, for example, DaPonte met Clement C. Moore, then just twenty-five years old. Moore — who would eventually compose perhaps the most widely known poem ever written, " 'Twas the Night Before Christmas" — not only encouraged DaPonte to begin giving Italian lessons to young New Yorkers, but also became one of his first pupils. More importantly, when Moore became a trustee of Columbia College, he convinced his associates to appoint DaPonte the first professor of the Italian language in America, albeit without salary.

Then in November of the same year, 1825, came an even more provocative — and for American culture — more significant meeting.

An opera company under the direction of Manuel Garcia arrived in New York for an American tour. The first season of Italian opera in the New World was opening, and Mozart's librettist, by now a tireless proponent of Italian culture, was there to witness it. No one is sure if DaPonte actually attended the gala opening performance of Rossini's *Barber of Seville* on November 29. But, after an early performance of this soon-to-be-beloved classic, he hurried backstage to meet the impresario and star, Manuel Garcia.

Now seventy-six years old, an eminence with courtly manners and the face and white hair of a Hebrew prophet, DaPonte must have swept into

that room with a flourish to announce himself: the author of *Don Giovanni*, the friend and collaborator of the great Mozart himself.

How could Garcia resist? Here in this primitive city, bankrupt of even an oboe player to fill out an orchestra, much less an audience to appreciate that orchestra — here was the most famous librettist in operatic history.

Garcia embraced DaPonte with what one writer calls "true Spanish fervor." And as he did so, he erupted into a song — "Fin ch'han dal vino" — the celebrated drinking song from *Don Giovanni*. It must have filled the old Italian teacher's heart with joy.

DaPonte soon became the chief propagandist for the company, as well as the singers' chief host, ever solicitous for their comfort. He took them to his favorite boardinghouse, Aunt Sallie's, where they could enjoy "soup, macaroni, and red wine, to say nothing of bread and vegetables, like those they had enjoyed in the trattorias of Florence and Rome."

He defended their performances ferociously. And, in time, he convinced Garcia to add his own masterpiece — *Don Giovanni* — to the repertoire.

On May 23, 1826, the main ambition of DaPonte's old age was realized. *Don Giovanni* was performed in America for the first time. Though it would be some time before Italian opera would be truly appreciated in America, DaPonte had succeeded in planting the seeds.

On August 17, 1838, Lorenzo DaPonte died at his home, No. 91 Spring Street. An eyewitness described the funeral as "impressive," which it may have been. His ashes, however, which DaPonte, in a last statement, agreed to consign to New York rather than Italy, never turned up to receive what he had hoped for: "vano conforto di tardi sospiri" ("the vain comfort of late sighs").

95

THE FATHER OF THE MODERN VARIETY SHOW

by Douglas Gilbert

Although they operated on different coasts and in different types of theater, Tony Pastor and Antonietta Pisanelli had this in common: Both were pioneers in bringing theater to more people — women and children specifically — than had been able to attend before. In their Italian conception of it, theater should be no less a family affair than life in the streets. That Pastor's influence had greater effect was probably because he operated in English. It may be, though, that Pisanelli's café-chantant is yet to have its day.

To TONY PASTOR go the honors for tossing variety's denimed frowsiness into the ash can and bringing out My Lady Vaudeville in starched organdy — a shining child, ready to meet its elders on something more than a gamin basis.

Tony (Antonio) Pastor was born in Greenwich Village in Manhattan.

A date — May 28, 1837 — appears in some of the data about him, but he was sensitive about his age and his forebears, and would never verify it. It is recorded that his father was a musician in Barnum's band, but there are other reports that his father sold perfume.

If 1837 is the year of Tony's birth, he made his first public appearance in the old Dey Street Church in New York at the age of six, singing duets. Apparently the boy's talent was marked even then, for his father, suspecting leanings toward a stage career, shipped him upstate as apprentice to a farmer. The farmer promptly returned him because his clowning disrupted the hired help. At this point his father gave up and Tony went on at Barnum's Museum in New York City as a child prodigy.

There is nothing to indicate that he ever saw his father again.

His precocity amazed — and dismayed — his employers. While he was with Delevan and Nathan's Circus, Tony rigged up a stage inside a tent, roped off a portion for intimate seating, and organized nighttime song and dance shows, a form of entertainment unheard of in circuses of those days because of the inadequate lighting. When the manager began to suspect that the boy's novelty was taking the larger share of the box office, he stopped it. Courageous and confident, Tony quit.

When the ringmaster of his next circus fell dead, Tony, at fourteen, assumed his duties, doubtless the youngest ringmaster under canvas. Singing, dancing, taking part in the afterpieces, Tony did well, playing circuses as ringmaster and performer until the Civil War broke out.

At the age of twenty-four, Pastor came back to New York and opened his first theater,

▶ **Some of Tony Pastor's roles for his singing act — a soldier, a bumpkin, and a clown**

SIGNORA IMPRESARIO

LARGE PLAYBILLS WERE circulated throughout the week in San Francisco. At Fisherman's Wharf, and up in Washington Square, groups congregated to discuss the news. A program in honor of the Neapolitan *canzonettista* — Signora Antonietta Pisanelli — was planned for Sunday evening, April 9, 1905, at the Teatro Apollo. The Signora — it was openly being said — possessed the personality to bring Italian theatre to San Francisco for the first time.

Pisanelli had come to California in 1904 with her orphaned son. She was not without theatre experience. In New York where she first immigrated, she had made her debut at the Società Fraterna at the Giambelli Hall. She at once became so popular that theatres seemed to be springing up everywhere in her tracks — first in New York, then in Philadelphia, Chicago, New Haven. In San Francisco, Pisanelli discovered to her amazement that there were sixty thousand Italians and not even one theatre. She moved quickly to rent the Apollo Hall for one night, rounded up all the available amateur actors, and announced a varied program of songs and sketches. Standing room was sold out and Pisanelli took in over $150. She had struck a bonanza.

Signora Pisanelli now had no doubts about the permanence of the Italian Theatre in San Francisco; she promptly discovered a larger and more substantial building — the Bersaglieri Hall — and leased it for ten years. Italian theatre was now in full sway, with actors and companies on their way to San Francisco from across the continent.

North Beach crowded the Teatro Bersaglieri every night. Then came the difficulties with the authorities. City officials claimed that as a theatre it did not comply with the regulations of the fire department and would have to close. Signora Pisanelli simply shrugged her expressive shoulders in resignation. The Teatro Bersaglieri was closed that evening. The next morning it was reopened as the Circolo Famigliare

Pisanelli — the Pisanelli Family Circle.

Instead of row seats, now there were little tables and chairs. But the stage was still there — it had become a café-chantant. On the stage the performers still sang, played instruments, acted in dramas, comedies and farces. Instead of admission charge, however, the admiring public now bought many drinks as the

fascinating Signora went from table to table, exchanging greetings, singing Neapolitan songs.

North Beach enthusiastically welcomed the innovation; things were — if anything — even more sociable than before.

During 1905 and 1906 the Circolo Famigliare Pisanelli reigned supreme in North Beach as an important social

institution — a combination of club, opera, theatre, and café. Its mainstay, always, was the Signora: "With the rise of the curtain, Signora Antonietta Pisanelli, the brightest star of the circle, trips out upon the stage amid bursts of applause," writes one contemporary reviewer.

"She is prettily dressed in black, the dress cut décolleté, revealing shapely shoulders and the bust of a model. Her Neapolitan cameo face is stamped with intellectuality and refinement. Heavy brows arch her piercing velvety eyes — as black as midnight, yet flashing with the brightness of the diamond — the kind that drive men crazy. . . ."

Her audiences seemed to completely agree.

Then came 1906, and the earthquake and fire. The desolate troupe contemplated the ashes of Circolo Famigliare Pisanelli and went on tour.

And the Signora? By some seismographic intuition, she had sold her theatre three days before the fire for the very profitable price of $20,000. She had already left for St. Louis.

She would return to San Francisco, however. Now Signora Alessandro, she would persuade Abe Reuf, an influential and later scandal-ridden politician, to supply the capital for the finest theatre the Italian colony was to have — the Washington Square. It was a thousand-seat theatre and all the greats of Italian theatre would play there.

And when that went into decline, the Signora Impresario would have yet another theatre — the Alessandro Eden — opened in 1924. For this one she would use circulars featuring comic strips to lure her customers to a night of diversion.

In the end, even the Signora Impresario had to yield to the inevitable decline. Americanization had done its work. But while it lasted, San Francisco Italian theatre, popular theatre for its immigrants, was second to none. And at its center was always the impresario, Antonietta Pisanelli.

— *Lawrence Estavan*

TONY PASTOR'S NEW 14th STREET THEATRE.

at 444 Broadway. It was a dive. There is no evidence that it was a rendezvous for bawds, though how it could have escaped cannot be deduced from the record. Tony starred as a singer. The plight of the workingman and the foibles of the day were both grist for his musical mill.

Before long, Pastor conceived the idea of a touring variety company. It was not precisely a pioneer venture, but his troupers were a compact unit offering specific entertainment with the accent on comedy, dancing, songs, and sketches. The show approached vaudeville as we were later to know it. Its success led Pastor to continue the tour as his annual feature for twenty years.

Then on February 8, 1881, Pastor moved to what he called Tony Pastor's New Fourteenth Street Theatre. A bandbox hewn out of Tammany Hall, it was not at first new or much of a theater. But in October he junked his musicals and opened with a real innovation: a straight, clean variety show, the first — as such — ever given in this country.

It was a daring venture. Only gals on the trampish side attended variety in the eighties. Pastor's move was mainly for profit, a canny bid to double the audience by attracting respectable women — wives, sisters, sweethearts. In boldface type Pastor announced his pride in offering unblushing entertainment. This gesture was not phony. Tony Pastor was a decent man.

At Tony's shows, and for the first time, vaudeville delivered its message to a mixed audience. And the mothers and wives and sweethearts kept coming to his shows. Sometimes Pastor resorted to tricks to lure them in — gifts of hats, dress patterns, and other feminine gewgaws. The haut monde seldom slummed at Pastor's.

Slowly, other managers followed Pastor's "clean" shows, and variety began to approach the financially stable enterprise known as vaudeville, its bookings secure, its salaries definite and sizable.

Pastor always mistrusted his high-sounding sobriquet, "The Impresario of Fourteenth Street." Regarding himself as a trouper rather than a manager, he was an indefatigable worker, learning upward of fifteen hundred songs — possibly the greatest repertory of

any performer — laboriously, a phrase at a time, nearly driving his pianists mad with insistent repetitions.

As a theater owner, Pastor literally ran his affairs in his hat. He had vision but never capitalized on it on a nationwide scale as did his competitors who were to engulf him — Keith, Albee, Poli, Beck, Proctor, and Murdock — sometimes unethically, sometimes dishonestly. One of his last statements indicates his attitude: "I owe my good health and good spirits to the fact that I am not worried by ambition. I frequently have been asked why I did not move up on Broadway. Once I listened to these suggestions and actually commenced negotiations. Then something or other went wrong and I never made another attempt. I look with amazement at the men who can run three or four playhouses and apparently enjoy it. This one [Fourteenth Street] is work enough for me, but it is congenial work after all. I come down every day and attend to the booking, etc., and when that is over I am free."

Since Pastor was largely, if indirectly, responsible for the success of the big-time operators, his statement should be heard more in the spirit of resignation than lament.

That Keith first took vaudeville out of the beer halls and wine rooms, bathed it in purity, and adorned it with silks is a press agent's lie. Unwittingly, or by design, Keith simply followed the lead of Pastor, whose "clean" vaudeville at Fourteenth Street came two years before Keith even entered the field. And the idea of the double audience — women and men — belonged to Pastor as well.

It was the reformation, and it was Pastor, not Keith, who became the Savonarola of the modern variety show.

Tony Pastor died on August 26, 1908, of a paralytic stroke. His estate was auctioned off for dimes. The good-natured, friendly father of "family" vaudeville had watched the more aggressive Keith, then Proctor, pick up the dropped handkerchief of "polite" comedy, and exploit it for the millions its true founder never made. ❧

MARIO LANZA'S NOSE

by Anthony Valerio

Mario Lanza's movies, for a brief time, made opera a form of popular culture once again.

▼

Only the special few reach that level of fame where their surname alone is sufficient to signal an entire genre. Caruso is one, for I can still hear, when I sing, the gentle put-down of my youth: "Whattayou, think you're a Caruso?" For a few golden years, Mario Lanza thought he was not only a Caruso, but the Caruso. Sadly for him, and for music, it seems Mr. Lucky Luciano did not agree.

OUR LOCAL CULTURAL station, Channel 13, recently aired a program called "Mario Lanza: The American Caruso." Mrs. Richard Tucker must have been extremely upset, refusing to tune in, because her husband was touted as America's heir to Caruso. "Richard Tucker: A Brooklyn Caruso," he was once tagged. "Forget about the Caruso thing, Mrs. Tucker," I'd like to tell her. "Caruso was Caruso — it's intimidating, even contemptuous, for a good tenor to be compared with him. I mean, do you hear Luciano Pavarotti calling himself 'The Italian Lauritz Melchior'? Or Placido Domingo calling himself 'The Spanish Luciano Pavarotti'?"

FOR THE MARIO LANZA show, I can imagine the Met saying to its principal tenor, Placido Domingo: "Thirteen is doing a thing on Mario Lanza. They want you to host it. You won't have to go out of your way — one afternoon after rehearsal we'll set up a camera in the orchestra pit, you stand on an empty stage, and in your best accent you say, 'Mario Lanza, he wanted this — the stage of an opera house, but he never got it. He was born in 1921, the year Caruso died. Mario Lanza believed that Caruso's voice passed into him.' Stuff like this.

"You won't be alone — we're sending over Robert Merrill, Anna Moffo, Rosalind Elias, and there'll be clips of Kathryn Grayson, Ann Blyth, Frances Yeend, Lanza's physical instructor, even Zsa Zsa Gabor.

"Then we'll shoot you down to Lanza's childhood home above his grandfather's store in South Philadelphia...."

"I'm not going to South

CARUSO IN THE BIG APPLE

IN DESCRIPTIONS OF Enrico Caruso's singing, the words *gold* and *golden* crop up constantly. "Molten gold." "Golden melody." "Gold swathed in velvet." His voice, experts of his era enthusiastically declared, combined beauty and power to a degree that no other voice had ever attained before and, in the thirty-odd years since his death, no other voice has ever combined since.

The uniqueness of Caruso's voice is almost impossible to define. Innumerable persons, who, like myself, heard him in his prime, are absolutely convinced that no voice ever had the clarion quality of Caruso's when he sang a dramatic aria in a dramatic opera. At such times his hearers felt that his throat must be made not of flesh and tissue but of solid, vibrant metal. Unique also to multitudes of his enraptured contemporaries was the rich, deep beauty of his tones when he turned from portraying fury and vengeance to conveying the tenderness of love. All such persons need to do, when they put on a Caruso record, is to call on memory and imagination, in order to be shaken again, as they were

in the past. But who can adequately describe a thunderclap — or a nightingale? And Enrico Caruso was both.

Giulio Gatti-Casazza, his manager and friend for many years, said of him: "He was a unique artist, with whom no other compared — and I do not see how we can ever have such another."

AMONG THE NUMEROUS cities in numerous countries visited by Caruso in his years of glory, only one held him more than a few weeks or days at a time — New York.

The American metropolis used to monopolize him for three or more months out of every twelve. In all, he sang at the Metropolitan Opera 607 times, a record unapproached anywhere else — to say nothing of his frequent appearances at concerts in the homes of rich New Yorkers. At the Met he sang Canio in *Pagliacci* — the role that brought him the most tumultuous ovations in his sensational career — a total of *seventy-six times.*

No wonder New York considered Caruso its own special property. No wonder New Yorkers got all puffed up at the realization that the greatest of all tenors could not sing anywhere else until they had had their fill every year of

his matchless voice. As early as his third or fourth New York season, his fame was already taking on that quality of uniqueness achieved by no other singer before or since.

He was recognized wherever he went. That broad smile, that pudgy body, and that peculiar gait and extravagant attire were unmistakable. "I have my name written all over me," he used to say. So dazzling was his local celebrity that, when admiring New Yorkers and out-of-town visitors found out where Caruso liked to take his meals, they used to flock to such places hoping to catch a glimpse of him. Whereupon, with Italian oaths of high temperature on his lips, Caruso would ferret out some other Italian restaurant.

For some time, his favorite eating place was Del Pezzo's. There he used to leave a standing order: "Reserve for me every night until further notice a private dining room and prepare enough Italian food for me and half a dozen guests." He might not show up. His guests might not show up. But Caruso didn't care. He paid the bill just the same.

MANY AND VARIED were the honors lavished on the famous singer in New York,

---

Philadelphia!" Domingo might respond. "You want another young dead tenor?"

"All right, all right," the producers might concede. "You have a fireplace in your condo?"

"Five of them."

"Then we shoot you in front of a mantel with a photo of Lanza on it. Nobody'll know — a mantel is a mantel. Look, you played *Butterfly* and *Tosca* on Channel 13. . . ."

"Well, okay. . . ."

THE KEY TO Mario Lanza's tragedy was his belief that his nose, his neck and his weight were interrelated.

Lanza was born with his mother's nose, a finely chiseled, uptilting nose, but Caruso, Gigli and even Richard Tucker had mushroom noses.

Mario Lanza could change his name from Alfredo Cocozza, which translated means Alfred Eggplant, but there was nothing he could do about his nose.

And his neck was thin, while the golden voices, including Richard Tucker's, had thick necks, like a bull. Mario Lanza believed that an appropriate nose dwelled somewhere inside his body and that it would surface to his face if he bloated that body.

And so he ate and ate, and he grew fat around the midsection, but his nose stayed fine and his neck stayed thin.

Early in his career Mario Lanza sang the role of Pinkerton in *Madame Butterfly* in a minor opera house in New Orleans. He sang with a fine nose and a thin neck, and when he got paid — a small amount because unfortunately Pinkerton is viewed as a minor role — Mario Lanza said to himself, "Fuck this!" and he went to Hollywood.

Joe Pasternak took one look at his girth and black curly hair and said to the studio beautician, "Take the kinks out of his hair, reduce him by eighty pounds, and I'll put him in *That Midnight Kiss.*"

The point is — he wasn't fat enough! But he kept trying. After *That Midnight Kiss* he sent for his mother and she brought to Hollywood her recipe for spaghetti sauce. As long as his mother lived she would make the sauce, and as long as she made the sauce there was the chance that it would stir the nose inside of him. It would rise up through his stomach, into his gullet, and then one morning he would look in the mirror and there would be his operatic nose.

He paraded his mother around Hollywood in her

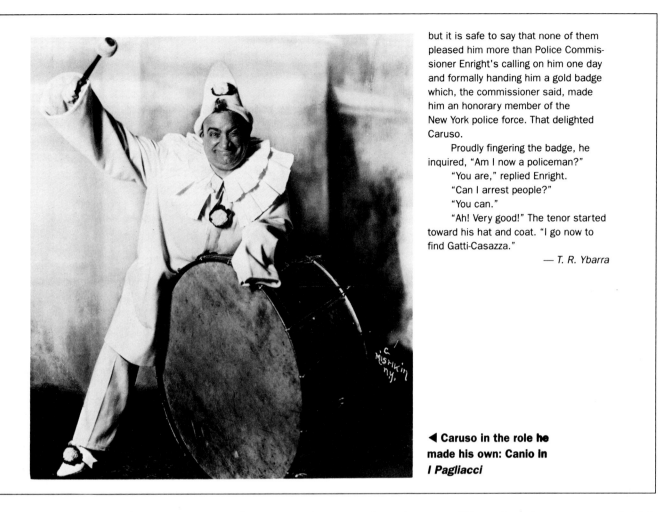

◀ **Caruso in the role he made his own: Canio in** *I Pagliacci*

apron, and he said to everyone, "Look at my mother. Look how great she is." He was so intent on changing his body permanently that he didn't understand the rivalry betwen his mother and his wife Betty. He'd say, "We have a big house in Bel Air, servants, custom-built kitchen — I don't understand what's going on."

Betty made a good plate of spaghetti, but her sauce came nowhere near his mother's in taste. After Maria Cocozza died, Lanza would finally come to relish his wife's sauce. But then Betty gave up eating entirely, let alone cooking. She drank and swallowed every pill in sight, including her husband's phlebitis pills.

Mario Lanza found some peace in the recording studio, away from mirrors, his wife's noncooking, and the viewing public. Except for a few technicians he was alone with his voice, and he recorded immortal songs, as well as a few pretty good arias. But he grew more and more frightened of singing live with his fine nose and thin neck. He reneged on a Las Vegas contract. His voice was dubbed on a supposedly live TV show, creating a scandal. In *The Student Prince*, Edmond Purdom's full nose stood in for his.

Mario Lanza broke down and moved to Italy in

order to be near millions of mushroom noses and thick necks. Nothing happened. He submitted himself to the cure of a twilight sleep lasting twenty days. His true nose would drop out of the twilight. He was fed intravenously — the true nose was lodged somewhere in his veins and would be drawn up to his face along with the fluid.

Lucky Luciano found the answer. He was going to attend a benefit in Naples, and he asked Mario Lanza to sing a few songs. But Mario Lanza went instead to the sanitarium for his twilight sleep. Mr. Luciano in his wisdom hit on the idea that the tortured young man's ultimate peace lay in dwelling permanently with the twilight, leaving only his voice behind.

A few trustworthy Neapolitans were dispatched to the sanitarium on the twentieth day, the day Mario Lanza was supposed to come out of his sleep with his new self. The men waylaid the chauffeur and the nurse and in the last intravenous bottle introduced a few bubbles of air. ❧

101

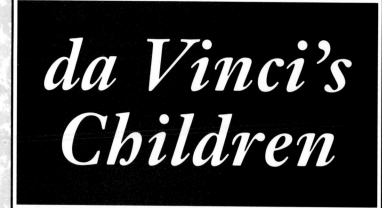

da Vinci's Children

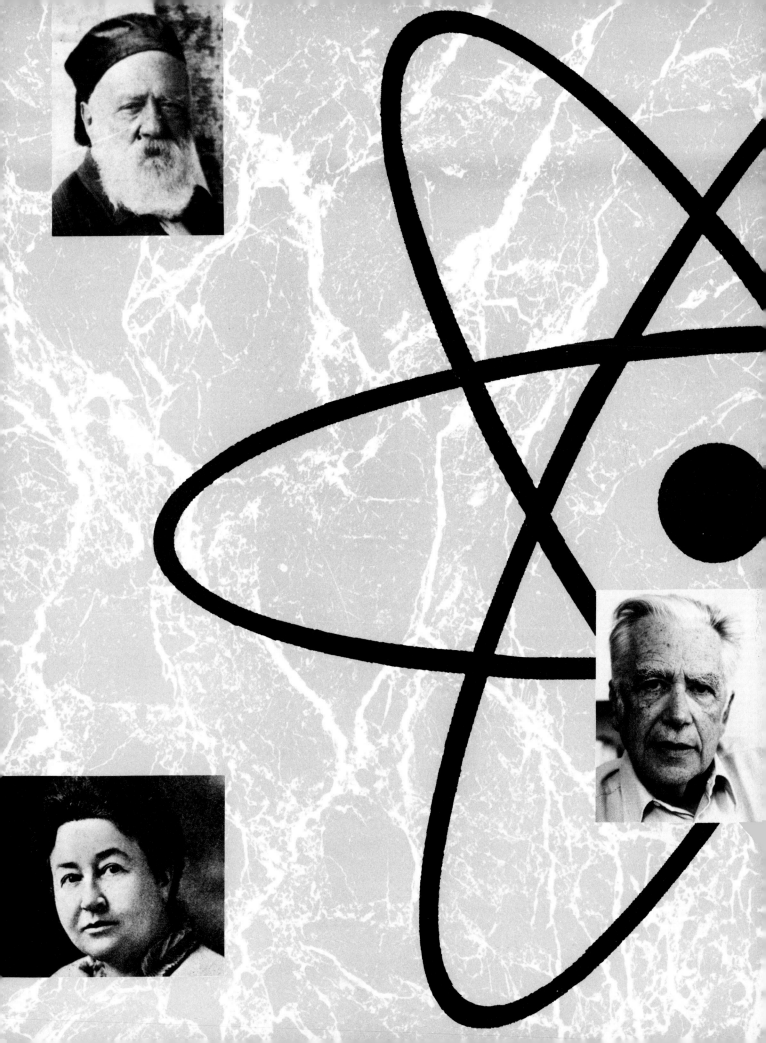

MEUCCI'S TELEPHONE

by Francesco Moncada

Few images have greater reso-nance in American mythology than the amateur inventor working in a backyard lab. Antonio Meucci fits the type in all but one particular: He could not speak or write English well enough to win final recognition. And so he goes down in Ameri-can history as an unknown, a failure — but one who, through his association with Garibaldi and his tenacity in seeking cred-it for his inventions, ranks as one of the more noble failures in the annals of science.

IN 1835 A young Floren-tine was engaged at the Tacone Theatre in Ha-vana as a theater machin-ist and property man. In those days a theater machinist had to know not only mechanics and design, but also physics and chemistry, since he had to pro-vide lights and colors for the stage and the theater. Still, life in Havana was placid and serene, allowing him to acquire a comfortable sum through sav-ings, and time to study.

The young man was the tal-ented Antonio Meucci, and before long various electrical treatises concerning galvanism came into his hands. Through the offices of the governor-general of Cuba, he was engaged to galva-nize, or electroplate, certain objects for the troops, such as swords, buttons, medals, etc.

The study of electricity soon began to engross him. Meditating over Mesmer's trea-tise on animal magnetism, he conceived of applying electricity to the cure of certain dis-eases, and his experiments had considerable results.

One day a man suffering from rheumatic pains in the head came into his laboratory, willing to try the electrical cure. Meucci had the patient sit in the parlor, hold in his hands two conductors that led to batteries, and in his mouth a little metallic tongue soldered to a copper wire conductor, also in communica-tion with the batteries.

In his laboratory, Meucci held the same paraphernalia in his own hands and mouth, so as to regulate the electrical strength that was to be administered. When the patient received the electrical charge, he gave out a cry — and at the same instant a sound was heard at the other end. This interrupted the operation.

The next day, after some thought, Meuc-ci covered the metallic tongue with some cork so as to isolate the electricity, and then he repeated the same experiment, asking his wife Ester to shout and to speak through this electric wire. Again he heard sounds.

The idea of the telephone was born.

This was in 1849. Meucci called his invention the *teletrofono*.

By 1860, after continuous experiments, Meucci succeeded in perfecting his tele-phonic instruments. Through the Florentine's efforts, the human voice was being success-fully transmitted by means of electricity.

Meucci realized the immense possibili-ties of his invention. He sought capitalists, wrote to Italy, but no one answered. Having moved to New York in 1850, where he tried several money-making ventures — including a candle factory operated jointly with the patriot Garibaldi, then in exile in New York — he succeeded only in losing his savings.

After an article in *L'Eco d'Italia* announc-ing his invention failed to attract backing, Meucci's financial difficulties began to increase. His property was taken over by creditors. He himself, while on the ferryboat going to Staten Island, was hurt so seriously when the boiler burst that he was bedridden for six months.

In a moment of desperation, Ester Meucci then sold her husband's telephonic instruments for six dollars to a scrap iron dealer named Fleming. They were never recovered.

THE REST OF the story is almost predictable. Meucci tried to protect his invention. He hired a patent lawyer, a Mr. Stetson, but could only afford a "caveat" — assuring his rights to the invention for one year pending a patent. But $250 was needed for the patent, and it was impossible to raise the sum.

Then in 1872 he thought of turning to

Edward Grant, president of the District Telegraph Company (a branch of Western Union) of New York. Grant took the designs and directions, translated them into English, promising to put at Meucci's disposal the other paraphernalia needed to conduct the experiments.

What Grant did, we do not know. We do know that both Alexander Graham Bell and Elisha Gray — almost simultaneous "discoverers" of the telephone — worked in the Western Union labs at this time, and it is strongly suggested that both used Meucci's papers as the basis for their subsequent work. This may be the reason that Bell Telephone and Western Union agreed to an out-of-court settlement in 1879: Both were dealing with the same stolen goods. In any event, Grant kept putting Meucci off for two years, and finally told him that the papers and designs in his charge had been lost.

Then, in February of 1876, Alexander Graham Bell announced to the world the great invention. Meucci's protests were to no avail; his caveat had run out for lack of money.

In 1883, Meucci made one last attempt to be recognized. He had friends publish in American newspapers an article declaring that he, not Bell, was the inventor of the telephone. The article interested the Globe Telephone Company, and preparations for a legal battle with Bell Telephone were prepared. An account of the life and inventions of Meucci, with his affidavits, his memorandum book, and the designs and the telephone instruments recently reconstructed were provided to the secretary of the state of New York.

In a judgment on January 15, 1886, the secretary declared that there were sufficient proofs to establish Meucci's priority in the invention of the telephone and he sent the case to the courts. Meucci's testimony lasted thirty-eight days and formed a volume of 172 pages. He explained how through his metallic diaphragm the human voice was transmitted by means of the electromagnetic current created, not by vibrations of the air.

Finally, on July 19, 1887, the court handed down a decision that can qualify as a solemn, lugubrious joke. It put its belief in the American Bell Telephone Company's technical expert, Professor Cross, that the Meucci telephone was a "string" telephone

or "lover's telephone" — that is, a mechanical, and not an electrical, telephone, of the kind in use among children.

Though the case was appealed, it was postponed from year to year, and finally died a lingering death in 1896.

Antonio Meucci died unrecognized on October 18, 1889. His funeral expenses were paid for by the Italian government, his name was given to a small street in Brooklyn, and his ashes, held for ten years, were finally interred on the grounds of his home in Rosebank. ✍

▲
Antonio Meucci in his Staten Island home, which is now the Garibaldi-Meucci Museum

105

DA VINCI'S CHILD

WITH A CUM LAUDE diploma in engineering from the Royal Institute of Milan, Giuseppe Mario Bellanca arrived in Brooklyn, New York, in 1912 to seek his fortune in aircraft design and construction, a field rich in dreams and poor in financial return.

The Italian community of Brooklyn rallied round the aspiring aircraft designer and financed Bellanca's first attempts at airplane building in the United States. Had they known of his previous history in the mother country, they might have been less generous. Intrigued by Leonardo da Vinci's sketches and encouraged by the Wrights' success, Bellanca built and promptly crashed his first airplane in 1908. Apparently he was aware of the odds, for he talked a friend into being the test pilot. Since the plane crashed on takeoff, one assumes the friendship was short-lived. The following year, his second attempt never got off the ground: The funds ran out before the engine arrived.

But three years later, Bellanca was at last airborne, studying aerodynamics in the Brooklyn skies in his 30-horsepower Anzani-powered "grasscutter" monoplane. Giddy with success, he opened a flying school and traded flying lessons for driving lessons with one of his students — Fiorello La Guardia.

In 1917, Bellanca refined the wind-blasted aviator image with America's first cabin monoplane, a giant step for aircraft design and no small step for Bellanca's reputation. Pilots, who perhaps preferred the scarf-and-goggles look, were skeptical of this taming-of-the-cockpit design, but it matured into the Bellanca CF and took first place in a dozen air races. The CF begat the Pacemaker and the Skyrocket, and Bellanca came

to be considered the first bona fide aeronautical engineer in the country.

"The Professor" established a reputation for building fast (and safe) long-range load-carrying airplanes. An ideal combination for a transatlantic flight, thought Charles Lindbergh, who arrived in Bellanca's office one afternoon with a check for $15,000. Here Bellanca and his partner Charles Levine made what is probably the worst marketing decision in the history of the aircraft business: They refused to let an unknown pilot fly the Bellanca craft and thus risk his reputation as a designer. Lindbergh was turned away.

Two weeks after Lindbergh's transatlantic flight in a Ryan, Bellanca's *Columbia* came in second, establishing a new distance record while carrying the Atlantic's first passenger: financier and *Columbia* owner Charles Levine.

When racing fever inflamed the aviation community in the 1930s, Bellanca obligingly turned out the low-wing Model 28-90, which cruised, mind you, at 275 mph; and the 28-92, a trimotor Bendix Trophy winner. And to keep a hand in the growing lightplane market, he produced the Cruisair, whose design is echoed in today's Bellanca Viking.

Giuseppe Bellanca died in 1960, but his only son, August Thomas, carries on. August's SkyRocket II, a fiberglass-and-aluminum composite design clocked at 285 knots, broke five speed records and established itself as the world's fastest single-engine lightplane.

— *Patricia Trenner*

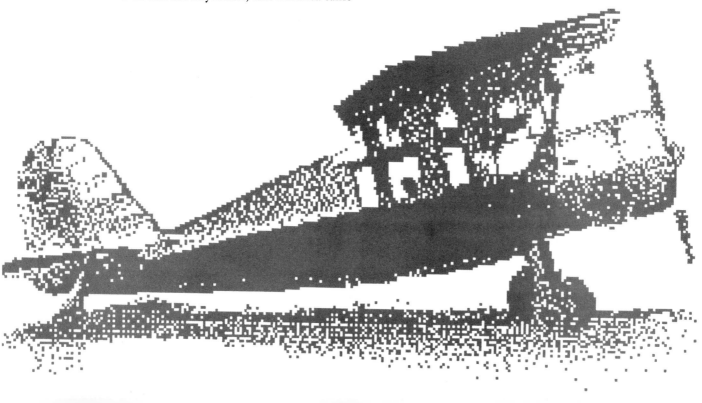

ENRICO FERMI AND THE ATOMIC AGE

by Ernest V. Heyn

IT WAS JUST before dawn in the desert near Alamogordo, New Mexico. For years, teams of scientists and engineers had been working feverishly to build the world's first atomic bomb. Now, on July 16, 1945, it sat on a slender steel tower as the final minutes before detonation ticked away.

Two scientists, Emilio Segrè and Enrico Fermi, were on station nine miles from Ground Zero. Then, just before the explosion that was to change the world, "Fermi got up and dropped small pieces of paper on the ground," wrote Segrè later. "He had prepared a simple experiment to measure the energy liberated by the explosion: The pieces of paper would fall at his feet in the quiet air, but when the front of the shock wave arrived (some seconds after the flash) the pieces of paper were displaced a few centimeters in the direction of the propagation of the shock wave. From the distance of the source and from the displacement of the air due to the shock wave, he could calculate the energy of the explosion immediately."

While readings from the elaborate network of instruments were not available for several days, Fermi had the answers within seconds. And, points out Segrè, Fermi's answer from his simple experiment was very close to the one the complex instruments eventually delivered.

"He had an unusual grasp of physics which he kept at his fingertips always ready to use," said Herbert L. Anderson, a coworker in the development of atomic energy. "When a problem arose, he had the knack to be able to go to the blackboard and simply work it out. The physics just flowed out of the chalk."

It is strangely fitting that the coded language used to report the success of the first nuclear reaction contained a reference to "the Italian navigator," Columbus. Enrico Fermi, too, led humanity into a new world: that of nuclear power.

THE MAN WHO was to launch the atomic age was born in Rome on September 29, 1901. He became fascinated by physics early, and by the time he entered the University of Pisa in 1918 he had little to learn; from his own reading and studying, he was more knowledgeable than most of his professors. Over the next decade, almost single-handedly,

▲

Enrico Fermi gave his name to the element with atomic number 100, "fermium."

he brought a new spirit into Italian physics. In 1926, while teaching at the University of Florence, he published a paper on the mechanics of small particles that became a worldwide sensation and ultimately resulted in one class of elementary particles being named fermions.

By the early 1930s he had published several more sensational papers and become internationally famous. In those days, physicists were just beginning to probe the atom in an attempt to discover the fundamental nature of matter. In a brilliant series of experiments, Fermi used slowed neutrons to bombard atoms, and discovered more than sixty new subatomic particles within a few months in the early days of 1934.

But in 1938 an event of great importance to Fermi's future — and to the world's — took place. Benito Mussolini, dictator of Italy, took a cue from his German allies and published a set of anti-Semitic regulations. Fermi's wife, Laura, was a Jew. At about the same time, Fermi heard that he was to be awarded the 1938 Nobel prize in physics.

He and his wife worked out a plan. Several universities in the United States had previously offered him jobs. So he quietly got in touch with one of them — Columbia University — and arranged for a position. Then he, his wife, and his two children left for Stockholm, where he was to accept the prize. Afterward, they calmly got on a ship and, instead of going back to Italy, sailed for the New World.

The United States physics establishment was in a state of excitement when Fermi arrived on January 9, 1939. Leo Szilard had conceived of the basic idea of a nuclear chain reaction in 1933. If he could find an element that, when split by one neutron, would release two, it would be possible to set up a self-sustaining reaction. But at that time, nobody had discovered such an element.

Just a few weeks before Fermi arrived in New York, two German scientists named Hahn and Strassman had bombarded uranium atoms with Fermi's slow-neutron technique and demonstrated nuclear fission.

Years before, Einstein had predicted that a small part of the mass of the atom would be converted in such a reaction into pure energy, and that the amount of energy would be incredibly large. With World War II getting under way, most physicists saw the development as a weapon — and as a race. Would German physicists be able to develop an atomic bomb before the United States? Einstein's famous letter to President Roosevelt started the United States on the road to developing a bomb.

The essential first step was to demonstrate a self-sustaining chain reaction.

FOR THE NEXT several years, Fermi and other physicists worked out the thousands of necessary details.

When the time came for the great experiment, Fermi, father of the slow-neutron process, was obviously the man to try. In 1942, under the Italian physicist's direction, a strange 500-ton structure of carefully machined graphite bricks began to grow in a squash court under the west stands of Stagg Field at the University of Chicago. Embedded in the graphite pile were pieces of uranium. Three sets of control rods were inserted into the pile to absorb neutrons and prevent a chain reaction. When they were withdrawn, according to calculations, the pile would "go critical" and the reaction would become self-sustaining.

Forty-two of the world's leading atomic physicists were on hand. Fermi gave the orders and inch by inch the rods were withdrawn. Each time the clicking of the radiation counters increased. Fermi constantly made calculations on a slide rule he held, checking predictions against the performance.

At 3:25 p.m., he gave the order to pull once again. "This is going to do it," he told physicist Arthur Compton.

Minute after minute the neutron count increased as Fermi manipulated his slide rule. "His face was motionless," said physicist George Weil. "His eyes darted from one dial to another. His expression was so calm it was hard. But suddenly his whole face broke into a broad smile."

Fermi closed his slide rule. "The reaction is self-sustaining," he announced quietly. "The curve is exponential."

Physicist Eugene Wigner brought out a bottle of Chianti he had kept hidden during the experiment. Fermi uncorked it and sent out for paper cups so everyone could have a sip. Silently, without toasts, they raised their cups and drank. There was almost no conversation.

Arthur Compton went to a telephone, called Dr. James B. Conant of Harvard, and delivered a message by prearranged code: "The Italian navigator has landed in the New World."

"How were the natives?" asked Conant.

"Very friendly," Compton said. ❧

108

EMILIO SEGRÈ AND THE NUCLEAR GHOST

I N HIS HILLSIDE home, Emilio Segrè answers the question everyone wants to know: What does it feel like to win the Nobel prize? "You push, push, push," the physicist, now eighty, says in his lilting Italian accent. He jumps forward in his chair. "All of a sudden — whoosh — you break through. There's a breach and you're through the wall."

His description seems somehow too simple for a man who helped develop the atomic bomb, and later codiscovered the nuclear ghost — the antiproton — whose momentary existence had eluded scientists for years.

For creating the antiproton, and making it "stand still" long enough to identify it, Segrè shared the 1959 Nobel prize with Owen Chamberlain.

Son of an industrialist in Tivoli, Italy, Segrè studied with Enrico Fermi in Rome during the conception and infancy of nuclear physics. They were at the frontier of science, and they knew it. But the secrets that would open a new world, both good and horrible, lay then behind what seemed an impenetrable wall. Segrè recalls feeling its resistance, then its give.

It was 1934. They were bombarding different substances with neutrons to smash atoms, but always getting different reactions.

One day at about noon they noticed that if they filtered neutrons through simple paraffin (wax), the neutrons worked more effectively. They went home for lunch and siesta. When they returned at 3 p.m. Fermi had a suggestion: Neutrons were slowed down in paraffin because they collided with hydrogen atoms abundant in the wax.

These slower neutrons, it turned out, were more likely to slam into heavy atoms such as uranium and cause them to split. This was a key discovery in opening the nuclear world.

"The scales fell from our eyes," Segrè wrote a few years ago of that day.

Stories of scientists discovering something great by accident are largely myth, Segrè says. "You know when you've discovered something important. You feel it."

SEGRÈ SAW MUSSOLINI'S Black Shirts march into Rome in 1922. While in the United States on a visit in 1938, he learned that he and all other Jewish professors had been fired from universities.

Segrè and his family never returned to Italy to live. Foreign scientists here were barred from working on war research, such as radar, so, Segrè recalls, they continued to pursue atomic energy. They knew their work could result in a bomb powerful beyond imagination. In 1942 the government agreed, and began the Manhattan Project.

"At the time our goal was to have one or two bombs to end the war. Nobody thought of ten thousand." He pauses, then tries to explain. "If you have a world war, you want to stop it. It's like a house fire. You want to put it out. Then, later, you worry about if you have enough water left over for irrigation."

— *Jayne Garrison*

▲
Emilio Segrè, collaborator with Enrico Fermi, won a Nobel prize in 1959 for discovering the antiproton.

NIGHT ON OAKDALE LANE

by Lawrence DiStasi

ALWAYS THERE WAS a peculiar enthusiasm to his coming home. It was not that he had brought toys or sweets for us, that Americanism to him not fit activity for a man. Rather it was that he always seemed to enter charged with a new passion of his own which he succeeded in making ours: a new provolone that he had bought entire, the whole forty pounds; which, whether we liked it or not, whether the white worms oozing from it revolted us or not (tiny milkworms that the more daring of us would gather stuck to predatory fingers, and eat), still filled us with the giddiness of ribbons and icing. Or the report of a house that he had seen, with a wine cellar — he always looked for that first, nevermind the plumbing or the yard, cool enough it had to be to store the wine we never made, to hang the fifty-pound prosciuttos we sometimes forgot — c'mon we'll take a look tonight, and we were gone. Or yet another Doberman pinscher someone had offered so cheap he couldn't refrain from taking even though the thing had been trained neurotic in the army, beautiful isn't she? And we would dance our agreement even though we knew she would soon be gone, they all were, the Dobermans and Great Danes and rabbits and baby chicks and everything else he carted through the door including a tribe of live frogs popping out of every pocket of his golf bag. Or sometimes he would have nothing in hand but simply the announcement to come on, we're going to Philly; to visit the relatives; a five-hour drive but no matter, bundle the kids in pajamas no need for a call, we're going. And we did.

Even so, that night on Oakdale Lane was special. He had nothing in hand. Nor were we going anyplace or contemplating any moves, having just done that. Still he was charged. His mustache when he kissed me bristled with static. His hat sailed, his coat flew, he plucked my mother off her feet and whirled an elaborate tango. She protested, laughed a little nervous (since Elena's birth she outweighed him by twenty-five pounds), "You're *pazzo.*" He only laughed more as he sent Carmela for the wine, some cheese, let Elena climb onto his lap.

"We've got it now. Sonofabitch, we've got it now," he laughs, kissing Elena in her hair. "This time next year we'll be in Italy. Guaranteed!" Then leaning to me with a gentle tap to the cheek, "Right, pal?"

I smile. Hell yes it's alright.

"What?" my mother dries her hands, "what is it?"

Again he laughs. "We've got more of this? And some prosciutt'?"

"What? For what? Will you tell me. . . ?"

"They'll be over about 8:30. Have we got enough?"

"Yes, damn it . . . tons . . . but what?"

He draws it out, nibbling slow on his cheese, insisting that I take a bite of the peach slice he's been marinating in his wine. Then suddenly confidential. "You kids now, I want nothing about this to get outside, eh? What goes on at this table is this family only. Period."

By now, though we know that he will be the one to spill it if anyone does, we are on fire to learn what it is. He remains cryptic. Takes Elena's four-year-old hair, lifts it. It still holds a slight wave from the test curl he gave her two weeks ago.

"Look at that," he smiles.

We all look.

"Two weeks," he goes on, "without even a neutralizer." We nod attentive, waiting for the revelation. "You realize? Right now, this one is the best? The best! None of them can touch it, *capisc'*? And you know why?" he is waving his hand toward his jacket, directing Carmela to bring it; searches inside for a folded-up letter, "This is why, sonofabitch! Here it is."

My mother and Carmela are behind him now, leaning to read over his shoulder. "Doc Venerino's report and you know what it says?" Held at arm's length so, farsighted, he can read it, the report takes on the aura of a proclamation. "Perfect it says. Not just clean, the stuff is perfect. The lab injected it, in*j*ected it, mind you, into rabbits, and nothing happened. Nothing! Not even a pimple. The first nontoxic solution ever which they couldn't believe it because they know, *capisc'*, that they're burning the scalps off them with all the rest, Toni, Hudnot, all of them, but this one is perfect." We are all bouncing up and down, fancying ourselves on ocean liners bound for Italian sun; he is hugging Elena, holding pieces of her hair in

strands for my mother to see, to feel, to yield finally to the thrill of it; of finding at last the solution he's been pursuing for years in various lab cellars piling high with curlers and beakers and drums full of pungent chemicals; the one that destructures hair without destroying it, takes its 'herited resistance to wave and makes of it a willing, a limp accomplice to his design; and all as he has wanted it, demanded it — without

break, without burn, benignly.

She sits holding the letter. Her lip line straightening, thoughful. He notices.

"Not good enough, eh?"

"No. It's terrific, but . . ."

"The neutralizer, hah? You're worried about the damn neutralizer."

She is. That, she knows, is the problem; to get a

neutralizer to hold the curl to its new shape. Which even Elena's won't do yet, which when washed will sag into straightness like the rest.

"Well we got that too."

Her eyes light up, incredulous. "But . . . how? When?"

"Remember I told you the other night I couldn't sleep?"

She doesn't.

"*Fa'n cul'*, I told you didn't I? About unhairing, I was reading about it?"

She shakes her head.

Mannaggia, he says, what a woman not to remember things of such importance. Anyway, it was there, the chemical he needed, and tonight they would get it, guaranteed. And gulping his wine, he lays it all out, his latest hunch. My mother, though, remains subdued. She has seen his hunches before, rushing toward the curl ever vanishing, the one that will stay through neutralizer and washing and combing, the one natural and nontoxic and perfect as his shoe size, benign as his mother's milk, that will rocket us to the top of the pile triumphant. The Cold-Wave Champions of the World. Which is yet only half realized. Which she will believe only when it is not just dreamed, but applied to a head. He is not daunted.

"This time," he talks at us now, "it's it. *Sfaccim'*, they gotta get up pretty early in the morning, eh kid? They all want to know, hey they say, how in hell do you figure this stuff out? Because I never went to school like them, they think I should be washing heads all my life. I don't tell them anything. I read. I use this," he digs his finger into his temple, hard, "and the whole damn bunch of them with all their degrees they still can't get a wave that isn't poison. But tonight, we get it, sonofabitch, and they can all *va a Napoli*!"

I imagine them lined up again, the ladies ejected outside his beauty shop; as he, eyes ablaze, grins hammering his fist to the table rattling wine jug, glass, the plates Carmela has just set, making him laugh even harder in his strength. For he is strong tonight. And he sweeps us along, my mother too though scolding that he's crazy has been won, seized again by the breezy mania of him that has got us all; who understand little about the chemical or economic resistances at issue except that he is the one battling sons of bitches out there, nefarious sonofabitches all against him we know not why or even who but only that we hate them as he does and long to have them deposed and muzzled beneath his hand bearing us to Italy for those oranges big as grapefruits that he always promised would be waiting as soon as the big wave broke and he got the curl.

And tonight, he declares, it is imminent.

And we believe . . . 🍃

One wonders if the exposure of children to the "natural science" of fermentation predisposes some of them to scientific pursuits later. However it may be, Mariana Bertola pioneered in medicine and social welfare after her father pioneered in grape growing and wine making in his district near Martinez, California. Pietro Rossi, also a pioneer, discovered a chemical approach to fermentation that changed the face of the California wine-making industry.

DR. CRUSADE

by Anna Sommer

EVERY COMMUNITY SINCE the days of Noah has had its measure of "strong" personalities, people who never explain, never retract, but get it done, then howl. They attract strong friends and stronger enemies, this Gibraltar clan. You can usually find them where the fight is at white heat.

Consider, for example, the extraordinary career of "Dr. Crusade," Mariana Bertola.

As one of the most active members of the Citizens' Vigilance Committee, during the reign of the "Howard Street gang" in San Francisco, Bertola received innumerable Black Hand letters threatening death if she failed to resign. As an avowed supporter of the progressive side of political reform during Hiram Johnson's campaign, back in 1910, she faced little short of social ostracism.

Both she brushed aside with something akin to indifference.

It is doubtful if Mariana Bertola remembers all the boards in which she has held office during her career. A list of them would take up the better part of a column in *Who's Who of California*. One of these boards — the Bertola Assembly of California Women — even bears her name.

In person, Mariana Bertola gives the lie to the popular theory that all Italians are excitable and volatile. No Englishman could be more self-contained, no Swede more stubborn. Yet she is of pure Italian extraction, her father having been one of the pioneer grape growers of Contra Costa County, and before that one of the pioneer miners in the state.

She speaks fluent Italian in addition to four or five other languages. Della Robbia plaques, majolica ware, volumes of Dante and a bust of Tasso in her sunny twelfth-story Mason Street apartment reveal traces of her early life in Martinez.

For before graduating from Cooper Medical College in 1899, she was principal of the Martinez

◀ Dr. Mariana Bertola was by turns teacher, obstetrician, political activist, social reformer, and clubwoman.

school which she had once attended. But always, as long as she could remember, she had wanted to be a doctor.

It is difficult to bring Dr. Bertola to speak of herself. "I loathe Pollyanna eulogies," she says, with one of her rare smiles. "Let my work speak for me."

Three pieces of social welfare work among the scores she has effected, she is inclined to regard with tolerant satisfaction. The first is the improvement and expansion of county hospitals under the California Federation of Women's Clubs. With this, the "California Plan" she inaugurated, every county hospital was equipped with both a children's ward and a maternity ward. People of moderate means were the chief benefiters of this.

"The very poor and the very rich are always taken care of," explains Dr. Bertola, who is ex-president and director of the federation. "It is the man of small income who usually bears the brunt of things."

Her second leading piece of work is the home on Baker Street for self-supporting working girls and old ladies of the Native Daughters of the Golden West.

Dr. Bertola has been chairman of that organization for thirty years.

As the third piece, she cites her presidency of the Travelers' Aid Society. "The greatest work in the world, after all, is teaching others to think for themselves," she declares.

San Franciscans, however, know Mariana Bertola best for her Americanization work among the Italians of North Beach to whom, in her capacity as physician, she has been mother confessor and a friend in need. She is still remembered for her tireless medical care to those injured in the 1906 earthquake. In November of 1909, she founded the Vittoria Colonna Club for Italian women. The club quickly established a "Settlement House" in a tenement apartment donated by one of its members where classes helped immigrant children and parents adjust to life in America.

As to routine, Dr. Bertola has delivered more than three thousand babies in her career as obstetrician. About this she says: "Child welfare has been my big life work." Like all her self-directed comments, it is something of an understatement. ◆

113

THE CHEMISTRY OF WINE

PIETRO ROSSI DID not start out in life as a wine-maker. He was a graduate in chemistry and pharmacy from the University of Turin. When he arrived in San Francisco in 1875, he went into partnership in a pharmacy in North Beach.

Had he stayed a pharmacist, Rossi would have done quite well; his business was thriving, his wife was rather well-placed socially, and the horses in the city were no doubt well-behaved. True, his father-in-law, Justinian Caire, had died after he had been thrown by a horse, but that was on Santa Cruz Island. Life in the city could be counted on to be much safer.

But Rossi met Andrea Sbarbaro, whose first wine-maker at the fledgling Italian Swiss Colony had produced vinegar. So the pharmacist, originally an investor, became Italian Swiss Colony's chief wine-maker and president in 1888. He must have known what he was doing, for, from that time on, the Colony's wines began to win prizes both in America and abroad.

At first he was a "weekend wine-maker," working in his pharmacy during the week and traveling by train to Asti on weekends to supervise. Soon he had to devote himself full-time to the winery.

His devotion paid off. Asti wines won gold medals at Genoa in 1892, at Bordeaux in 1895, at Paris in 1900, and at Milan in 1906. This was heady stuff for American wines in those days. Europeans, particularly the French, had nothing but contempt for American attempts to produce anything but vin ordinaire of the most ordinary type. As a Paris journal noted: "The fact is that there are still in this world many, many things that they [the Americans] can never achieve. For example, they have not been able to manufacture champagne or even produce a sparkling wine that suggests the champagne of France."

The occasion for this outburst was the discovery that Pietro Rossi had snared for his winery one Charles Jadeau, a noted champagne-maker. The French were outraged, but confident that no amount of American gold could buy the one thing necessary

Pietro Rossi

for champagne: the soil of France.

As it turned out, Jadeau helped Italian Swiss produce a prizewinning champagne. But it was another product of Rossi's European trip of 1909 that proved of truly lasting value.

He had gone to Europe with his twin sons to research French methods for making table wines in Algeria's hot climate — a climate that resembled California's hot valleys where Italian Swiss had many of its vineyards. The first thing Rossi learned was the use of attemperators to control fermentation temperatures. As his son later attested, "My father was one of the first to establish a refrigerated system at Asti."

As a chemist Rossi was intensely interested in another wine-making experiment which his sons had learned about, theoretically at least, in the enology department at the University of California at Davis. The French at this time were talking about the "pure yeast culture" and "sulfur dioxide" methods of making wine. This was a method to innoculate, via sulfur dioxide, the unwanted wild yeasts that occur naturally on grapes, thus allowing the "good" wine yeasts time to take hold for proper fermentation.

Rossi on that 1909 trip made connections to buy sulfur dioxide in its available forms: from Germany as potassium meta-bisulphite; from France as liquid sulfur dioxide in drums. When he returned to California at the start of the vintage season, he began the chemical practice that would revolutionize commercial wine making in California.

Rossi's experiment with champagne bore fruit as well. Sadly, he was not to see it. Charles Jadeau's "Golden State Extra Dry," produced in a lot of 150,000 bottles, was awarded the Grand Prix — the highest award possible — at the international exposition in Turin. This was in October of 1911.

Only days before, Pietro Rossi had been taking a Sunday morning ride in a carriage at Asti. The horse bolted as Rossi was trying to step from the carriage; falling heavily, Rossi's head was struck by the wheel.

He was dead before the triumphant news from Turin could reach California.

— *Michael Bellini*

A GENETIC JACKPOT

by Joan Rachel Goldberg

"I AM NOT A very curious person," says Salvador E. Luria.

It's a curious statement from a Nobel laureate who has turned such serendipitous events as a friend's slot-machine winnings and a shattered test tube into landmark scientific discoveries.

So important is serendipity to the seventy-two-year-old molecular biologist that he vehemently eschews the attention usually linked with scientific achievement.

"Creativity is a certain delusion," he insists as we converse in the roomy office he occupies as director of Massachusetts Institute of Technology's Cancer Research Center. "It's really a matter of chance and luck and a certain energy in facing difficulties."

Despite his modest statements, Luria was awarded the Nobel prize in 1969 for his work in the 1940s showing that the resistance of clusters of bacteria to bacteriophages — viruses that attack them — is due to spontaneous mutation. This discovery helped to lay the foundations of today's genetic engineering techniques, and also improved the use of chemotherapy to treat cancer.

Yet Luria remains unfazed by the accolades. Instead, he comments that he has "always found scientific work very hard and not particularly pleasant."

LURIA HAD TO overcome tremendous obstacles to secure his place in science. Born in Turin, Italy, he rebelled against his parents' wishes that he become a physician. Though he earned a medical degree from the University of Turin, he never practiced. Instead, he was captivated by research and associated the "academic life with the good life," as he says in his recent autobiography: *A Slot Machine, A Broken Test Tube.*

Following romantic notions of a career in physics, Luria studied for a year in Rome under Enrico Fermi. It soon became apparent that physics was not his métier, but Luria was not discouraged. He took up biophysics as a bridge between his medical training and his interest in physics.

Inspired by the writings of the physicist Max Delbrück, with whom he eventually shared the Nobel prize, Luria set out to study bacteriophages. However, as a Jew, he was forced to flee Fascist Italy in 1938. Then, just before the Nazi invasion, he left Paris for America.

Soon after his arrival, Luria joined the faculty at Indiana University. Molecular biology — the study of the chemical basis of inheritance — was still in its infancy. Little was known about how genes govern the activities of cells, DNA was not yet discovered, and bacteria were thought to have no genes at all.

While at Indiana, Luria put forth a daring theory. He said that bacterial resistance to attack by phages (or viruses) is due to genetic mutation, not to activity on the part of the virus itself. In proving this, he would also show that bacteria did, in fact, possess genes.

But how to prove it?

A chance observation at a faculty dance gave him an idea. When a friend hit the jackpot on a slot machine, Luria began to speculate about a possible connection between the statistical distribution of jackpots (how often a winning number came up) and the pattern of gene mutations in a series of cultures.

If, on the one hand, resistant bacteria in the cultures were distributed in *clusters*, then

Some scientists keep themselves tuned exclusively to the world of their specialties. Others are like Salvador Luria. He used to hold evenings for his graduate students at which great books of literature were read and discussed. He helped organize fellow scientists to oppose the Vietnam War — a move that got him blacklisted by the Department of Health, Education and Welfare when he was recommended for an advisory position. Typically, the move proved more embarrassing to HEW than to Nobelist Luria.

115

the resistance could be attributed to mutation — mutant bacteria would have duplicated themselves before their exposure to the invading virus.

If, instead, they were evenly distributed throughout the culture, then the resistance would have to be due to the action of the virus.

Luria mixed several cultures of identical bacteria with a phage, and then waited to see if his hypothesis would be supported. Two days later, his moment of triumph arrived. Clusters of resistant bacteria meant mutation.

This conclusion was contrary to the then-current teachings of bacteriology, which, according to Luria, was the "last stronghold of Lamarckism." It began to focus attention on the genetics of bacteria, and led ultimately to the explosion of DNA research — led, not incidentally, by Luria's famous student, James Watson.

The experiment itself became known as

the fluctuation test. Since it can be used to forecast how quickly cancer cells mutate and become drug-resistant, the test has proved invaluable in prescribing effective chemotherapy.

SERENDIPITY AGAIN THREADED its way into Luria's research in 1952 at the University of Illinois. He had been observing another type of mutant bacteria which, when invaded and killed by a phage, did not serve as hosts for the virus's replication — the usual course of events.

When a test tube of these bacteria broke, Luria borrowed another tube filled with a different type of bacteria. In the new culture, the phage unexpectedly went wild.

This led Luria to conclude that the mutant bacteria had somehow modified the phage, thus limiting it to reproducing itself in another host. The cause of this phenomenon — enzymes snipping the virus's DNA and changing it — is now known. And

THE BRAIN DOCTOR

BRAIN RESEARCH SOUNDS like the most technical of all disciplines, requiring, we imagine, sophisticated laboratories filled with twenty-first century equipment flashing and crackling with eerie lights.

For Dr. Michael Gazzaniga, this seems not to be the case. He does his major work in a twenty-six-foot motor home. It is a movable laboratory for testing the bizarre responses of split-brain patients — people who, usually to control epileptic seizures, have had the two halves of their brains surgically separated.

Testing such people long ago revealed that the two halves of the human brain work separately. The right brain in general controls nonverbal functions such as pattern discrimination; the left brain controls language. By flashing messages to one or the other half separately, Dr. Gazzaniga and his colleagues have for years been recording strange results like the following:

A picture of a chicken claw is shown to the left, or verbal, hemisphere of the brain. Simultaneously, a snow scene is shown to the nonverbal right brain. In front of the patient is a series of cards that serve as possible answers to the question of what goes with what: for the left half a chicken, for the right half a shovel.

The patient correctly points to the chicken with his right hand and the shovel with his left.

But now comes the surprise. When asked why he does so, the patient immediately says: "Oh that's easy. The chicken claw goes with the chicken, and you need a shovel to clean out the chicken shed."

Here, according to Dr. Gazzaniga, is the critical situation: The left brain has to explain an overt behavior initiated by a part of the brain it has no awareness of.

In this case its left hand is pointing to a shovel when the only picture the left brain recalls seeing is a chicken claw. Yet the patient's very own body is pointing to a shovel. Why?

According to Gazzaniga, the left brain's cognitive system needs a theory, and instantly supplies one that makes sense, given the information it has. It explains the shovel in terms of the chicken claw.

DR. GAZZANIGA, TRAVELING in his motor home to split-brain patients all over New England, has done countless similar experiments, each more refined than the last. In some cases, he has found that the normally language-blind right brain can even understand some few nouns. But in every case the basic situation is the same: the right brain receives a stimulus, for example a direction to "walk," that is completely hidden from the left brain. The left brain then sees itself "walking" and talks itself into a logical explanation.

Gazzaniga believes this illuminates some of the mysteries about all human behavior. Much of the time we humans find ourselves doing things that seem to defy our own intentions or beliefs. We violate our own moral codes; we wake up some mornings feeling unaccountably blue. Our conscious selves — our language-generating selves mainly — can make no sense of this at first.

Then the left brain — Gazzaniga calls it "the interpeter" — makes hypotheses to rationalize its own

actions. Sometimes these hypotheses, if we could see them for what they are, would seem as bizarre as the explanation of one of Gazzaniga's patients.

"Last year we saw a patient, M.S., who had a lesion in her right parietal zone. Lesions in this location can produce a wide variety of disturbances, among them M.S.'s translocation of place. Although a woman of great charm and intelligence, she believed herself to be in Freeport, Maine, when she was actually in a New York hospital for surgery. She sat in hospital garb in her wheelchair with intravenous tubes in place and carried on an informed conversation; but when asked where she was she would respond, 'I'm in Freeport, Maine. Where are you?'

"When I pointed to the elevators and asked, 'What are those things over there?' she responded, 'Those are elevators. Do you know what it cost me to have those put in my house?'"

— *August Gaudino*

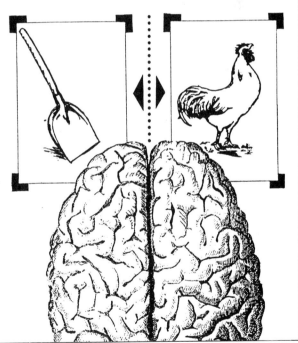

it is the primary tool of recombinant DNA work.

In spite of these revolutionary findings, Luria insists that he has limitations as a scientist: "I don't have the self-image of a great problem solver. I prefer to have data on a small domain." And unlike physicists, who "have a certain confidence that they can solve anything," Luria contends that he is far more timid.

While Luria still finds time to teach at MIT, his life as a researcher is largely over. But he still retains a clear perspective on what has always made science compelling for him.

"You want the success of your own efforts against a challenge," he says. "One invests emotionally — it's a reward." ❧

Saints

A Saint for the New World

by Lilian Gerard

I N A TINY chapel on Manhattan's highest hill, overlooking the Hudson, the enshrined remains of Mother Francesca Cabrini lie in perpetual adoration. Here thousands of pilgrims arrive from all around the world to pay homage to a woman canonized by the Roman Catholic Church as the first American saint.

The sanctity of Mother Cabrini became evident to members of her faith only after her death less than thirty years ago, when numerous miracles attributed to her divine intercession were reported from all parts of the world. Largely on the strength of these reports, a movement for her canonization was started, although according to church decree, sainthood proceedings may not be instituted until fifty years after a candidate's passing.

For Mother Cabrini the Vatican waived this requirement "in view of the need for strong spiritual currents" in the world today. In 1937 she was declared venerable, the following year beatified and accredited by the church with two miracles, winnowed out of thousands of cases reported by beneficiaries of her intercession.

Now Francesca will join her namesakes, Francis Xavier, Francis de Sales, and Francis of Assisi. Thousands of candles will burn in Rome as her canonization is celebrated in St. Peter's with a high pontifical mass attended by cardinals and prelates, statesmen and government officials, all to pay tribute to a naturalized American citizen, who told her bishop in Italy when he first advised her to go to America, "New York is too small a place for me."

"Surely," he answered, "the whole of the United States is not too small."

To which this indomitable woman, the last to consider herself a saint, replied: "The world is too small."

IT WAS THE last day of March, 1889, when she arrived in New York's Lower East Side with a band of five sisters. She spent her first night in America in a mouse-infested, vermin-ridden back room on the brink of Chinatown. Expecting to find a convent ready to house her small order, Cabrini called the following day on New York's Archbishop Michael Corrigan.

Although the country from which they came was the home of the Catholic religion, the country to which they came considered them, if not pagan, as close as Christians can come to that designation. So it must have given Italian Americans no little satisfaction to realize that a saint had emerged in their midst. She was Mother Cabrini, and her mission was to that Orient of the West, the slums of the New World. Appropriately, she combined Old World sanctity with a shrewdness and business acumen that could have been honed on Wall Street.

"My advice to you and your sisters," the archbishop stated, "is to take the next boat back to Italy."

Instead, in a lower-Manhattan basement, Sister Cabrini opened an embroidery school to teach adolescent girls a trade. In a couple of empty stores, hot in summer and heatless in winter, she established a day nursery to keep four hundred slum children off the street. With $250, enough to pay one month's rent and buy ten beds, she launched a hospital in two adjacent buildings on Twelfth Street.

The future Mother Cabrini named the hospital Columbus after the "first Italian immigrant" to inspire the support of his proud countrymen and of loyal Americans as well, and the nuns became known as Sisters of Columbus. It was her first major undertaking; today there are seven Columbus Hospitals, three in Chicago alone.

Her method soon established itself. Once she had gained the confidence of a community, Mother Cabrini left her sisters behind and moved on to another locality. The sudden appearance of this black-clad, blue-eyed figure often dismayed bankers and bishops, politicians and philanthropists. She seemed at first a hopeless enthusiast, but proved to be a most practical woman. Her real estate investments alone now run into the millions, largely because she had an uncanny instinct for knowing in what direction a city would eventually spread.

Essentially she was a bargain hunter, and instead of relying on agents or resorting to maps, she personally got acquainted with every section of a new community. With her lunch under her arm, she would sometimes board a trolley car at six o'clock in the morning and ride all day from one end of the line to the other. More often, though, she prowled through strange cities on foot, exploring outlying regions to find some dilapidated home, abandoned mansion or run-down hotel that she could transform as she saw fit.

Those who tried to take advantage of the Little Mother were seldom successful. While dickering for the purchase of the North Shore Hotel in Chicago, she suspected the operators of unfair dealings. And, the story goes, at five o'clock one morning the policeman on the beat saw a strange sight.

Two nuns were outside the empty hotel, every now and then bending double, holding some string to the ground, then making a chalk mark on the sidewalk. This performance was repeated again and again, and the policeman signaled for the sergeant around the corner.

The two finally concluded that the sisters were merely measuring the property, as indeed they were. For Mother Cabrini feared that the hotel owners were reducing the value of the property by secretly cutting off a corner strip, twenty-five feet wide. When the documents of sale were ready, she produced her measurements, demanded the whole length of the block, and got it.

At the age of sixty, Mother Cabrini was still active, still measuring the domain of her concern, whitewashing the outer walls of the Dobbs Ferry Orphanage, buying a farm outside Chicago to supply her hospitals with company-owned farm products, even selecting the cows herself.

But her health was rapidly failing and she gave thought to retiring. Unknown to her, however, the sisters of her order conducted a plebiscite and agreed unanimously not to accept a successor as long as Mother Cabrini was alive. In her last years her body was often racked by fever and pain from malaria contracted during a stay in Brazil. The illness recurred frequently and with increasing intensity.

In 1917, she suffered a malarial attack while wrapping presents for five hundred children in the Chicago hospital she had founded.

She died a few days before Christmas, the New World's first Catholic saint. ❧

THE PADRE OF BASKETBALL

HOW DO WE recognize the folk hero? I don't know the formal criteria, but certainly a good name helps. Billy the Kid, Pretty Boy Floyd — these are memorable monikers that fit into a ballad or atop a comic strip. In America, it also helps to be boyish, good with a gun, and a loner with a yen for wide open spaces.

Clearly, your average cleric doesn't fill such a bill.

And yet, Father Oreste Trinchieri, second pastor of Sts. Peter and Paul Church in San Francisco, Provincial of the Salesian Order in the West, was surely a folk hero.

To begin with, he had the names. Sportswriters called him "The Padre of Basketball." Others titled him "The Don Bosco of North Beach" and his parish a "neighborhood Boys Town." To his boys, he was always "Father Trink."

And he was young — at least in 1914 when he arrived in a North Beach riddled with juvenile gangs. Where others wrung their hands over the problem — 60% of San Francisco's juvenile crime took place in North Beach — Father Trinchieri saw it as an opportunity. He immediately began prowling the streets, recruiting for altar boys first, then for the new Boy Scout troop he founded, and finally for his beloved basketball teams. Quiet and unassuming, he yet had a pied-piper quality that made him irresistible. His boys followed him on overnight camping trips and into ambitious building projects. He followed them down secret alleys, rescuing them from the lures of the street and scrapes with the law. "How did you know we were in trouble?" they would ask. "My detectives told me," he'd answer.

Before long, there was hardly a kid in North Beach who didn't consider Trink's Salesian Boys Club a second home. The basketball teams that poured forth began winning everything in sight — including a run at a National Basketball championship. Joe DiMaggio was a graduate of the Club. So were Frank Crosetti, Hank Luisetti, Fred Scolari, and others nearly as great. The neighborhood became almost legendary, its juvenile delinquency virtually absent.

Oddly, all this success led to the trouble that would cap the legend. Beginning in 1926, the new church and adjoining Boys Club were bombed five times. Some said the attackers were anarchists, some that they were criminals disgruntled with Father Trink for keeping all their recruits off the streets. No one ever found out, for the two bombers who died in the last attempt in 1927 never talked.

But the pivotal episode had been written. He who had done nothing but good had been repaid with secret violence. And the violence had backfired. The myth of the hero was taking shape.

▲
Father "Trink" with some of his boys in 1934

THE LAST, CRUCIAL element in the making of a folk hero comes after he dies. His deeds live on — "Once you knew him," wrote one of his boys, "something, something indefinable kept him forever in your memory" — growing in stature until they are distilled in some popular form.

When I went to parochial school, that form was comic books which illustrated the lives of key saints — Ignatius Loyola, the Little Flower — as impossibly moral people whom no one on our block ever hoped to meet.

This is the form that apotheosizes Father Trink. A comic booklet empanels the major events of his life: He arrives in North Beach, begs the police to release neighborhood toughs into his care, and outfits them in basketball whites. The bombings are illustrated in detail.

The last panel shows him seriously ill, arguing with a nurse to keep his bed near the window outside which his boys play a noisy game of basketball. As if only there can he get the healing energy he needs.

His death, a heart attack at a 1936 dinner for Mayor Angelo Rossi, is mentioned briefly as the occasion to note that Father Trink's spirit lives on. For the folk hero, death is but another step to new life.

And so it is, even today on the streets of North Beach, with the Padre of Basketball.

— *August Gaudino*

BILLY THE KID

by Sister Blandina Segale

Born Rosa Maria Segale, Sister Blandina immigrated with her parents to Cincinnati and joined the Sisters of Charity at age sixteen. Sent to Trinidad in the Colorado Territory, she spent twenty-one years on the frontier, building and working in schools and hospitals with the local Indians. Her observations — including those about her encounters with Billy the Kid — were published in 1932. She spent the last years of her life in Cincinnati, working among Italian immigrants.

YESTERDAY ONE OF the Vigilant Committee came to where I was — I was acting as umpire for a ball game at the time — and said: "Sister, please come to the front yard. I want you to see one of Billy's gang, the one who caused such fright in Cimarron week before last."

When we reached the front yard, the object of our curiosity was still many rods from us. We stood there, everyone trying to look indifferent, while Billy's accomplice headed toward us.

He was mounted on a spirited stallion of unusually large proportions, and was dressed as the *toreadores* dress in old Mexico. He had a cowboy's sombrero, fantastically trimmed, red velvet knee breeches, green velvet short coat, long sharp spurs, gold and green saddle cover. His intention was to impress you with the idea "I belong to the gang." The impression he made on me was one of intense loathing. He also left me frightened.

The figure passed from our sight. I tried to forget it, but it was not to be. William Adamson came to me excitedly some days later to say — "We have work on hand."

"What kind of work?" I asked.

"You remember the man who frightened the people in Cimarron, and who passed our schoolhouse some weeks ago? Well he and Happy Jack, his partner, got into a quarrel, and each got the drop on the other. He received a bullet in his thigh, and has been brought into Trinidad, thrown into an unused adobe hut, and left there to die. He has a very poor chance of living."

At the noon hour we carried food, water, castile soap and linens to the wounded man. After placing on a table what we had brought, my two companions withdrew. I walked towards the bed and, looking at him, I exclaimed, "I see that nothing but a bullet through your brain will finish you."

I saw a quivering smile pass over his face, and his tiger eyes gleamed. My words seemed heartless. I had gone to make up for the inhuman treatment given by others, and instead, I had added to the inhumanity by my words. It was only after a few days of introspection that I concluded it was not I who had spoken, but Fear — or so psychologists say.

I continued my daily visits. One day he informed

123

Billy the Kid — behind those hard eyes Sister Blandina saw a human being.

me that his old gang was on its way into Trinidad to scalp all four doctors there, because none had had the courage to remove the bullet from his thigh.

I looked at the sick man for a few seconds, then said, "Do you believe that with this knowledge I'm going to keep still?"

"What are you going to do about it?"

"Meet your gang at 2 p.m. next Saturday."

He laughed as heartily as a sick man could and said, "Why Sister, Billy will be pleased to meet you."

Saturday came. When I got to my patient's room, the gang was already around his bed. The introduction was given. I can only remember, "This is Billy, our Captain, and Chism."

Billy had steel-blue eyes, and a peach complexion. He was very young, one would take him to be seventeen — innocent-looking, save for the corners of his eyes, which foretold a set purpose, good or bad.

"We are all glad to see you, Sister," Billy said. "And I want to say, it would give me pleasure to be able to do you any favor."

I answered, "Yes, there is a favor you can grant me."

He reached his hand toward me with the words: "The favor is granted."

I took his hand, saying, "I understand you have come to scalp our Trinidad physicians, which act I ask you to cancel."

Billy looked down at the sick man, who remarked, "I told you she was game."

What he meant by that I am yet at a loss to understand.

Billy then said, "I granted the favor before I knew what it was, but it stands."

A YEAR OR so later, I decided to take a trip to Santa Fe. I was warned against attempting the visit. "The Kid is attacking the coaches or anything of profit that comes in his way." I knew they meant Billy and his gang.

The first day we traveled to Sweetwater, reaching it at about 4 p.m. "Billy's gang is dodging around, and we expect they will attack us tonight," Sister Augustine and I were told.

The Kid arrived the next day around noon.

"Please put your revolvers away," I said to our guards in a voice which was neither benign nor aggressive, but was the outward expression of my conviction that we had nothing to fear. The light patter of hoofs could be heard as the gang drew near the carriage opening. As the rider came from the rear of the vehicle, I shifted my big bonnet so that when he did look, he could see the Sisters.

Our eyes met; he raised his large-brimmed hat with a wave and a bow in recognition. The rider, of course, was the famous Billy the Kid. He stopped to give us some of his wonderful antics on bronco maneuvers before he left.

IN APRIL OF the following year, Billy was once again captured. That May I decided to visit him in prison. Besides being cuffed hands and feet, I found him also fastened to the floor. You can imagine the extreme discomfort of the position. When I got into the prison cell, and he saw me, he said, "I wish I could place a chair for you, Sister."

Billy escaped from that prison not long after I visited him. In escaping, he killed two of his guards. The next time I heard about him it was only to learn that he had been shot and killed by Mr. Pat Garrett. I have often thought about how many crimes might have been prevented, had someone had influence over Billy after his first murder. The plains are broad. His ascendancy was instantaneous over the minds of our freelance cowboys. Finding himself captain and dictator, with no religious principles to check him, he became what he became — the greatest murderer in the history of the Southwest. ✺

THE HYPOTHESIS OF THE BLUE SHELLS

EXPLORER, GEOGRAPHER, astronomer, farmer, town-builder and missionary, Eusebio Francisco Chino (he changed his name to Kino as a concession to Spanish pronunciation shortly after arriving in the New World in 1681) accomplished more in thirty years than most men do in several lifetimes. He is credited with mapping much of northern Mexico, southern Arizona and New Mexico; founding a chain of missions, towns and cattle ranches upon which the Southwest eventually based its economy; introducing European grains, fruits and grapevines; and discovering once and for all that Baja California was a peninsula, not an island. Chino's Baja discovery came by virtue of his own "Hypothesis of the Blue Shells."

Since the days of Cortés and Cabrillo many views had been held regarding the geography of California, some regarding it as a peninsula and others as an island. Kino had been taught by Father Aygentler, in the University of Ingolstadt, that it was a peninsula, and had come to America firm in this belief; but in deference to current opinion, and as a result of certain observations of his own, he had given up the notion, and as late as 1698 he wrote of California as "the largest island of the world."

But during the journey of 1699 to the Gila River an incident took place which caused him to turn again to the peninsular theory. It was the gift by a few Yuma Indians of certain blue shells, such as Chino had seen in 1685 on the Pacific coast of the Peninsula of California, and there only.

If the shells had come to the Yumas from the South Sea (the Pacific), Chino reasoned, could there not be a land connection with California and the ocean by way of the Yuma country?

KINO DIRECTED HIS efforts to learning more about the source of the blue shells. For this purpose he made a journey in 1700 to San Xavier del Bac. He spoke with the Indians from all the villages for hundreds of miles around. In "long talks" he learned that the only known source for blue shells was the South Sea.

This assurance was the inspiration of his remaining journeys. In the same year, 1700, for the first

time, he reached the junction of the Yuma and Gila rivers, and learned that he was now directly above the head of the Gulf — a fact which greatly strengthened his belief in the peninsular theory.

In the next year he returned to the same point by way of the Camino del Diablo, passed some distance down the Colorado River, and towed on a raft by Indians while sitting in a basket, he crossed over to the California side.

Finally, in 1702, his triumph came, for he again returned to the Yuma junction, descended the Colorado to the Gulf, and saw the sun rise over its head. "California no es isla, sino peninsula," he wrote in triumph.

FATHER KINO DIED at the age of sixty-six, at Magdalena, one of the missions he founded. A contemporary, Father Luís Velarde has described Kino's last moments: "Father Kino died in the year 1711, having spent twenty-four years in glorious labors in this Pimeria. When he died he was almost seventy years old. He died as he had lived, with extreme humility and poverty. In token of this, during his last illness he did not undress. His deathbed, as his bed had always been, consisted of two calfskins for a mattress, two blankets such as the Indians use for covers, and a pack-saddle for a pillow. Nor did the entreaties of Father Agustín move him to anything else."

— H. E. Bolton

◄ Father Eusebio Kino's monument in Nogales, Arizona — part of the territory he missionized in the seventeenth century

The Crucifixion of Nazone

by Pietro DiDonato

NAZONE FINISHED A long drink, reeled into the center of the shanty and proclaimed eloquently with hand over heart, "In this world there is no animal more beautiful than the Woman." He rolled his eyes upward and kissed his fingers.

Hunt-Hunt shook his head.

"Now look at this schoolboy poet; are we Englishmen who talk-talk and sport caramel in eye? 'Bye-bee,' I feel like a tasty bit of whore proverbially now!"

Alfredo put finger to mouth and winked.

"Happy thought! . . . Only around the corner," he whispered, "a Polish woman and her two daughters — ah, specimens of femalia — very fine! Polite, and character sympathetic! Very fine! The mother even wears silk stockings — sometimes a veil, like a noblewoman — fine! First-class!"

Nazone's huge nostrils went up; the Lucy's fierce eye gleamed. Alfredo puckered his lips.

"And as clean as a whistle, I tell you." He pushed back his cap, placed palms on knees. "What say you — make we this little voyage?"

Sturdy spines bent forward, molars clamped, horny hands clutched jug handle, wine rivered, knees pressed together, and lust spread as scalding enema in bowels.

Pietro DiDonato's Christ in Concrete *is a novel that both overtly and covertly applies Christian symbolism to the plight of immigrant construction workers. The opening event is perhaps the most brutal rendering of the death of a worker — the Christ buried in concrete — ever recorded. The scene excerpted here, again a crucifixion, is more humorous, though no less revelatory of the Italian peasant's earthy, and easy, play with his faith's most sacred symbols.*

NEAR MIDNIGHT THE nineteen of them headed back to the shanty arm in arm, stogies blazing against the night, cap a-jaunt, footstep slack and manner philosophic.

"We should not have gone," muttered Santos.

They filed into the shanty. Orangepeel-Face heaped the stove with wood and warmed his front. "Ah she kissed me with a sentiment — mother mine, what a mouth! what a feeling!"

"Hush," said Nazone. "There sound the chimes of the midnight service. . . . For pity that we are like rabid swine and not with knee in pew . . ."

They became silent.

"And our God Jesus the Son of Mary," continued Nazone, "is now born. This is a sin, really a sin."

"Cocko," said Fausta softly, "you know, it appears our dear little Nazone should have donned the cassock . . ."

Remorse is a precious instant and then — no more. Praise brought the nod to Nazone's chin and flickering sparks to eye.

Said Alfredo: "Put a finger in his mouth."

"Ah, sweet is our Nazone . . ."

"Patron Saint of the whorehouses."

Nazone struggled to keep somber.

"Face of priest . . . veritably," remarked old Santos.

"Look at him," said the Lucy, "the shame-faced Tartuffe." And he jammed his finger into Nazone. Nazone howled, and each way he turned another fingered him.

"Blasphemy! Animals, you'll roast forever in Purgatory!"

Hunt-Hunt measured Nazone dreamily. He whispered to Fausta. Fausta's eyes opened, and he twirled his mustaches.

"And why not?"

The Lucy heard, and grinned, "He merits it."

They motioned to Octavio and instructed him on the side.

"Sure-sure . . . it will only take five minutes." He gathered his tool sack and left the shanty.

The men paid special attention to Nazone. He gloried.

"Man," he lectured, "though of the basest class, should observe the spir-it-tual . . ."

Fausta feigned tears and wailed raucously, "He is a good man — nay, a sainted one . . . oh oh — what a man beatific!"

Nazone lifted the jug and drew heavily.

"Ah paesans, this is not subject that one jokes

with, for —"

The shanty door opened and Octavio lugged in a clumsy timber.

"What has he there?" asked Santos.

It was a large stout cross made of two cement-studded scaffold planks.

"J-J-J-Jesu G-Giuseppe e Mari," exclaimed Bastian, "what have we . . . a c-c-crucifixion! Who is to adorn the scaffold cross?"

Nazone clung to his jug and looked about.

"Nazone sonofabitch!" cried Fausta, "prepare yourself, for only the good are crucified!"

They fell upon him and began undressing him.

"Stop! You do not realize — for charity's sake — I'll die of cold — oooh — bastards!"

They soon had him down to his long red underwear and shoved the cross upon his shoulder.

"Please, for the love of those children who depend on me in the old country — do not permit this outrage — this is immortal sin — let not your souls be soiled with this sacrilege — I say enough is enough — I shall lose this patience and blood will fly!"

They pushed him around the shanty and followed in drunken procession. He protested, then compromised that for each length of shanty he be refreshed from the jug. They did likewise. Through besotted tears they fixed the cross to the wall and roped him to it. The Lucy fashioned a crown of rope with nails pointing upward and placed it upon his head.

"I am dead of cold . . ." Nazone wept maudlinly. Orangepeel loaded the stove with dry timber. It roared, and the shanty became thick with smelly heat.

"Now I am dead of fire . . . oh oh this poor Christ," wept Nazone. Fausta pulled the long red underwear from him and left him tied to the cross plump naked and wearing only shoes and socks. They held the jug to his mouth and he drank and drank. Near the blazing stove, belly round with red drink, Nazone looked about at the revolving faces and then dropped head to breast.

They forgot him and gurgled wildly from the few remaining jugs. Alfredo opened his mouth wide and sang "Without a Mother"! As he sang he wrung his hands and cried with rending woe. They sang and fell against the shanty walls. One sang a bawdy tale, another a hymn.

"Allay! Our Nazone makes the slumber-ell."

"Let's awaken Nazone, our dear Nazone!"

"He doesn't move . . . perhaps he is gone!"

Octavio emptied a jug over Nazone's head. He raised heavy head, shivering and gasping, "What has happened? What goes on? What is this?"

Fausta tickled him. They all tickled him and he laughed and cried and wriggled and moaned: "Stop — I am dead — my arms are broken off — hahaha — stop I am sick . . . He he ho haha — police! — oh, my death on your heads — ha ha ha — oooh — "

The louder he bawled the more they laughed. His nose dripped and tears rolled all over his shiny flush cheeks. Fausta dipped biscuit in wine and painted circles on him. He yelled unintelligibly until he gulped and vomited gushes of sour wine and lunch into Fausta's face. Then tight reeling muscles pushed out storms of open throated laughter stomach kicking laughter fist clenching chest shaking laughter that made the stove laugh and the cross laugh and bulged the shanty walls with crazy laughing laughter. ❧

MISSISSIPPI HEAT

by Thomas E. Blackburn

THE FIRST TIME I heard Jim Groppi's name, it was in this context.

Someone in our Christian Family Movement group had met the new priest at St. Boniface parish in Milwaukee. It was an old German national parish now completely engulfed in black Milwaukee. The priest seemed "at a loss" about what to do with the situation, but he was asking for help on a parish census to get something started.

The priest, Father James Groppi, was described that night as "not very forceful, but well-intentioned."

The first time I saw him was one afternoon at that program. He had slipped quietly into his church basement and was standing at the door while a half-dozen adults worked in small groups with the kids at those long, gray setup tables and folding chairs without which the church couldn't function.

He didn't say anything to anyone. But I'd had a pretty good session on American history, and as I was leaving I brightly said we had accomplished something that afternoon.

"We have so little to offer them," he said.

It wasn't long after that Groppi hit the streets with his National Association for the Advancement of Colored People (NAACP) Youth Council and became the Mouth that made Mayor Maier antsy. Two hundred consecutive days of street marches for open housing; sermons urging that, "You must be revolutionaries; Christ was a revolutionary; that's why he died on the cross" — maybe he was looking for a little more "to offer them."

The last time I saw him was on the Meredith march in Mississippi in 1966. By then, the "not very forceful" priest had become a force in Milwaukee and a national figure. For some, Groppi was a six-letter epithet.

I had followed his career, and I had even watched one night when some priests, meeting with his pastor in the St. Boniface rectory, had carefully worked out a plan to cool a school boycott in Milwaukee and then turned on the television to see Groppi saying

▶
Father James Groppi being arrested at a Milwaukee civil rights march in 1967

Father James Groppi lived amid controversy: He led the marches that resulted in Milwaukee's first open housing law in 1967. He married Margaret Rozga in 1976 and was suspended from the priesthood. He drove cabs and a city bus to earn money for law school. Only in 1985, while he was dying of cancer, did Milwaukee acknowledge his contribution. But even in death Groppi ignited controversy. On the day of his funeral calls flooded the archdiocese objecting to the decision to give the ex-priest a Christian burial.

things that superseded their planning and forced them back to the drawing board.

One of the high-powered priests present quoted Martin Luther King, Jr.: "There go my followers. I'll have to hurry to catch up to them."

Groppi had heart and guts, but he never claimed to be a brilliant theoretician and he was a lousy politician. Which brings us to the Meredith march, where all the civil rights movement's big feet were collected and where the movement was undergoing one of its turning points. On that march, "black power" went nationwide.

While the movers and shakers argued from Memphis into the Mississippi Delta, Groppi disappeared one afternoon, and I went looking for him.

I found him down a dusty road past some shacks. He was in his clerical blacks and Roman collar, down on his knees playing a game that involved drawing pictures with a stick in the dust. Four or five kids, the oldest no more than nine, were his playmates.

When the game was over, I walked with Groppi to the church where the marchers were being fed. He had dust on his knees. He said the kids were the "real story" of the march and made some small talk, but his mind was still half on the game. When I think of him these days, which is often, I think of black kids laughing and horsing around with their buddy with the bug eyes and the big nose who had dirt on the knees of his clerical suit. They probably didn't know he was a priest, and an Italian priest from the Yankee North at that. ❧

129

OBITUARY FOR AN ACTIVIST
The Death of Father Baroni

MSGR. GENO BARONI died in Washington, D.C., in August 1984, after a long struggle with peritoneal mesothelioma cancer. He was rightly known as one of the most effective and innovative Catholic social activists of his generation.

Born of an immigrant coal-mining family in Acosta, Pennsylvania, Baroni brought the stamina of the laborer to all he did, and a relish for ethnic variation. He was ordained in 1956, and soon stationed in a Johnstown, Pennsylvania, steel-mill parish where "the pastor spoke for the company, and I spoke for the union." When wealthy parishioners chided him for his outspokenness, warning such forwardness would limit his ecclesiastical rise, Father Baroni wryly responded: "Me, a bishop? I'm just an Italian kid lucky to be ordained at all."

In Johnstown he initiated a credit union ("Man does not live by bread alone, but by credit as well") that today includes seven thousand members.

In the 1960s Baroni became the pastor of a racially diverse parish in Washington, D.C. Such diversity was salt to him, and his naturally cheerful spirit combined with a tactical gift for building concordances. "I am interested in legitimizing pluralism," he said.

So he marched with Martin Luther King, Jr., founded the Campaign for Human Development and the National Center for Urban Ethnic Affairs, established neighborhood development groups in over forty-five cities, and served as undersecretary of the Department of Housing and Urban Development under President Carter — the first Catholic priest to hold a subcabinet policy-making position.

On Labor Day, 1983, in his last public homily at the Shrine of the Sacred Heart in Washington, D.C., he shared a prayer that embodied his life and faith: "On this Labor Day, Lord, I pray: 'Help me to know that our limited charity is not enough. Lord, help me to know that our soup kitchens and secondhand clothes are not enough. Lord, help me to know that it

▲
Msgr. Geno Baroni, while an assistant secretary at HUD

is not enough for the church to be the ambulance service that goes about picking up the broken pieces of humanity for American society. Lord, help us all to know that God's judgment demands justice from us as a rich and powerful nation.' "

Not simply an activist or social mover, Baroni showed concern that was genuinely pastoral for the life of parishes and his fellow workers. He was concerned for their sense of rootedness and continuity. "I think that the sense of identity and heritage is very important to the life of the church," he told the *Notre Dame Journal of Education* in 1973. "Many of our priests and nuns are moving away from their heritage, their culture, and their traditions. They are giving up identity with those values and goals traditional to the church, and consequently are causing a crisis within themselves."

His own last illness, after repeated bouts with cancer, was the mark of his own mettle. Weekly, for over two years, he met with other cancer patients at the Washington School of Psychiatry for attitude therapy sessions. He called these "the best medicine I've got." He conducted healing services at his old parish, and told friends, "There's a great tension between the will to live and the will to die. You've got to have both."

We have now had both — his life and his death. Both were exemplary.

— *Peter Steinfels*

Chicago's Activist Cardinal

by D. J. R. Bruckner

Joseph Cardinal Bernardin has become a significant leader of American Catholicism for many reasons: his positions on peace, on economic justice, on AIDS. But finally these involvements all come down to this statement: "Human life is both sacred and social." Sacred is not new for the church; social is. For it means developing the kind of society that protects and fosters life. It means a church concerned with not just personal but social morality. Cardinal Bernardin is talking transformation.

WHEN THE ROMAN Catholic bishops of the United States convene in Chicago on May 2, 1983, to vote on a pastoral letter on nuclear warfare, their action will climax a two-year battle led by Joseph Cardinal Bernardin, principal architect of the controversial declaration, who has fought for this declaration as the head of the bishops' committee which has already seen the letter through three previous drafts.

On that front, Bernardin understands that another and longer campaign is just beginning. Indeed the cardinal has drafted this document as a platform for continuing instruction and debate among the nation's 50 million Catholics. His long-term objective is still the transformation of the Catholic Church in the United States into a "peace church."

This leader of the "peace church" is a man who by virtue of his office might once have been called "a prince of the Roman Church." But there is little about Cardinal Bernardin that one would associate with royalty, except, perhaps, for the rambling brick mansion bristling with towering chimneys where Chicago archbishops have lived for one hundred years and where his predecessor Cardinal Cody lived all alone.

The new cardinal has made changes: Heavy draperies were pulled aside, windows opened and ceremonial rooms and offices dismantled. The cardinal invited two priests to occupy quarters in the big residence and has welcomed a broad spectrum of Chicago society as visitors.

The cardinal seems at home here. He pulls his chair up closer to a visitor's and sits sideways in it, so that when his black jacket falls open it reveals a lining patterned with tiny white quatrefoils.

Sitting does not describe his posture: there is more movement in his chair than in most joggers' routines, and as he talks, he uses both hands to shape and caress words and ideas. He has a tendency to be serious about everything, but heavy-handed about nothing. Asked about his cardinal's ring, he took it off and handed it to his visitor, telling a story about how it was made and commenting "I like it."

For all his sophistication in church affairs and in politics, there is a lot of the small town in Cardinal Bernardin, and it works to his advantage when he is dealing with people.

He was born in Columbia, South Carolina, to Joseph Bernardin, an immigrant stonecutter from northern Italy, and his wife Maria, and attended public and Catholic schools there before going on to the University of South Carolina, where he intended to prepare for a medical career.

(One of the jokes making the rounds in Chicago these days is that there, but for the grace of God, goes a potentially fine doctor.)

Like many children of immigrants, he has become more interested in his roots as he grows older. He says that when they were young, he and his sister Elaine, now Mrs. James Addison, did not learn Italian, "because we were too busy becoming American," and it was only recently that he became proficient in the language. He did not visit Fiera di Primiero, the little town in the Dolomites, near the city of Trento, where his parents came from, until long after he had become a priest. But when he received his cardinal's hat last February, his Primiero relatives rented a bus and drove to Rome for the ceremony.

ASK HIM WHAT Joseph Bernardin is deeply,

essentially, and he says: "A priest."

"My principal role," he says, "is to proclaim the Lord and the Gospel, and it has a very evangelistic thrust. I have tried to witness to that not only in preaching, but in the way I live and relate to people. There is a great spiritual hunger in this country. For some years we have gone through a period of questioning and a great loss of faith, but I see a reawakening."

That the rebirth he sees is a faith found on the other side of disillusionment does not trouble him.

"People may be tired of the institutions, but they want the Lord. We may come out of this with a much stronger faith than before."

Challenged about his traditional views on moral questions, especially sexual mores, he says: "People have been given some strange notions, not only about sexuality, but about their own purposes and identities. I am not so much interested in dos and don'ts. I support the rules, but I really want people to come to church, to have a relationship with the Lord. If they do," he says, "they will find it is much more demanding than the rules."

That kind of view is almost certain to bring the church into increasing conflict with the rest of society, if not with the civil order, and the cardinal acknowledges that "if we live a religious life and encourage others to do that, there is no doubt we will come into increasing conflict with the prevailing values of this society."

Bernardin's effect on crowds of Chicago Catholics is difficult to define. It is more than celebrity, although he knows how to use that very well, and there is a terrific excitement about him. The cardinal does not seem to be running for anything except the next meeting on his busy schedule, but there is an extraordinary amount of speculation about his future among people in and outside the church. Dr. Gottschalk of Cincinnati's Hebrew Union College offers what he calls a Jewish perspective on the matter: "If ever an American could be pope, Joe would be wonderful."

Chicagoans have their own perspectives. There is the applause, the admiration, the apprehension, the questioning, many individual judgments. In a basement bar a block away from Holy Name Cathedral, a sometime usher pondering a second Scotch offers this one: "The cardinal's a terrific guy, all in all. I guess he'll make it here. I hope he does. We need it. But I would find it all easier to take if his parents hadn't been named Mary and Joseph." ❧

GOLDEN GATE BRIDGE

Born in the village of Predazzo in 1921, Fr. Efrem Trettel was ordained a Franciscan priest in 1944. After serving first in his native Trentino and then in Calabria, he joined a mission in Hupeh, China, from which he was expelled by the communist regime in 1951. It was then that he came to San Francisco to begin his radio and television ministry.

Beginning in 1954 as host of a local radio program for Italian immigrants, he founded in 1964 the Apostolato Radio Cristiana, or ARC — a San Francisco ministry designed to bring Catholic Mass to shut-ins by means of television broadcasts. The ministry was extended in 1969 to stations throughout northern California and Nevada and as far as Tucson, Arizona. His daily work also includes ministering and organizing outings for the aged. In between, Father Trettel finds time for his twin avocations, photography and poetry: He has published several books of poetry as well as a biography of St. Francis of Assisi. The following poem is from "Armonie senza spazio," a recent poem collection.

Vorrei essere immesso nelle tue strutture
o ponte del Cancello d'oro.

Nascosto nell'immensa arcata
vorrei provar le vibrazioni
dell'acciaio sospeso
sopra l'acque pacifiche;
vorrei sentir il rombo dei motori
sulla strada oscillante;
vorrei tremare all'urlo dei venti
nell'arpa poderosa;
vorrei rabbrividire all'umidore
delle nebbie striscianti
lungo il tuo corpo in frigida carezza.

E forse sentirei la forza
di quell'umanità in cui vivo,
l'armonia del creato
e i destini di Dio.

I would love to be immured in your very struts
o bridge of chancelled gold.

Hidden in the endless arc of you
I would resonate to each vibration
of your steel suspended
over the pacific waters;
I would move with the roar of engines
on your swaying roadway;
I would tremble to the winds howling
through your mighty harp;
I would shudder in the dampness
of fogs creeping
along your body frigid, caressing.

And there perhaps I'd feel full the force
of this humanity in which I live,
the harmonies of creation
and the geometries of God.

— Father Efrem Trettel
(translation by Lawrence DiStasi)

Sinners

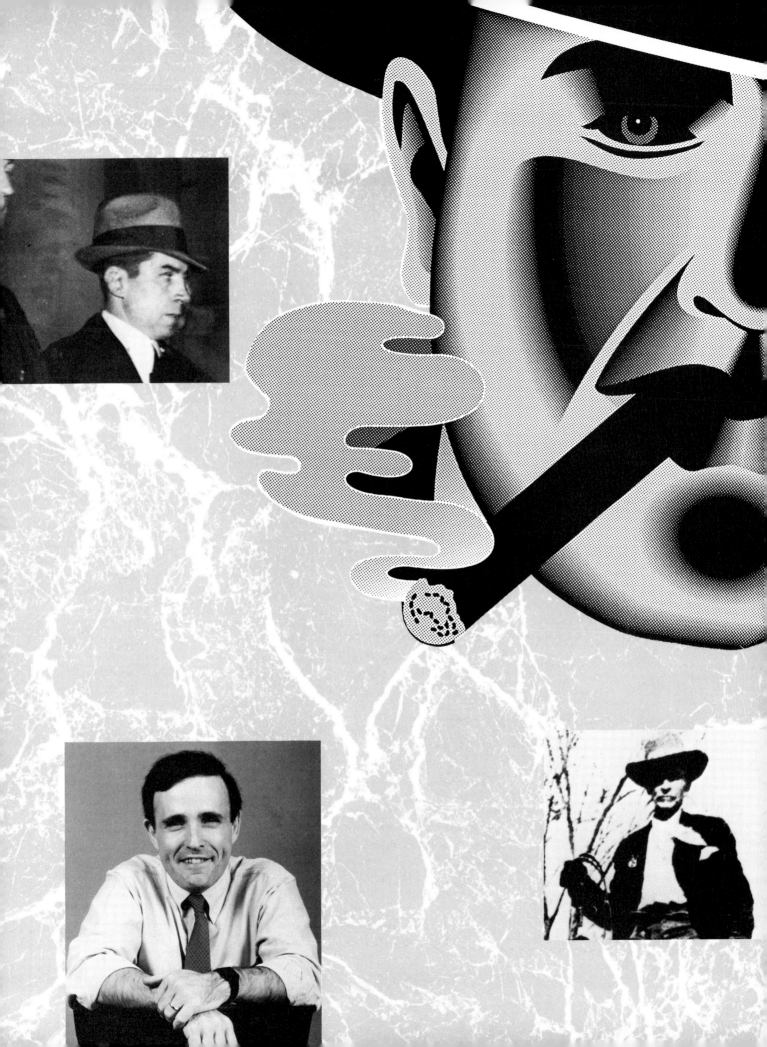

THE LUCIANO PROJECT

by Rodney Campbell

I
N ONE OF the most sensational decisions of the postwar years, on January 2, 1946, Gov. Thomas E. Dewey of New York commuted the thirty- to fifty-year sentence of Charles "Lucky" Luciano. In a month, Luciano was aboard the S.S. *Laura Keene,* deported to Italy. Dewey's message to the state legislature read, in part: "Charles Luciano was convicted in New York County of compulsory prostitution of women and sentenced, June 18, 1936, to a term of thirty years minimum, fifty years maximum.

"He has previously been convicted of the possession of drugs.

"He is now forty-eight years old.

"Upon the entry of the United States into the war, Luciano's aid was sought by the Armed Services in inducing others to provide information concerning possible enemy attack. It appears that he cooperated in such effort, although the actual value of the information procured is not clear."

CHARLES "LUCKY" LUCIANO had clawed his way to the top of the Mafia in the eastern United States in the 1930s. As one of the crime reporters of the period wrote: "For years, like some deadly King Cobra, this droopy-eyed thug coiled himself about the Eastern underworld and squeezed it implacably of its tainted gold. He was the bookmakers' joy, a torch singer's delight, Dracula masquerading as Good Time Charlie."

Why had Tom Dewey — who had mobilized, planned, and led the most successful onslaught against crime ever seen in America — commuted Luciano's

While mainstream American culture has always been intrigued with its underside — its outlaws and criminals — American subcultures have been equally intrigued with the way the underside of the underside becomes the inside. The pardon of Lucky Luciano by that apostle of rectitude, Thomas E. Dewey, fairly reeked of the inside. The Navy-Mob alliance was its name. What has yet to emerge is how far and how high such unholy alliances still go.

sentence? What was this reference to Luciano's "aid" being "sought" by the armed services all about?

It took thirty years to find out. In the interim, rumors filled the newspapers. Governor Dewey — who had appointed William B. Herlands to undertake a study of the matter — suppressed his own report for twenty years. Then in the summer of 1976, against the wishes of Naval Intelligence, the estate of Thomas Dewey decided to release the report after all.

BACK IN 1942, the report indicated, U.S. Naval Intelligence had been understandably worried about the huge toll of allied ships succumbing to German subs. Between December 7, 1941, and the end of February 1942, the United States and its allies had lost a total of seventy-one merchant ships to marauding Axis U-boats.

It was then that the Navy went to New York's district attorney Frank Hogan with the Navy's major concerns: Information as to convoy movements and assistance in refueling German submarines could possibly be obtained from criminal elements of Italian or German origin on the waterfront in the metropolitan area. Torn between their loyalty to both their new and old countries, the theory went, some of those very same Germans or Italians who had been rumrunners during the days of Prohibition might be in the business now of running contraband oil supplies to the German submarine fleet.

The New York DA's office decided it was worth a try. Not a month earlier, on February 9, the SS *Normandie* had burned and rolled over at her moorings on the Hudson River. There was speculation that either Axis saboteurs, or criminal elements had set the fire.

Assistant DA Murray Gurfein, head of the rackets bureau, was chosen to make contact

with the underworld, specifically with Joseph "Socks" Lanza, the business agent for the United Seafood Workers Union, and the de facto rackets boss of the Fulton Fish Market. Lanza began the operations, but for an undertaking of this size, his power was limited. The man you should be talking with, Lanza soon told the DA, is Lucky Luciano.

Within weeks Luciano was transferred from Dannemora Prison to Great Meadow Prison at Comstock, not far from Albany. Meyer Lansky was chosen to make the initial proposal to Lucky.

At their first meeting, Lansky and attorney Polakoff attempted to convince Luciano that he should cooperate. At first Luciano was skeptical. It was not a question of patriotism; but, according to Lansky, "Luciano had a deportation warrant attached to his papers . . . and he didn't want his cooperation with the U.S. government to become known because whenever he would be deported and went back to Italy, that he might get lynched. We told him we would stress that this will be kept secret so he is not in danger at any time."

It took one more meeting, this time including Lanza, for the "summit" to be a success. Lucky Luciano by then had his organization primed: New York Harbor was going to go all the way for the Allies. The terms of this "Devil's Pact" were, of course, left unspoken: The Navy was going to secure its convoy base for victory in Europe but only in return for tacit acceptance of continued underworld control of the waterfront.

THE DEAL HELD tight throughout the course of the war. "Before the contact with Luciano," Lieutenant Kelly of Naval Intelligence later commented, "we ran into great difficulty in obtaining reliable informants along the waterfront, or people who would give us an honest answer to any question we had there. But after the contact was made, it definitely changed."

After Luciano's entry into the alliance, there was no active sabotage, no labor disturbances, no disruptions, nor delays of shipping out of the Port of New York.

There was, in fact, a decided decline in the rate of sinkings by the end of 1942, especially when measured against the vast increases of shipments of men, weapons, ammunition, and supplies across the Atlantic.

The Allies were safely ashore in North Africa, and, unquestionably, the tight security in the Port of New York, along with the Allies' improving technology and tactics of submarine warfare, had helped make that invasion a success.

On VE Day, May 8, 1945, in New York City, attorney Moses Polakoff swore out in his office at 475 Fifth Avenue a petition for the grant of executive clemency for Charles "Lucky" Luciano. And on January 6, 1946, it was granted. Lucky Luciano — a bona fide American patriot — sailed to Italy. ❧

FIFTYSOMETHING

"**W**HY THE COVER up?" has always been an important, unanswered question in terms of the Navy-Luciano Project. Even if the Navy did use criminals to stop sabotage in American ports, and to supply lifesaving intelligence during the invasion of Sicily, why were the details of this operation so long suppressed?

As Dorothy Gallagher makes plain in her book *All The Right Enemies: The Life and Times of Carlo Tresca,* the answer may well lie in the government's final hidden pay-off on the original "Devil's Pact."

Lucky Luciano had been arrested for narcotics trafficking in 1923. He thereafter always claimed that it was never he but Vito Genovese who was the drug kingpin: "Every one of them pipelines [i.e., from North Africa through the Italian and French processing centers] had been tied together by Vito."

On the other hand, Luciano apparently tried to turn Cuba into a center for narcotics smuggling shortly after his deportation to Italy in 1946. It was only a threat by the Narcotics Bureau to shut off Cuba's medical supplies that forced then Prime Minister Batista to shut the door on Luciano. According to the Narcotics Bureau Luciano, booted out of Cuba, simply switched his operations to Naples and Palermo — at one point outfitting a candy factory where drugs, rather than almonds, were inserted into its candies.

Kingpin or no, it is clear that Luciano, Genovese and the Sicilian Mafia were, both before the war and after, involved in drug smuggling. And the route — raw drugs from North Africa to be processed in Sicilian and Italian port cities, as well as Marseilles, and then sent to America — was precisely the route that the Allies would use for the Sicilian invasion.

The missing piece to the deal has finally surfaced.

Lieutenant Titolo — one of the Italian American Naval Intelligence officers involved in the Sicilian invasion — has testified: "I had heard at the time that information was being received through small fishing vessels plying between North Africa, Sicily and the Italian mainland. I had heard that most of them were drug smugglers."

Michele Pantaleone, a Sicilian and a Socialist deputy in Palermo, is even more specific: "It is a historical fact that the Mafia, in agreement with American gangsterism, did its best to clear the way right across the island [Sicily] and so enable the invading troops to advance into central Italy with remarkable safety.. . . Clandestine landings also took place in the small Mafia-controlled fishing ports between Balestrate and Castellammare . . . these are ports which years later would play an important part in the drug traffic between American gangsters and the Sicilian Mafia."

Thus, Dorothy Gallagher suggests, this same "network of men on small fishing boats," which was transformed from drug smuggling to intelligence work during World War II, was reborn, stronger than ever, in its primal form after the war. As Gallagher writes: "The 'technical' details of the Luciano project that the Navy was anxious to keep secret may have been the existence of such a network — one that did not disband after the war, but continued to smuggle drugs, perhaps even with some grant of immunity from the authorities, while the use of narcotics became epidemic in the cities of the United States."

If Gallagher is correct — and recent revelations about similar "pacts" in Central America offer their own haunting kind of confirmation — the devils have indeed had their due, and drugs continue to move through historical networks constructed by mob bosses in cooperation with American government officials slightly more than fifty years ago.

— *August Gaudino and Bob Callahan*

THE FIRST OF THE GANG LORDS

by Jack McPhaul

IN 1925 IN a wealthy neighborhood of Chicago's South Shore, a man stepping from a Cadillac was ambushed and left for dead. He was known to his neighbors as Frank Langley, businessman.

His real name was John Torrio.

In time, Johnny Torrio recovered, and left town; and a New York hood by the name of Al Capone succeeded him as boss of the Chicago mob. Capone would leave behind a famous name. Torrio, however, would leave behind an institution.

Less than a decade after the surgeons in the Jackson Park Hospital patched him up, Torrio set in motion a crime system that places him in the number-one niche in the American Hall of Ill Fame.

Torrio founded the national crime Syndicate — the Outfit, the Mob, the Cosa Nostra. Call it what you will, to this day it is still following the blueprint laid down by Johnny Torrio.

"Torrio was the father of modern American gangsterdom, the smartest of all the hoodlums," said Elmer L. Irey, chief of the Treasury Department's enforcement branch. Virgil W. Peterson, onetime FBI district chief, termed Torrio "an organizational genius." The *Chicago Tribune* described him as "the criminal in business who put businessmen in crime." According to the late Herbert Asbury, "Torrio was probably the most efficient organizer of criminal enterprises on a large scale that this country has ever produced. He came very close to being the mythical mastermind."

There have been biographies of Capone, Frank Costello and Lucky Luciano. There has never been a biography of Torrio. "JT" preferred it that way. He had a passion for anonymity. He shied away from

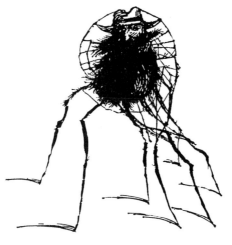

Johnny Torrio and Charles Ponzi were alike in some respects, especially where making money was concerned. But fundamentally they embodied opposing styles of crime. Ponzi courted publicity, relying on it to feed his scheme. He gave his name — the Ponzi scheme — to the con game he mastered. Torrio shunned the limelight and gave his name to nothing. But his legacy — the organization of crime as big business — secures him a lasting place in the American Hall of Ill Fame.

headlines like a burglar dodging a cop's flashlight. To his way of thinking, an outlaw should neither be seen nor heard.

Prohibition was the launching pad for Torrio and his opposite numbers in other metropolitan areas. With bootleggers' gold, they ensnared the politicians whom, before, they had served as lackeys in election day terrorism. Beer barons like Torrio — his 1923 Chicago earnings from his brewery interests in Chicago were estimated at $12 million a year — put bribery into mass production.

Earlier, corrupters dealt solely with the upper echelon of politics and the top brass of police. Torrio and his fellows were more democratic. On his payroll the private shared space with the generals. A governor opened the doors of a state prison to people his mob; a mayor gave him a wide-open town; a sheriff led the way in his conquest of a suburb.

Torrio had had a sound grounding. He had learned the rudiments of his trade out in the field, an apprentice in the second oldest profession. Pimping taught him how to recruit women, interest men and protect them against that most annoying of intrusions: a cop popping into the bedchamber.

But even here he was a pioneer.

Many a fortune has been founded on the automobile. JT was the first to capitalize on the motor car as an adjunct to whoremongering. He established countryside brothels. You might call him the creator of the drive-in whorehouse.

It happened around 1912 when Mayor Harrison of Chicago began a campaign to clean up the city's notorious red-light district. Torrio's saloon license was revoked; his whorehouse business was shaky.

JT got himself a map. He drove into suburbs and villages introducing himself as one seeking a site for a restaurant, chatting with mayors and police chiefs.

In Johnny Patton, village president of Burnham, eighteen miles southeast of Chicago, he found his man. Patton showed his visitor a two-story structure in use as a restaurant and dance hall. Winking, Patton pointed out its location: It straddled the Illinois-Indiana line.

Torrio's then boss (he was later murdered at Torrio's instance by Frankie Yale), Diamond Jim Colosimo, saw the beauty of the location: "I get it. The Indiana cops come in the kitchen and the broads run into the front room. That's Illinois. The Chicago cops come in the front and the girls run into Indiana."

A score of girls were imported from Chicago, Patton became the manager, and the police chief was hired as a bartender. Judiciously, Torrio opened Burnham to other whorehouses, saloons, and gambling rooms. His thinking anticipated the modern suburban shopping center by thirty years: Variety and number draw greater crowds than a single establishment.

In careful stages Torrio established a chain of suburban brothels — in Stickney, Chicago Heights, Posen, Forest View, Burr Oak, Blue Island, and the Indiana towns of East Chicago, Gary and Whiting.

About this time Torrio got a request from Frankie Yale in Brooklyn.

A young punk had stabbed another youngster in a dance hall brawl and needed to skip town. Would JT find him a job? The kid was nineteen, a hulking fellow with a knife scar on his cheek. Torrio hired him for thirty-five dollars a week as bouncer in the Four Deuces brothel. The kid's name was Al Capone.

TORRIO SPENT MOST of his later years in Brooklyn (he had begun in New York as leader of the notorious Five Points Gang) as a gangland elder statesman. He established himself in real estate and was a silent partner in a legitimate liquor business, Prendergast & Diamond. Only once, in 1939, was he jailed for two and one-half years and fined $86,000 for back taxes.

Paroled in 1941, he entered a virtual retirement. Torrio died of a heart attack in a barber's chair on April 16, 1967. In Green-Wood Cemetery in Brooklyn, the headstone is modest and the name is no magnet for the curious. JT simply preferred it that way. ❧

THE FALL OF MISTER PONZI

WHEN HE LEFT Italy for America in 1903 he had nearly $200 in his pocket and unlimited hope in his heart. By the time he hit New York he had only $2.50 left; he had lost the rest to card sharks on the boat.

It was a disappointing start, as were his first dishwashing jobs in New York, and his job as manager of the immigrant Zarossi bank in Montreal: he was caught forging checks and sent to prison for twenty months. Released, his first job in Boston — as a stock boy with J.P. Poole, import and export brokers — seemed little better.

But in two years, by the summer of 1920, Charles Ponzi was being hailed as Boston's "Wizard of Finance," and "a modern King Midas." Investors were lined up outside his Securities and Exchange Company office at 27 School Street begging him to take their money. Sixteen clerks spent their days doing just that, and handing out notes of deposit in return. Often they couldn't find space for it all — one day an astonishing $2,000,000. poured in — and cash overflowed from drawers, closets, even waste baskets.

Outside, Charles Ponzi would arrive in his cream-colored limousine driven by a Japanese chauffeur and the crowds would cheer him like a movie star. Always jaunty, always with a flower in his lapel and a gold-headed cane in his hand, he would tip his hat to the crowd, and sometimes make a little speech—usually about how he was doing what bankers had always done, only this time including the little guy in the profits.

The crowds cheered. One fan called him the greatest Italian of all.

"But what about Columbus," Ponzi replied modestly. "He discovered America."

"But you discovered money!" came the reply.

And the cheers got louder, for Charles Ponzi truly seemed to have discovered perpetual money. He promised a rate of return that no bank could approach: 50% in 45 days, 100% in 90 days. The Wall Street Journal calculated that at Ponzi's rates, a $100 investment, reinvested for three years, would expand to a miraculous $1,680,000. How could it be?

Ponzi told all. He had discovered, he said, the simple fact that postal reply coupons bought in foreign countries, such as Spain, for one cent

could be redeemed in the United States for a nickel. He claimed to have agents all over Europe buying up these coupons and redeeming them for a five-hundred percent profit. And unlike other bankers, he was sharing his wealth with his investors.

Of course the financiers objected. They suspected his was the old scam of paying off early investors with later investors' deposits—which it was—and all would soon go broke. But Ponzi confounded them by always paying off on time, and the more he paid off, the more the public was dazzled. Policemen, judges, even bankers began to invest.

By late summer, Charles Ponzi had taken in between $10 and $15 million and bought out both his first bank and the J.P. Poole Co. where he'd made his initial discovery. Boston's get-rich-quick frenzy was going nationwide.

THEN, AS ABRUPTLY as it began, Ponzi's bubble burst.

On August 11, 1920, the Montreal Police identi-fied Ponzi as the Zarossi clerk once jailed for forgery. Two days later Federal agents siezed both Ponzi and his holdings. Swarms of investors stormed the School Street office, screaming for their money or his head. They got neither.

Ponzi spent the next years fighting both jail and deportation, but to no avail. Having served a seven-year sentence, he emerged in 1934 only to be deported to Italy for an immigrant violation. He managed to impress the Fascists so much that he was given a job as business manager for Mussolini's Latin Airlines in Rio di Janeiro.

Then Mussolini fell, and Ponzi was again out in the cold. He tried to eke out a living teaching English but in the end, half blind and partially para-lyzed, he was committed to a charity ward in Rio. He died there in January 1949 at the age of 66.

His legacy was a paltry $75 — barely enough to cover his burial — and an unfinished manuscript: "The Fall of Mister Ponzi."

— *Richard Leonetti*

THE POETICS OF GANGSTER ART

by Marshall Fishwick

"Dere's little stealin' like you does, and dere's big stealin' like I does.

"For de big stealin' dey makes you Emperor and puts you in de Hall o' Fame when you croaks."
—Eugene O'Neill, *The Emperor Jones*

MAJOR AMERICAN VILLAINS are scarce. Lacking the dramatic flare and timing that would make them memorable, most evil-doers are soon forgotten. T. S. Eliot noted that few contemporaries err with enough purpose or awareness to land in hell. Most of them deserve no longer epitaph than that on a young gunman's grave in Arizona's Tombstone Cemetery: "He done his damndest."

A real villain, however, must be able to talk, think, and act in the "grand manner," so that defiance lends symbolic significance to his crime. He must be able to obstruct the hero, to come dangerously close to succeeding, and to descend to his deserved fate open-eyed. The real villains of history are unforgettable.

Sired by that fourteen-year orgy, Prohibition, the American urban gangster comes closest to fitting this mold. An individualist like the cowboy, he traded six-shooter for submachine gun and tooled leather belt for bulletproof vest. That he was resisting a national law that most people opposed gave him a romantic sanction. Gangsters became public idols as well as public enemies.

The individual who epitomized the type was Al Capone, alias Boxcar Tony, Scarface, and the Big Fellow.

Born in Naples in 1899, and brought to America as a child, he became involved in a Brooklyn pool-hall fight, and fled to Chicago. He specialized in the vice business until bootlegging became more profitable. His syndicate's income became so great that others began to horn in. The result was nine years of gang warfare and over five hundred violent deaths. From the suburb of Cicero, where Capone ran his intricate business, orders went out that affected the lives of thousands.

Al was no punk. He had a London tailor, a French cook, and a fine library. In his own eyes he was practically a public servant.

"I've spent the best years of my life giving people the light pleasures, and all I get is abuse," he complained. "Well, tell the folks I'm going away now. There won't be any more booze. You won't be able to find a crap game, let alone roulette, or faro. Public service is my motto. Ninety-nine percent of the people in Chicago drink. I've tried to serve them decent liquor and square games. But it's no use. I'm going."

Of course, Al didn't go. When his friend Lombardo was killed by North-siders, he directed the machine gun execution of seven Moran men in a beer truck garage on Saint Valentine's Day, 1929. "Bugs" Moran retaliated; after murdering three Capone men, he ordered several attempts on Capone's life, all unsuccessful. They only furthered the myth of Scarface's invincibility.

Much impressed, Yale University seniors in the class of 1931 voted him the "second most interesting personality of the present age."

Sensational newspapers described his trips about the country as "Capone's Odyssey." A French best-seller called *Une Grand Figure: Al Capone* enhanced his European reputation, and he became a minor hero in Hitler's Reich. Such was his importance that in 1930, F. D. Pasley published *Al Capone, Biography of a Self-Made Man.* Even Horatio Alger would have found it hard not to extol Scarface's rise to fame.

The movie *Scarface* (starring Paul Muni) was a success, painting the killer's life in bloody but thrilling hues and leaving the impression that he was a martyr to his principles. A folk hero was definitely shaping up. *True Detective, Harper's, Newsweek, New Republic,* and *North American* heralded his daring. The federal government finally convicted him of income tax evasion and shipped him off to Alcatraz. The Al Capone who died peacefully in 1947 was but a shadow of the once invincible Big Fellow; but his imprint on the American mind was deep and lasting.

THE PERSISTENCE OF the gangster type in the popular mind long after the repeal of Prohibition shows that real cities produce criminals, and imaginary cities gangsters.

Or, as Robert Warshow put it, "The experience of the *gangster as art* is common in America, even though

most Americans have never seen a gangster." Only in an ultimate sense does the movie gangster invade our own experience of reality. Much more immediately, he appeals to our previous and no less vicarious experience of the type itself. The type has created its own field of reference.

Nervous, enterprising, skillful, the gangster moves like a dancer among the crowded dangers of the city. His story is a nightmare inversion of the traditional success story. He is doomed to be punished because he has succeeded by his own unsocial Darwinian standards.

Gangster films invariably resolve the dilemma by making sure the hero is disposed of relentlessly. Thus, in *Scarface*, outside the gangster's bulletproof apartment is a big neon sign reading "The World is Yours." It is the last thing we see after the protagonist's death.

The world is *not* his, any more than it is ours. By dying, he pays for our fantasies, and even releases us for the moment from the concept of success. His death seems not so much punishment as defeat. Lonely and melancholy, he "has to do" what he does, just like the heroes of Greek tragedy.

He is perhaps the closest approximation to a tragic hero our urban folklore has yet produced. ❧

ON FRANK COSTELLO

by Gay Talese

FROM THE 1880s through the early 1900s they crossed the Atlantic in filthy ships, because they were poor; and dug ditches, because they were ignorant. They were not from the Italy of da Vinci or the Medicis; they were mostly from Sicily and the South; people who, from pre-Roman times, seemed always to be mourning something: mourning the murders and rapes by the invading Saracens, Greeks, French; mourning the erupting volcanoes, malaria, taxes, and endless poverty. Finally, many of them had enough, and they sailed to America. Two who did this were named Castiglia, and from their town of Cosenza they brought their four-year-old son, Francesco, who never dreamed he would someday have an Anglo-Saxon doorman.

HE NEVER DREAMED that, as Frank Costello, he would someday spend $50 for a hat, $350 for a suit, and be capable of forgetting $27,200 in the backseat of a New York taxicab. Nor did he ever dream that the mere mention of his name would whet the appetites of crime busters, and make thousands of Italian Americans slightly uncomfortable with *their* names, and hypersensitive to slurs and questions. . .

Frank Costello for many years epitomized the dapper gangster with influence in high places. He was surpassed, at least for a few years in the 1960s, by Sam Giancana. Enlisted by the CIA in a plot to kill Fidel Castro, Giancana is also suspected of involvement with CIA operatives in the assassination of President John F. Kennedy, the man whom he had earlier helped to win Chicago and hence the entire presidential election. As if sharing the president's electoral victory weren't enough, Giancana also apparently shared the president's girlfriend, who here casually discusses her pivotal position between the two most powerful men of her time.

You Italian?
"Half and half."
You Italian?
"None a your goddamn business."

FRANK COSTELLO GREW up in a New York slum with other peasant children whose parents understood neither the language nor the law. Their mothers relied entirely upon God.

And their fathers relied on those better-educated but unreliable countrymen, the padrones, with the same blind faith that in later years led them to believe that Primo Carnera would beat Max Baer. These fathers were short and humble men — too short to become cops, but just right for collecting garbage and building subways, although some preferred to tend farms upstate, and still others moved into Ohio and Pennsylvania and pushed wheelbarrows filled with rocks up hills to build homes. And at the top of a certain hill in Ambler, Pennsylvania, panting and sweating, a parrot at the window of a roadside home would shrill: "Dago-dago-dago-dago-dago!"

Why couldn't you go straight,
    Frank Costello?
Why couldn't you get a shovel and identify
    with Christ in Concrete?

HE NEVER COULD. Like many sons of these peasants, Costello despised his father's humility and inadequacy, and sought easy money and escape from his father's grocery stand. In 1908, he was arrested for assault and robbery. In 1912, he was arrested for the same thing. On both occasions he gave his name as Castello. In 1914, when he got his marriage license, he said he was born Costello and was a "plumber" by trade. In 1915, when he served ten months for carrying a concealed weapon, he gave his name as Frank Saverio and his occupation as steamfitter. But when he appeared before General Sessions Court for sentencing, he gave his name as "Stella." He had little capacity for the truth.

By 1923 he was a rumrunner; he worked under the notorious ex-longshoreman, Big Bill Dwyer, and helped command a vast operation that illegally shipped liquor down from Canada via a dozen steel-plated speedboats

they had learned the art of silence — learned it through centuries of biting their lips.

To survive amid the pestilence, poverty, impossible taxes, and torture, the peasant had to live by his wits, often remain silent, and wait for revenge — as had that vengeful band of Sicilians in 1282 before butchering an entire French garrison after a soldier had raped and murdered a Palermo maiden on her wedding day. It is said that out of this incident, glorified in a Verdi opera, came the inspiration for the Mafia — a union pledged to avenge offenses to a brother, never appeal for police protection, and never — on pain of death — to reveal anything about the organization.

This was Frank Costello's background. And so it was in New York in the twenties that the police encountered silence in Italian Harlem, Brooklyn, and on Mulberry Street in Manhattan. After the police had gone the men would mutter among themselves, "We want no trouble." And they would agree that Costello had done no wrong — the law was merely picking on him because he was Italian.

Frank Costello himself felt he had done no wrong. And, in 1925, he became an American citizen. When asked his occupation, he answered with a straight face and a clear voice, "real estate."

armed with machine guns, and aided by corrupt Coast Guardsmen. Once Costello's swift vessels accidentally strayed into the path of a speedboat race — swished across the finish line first, and kept going.

Detectives began to trail Costello. They visited Italian ghettoes and asked questions. But the neighbors would not talk. These people would no more squeal on a countryman to the New York police in the twenties than they would to the Saracen conquerors in the ninth century or the French in the thirteenth. Suspicious of all alien authority,

IN 1951 AFTER stalking out of a Congressional hearing before a national television audience, Frank Costello was sentenced to a year in prison for contempt.

No sooner had Costello completed his year in prison than he was hauled back on charges of tax evasion. His high-priced attorneys tried hard to beat the case in court.

"Now for God's sake, Frank," one of them said, "when you appear in court tomorrow don't come in wearing one of your $350 suits, and appear so affluent."

145

Sam Giancana and the President's Girl

In mid-October 1961 I leased a house in Palm Springs for three months. By now there seemed to be countless people who knew about Jack. Complete strangers would come up and say, "Are you the Judy that's going with Jack Kennedy?" The "ladies" at the Racquet Club, particularly Gloria Cahn, who had a terrible crush on Jack, would always ask me about him. Gloria would be sitting by the pool, and as I walked by, she would say in her bitchiest tone: "Been to Washington lately?" I would look directly at her and sweetly reply, "Oh yes, just returned." Even Walter Winchell got his two cents in. In his May 8, 1962 column, he wrote: "Judy Campbell of Palm Springs and Bevhills is Topic No. 1 in Romantic Political Circles."

But I found that I was happier with Sam. It took such a long time to work up to an intimacy with him that I don't remember just when it happened. I always enjoyed being with Sam but now I was anticipating seeing him. I completely stopped thinking about Jack when I was with Sam.

I must say that Sam was entirely different in my eyes than the Sam Giancana reported in the press. He was so gentle with me. I have since read that he and Phyllis (McGuire, of the McGuire Sisters) used to have rip-roaring battles. I never once had any kind of a battle with Sam, and I've got a pretty fair temper. I would be angry with him, but it never amounted to anything. If he got mad at me for any reason, he was silent. But it was a strong kind of no-nonsense silence.

Only once did he walk out in anger. We were kissing and it became a little too passionate, and when I refused to go any further, he walked out without saying a word. I left for New York the next morning, and no sooner had I walked into my room at the Plaza than he was on the phone apologizing. A moment later he had a piece of jewelry delivered to my room.

It was not long after this incident that we made love for the first time.

Love with Sam was not as exciting as it had been with Jack, but it was gentle and tender and emotionally fulfilling. It left me with a comfortable feeling instead of a gnawing emptiness.

Was Sam using me because I was the president's girl, as many writers have suggested?

All I can say is that Sam had been after me to leave Jack for a long time. He would point out that Jack was married and try to make me understand the futility of the situation. As I said, I had a hard time letting go of Jack. Sam wasn't too thrilled the few times I saw Jack in 1962. Before we were intimate he would kid me about Jack, but now it wasn't funny anymore. He listened when I explained that I was confused, he promised to be patient, but I knew it was eating away at him. Sam couldn't have been more delighted when I finally stopped seeing Jack.

— *Judith Campbell Exner*

"What do you want me to wear?"

"What you have on," the attorney said, nodding toward Costello's blue denim prison suit.

Costello thought it over for a second, then frowned and said, "I'm sorry but I'd rather blow the goddamn case."

He did. On May 14, 1954, the headlines read: "Costello Guilty in Tax Fraud Case!"

Before getting into an automobile that morning, he turned to reporters on the sidewalk and said, "I think this is a political thing. A lot of guys trying to get ahead by climbing on my back. And that's the way the world goes."

"What was the first mistake?" Walter Winchell asked.

"If you call it a mistake," Costello said, "I guess it was being born of poor parents and raised in a tough neighborhood. If things had been different I might have gone to college and been sitting up there with Mr. Kefauver."

Today as Frank Costello approaches his seventy-fourth birthday, the present-generation Italians are celebrating his decline, in a sense, because his notoriety reminds them of an era they wish to forget.

Costello never understood the rules of the New World because he was influenced by a tradition of a land that exists in the past. His father, who might have dominated family life in Italy — as fathers do there — was illiterate and incapable here. His father was *scemo* — the unforgivable sin of the Southern peasant and Sicilian. Costello had no respect for him. At sixteen he ran away from his home in the slum and regarded those who were not his friends as Saracens. He justified his thievery by his kindness to his wife, and by giving money to panhandlers and for stained-glass windows to churches.

And he will die thinking he has done no wrong. ❧

The Cowboy Detective

by J. Frank Dobie

ONE COLDISH, MISTY December day, towards sundown, in the year 1931, I rode up to a ranch house on the San Bernard River, in Brazoria County, Texas. A white man of advanced years was out in a pen with three black cowboys. When the white man told me that his name was Jim Keller, I immediately remembered the name. Charlie Siringo had once spoken of a Jim Keller who once loaned him a saddle horse. Yes, this was the same man.

We went inside the house to drink coffee and talk. Keller spoke of Siringo at length, and what he told me once more lit up the Charlie Siringo of mavericks, mustangs, mossy-horned steers, fenceless coastal ranges, hide and tallow factories, and other legendary exploits. Keller had known Siringo as a boy and worked with him on Grimes's Rancho Grande.

"His father was Italian and his mother's name was Bridget. He was happy-go-lucky and usually out of luck. He could let more horses get away with the saddle on than any other cowboy in the country. That first book of his told things just like they was."

Keller said Siringo was the most fearless, coolest man he ever knew. One time on a cow-work Siringo and a cowboy named Otto had a quarrel. Soon afterwards Siringo was in camp squatting down on the ground eating dinner when Otto suddenly called out to him from behind, "Charlie, I'm going to kill you. Don't move."

Siringo turned his head just enough to see the barrel of a six-shooter.

"All right," he said, not interrupting eating on a calf rib, "but I have a favor to ask before I die."

"What is it?"

As novelists have long known, the cop and the criminal are closer than either would care to admit. Charlie Siringo, being a writer himself, did admit it. He showed an alarming (to some) empathy for the cowboy criminals he pursued, along with a rather un-American reticence to use his license to kill. More recently, Rudolph Giuliani has charged about on the white horse of the law with an almost religious fervor. The question for him now becomes: Can such pure heat be maintained in the foggy bogs of American politics?

▲
Charles Angelo Siringo: His life in print fuels the myth of the cowboy-lawman as archetypal Western hero.

"You've heard me say more than once that I hoped I'd not die hungry. I dread dying on an empty belly."

Without saying anything but still holding his six-shooter on the target, Otto apparently agreed to let Charlie finish his last meal. Charlie did not seem to slow down the process of filling up on beans, calf ribs, and skillet bread in order to put off the act of dying.

"And I have another favor to ask," Charlie went on, his back to Otto, his squatting position unshifted.

"What's that?"

"When you shoot, don't quit till you've killed me dead. Don't just wound me and leave me wallering around to bother other people. Even if you have to reload to finish me, keep on shooting."

Meanwhile, out of Otto's sight, Charlie's hand was deftly working towards his own six-shooter, which he wore frontward. In a flash it was out and Charlie whirled around, covering Otto.

"Otto," he called, "put that gun up. It might go off and shoot a horse or something. Put it up and eat your dinner."

Otto put it up and ate his dinner. As Jim Keller concluded the story, "A man's wrath cools on a full stomach."

SIRINGO'S REPUTATION AS a fearless cowboy led to his work for Pinkerton's National Detective Agency. By 1910 he had written a book on his experiences as a detective tracking such desperadoes as Billy the Kid

▲
Siringo as a Pinkerton detective

and Butch Cassidy's Wild Bunch.

For two years, however, publication of *Pinkerton's Cowboy Detective* was held up in the superior court of Chicago — until Siringo finally agreed to change the title to *A Cowboy Detective*, change the name of Pinkerton's to the fictional Dickenson Detective Agency, substitute other fictitious names, and cut out a good deal of material.

SIRINGO WAS NOT through with Pinkerton's, however. In Chicago, three years later, directly under the nose of Pinkerton's headquarters, he finally published exactly what he felt concerning "the most corrupt institution of the century": *Two Evil Isms: Pinkertonism and Anarchism.*

More than anything else that he wrote, *Two Evil Isms* reveals the workings of Charlie Siringo's mature political mind. In the beginning, his sympathies were with labor, and it was only when he saw anarchists betraying labor that he took a job with Pinkerton's to bring them to justice.

Very soon his eyes were opened. The falsities in reports about anarchists made by Agency men "would make a decent man's blood boil." Perjured testimony, "third degree" brutality, and padded expense accounts were other Agency evils he felt called upon to expose.

In *A Cowboy Detective* he had called Tom Horn, of Johnson County War fame, "Tim Corn," claiming that Horn was working for "private parties." In *Two Evil Isms* he boldly says that Horn was hired by the Agency to help "wealthy cattlemen get rid of small ranchmen" at six hundred dollars a head. A later biography of Tom Horn corroborated the statement.

Siringo's years of sleuthing left "one dark blot" on his conscience. That was his work against coal miners in their fight to wring justice from "greedy corporations."

Remembering him out of the days of the bloody Coeur d'Alene strike in Idaho of 1891–92, John Hays Hammond describes him as "a slender wiry man, dark-eyed, dark-mustached, modest . . . the most interesting, resourceful, courageous detective I ever dealt with."

A lawyer who worked with Siringo in the "Silver Mining War" adds this to the portrait: "He was deadly with a Colt 45, a weapon he carried at all times. I have thrown up an empty bean can and watched him, shooting from the hip, riddle it in flight, yet he had never, so far as anyone knows, taken a human life. . . .He was shrewdly intelligent, infallible in his judgment of human nature, and courageous to the point of recklessness; he was quick and nervous normally, but in a critical moment, or an emergency, cold and steady as a rock. He was relentless on a scent. He was a rattler who never struck — a personality as interesting as any I have met along the frontier." ❧

SENDING A MESSAGE

WHEN RUDY GIULIANI was graduating from Bishop Loughlin High School in Brooklyn, many of his classmates inscribed "Good luck in the seminary" in his yearbook.

It was the natural thing to write; the high-spirited, high-minded senior was planning to begin studies for the priesthood in the fall. But that summer he changed his mind and decided instead to go to Manhattan College. Giuliani found his particular calling anyway. After college he entered New York University law school, and it was there, as his old friend Father Placa puts it, that "he was *converted* by the law."

As U.S. attorney for the Southern District of New York, the showcase office of the federal legal system, Rudolph Giuliani, forty-one, has a mission: "To make the justice system a reality for the criminal."

He has done just that by snaring high-living mobsters, low-life drug dealers, quiet white-collar criminals and loud banner headlines. Like Thomas Dewey and Henry Stimson, earlier New York prosecutors who parlayed their convictions into prominent national careers, Giuliani has become a high-profile gangbuster in an age when the public yearns for someone to prove that crime doesn't pay.

A thoughtful, driven man who rarely sleeps more than five hours a night and resembles a fresco of an obscure saint, Giuliani has put the Southern District into overdrive. And it is the cluster of cases against the Mafia that is turning Giuliani into a national figure. "Our approach," he declares, "is to wipe out the five families."

Giuliani's father, who ran a small restaurant in Brooklyn and set about to teach his son to box almost as soon as the boy could make a fist, instilled in him a hatred of bullies and an anger at the way in which a few Italians had besmirched the name of a great culture. Unlike many Italian Americans, Giuliani makes a point of using the term *Mafia*. He has no tolerance for those who say it does not exist.

"By using the word *Mafia* correctly, you actually help to end the unfair stereotype. By playing word games and denying reality, you increase the prejudice. The most effective way to beat down the prejudice," he says resolutely, "is to beat *them* down."

▲
Rudolph Giuliani: He always goes for the long ball.

Giuliani now supervises 130 lawyers, about 90 of whom are in the criminal division. Rare is the day that Giuliani's name does not appear in the papers. Media savvy, he is a modern haiku master who can distill a complicated answer into a crisp, fifteen-second sound bite. His critics suggest that he is a glutton for publicity, and that his press conferences are part of a political campaign, the office to be determined later. But Giuliani responds that it is not a crime to want to go into politics; anyway, that is for the future. For now, publicity is a necessary weapon in his crusade against organized crime. "The only way to deliver a deterrent effectively is to publicize it. I want to send a message."

Giuliani believes that the legal system has come to favor the rights of the victimizer over the victim. "During the fifties and sixties," he says, "we socialized the responsibility for crime." The individual, he stresses, not the group, must be held morally responsible.

"Ultimately, you diminish human individuality and importance when you say, 'Oh, well, you're not really responsible for what you did. Your parents or your neighborhood or society is responsible for it.' In fact, if you harm another human being, you're responsible for that."

Giuliani still takes time out for the unexpected. Not long ago, he attended a memorial Mass for Roger Maris at St. Patrick's Cathedral.

Giuliani was that rare thing, a fan who preferred the saturnine Maris over his more popular teammate Mickey Mantle. "Mantle was a better natural hitter," Giuliani explains. "But Maris always went for the long ball, for home runs."

The scouting report on Giuliani would say the same thing.

— *Richard Stengel*

The Electronic Puppet Show

THE MOUSE PRINCESS

by Jerry Bowles

One embodied the barely repressed sexual longings of a newly suburbanized generation. The other represented the urban fears many still had that they would never be more than clumsy, unglamorous, and alone. Apparent opposites, Annette Funicello's Mouse Princess and Penny Marshall's Laverne are, in a sense, the same: electronic updates of that classic archetype of Italian commedia, the dual-natured Pulcinella.

ANNETTE FUNICELLO, dream girl of the fifties, first love to a generation, a breathing reincarnation of malt shops, sock hops, penny loafers, ponytails, and slumber parties, sits in a high-backed wicker chair sipping scotch and smoking a Lark on an ordinary afternoon in Encino.

She is a beautiful child-woman. The afternoon California sun filters through the drapes behind, casting pools of light on her dark brunette hair and accentuating her porcelain-like face and oversized eyes. She seems, at this moment, a perfect product of an artistic union of Botticelli and Walter Keene. The innocence has returned. American International nearly destroyed that forever with those beach party pictures in which Annette came across as a fat, disingenuous little creature with horribly teased hair and skin that never tanned. What we have here is an older, more mature Annette, who, at thirty-two, seems to have regained that peculiar charm that dazzled fourteen million kids daily on the "Mickey Mouse Club."

"The Mouse Club was the happiest time of my life," she says. "I know people think this is goody-goody. They say 'Annette, you're sugar-coating it. It couldn't have been that good.' But it really was the happiest days of my life."

To understand just what she meant to her generation, you have to go back a bit and pick up a little history.

Joe and Virginia Funicello moved their family out from Utica, New York, in 1947, settling in Studio City where Joe opened a filling station and garage. The Funicellos were, and still are, a close-knit Italian family. They had two boys, Joey and Mike, and a pretty, dark-eyed girl named Annette, who wanted to be a ballerina. She took dance lessons.

Walt Disney saw her dancing at the Burbank Starlight Bowl one night and asked her dance teacher to bring her in to audition for the "Mickey Mouse Club." It was to be his major contribution to the show.

"I worshipped Mr. Disney," Annette says. "I loved everything he stood for. I could see his love for children. I found him very shy. If there was a member of the crew who said 'damn' or 'hell,' he was gone the next day. He was so protective of the kids."

THE "MICKEY MOUSE CLUB" premiered on ABC on October 3, 1955, and became an immediate sensation with the kids, though the critics were cool. The Funicello kid, particularly, worked out better than anybody could have imagined.

"Until the mail started coming in," one studio exec recalls, "everybody in the studio expected someone like Cubby O'Brien to steal the show.

"Annette was the last person anybody at Disney's or ABC would have picked. She had a nice smile and a sweet personality and that was all." But by the end of the first week, the mail response was such that Annette was on her way to becoming a genuine 1950s-style legend.

The irony, of course, is that Annette really was the least-talented first-string Mouseketeer. Bobby Burgess, Lonnie Burr, and Sharon Baird were better dancers; Darlene Gillespie could sing better. But Annette . . . wow, Annette had that certain magic something. Just what that something was, exactly, nobody ever quite figured out. But it quickly became obvious to all that Annette was the star of the show. Within a few weeks she was getting close to four thousand letters a month, nearly one-third of the total for the entire cast.

Disney quickly recognized Annette's enormous capacity to stir the awakening fantasies of a generation of twelve-year-olds. It was all there in those moist letters that poured in. Annette was hot; she was a property that could be sold and, miracle of miracles, she needed almost no packaging. She was exactly what she appeared to be.

Disney was always protective of her image. Several years later it was he who persuaded her not to wear a bikini in those beach pictures, but to opt for a modest one-piece instead.

Although Annette was clearly Uncle Walt's favorite, not everything remained entirely rosy at the studio as an item in the December 18, 1959, *Los Angeles Times* indicates: "Annette Funicello, 17-year-old singer, yesterday made a futile attempt to have Superior Judge Benjamin Landis set aside the 1955 court approval of her seven-year contract with Disney Productions, Inc. The agreement started with $160 weekly salary and rose by option to a present $325.

"Miss Funicello, whose current record, 'First Name Initial,' is among the top 10 hits, complained that the pact was inequitable and that she was without an agent or legal counsel when she signed it.

"Judge Landis dismissed her motion."

The Disney victory was brief, however. A year

153

STILL COMIN' FROM UNDER

THE HOTSHOT DIRECTOR whose career has just been rekindled with a big — make that *BIG* — box office bonanza is barefoot and sitting, her feet tucked up under her, in an overstuffed chair in her Hollywood Hills den.

Behind her hangs a brass wall plaque with the inscription, "Whine Bar." Within minutes it's clear she has earned the medal. First of all, she says, she doesn't like talking about herself. She doesn't like sitting still, can't bear the sound of her own voice (her answering machine greeting is recorded by a housekeeper) and doesn't like having her picture taken: "I'm all nose and teeth," she complains. "I thought directors didn't have to do this."

As the sign says: whine, whine, whine. Does Penny Marshall sound a little like the character she played for so long on "Laverne & Shirley"? Not even her transition from costar in that top-rated TV series to director of the Tom Hanks comedy *Big* has helped bolster her notoriously low self-esteem. No matter that *Big* is a huge hit — the most successful feature ever directed by a woman.

Big deal, shrugs Marshall, now forty-five. "I'm used to comin' from under, so I get a little nervous about people liking something," she says in her Bronx twang. "The whole thing's a crapshoot. I was just tryin' to make a movie. I don't know if it'll mean I'll be more confident on my next job. I've just been lucky in some of the things that walked into my hands."

That luck, the Hollywood grapevine once hissed, stemmed from nepotism. Penny's brother, Garry Marshall, produced *The Odd Couple* and launched her career in 1971 in the role of Jack Klugman's secretary. When that series died, Garry placed Penny in her most infamous role, the loud-mouthed bottle-capper in

▲
Penny Marscharelli, tap dancer, became Penny Marshall/Laverne, bottle-capper.

"Laverne & Shirley" — which he created and produced. Yet Penny still bristles at the "she's-the-boss's-sister" jibes.

"This is a factory business; of course the sons and daughters of people in it are going to go in it." Penny Marshall's family did just that with a vengeance. Penny was the youngest of three children born to Tony Marscharelli, an industrial filmmaker, and his wife, Marjorie, a dance teacher, in the Bronx. Marjorie taught Penny — the whole neighborhood in fact — how to tap. Despite appearances on "The Jackie Gleason Show" and Ted Mack's "Amateur Hour," however, Penny grew bored with dancing. She went off to the University of New Mexico to study math and psychology but dropped out before graduation, married a

football player, had a child, Tracy, and divorced after two years. In 1967, she moved to L.A., met director Rob Reiner, and married him in 1971.

By 1976, when she debuted on "Laverne & Shirley," most of Marshall's family joined Penny and Garry in the credits: sister Ronny as casting director, Dad as coproducer. For the next seven years, until 1983, Penny Marshall as the wisecracking Laverne was as familiar in most households as a well-worn pair of slippers.

Then came a series of breaks — from Rob Reiner in 1979, from "Laverne & Shirley" in 1983, and from the furious social scene with close friend John Belushi in the late 1970s.

"The 1970s was a party period for most of the people I know," says Marshall. "We couldn't deal with being famous. We were all holding on to each other. But the party's over now."

Now Penny Marshall spends her time pondering scripts and projects, an activity that upsets the image she projects — to herself mainly — as lazy.

"Some part of me must be ambitious because I keep doing things," she muses. Not *any*thing. No Shakespeare: "I can barely speak English," she quips. "And I won't ever act in a movie I'm directing. I could never look at myself that long."

The Whine Bar is open and Penny Marshall is still serving.

— *Tom Cunneff*

---

later Annette was back in court and this time she won. Her salary was immediately raised to $500 a week with regular increases up to $1,050 a week at the end of four years. She was also guaranteed forty weeks employment a year.

Altogether, during her nine years under contract to Disney Productions, Annette earned a quarter of a million dollars.

On January 9, 1965, at the age of twenty-two,

Annette married her agent, Jack Gilardi. Her marriage, however, was the beginning of the end of Annette, the performer. "When I have babies," Annette said, right after her marriage, "I don't want them brought up by a nurse. I'll either quit the movies entirely, or limit my pictures to one a year."

Unlike the thousand other starlets who have taken the pledge, Annette really meant it. ❧

GROWING UP WITH PERRY

by Lorenzo Carcaterra

If television is theater in the home, then it is to Italian American entertainers such as Perry Como that we are indebted for evolving a style of theater suited to the living room. A relaxed intimacy is the hallmark of the style. The content may well owe something to Tony Pastor and his "clean" variety shows. It is on television where this "cool" personality — itself evolved out of the "hot" character typical of earlier immigrants — finds its ideal forum.

Perry Como, first of the South Philadelphia crooners

▼

THE FAMILY SAT together. My mother settled in at the far right of the couch, next to the battered bureau with the cracked lamp. My father sat toward the left, a mug of bubbling seltzer balanced on his knee. I was crunched in the middle, facing a nineteen-inch Zenith black-and-white, topped by a Christopher Columbus flower boat and the framed pictures of three grandchildren. My parents' best friends, Ada and Louie, sat on the second couch, next to the small bookcase, under a portrait of a Venetian gondolier, a bowl of pretzels between them. It was 9 p.m. on a cold midwinter night, one week before Christmas.

We sat and waited for the start of the "Perry Como Special," with guest star Claudine Longet.

In Italian American homes, watching Perry Como, a former South Philadelphia barber turned crooner, was a twice-a-year Easter and Christmastime ritual. Italian moms saw him as the complete man — religious, devoted to wife and family, a gifted singer. Italian fathers sat and watched out of habit, ending up as teary-eyed as their wives when Como hit those "Ave Maria" high notes. Italian children watched because they had no other choice. He appeared on screen, surrounded by well-lit trees and fake falling snow, the sounds of an off-camera chorus filling the room, a dignified white-haired man with a gentle face and cream-colored sweater. The first song, sung softly and with passion, was "Silver Bells."

"He looks so young," Ada said with respect, and in Italian. "He never seems to get old."

"He leads a good life," my mother said, shooting a negative glance at my father. "He really loves his wife."

My mother had never even seen a picture of Mrs. Como. Perry himself never talked about her. The Italian women of the neighborhood held her up as a model of a perfect wife. In truth, for all we knew, Perry Como could have been living with Diana Ross.

"The money never went to his head," my father said, as Perry and little Donny and Marie plowed into a rousing rendition of "Jingle Bell Rock."

"Not like Dean Martin," my mother said, sipping a cup of hot tea with milk. "I don't watch his show since he left Jeannie."

155

Como mixed his seasonal songs with timeworn routines and heart-tugging dialogue. For the people in my living room and in the East Bronx, a predominantly Italian neighborhood, the one-hour special served two purposes — the music brought them back to native soil and memories of happier holidays, while the quiet dignity of Perry Como showed them that success in America could still keep a good man simple and pure.

Claudine Longet came on to sing something in French. Her hair was in the flipped-up Alberto VO-5 fashion of the day, the dress tight and short, the voice an Alvin & the Chipmunks squeak. This was pre–Spider Sabich time, when she was married to Andy Williams, a full-time wife who sang holiday songs for Andy and his friends.

"She's not a bad actress, this kid," my father said.

"She played a blind girl on 'Combat'," my mother said.

"Vic Morrow saved her from the Germans," my father said.

"I can't watch that show," Ada said. "Vic Morrow looks like my brother Dominick, God rest his soul."

In the years prior to the TV specials, Perry Como had his own weekly show. In fact, he had several musical variety shows; they were very popular. They made Como a millionaire and gave us Italian Americans something to watch in the days before "The Untouchables."

Perry would always, at some point in the program, sing a song with a group of young children, further fueling his Mr. Good Guy image. To my family, these little children were not professional singers hired by the network to work, for scale wages, on the special. They were his grandchildren.

"That's his grandson," my mother said, pointing out a smiling boy no older than ten, dressed in a button-down shirt and black bow tie. "Looks just like him."

"How many children does he have?" my father asked.

"Five, I think," Ada answered. "Maybe six."

"And they all love him," my mother said, looking directly at me. "A good man is always loved."

During the commercials, Louie would stretch, yawn and ask Ada for a refill of his glass of grappa.

At 9:50 p.m., the small, crowded living room with the cracked ceiling turned silent. Louie put out his cigarette and stopped munching pretzels. My father put down his seltzer glass. My mother emptied her teacup. Ada rolled her gum into the ashtray. I was told to sit up and pay attention. Perry was going to sing the "Ave Maria."

At 9:56 everybody was crying. My mother cried because the song brought back memories of her mother who was still alive and had never heard of Perry Como. Ada cried because it made her wish she had become a nun. My father cried because the "Ave Maria" made

him feel pious and allowed him to skip Sunday Mass for another year. My eyes welled with tears because I had taken a hit from Louie's glass of grappa.

And though we all got older, grew further apart, started careers or retired from jobs, every year we could count on Perry staying the same. The voice a mellow hum, the manner as soothing as a sauna, the snow-gray hair relaxed and in place. A hero from another time. The specials still arrived, bundled up for Christmas, springlike for Easter. Only that the audience is older, the set volume played higher, the memories even stronger.

I think of Perry Como during the holidays. I even tried getting my own family to watch the special this past Christmas — without much success. My German/WASP wife prefers Lou Reed, Dave Edmunds and Waylon Jennings, three very definite non-Como holiday guests. It took me an entire year to get my five-year-old daughter, Kate, to appreciate "The Three Stooges," so Como would be a definite stretch. My nine-month-old son, Nick, would rather chew the edge of a dining-room chair.

So I watched alone, in my living room, a bowl of pretzels to my left, a glass of grappa balanced on my knee. It wasn't the same. My mother wasn't jangling her rosary beads between commercials. My father wasn't sucking a mouthful of seltzer-soaked ice cubes. Ada wasn't taking coin-shaped earrings on and off. Louie wasn't sneaking shots of grappa in between pretzel bites.

The house was quiet, the kids asleep, my wife in bed reading. It was 9:50 when Perry Como began the series of songs which would culminate with the "Ave Maria." He sat on a bar stool, hands folded across his lap, and sang with an eye toward the studio heavens. At 9:56, as my family and friends before me had done, I wiped a handful of tears from my eyes. It must have been the grappa. ❧

LIFE AFTER GODFREY

AT APPROXIMATELY 11:28 on the morning of October 19, 1953, Arthur Godfrey brought an era to a close in just thirty-seven words.

"That was Julie's swan song with us," Godfrey announced, as his Italian golden boy finished singing. "He goes now out on his own, as his own star, soon to be seen on his own program, and I know you wish him Godspeed. I do. 'Bye, 'bye!"

And so twenty-three-year-old Julius LaRosa was fired on live television, in front of seven million viewers — a public firing without precedent in the history of the industry. Dazed by the outraged reaction of newspapers and public, Godfrey told the press he had fired LaRosa because the boy had "lost his humility."

Julie was a frightened and sobbing figure. Panic seized him; he forgot that, quite apart from his paycheck from Godfrey, his agent had guaranteed him $100,000 annually.

"All I knew was that my steady job was gone," Julius says. "I kept telling my family that now Mama would have to go back to work, and we'd lose our new house in Mount Vernon, and I couldn't buy that extra suit of clothes. All my publicity was negative publicity — I was Julius LaRosa: freak."

TWO YEARS LATER Julius LaRosa, solo entertainer, had built himself into a million dollar Las Vegas annual showroom act. Since then, he seems to be thriving. The new world of luxury is still new to LaRosa, particularly his six-room plush office in Manhattan. He grew up in a four-room railroad flat on Jefferson Street, in the Ridgewood section of Brooklyn. Both his parents were immigrants from Sicily; his father, Salvatore LaRosa, was a radio repairman, and his mother, Lucy, worked in a clothes factory, sewing sleeves on coats.

There was a big kitchen where they ate, the living room, the parents' bedroom and the room where Julie and his sister slept. Says Julius, "Sadie is two years older than I am, but because we couldn't afford a bigger apartment, she slept in the same room with me until she was nineteen and I was seventeen. I finally got out of her bedroom by

joining the Navy."

Sal LaRosa used to bring records home, and Julius would sing along with his heroes, Frank Sinatra, Perry Como and other top singers. At school dances and weddings, he was often informally pushed in front of the crowd to sing with the musicians.

His only voice training came in his last year of high school when he rehearsed for months with the two-hundred-strong All-City Chorus for its yearly concert. The idea of taking singing lessons never even occurred to him. "I didn't take lessons until I'd been six months on the Godfrey show," he shrugs eloquently. "Who believed in lessons?"

AS FOR THE firing, most of the time Julius LaRosa is delighted with everything that has happened to him since he first met Arthur Godfrey — and especially since he last met Arthur Godfrey.

"I wasn't really twenty-three when I was fired — I was really an infant, a baby," he says. "I was stunned, and after that, I was terrified. I had to change from being the sheltered Julius LaRosa of the Godfrey show to Julius LaRosa, period.

"I owe Godfrey. Being fired was the greatest thing that could have happened to me."

— *Eleanor Harris*

**Julius LaRosa:
the paradox of
the fortunate
firing**

▼

157

MEDIA ITALIANS WHO AREN'T

I'M NOT SURE why but there's something about non-Italians playing obviously, stereotypically Italian characters that sets my teeth on edge.

Maybe it's just the stereotype. Maybe, that is, if the character were a true flesh-and-blood Italian, it wouldn't matter who played it. But when I'm presented with some script department's need for a spaghetti persona who must be as instantly recognizable as a dancer in blackface, then I bridle.

Admittedly, it's not always that simple. The earliest, and purest, samples of the genre seem now to be the least offensive. Edward G. Robinson as "Little Caesar," for instance, really set the whole crime stereotype rolling. Compared with the real thing in the Televised Crime Hearings — Joe Valachi's blunt face, Frank Costello's disembodied hands dancing to his gravelly voice — Robinson's portrayal is an act of such broad caricature that he might as well be playing Julius Caesar.

Somehow, too, J. Carroll Naish in radio's "Life With Luigi" always managed to pass. Maybe this was due to the lack of a visual component; the program bombed on television. But I remember sitting around the radio with my whole family laughing helplessly at Luigi's efforts to talk (in mangled English) his way out of the amorous clutches of his landlady's daughter, the hungry and homely Rosa.

And when Marlon Brando stuffed his cheeks with cotton and brokenly mumbled his lines as Vito Corleone, there was no gap at all — he was, beyond Italianismo or anything else, the Godfather. As Peter Falk was, beyond all typology, the rumpled and walleyed Italian detective, Columbo.

Somewhere along the way, though, possibly with the pretentious, Walter Winchell–narrated verismo of "The Untouchables," but more noticeably with the Fonz — Arthur Fonzarelli of "Happy Days" — the traditional caricature took on a new and less-amusing cast; or, perhaps one should say, reached a new and even more ludicrous level of parody.

It's still not clear to me what the problem was. Henry Winkler is a fine actor. The character he created as the Fonz rapidly became a pop icon.

And yet . . .

Something is missing. Something is off center.

Beneath the classic Italian stereotypes of lover, wise guy, working-class hero, and untutored philosopher, the guy is just too cozy. Too domesticated. He lacks some Italianate center of gravity that immediately reveals him to be a hybrid — a suburbanite rendering of an old ethnic neighborhood tough. This is all the more curious as the show itself is the brainchild of Garry Marshall — né Marscharelli — who ought to know. And yet anyone who came out of any eastern city where such toughs flourished knows that the Fonz is so milk-fed and designer-bred as to be insupportable

outside the Hollywood hothouse where he grew.

After the Fonz, the disease becomes almost viral. We get Rhea Perlman as Carla on "Cheers," and Estelle Getty as the Sicilian grandma on "The Golden Girls." The problem with both is similar. They play for all the right laughs, and mouth all the right "tough broad" lines. But aside from the obvious parody, something is by now noticeably lacking. Again, I think it is that center of gravity. Estelle Getty is simply too light — too lighthearted, too lightning-tongued, too light of limb even — to convince anyone who knows. A true Sicilian nonna has weight — weight of tone, of mind, of flesh. She doesn't crack jokes; she crackles, she sneers, she rumbles over opposition like runaway lava.

The worst part of all this is that the virus seems to have infected even those characters who might be called "authentic." John Travolta as Vinnie Barbarino in "Welcome Back, Kotter" and Tony Danza as the domestic houseboy in "Who's the Boss?" seem to draw far more from the new, essentially suburban, bloodlines of television than they do from the urban pipelines from which they purport to derive.

Is all this due to ethnic backlash? A general suburbanizing of culture? The wholesale sanitizing of character for teenage minds? It is hard to know.

What does seem clear to me is that the parody has begun to feed on itself to such an extent that the original type — if one can even be said to exist — has got dizzied by its own reflection. In other words, it is no longer discernible, or perhaps even of any concern to those who do such portrayals, who is in fact being portrayed. That being the case, what does it matter whether the actors are Italian or Jewish or Irish or Hindi?

And that is the case in two recent films that consummate the syndrome. In one, *Prizzi's Honor*, neither Jack Nicholson, as the hit man, nor William Hickey as the aged patriarch of the Prizzis, even makes much pretense about being Italian. *Prizzi's Honor* is pure burlesque.

In the other film, *Moonstruck*, some of the major characters are Italian; but the two female leads, Cher and Olympia Dukakis, are not. In Cher's case, particularly, it shows. But does it matter? Do the real Italians in the film, Nicholas Cage — of the Coppola family — or the veteran Vincent Gardenia, play any truer in such a vehicle? Not that I can see. Given the argument, the tone, the self-parodying nature of the whole, it doesn't much matter.

And this perhaps is where it gets to after all, as inevitable as the wholesale proliferation of Pizza Huts, of Pasta Shops run by Peggy Sues. In contemporary America, rough cultural edges must melt away in the microwaves of mass marketing; identifiable ethnic characteristics must eventually lose themselves in ever more stylized mirrorings of what was never more than a scriptwriter's shorthand anyway. As for those of us who still remember what the shorthand once meant, we will have little choice but to join in the laughter.

It doesn't mean we have to like it, though.

— *Lawrence DiStasi*

THE UNFORGETTABLE DURANTE

by Frank Capra

THE WORLD WAS sunk in economic depression during the late 1930s, so it was easy to understand the grim mien of the passengers on a memorable flight I took across the Atlantic.

Suddenly, one man leaped to his feet and began strutting up and down the aisle like a demented penguin, flapping his arms and hollering in a voice like a jailbreak in Brooklyn: "What holds it up? What holds it up?"

We looked at that merry-eyed man with the Punchinello nose and the hands that kept trying to strangle his battered fedora, and we burst out laughing. And when we laughed, we forgot our worries.

By the end of the flight we were all friends. I have forgotten many of the people I met that night, of course; but I will never forget the one whose antics brought us all together — "Schnozzola," the unforgettable Jimmy Durante. It was his first flight on an airplane, and he did what he did everywhere he went — he made people laugh.

Jimmy was a compassionate clown: He let you know he was bothered by the same things you were, but that if you couldn't change them, you might as well laugh at them. As he often said, "Dem's da conditions dat pervail."

I really came to know Jimmy as a result of a film idea — *The Jimmy Durante Story* — proposed by Frank Sinatra. The film never materialized, but I spent many hours of reminiscence with Jimmy, hovering between laughter and tears as he told me the story of his life.

According to Jimmy, who claimed to remember the event vividly, a distraught midwife attending his birth on February 10, 1893, protested, "Dis ain't da baby — it's da stork!"

Jimmy always joked about it, but his world-famous nose was a secret sorrow to him all his life. Maybe the reason that his comedy was so good-natured was that, from his childhood days on New York's Lower East Side, Jimmy knew what it felt like to be laughed at.

"Every time I went down the street I'd hear, 'Look at da big-nosed kid!'" he said. "And if they said nothin', nothin' at all, I'd shrivel up and think they was sayin', 'What an ugly kid!' Even when I am makin' a fortune on account of the big beak, and while I am out there on stage, laughin' and kiddin', at no time was I ever happy about it."

At the age of ten, Durante enjoyed the distinction of having the loudest newsboy's voice ever heard in lower Manhattan. But he already had his heart set on another job. "I'm passin' the joints on Fourteenth Street between Tird and Fort' avenoos," he remembered. "I peeps under da swingin' doors and keeps thinkin' that the swellest job in da world is da guy what bangs on the pianna. I want to be him!"

Bartolomeo Durante, Jimmy's father, was struggling to raise a family of four children in the three-room apartment behind his barber shop. When Jimmy was sixteen, his father celebrated the occasion by giving his son his first shave. And when he learned that Jimmy had musical ambitions, he bought his boy a "pianna" and engaged a music "perfesser."

But soon Jimmy had a confession to make. "Pop," he said regretfully, "I can't play classical music like you want me to play. I don't feel it. I'd rather go to Coney Island and play ragtime."

"Coney Island? No, no, my son. Carnegie Hall."

"Pop. Imagine what dey'd do if I came out in Carnegie Hall and dey see dis nose. Dey'd laugh at me, Pop — no matter how

Durante. The very name revives the feeling of one of the most beloved performers in memory. No one can say quite why, but it must have something to do with the expressiveness of the face. The Durante look was the look of Everyman. It said, whatever you have suffered, I have suffered too, and more — for my nose is bigger, my language more fractured. And yet I laugh.

▶

Durante began as a piano player and nightclub owner in the 1920s.

160

good I played."

After a pause, Bartolomeo said, "God works in inscrutable ways. He'll take care of you. Go ahead. Go to Coney Island."

BY 1923 JIMMY DURANTE had a nightclub, the Club Durant on Fifty-eighth Street just east of Broadway, and two partners — a singer and dancer named Eddie Jackson who didn't read music, and a former vaudevillian and singer named Lou Clayton.

The comedy team of Clayton, Jackson and Durante became the toast of the town. The columnists raved about them. "A good part of the fun of watching Durante," wrote an admirer, "is in the way we're with him and love him, the way we spot him for a good and happy guy."

But Clayton said it best: "You can warm your hands on this man."

Now their jokes were getting a reputation. It was Clayton who called Jimmy's proboscis his schnozz and dubbed him The Great Schnozzola — a nom de guerre listed in *Who's Who in America*.

One of the funniest bits about it was Jimmy telling of a hot, muggy day at the beach. Flies landed all over him. He suffered them without complaint until one walked on his nose.

"Just for dat," said Jimmy, "you *all* get off."

The act was funny and Hollywood noticed; so did Broadway. The trio's Broadway debut was in 1929 in Ziegfeld's *Show Girl*, and their movie debut in Paramount's *Roadhouse Nights*. Then Jimmy got a long-term Hollywood contract, and the team broke up. Clayton became Jimmy's business manager, and there followed over twenty films in ten years, and several more Broadway musicals.

BAD TIMES CAME to Durante in the early 1940s. His career had waned so badly that the only part he could get was in a Gene Autry Western called *Melody Ranch*.

"I'd never rode a horse, and the horse had never been rode," said Jimmy, "so we started on even terms. It was a catastrastroke."

Clayton got Durante two weeks of radio and nightclub bookings in New York, but Jimmy didn't want to leave his wife Jeanne, by then terminally ill with cancer. She insisted he go.

After the first radio show, he anxiously telephoned her across the continent. "I liked the program, Jimmy," she said. "It was very good."

That night he slept soundly for the first time in weeks. But in the morning a call came from Jeanne's mother telling him his wife of twenty-two years was dead.

Durante entertained to forget his grief; watching him, the war-weary crowds forgot theirs. It was a time of terrible casualty lists: The whole country needed to take its mind off its troubles, and at age fifty Durante found himself making a sensational comeback. Before 1943 was over, he had a network radio show.

Radio was the perfect medium to capture what critic Gilbert Seldes called "Durante's inspired, head-long rush at a word — let the consonants fall where they may." His writers were under strict orders to write the real words in the scripts — and let Jimmy bollix them up naturally. Durante could be counted on to turn "corpuscles" into "corpsuckles," "non-fiction" into "non-friction," "cataclysmic" into "casamclysmic." For Durante, sight reading was a constant catas-trastroke — and a joy forever.

But at the end of each program he changed from his clowning manner to an attitude of utter serious-ness, and said tenderly, "Goodnight, Mrs. Calabash — wherever you are."

The identity of Mrs. Calabash became what the *New York Times* called "a national mystery" — but Durante never told. Even clowns have their secrets.

Still, if radio and the stage had launched Jimmy's comeback, it was on television that we could all see his unforgettable facial expression and body language. As critic Philip Hamburger said in the *New Yorker:* "I have known for many years that Durante is a great man, but it has taken his television appearances to make me aware of the extent of his greatness. He seems to have an uncanny instinct for this new and baffling medium. He knows, for example, that the tele-vision camera picks up the slightest gesture and the faintest expression, and gives each special emphasis by reducing it to something bigger than life. Durante has caught on to the fact that when a television performer blinks, that blink is the equivalent of a toss of the head on the orthodox stage."

He wrote songs to fit his unique personality: "I Ups Ta Him, And He Ups Ta Me"; "I'm Jimmy That Well-Dressed Man"; and "Did You Ever Have the Feelin' That You Wanted To Go, Still You Have the Feelin' That You Wanted To Stay?"

And he had been right when he talked with his father about his choice of career — practically any jux-taposition of Jimmy Durante and classical music struck audiences as hilarious. In his TV specials of the fifties and sixties he clowned with concert-hall greats — the Met's Lauritz Melchior and Helen Traubel; concert pianist José Iturbi.

When Miss Traubel arrived in the armor of Brun-hilde, complete with metal breastplate and spear, Jimmy cried: "Holy smoke! She's been drafted!"

And when he declared in a song called "Toscanini, Tchaikovsky, and Me" that "We are definitely da Big Three!" it brought down the house.

In those days in the fall of 1959, when I was listen-ing to Jimmy tell me the story of his life, he was a happy man. He had ended his regular Saturday-night, half-hour television show at the height of its popularity. He still appeared on TV once or twice a year as a guest on variety or comedy shows or in specials.

He was so well fixed financially, he said, that his house had two swimming pools — "one for swimmin' and one for rinsin' off."

Maybe it was for the best that a film was never made of Durante's life. He had a wonderful life, it was a wonderful story — but what actor could really do justice to The Great Schnozzola? ❧

NICE GUY FINISHES FIRST

by Carey Winfrey

ALAN ALDA WAS born Alfonso D'Abruzzo in an apartment on Manhattan's Third Avenue at Thirty-second Street. In that Depression year of 1936, his father, Robert Alda — then only twenty-one and far from being a star — was a singer and straight man at various Catskill watering spots.

Alan Alda made his debut in a high chair in one of his father's sketches at the age of six months. It was there, the elder Alda recalls, "that he got his first laugh in the business."

By the age of three, the younger Alda had become a backstage regular at the burlesque theater where his father was master of ceremonies. "It's a wonderful place to learn about the theater," he remembers, "the place where you see both the trick and how the magician does it. It's also a wonderful place to learn about people. The strippers and chorus girls were just people to me."

As for his father, "I adored him," says Alda. "Some of my earliest memories were walking in the street, holding his hand next to my cheek, just loving his presence. He was a very sweet, warm father."

In 1943, having landed a contract with Warner Brothers, Robert Alda installed his family in what the son remembers as "an ugly little shack in Hollywood," and had just begun portraying George Gershwin in *Rhapsody in Blue* when his seven-year-old son was stricken with polio.

During Alan's long, painful convalescence, his parents had to apply boiling-hot blankets to his stiffened muscles every waking hour for the better part of a year.

He spent most of the next two years in a swimming pool, strengthening his weakened muscles. Alan Alda not only credits his full recovery to the treatment, but traces his strong feminist sympathies to it as well.

"I came to realize," he said, "that I probably owe my life — and if not my life, the fact that I'm not crippled — to two women: my mother, who recognized polio's symptoms, and to

The comic face is often a mask, its tension derived from the contrast between play and reality. Although Alan Alda portrayed the womanizing, wisecracking cynic, Hawkeye Pierce, on TV, in real life he is a committed feminist and nice guy. Conversely, Lou Costello's overweight, hapless clown revealed little of the gifted athlete who not only resented every slap he got from Bud Abbott, but took every opportunity to get even behind the scenes.

▶
Alan Alda as Hawkeye Pierce of "M*A*S*H"

Elizabeth Kenny, the famous Sister Kenny, who figured out the treatment. Which to me shows that sexism is not just impolite, it can be lethal."

ALAN ALDA'S FIRST major Broadway success came as the male lead in the 1964 production of *The Owl and the Pussycat*, and two years later he received a Tony nomination as the best musical actor for his role in *The Apple Tree*. When that show closed, he headed west, there to all but drop out of sight in a festival of forgettable films.

Then came the script for a new television comedy series, based on a Robert Altman film called *M*A*S*H*, about life in a mobile Army surgical hospital during the Korean War.

Alda thought the pilot script was the best he'd ever read, but was reluctant to move to California (home by then was New Jersey). He also worried that the show would turn into a "thirty-minute commercial for the Army." At his wife's urging, however, he finally accepted the part of Capt. Benjamin Franklin (Hawkeye) Pierce, the skirt-chasing, brass-baiting surgeon who wields a sense of humor as sharp as his scalpel.

"M*A*S*H" became an authentic television classic. Alda himself, elevated to superstardom, won four Emmy awards for his contributions to the series. He is the only person to be honored by the National Academy of Television Arts and Sciences as an actor, a writer, and a director.

While he is properly grateful for the role of Hawkeye, he believes it has affected perceptions of him and had something to do with why he was pilloried in *Same Time, Next Year*, ignored in *California Suite* and labeled "bland" in *The Seduction of Joe Tynan*.

In those films, he complained to me, "I tried to play characters that were distinct, true to the characters as written. My impression is that if I had played them like Hawkeye, I would have been better accepted. Some critics were thrown by the fact I wasn't this person they had come to like."

If Alda has one obsession in a life divided between acting and directing and writing, between Los Angeles and suburban New Jersey, it is time, or the lack of it.

"I do seem to be driven," he admits. If a movie doesn't grab him in the first few minutes, he will leave; he will not sign autographs because it takes too long.

"One of the reasons I work so hard," he says, paraphrasing Jean-Paul Sartre, an early hero, "is to hold off despair and meaninglessness another day. Life is, after all, essentially absurd, and I think that by working you have less time to think about that." ❧

WHEN HE WAS GOOD . . .

HE WAS BAPTIZED Louis Francis Cristillo. Reared in Paterson, New Jersey, he was instilled with the American success story: He wanted to be loved, enjoyed, acclaimed.

Everyone adored Charlie Chaplin, so Lou studied the little tramp, seeing *Shoulder Arms* twenty-five times until he could repeat every scene, every gesture. The later Chaplin estimate — that Lou was the best clown since silent films — must have pleased him.

He was intensely human, in both his faults and his virtues. Morrie Davis, business manager at Universal Studios, favored the analogy of the little girl with the little curl in the middle of her forehead.

When he was good . . .

At Christmas, for instance. Besides the festival of giving he made it, he had another ritual. Weeks before the holiday, he went to nearby grocery stores and said to the manager, "I'm going to spend a thousand dollars in your place; what kind of deal can we make?"

The goods were assembled on picnic tables at the Costello house. Lou then made a list of families in need: studio workers, burlesque buddies down on their luck. The bags were loaded into a station wagon and delivered on the day before Christmas — always with instructions that under no circumstances could the donor's identity be revealed.

BUT WHEN HE was bad . . .

The Dean Martin affair illustrates Lou's dual nature. It began in Philadelphia in 1946, when Bud and Lou were appearing at the Earle Theatre. After their final appearance each night, Lou and Eddie Sherman visited the nightclubs Eddie had known as a Philadelphia booker.

One club was called the Walton Roof. Lou and Eddie arrived for the show, which featured a singer with handsome Italian looks marred only by a large, aquiline nose. The owner confided: "I noticed you watching that guy Martin. I want to give you a tip: steer clear of him. He's got thirty different managers and each has got a piece of him. And . . . he drinks."

Upon returning to California, Sherman

▲
**Lou Costello: His
"Who's on First?"
routine with Bud Abbott
became a classic.**

was telephoned by Lou's New York lawyer. "Lou had me go to Philadelphia yesterday to sign a contract for him to manage Dean Martin," he said. "I think Lou is going to want you to represent the guy. By the way, Lou wants to get Martin's nose fixed, and I've got to find a surgeon who can do the job."

The surgery was performed, and Martin went to work for a very short while for Lou Costello. After only a few engagements, Lou's lawyer called Costello to report that the singer had charged merchandise amounting to $2,000. Costello instantly soured on his new singer. "Get rid of him," he said.

Dean Martin joined with Jerry Lewis in 1946, and Martin and Lewis soon became the hottest team since . . . well, since Abbott and Costello. Curiously Lou seemed pleased, and when Martin and Lewis opened at Ciro's in Hollywood, he reserved a front-row table. At the end of the performance, while Jerry Lewis hurried to pay respects at the Costello table, Dean Martin didn't even stop to say hello.

Costello telephoned Eddie Sherman the next day. He was irate. "Look, I got out that contract I had with Dean Martin," he said. "It still has two years to run. I'm gonna sue the bastard for breach."

"What are you talking about?" Eddie said. "You said drop the guy. People heard you say drop him."

"That don't matter. I still got a contract."

Sherman argued that a suit would be a mistake. It would only be construed as an act of professional jealousy.

"I don't care. Nobody's gonna slough me off. If he had just come over and sat down at the table, okay," Costello said. "But now I'm gonna make him pay."

Lou filed his suit. Martin's lawyer said the singer was broke. Eddie Sherman suggested borrowing from Hal Wallis, who had Martin under contract for films. The $20,000 was paid.

"Now make yourself a big man, and tear up the check," Costello was urged.

"Like hell I will," Costello said.

He then bet the entire $20,000 on a horse that ran eighth.

— *Bob Thomas*

The Legends of Sport

CHEERS FOR THE CLIPPER

by Gay Talese

ACROSS FROM HER portrait in the living room, on a coffee table in front of a sofa, is a sterling-silver humidor that was presented to him by his Yankee teammates at a time when he was the most talked-about man in America, and when Les Brown's band had recorded a hit that was heard day and night on the radio:

> . . . From Coast to Coast, that's all
>   you hear
> Of Joe the One-Man Show
> He's glorified the horsehide sphere
> Jolting Joe DiMaggio
> . . . Joe . . . Joe . . . DiMaggio . . .
> We want you on our side . . .

The year was 1941, and it began for DiMaggio in the middle of May after the Yankees had lost four games in a row, seven of their last nine, and were in fourth place, five-and-a-half games behind the leading Cleveland Indians. On May 15th, DiMaggio hit only a first-inning single in a game that New York lost to Chicago, 13-1; he was barely hitting .300 and had greatly disappointed the crowds that had seen him finish with a .352 average the year before and .381 in 1939.

He got a hit in the next game, and the next, and the next. On May 24th, with the Yankees losing 6-5 to Boston, DiMaggio came up with runners on second and third and singled them home, winning the game, extending his streak to ten games. But it went largely unnoticed. Even DiMaggio was not conscious of it until it had reached twenty-nine games in mid-June. Then the newspapers began to dramatize it, the public became aroused, they sent him good-luck charms of

He may well have been the greatest of them all. His grace, his courage, and the apparent ease with which he played the game made him a hero celebrated as often in novels, songs, and movies as he was in Little Italys across the land. When this son of a Sicilian fisherman landed the premiere female icon of the age, it was as if the dream merchants had conspired to crown Horatio Alger with the luck of Sir Lancelot. After that, who knew what was possible?

every description, and DiMaggio kept hitting, and radio announcers would interrupt programs to announce the news, and then the song again: "*Joe . . . Joe . . . DiMaggio . . . We want you on our side. . . .*"

Sometimes DiMaggio would be hitless his first three times up, the tension would build, it would appear that the game would end without his getting another chance — but he always would, and then he would hit the ball against the left-field wall, or through the pitcher's legs, or between two leaping infielders. In the forty-first game, the first of a double-header in Washington, DiMaggio tied an American League record that George Sisler had set in 1922. But before the second game began, a spectator sneaked onto the field and into the Yankee's dugout and stole DiMaggio's favorite bat. In the second game, using another of his bats, DiMaggio lined out twice and flied out. But in the seventh inning, borrowing one of his old bats that a teammate was using, he singled and broke Sisler's record, and he was only three games away from surpassing the major-league record of forty-four set in 1897 by Willie Keeler while playing for Baltimore when it was a National League franchise.

An appeal for the missing bat was made through the newspapers. A man from Newark admitted the crime and returned it with regrets. And on July 2, at Yankee Stadium, DiMaggio hit a home run into the left-field stands. The record was broken.

He also got hits in the next eleven games, but on July 17th in Cleveland, at a night game attended by 67,468, he failed against two pitchers, Al Smith and

◄ Joe DiMaggio: his stoicism while playing on painful heel spurs near the end of his career impressed some fans more than the records he set.

Jim Bagby, Jr., although Cleveland's hero was really its third baseman, Ken Keltner, who in the first inning lunged to his right to make a spectacular backhanded stop of a drive and, from the foul line behind third base, he threw DiMaggio out. DiMaggio received a walk in the fourth inning. But in the seventh he again hit a hard shot at Keltner, who again stopped it and threw him out. DiMaggio hit sharply toward the shortstop in the eighth inning, the ball taking a bad hop, but Lou Boudreau speared it off his shoulder and threw to the second baseman to start a double play and DiMaggio's streak was stopped at fifty-six games. But the New York Yankees were on their way to winning the pennant by seventeen games, and the World Series too, and so in August, in a hotel suite in Washington, the players threw a surprise party for DiMaggio and toasted him with champagne and presented him with this Tiffany silver humidor that is now in his San Francisco living room. . . .

JOE DIMAGGIO WAS not born in San Francisco but in Martinez, a small fishing village twenty-five miles northeast of the Golden Gate. Zio Pepe had settled there after leaving Isola delle Femmine, an islet off Palermo where the DiMaggios had been fishermen for generations. But in 1915, hearing of the luckier waters off San Francisco's wharf, Zio Pepe left Martinez, packing his boat with furniture and family, including Joe who was one year old.

San Francisco was placid and picturesque when the DiMaggios arrived, but there was a competitive undercurrent and struggle for power along the pier. At dawn the boats would sail out to where the bay meets the ocean and the sea is rough, and later the men would rack back their hauls, hoping to beat their fellow fishermen to shore and sell them while they could. Twenty or thirty boats would sometimes be trying to gain the channel shoreward at the same time, and a fisherman had to know every rock in the water, and later know every bargaining trick along the shore, because the dealers and restaurateurs would play one fisherman off against the other, keeping the prices down. Later the fishermen became wiser and organized, predetermining the maximum amount each fisherman would catch, but there were always some men who, like the fish, never learned, and so heads would sometimes be broken, nets slashed, gasoline poured onto their fish, flowers of warning placed outside their doors.

But these days were ending when Zio Pepe arrived, and he expected his five sons to succeed him as fishermen, and the first two, Tom and Michael, did; but a third, Vincent, wanted to sing. He sang with such magnificent power as a young man that he came to the attention of the great banker, A. P. Giannini, and there were plans to send him to Italy for tutoring and the opera. But there was hesitation around the DiMaggio household and Vince never went; instead he played ball with the San Francisco Seals and sportswriters misspelled his name.

It was DeMaggio until Joe, at Vince's recommendation, joined the team and became a sensation, being followed later by the youngest brother, Dominic, who was also outstanding. All three later played in the big leagues and some writers like to say that Joe was the best hitter, Dom the best fielder, and Vince the best singer.

JOE DIMAGGIO LIVES today with his widowed sister, Marie, in a tan stone house on a quiet residential street not far from Fisherman's Wharf. He bought the house almost thirty years ago for his parents, and after their deaths he lived there with Marilyn Monroe. There are some baseball trophies and plaques in the small room off DiMaggio's bedroom, and on his dresser are photographs of Marilyn Monroe, and in the living room downstairs is a small painting of her that DiMaggio likes very much: It reveals only her face and shoulders and she is wearing a very wide-brimmed sun hat, and there is a soft sweet smile on her lips, an innocent curiosity about her that is the way he saw her and the way he wanted her to be seen by others — a simple girl, "a warm bighearted girl," he once described her, "that everybody took advantage of."

The publicity photographs emphasizing her sex appeal often offended him, and a memorable moment for Billy Wilder, who directed her in *The Seven-Year Itch*, occurred when he spotted DiMaggio in a large crowd of people gathered on Lexington Avenue in New York to watch a scene in which Marilyn, standing over a subway grating to cool herself, had her skirts blown high by a sudden wind below. "What the hell is going on here?" DiMaggio was overheard to have said in the crowd, and Wilder recalled "I shall never forget the look of death on Joe's face."

He was then thirty-nine, she was twenty-seven. They had been married in January of that year, 1954, despite disharmony in temperament and time: He was tired of publicity, she was thriving on it; he was intolerant of tardiness, she was always late. During their honeymoon in Tokyo an American general had introduced himself and asked if, as a patriotic gesture, she would visit the troops in Korea. She looked at Joe. "It's your honeymoon," he said, shrugging, "go ahead if you want to."

She appeared on ten occasions before a hundred thousand servicemen, and when she returned she said, "It was so wonderful, Joe. You never heard such cheering."

"Yes I have," he said. ❧

THE KID RING LARDNER MISSED

IT IS PLEASANT to contemplate the good fortune which has come the way of Lawrence Peter Berra. If it is coming to any athlete, he has it coming to him. Aside from being a person of unusual decency and natural charm, he has, from a fairly inauspicious beginning in the big leagues, achieved over the last dozen years a place among the memorable players in the long history of the game — one of that extremely small number of players who have performed in the years following World War II who is a certainty to be elected to the Hall of Fame. Over and above this, Berra is a personality of such original force and magnetism that sometimes it has even obliterated his real stature as a player. He is, as Joe Trimble has called him, "The Kid Ring Lardner Missed" — the last of a glorious line of baseball's great characters.

While there is assuredly little aesthetic splendor about the way Yogi bunches himself at the plate, he handles the bat beautifully, with a delicacy and finesse which few place hitters approach and which is rarer still, of course, for a power hitter. He has magnificent timing, releasing his wrist action at the last split second. This explains why when Berra is hitting, he can hit anybody or anything, including more bad balls than anyone since Joe Medwick. In the 1955 Series — not the 1956 Series, in which he hit three home runs and batted in ten runs, but the 1955 Series, in which he made ten hits and batted .417 — Yogi put on one of the finest demonstrations of straightaway hitting in modern times, meeting the ball right between the seams again and again and lining it like a shot over the infield, very much in the fashion of Paul Waner and Nap Lajoie. "There's no one more natural or more graceful than Yogi when he's watching the pitch and taking his cut," Phil Rizzuto said not long ago. "He's all rhythm up there, like Ted Williams."

Williams and Berra are alike in one other respect: They are talkative men. Splendidly endowed as Williams is in this department, he is simply not in Berra's class. In truth, no player in the annals of baseball has been, and those who potentially might have challenged his preeminence made the mistake of playing the wrong position. Stationed behind the plate, Berra has a steady flow of new

faces to ask how things are going, and during lulls between batters there is always the umpire. Early this year Casey Stengel, a fairly articulate man himself, had a few words to say about Berra's verbosity. Asked if he considered Berra to be the best late-inning hitter in the game, a claim many have made for him, Casey replied that he didn't know about that.

"I'd have to look into it," he said. "He could be the best late-inning hitter in baseball because he's got to hit sometime during the game, and he is a very bad early-inning hitter.

"Sometimes Mr. Berra allows himself to grow careless. He forgets to start the game with the first inning. He's out there behind the plate saying hello to everybody in sight. Oh, Mr. Berra is a very sociable fellow. He acts like home plate is his room."

— *Herbert Warren Wind*

▲

Berra the wit: Upon buying his first star-quality mansion, Yogi told a friend, "Wotta house — nothin' but rooms!"

Fast Eddie

by Jim Murray

When I was going to the track every week with my father, it never occurred to me to ask why the horses ran so fast. Having read The Black Stallion, *I figured they just liked to, especially if they loved their jockeys. But for Eddie Arcaro, it was simpler: Go fast, and you win; go easy, or be ambivalent, or scared, and you lose. Fast Eddie won a lot. My father and I didn't.*

I F I WERE a horse today, I'd be tempted to throw a party — champagne, fillies, barn dancing, all kinds of horsing around.

You see, George Edward Arcaro, the well-known bongo drummer and horseback rider, has decided to hang up his tack. To understand what this can mean to a horse, just imagine the feelings of the crew of the *Bounty* when they put Captain Bligh to sea in that lifeboat, or the Russians when they got word Stalin was running a temperature.

There are two ways to win horse races — by guile or by terror. Eddie Arcaro chose the knout. His riding style, as far as the horse was concerned, was early cossack, a combination of Genghis Khan, Attila the Hun, and Jack the Ripper in goggles and silks. The horse was running not for his oats but for his life because he knew the quicker he got to the finish line, the quicker he could start to heal. There might have been times when the trainer or the stable wasn't trying. But there never was a time when G. Edward Arcaro wasn't. There were times, in fact, when the horse seemed superfluous.

Eddie Arcaro never actually carried a dying-run horse across the finish line but he strained so hard his nose frequently made the photo in a dead heat with the horse's. The Arcaro nose, inadequately described as a "banana," was as fine a utensil for sniffing out rancid horseflesh as for good steaks. A jockey's secret of winning is usually the simple "Stay off bad horses." But the Arcaro method was such that even bad horses extended themselves — like deer fleeing a fire.

It is well-established that fear makes supermen of tabby cats, something to do with adrenalin. I don't even know whether a horse has adrenalin. Neither did Eddie Arcaro. But he did know that when they ran scared, they ran faster. He set out to make himself the Dracula of the home-stretch. He steered 4,779 terror-striken horses into the winning circle for a gross take of $30,039,543.

It wasn't only the horse Signor Arcaro terrified. It was also the other riders. A man with the nice gentle disposition of a bear with cubs — or ulcers — Eddie possessed riding tactics that were legend. He took the position that whatever he couldn't run past, he could run through. Impartial observers say his technique for snatching saddlecloths showed that pickpocketing lost a first-rate suspect when someone hoisted Arcaro into a saddle.

He knocked so many riders in the infield in the early days that there wasn't a boy in the tack room who would dare let Eddie Arcaro get outside him. As a result, he was on the ground every other month, which had the effect of keeping his weight down, since it is commonly known that the simplest way to keep the weight down is not to eat and the simplest way not to eat is not to be able to afford it. Eddie spent one whole year on foot in 1942 for trying to deliver a rider, Vincenzo Nodarse, to his Maker prematurely, by way of the infield. What happened in the Cowdin Stakes that year was that Nodarse (pronounced Nodarcy) almost became No-Dicey when he came on Arcaro leaving the gate. Arcaro, with blood in his eye, gave chase and drew alongside. "No! No! Eddie! No mean it!" cried Nodarse. "Neither do I," Eddie told him as Nodarse went through the rail.

Eddie won five Kentucky Derbies but he won 4,774 other races because he rode every race as though it were a Kentucky Derby — or as though a lynch mob were after him. It's an axiom around the track that a good rider

172

cannot make a bad horse good but a bad rider can make a good horse bad. Arcaro was the good rider who frequently made bad horses good — or good and scared. In later years, he learned to control his temper. But he never let his horses know it.

He didn't always win races like a fullback on horseback. Sometimes he snatched them like a cutpurse, other times like a card shark. His theory was that 90 percent of the thoroughbred horses didn't give a damn whether they won or not — nor did 10 percent of the jockeys. This percentage leeway gave E. Arcaro plenty of room to become the top race rider of his day. He never took the safe way home but he sometimes took the sneaky way. He won the Manhattan Stakes once with a sprinter in 2:36 1/2. Most horses can walk faster than that but Eddie slickered the routers by pretending his horse was all out to stay in front, a tactic which would never work with Arcaro, who had a built-in clock

in his own brain.

Born the son of a fruit peddler in Cincinnati, Arcaro was never a born rider, except on the back of streetcars. But he was a born competitor. The famous story about him recounted by Roger Kahn concerns the trainer who first watched him scrambling all over a horse's back at Caliente. "You'll kill yourself," the trainer told him coldly. "If you can ride a horse, then I can make a watch." Arcaro said nothing but continued to accept mounts. Later, after he had won cups and a stable contract, he turned to the trainer innocently and said, "OK, now let's see you make a watch."

I got a better idea. Let's see them make another Eddie Arcaro. ❧

▲

Eddie Arcaro: in later years, he learned to control his temper, but he never let his horses know it.

DE PALMA AT INDIANAPOLIS

by Captain Eddie Rickenbacker

THE SAME DAY I saw a picture of Ralph de Palma pushing the gray Mercedes up to the finish line at the Indianapolis speedway in 1912, I read in the newspapers that a young RAF ferry pilot had flown across the Atlantic in less than six hours.

I thought to myself: It's all a question where you're going and what the competition is. The airman left Newfoundland and presently turned up in Scotland, saying the trip was uneventful and all the winds were tail winds. De Palma, on the other hand, chased around a two-and-a-half mile track for more than six hours and after nearly five hundred miles he ended up exactly where he had started. Clear to the end he was the fastest thing on earth that day; then a piece of metal failed and in the time it takes a piston to travel seven inches he was reduced from a sure champion with $20,000 in prize money in his grasp to an empty-handed tail-end Charlie.

That would have crushed most men. But de Palma answered with a show of character that will be remembered as long as the concrete foundations of the Indianapolis Speedway stand. I was there and saw it all. I raced against Ralph de Palma in the Indianapolis 500 on that particular day.

We have to go back many years. William Howard Taft was in the White House; Franklin D. Roosevelt was an unknown New York assemblyman; Christy Mathewson was the sporting hero of the day when de Palma appeared at the five-hundred-mile Memorial Day race with a Mercedes that had the gleam of something taken from a Tiffany showcase.

De Palma had raced the car in Europe. The German builders had given it a watchmaker's care. It hugged the ground and could do 120 miles an hour on the straightaway. But Ralph, besides being a sweet character, and real gentleman, was known to have a heavy foot. He always gave the customers what they wanted, but machinery will take only so much and the spills and breakdowns that came with monotonous regularity gave him the reputation of a hard-luck guy.

Twenty-four cars came up to the line that morning, driven by some very fine sportsmen. Bob Burman was the popular favorite. A rangy, broad-shouldered, handsome guy, he drove a car cut to his measure — a Cutting with a whopping piston displacement. He'd spent a fortune on it. But the grease monkeys in the pit thought it would be a toss-up between him and Bruce-Brown of the National team. Working with Bruce-Brown were Wilcox and Dawson, the latter a test driver for the old Marmon company. Bruce-Brown was all hell-for-leather. The strategy called for him to run the rest of the field to the ground; then one or the other of his teammates would come up from nowhere and win. However, that was not the way things worked out.

I remember the bands were playing "Everybody's Doin' It Now" as we lined up. So as to get the pack off to a flying start Carl Fisher took us around once in a gray Stoddard-Dayton roadster; then he scooted out of the way as the speedometers touched sixty. The morning air was fresh and cool. But in a few minutes the cockpit was as hot and noisy as a foxhole.

De Palma worked out in front in the third lap. The two millionaires' sons, Wishart and Bruce-Brown, were close on his tail and Tetzlaff bounded along in fourth place like a jackrabbit in his Fiat. De Palma soon pushed it up to eighty-three miles an hour — a lap in one minute and forty-nine seconds. He was playing for keeps. The pace was too fast for Knight. On the sixth lap, his Lexington blew a cylinder and he was through. A couple of minutes later Ormsby's

Opel was forced off the track with a busted connecting rod. On the twenty-fifth lap, Bruce-Brown had to go it with broken piston rings. My turn came on the forty-third lap — a broken valve.

So with nearly four hundred miles still to be run, I joined the spectators. I could have used some of the prize money, but if I had to look on, this was certainly the race to see. De Palma was driving with plenty of style, hurling across the turns with little loss in speed. His pit work, too, was the best on the track. The rest of us were lucky to change a tire and clear the pit in sixty seconds. Ralph was in and out in thirty. He looked fine and you felt nothing could stop him. The clock-watchers spread the word that the records were going by the boards. Two days of rain had cooled the brisk track and tires were lasting longer, the cars were going faster. The crowd, which always goes for the winner, gave Ralph a cheer every time he went by the grandstand.

The sun climbed high. You could smell rubber burn as it shrieked over the hot bricks. The pit crews started to flag in the crews at the first sign of wear on the treads. God, it was hot. Only once in my life did water ever again taste as good as the ice water in the galvanized iron buckets at Indianapolis.

De Palma kept his foot down on the floor. In the fourth hundred he raised the average speed to eighty-one miles and increased his lead to seven laps. By then Bob Burman was done for. He jockeyed Tetzlaff out of third place; then two tires let out and the Big Cutting rolled over, but not fast enough to catch him. That left eleven cars. And with de Palma's Mercedes charging around the track making a noise like a battery of five-inch guns, and with that fine lead, it certainly looked as if de Palma had licked the field.

The others were slamming around the track as methodically as Lionel trains; the racket kept up; the grandstand was emptying; everything was as it should be and then a hush fell and you could feel the question forming in eighty thousand minds: "Where's de Palma?" Then the news came from the spotters in the backstretch. De Palma was in trouble; the Mercedes was hitting on two or three cylinders — a broken piston. Dawson caught the frantic signal from his pit men

and poured on coal. The speed went up to ninety miles an hour. But Ralph, when he finally hove in sight, was crawling at dump-wagon speed and from the engine noise you would have thought it was being pounded with sledgehammers.

Ralph started to turn into the pit, but his men waved him out; if he shut off the engine, he was out for good. He went back on the track and crawled, like a hurt animal, up the straightaway. The crowd groaned. He didn't appear for a long time and Joe Dawson and the others kept going round and round. The next time he passed the pits, to start the 199th lap, he was making less than twenty miles an hour.

The books show that the flag went down in front of Dawson at 381.06 minutes — a new record, incidentally. Ten minutes later Tetzlaff finished and won $10,000. And right behind him was Merz in a Stutz, to take third place and $5,000. Then several others rolled home. About that time the Mercedes showed up in the backstretch. It was barely moving. Ralph was steering and pushing from the side, and his mechanic was shoving from behind. I'd say they pushed a mile and a half, clear to the finish line; while the field went by.

The rules say that the car must complete a race under its own power and so de Palma is down on the record book as not finishing. The popular legend is that he pushed the Mercedes to the finish line. Not quite. Technically, he was still one lap short. But eighty thousand people were there; they saw the sweat on his face; they knew what was going through his mind; and I doubt that they cared about the missing lap. They roared out a cheer that has never been heard again in Indianapolis. You have to fail in a peculiar and wonderful way to earn such a cheer. ❧

MASTERS OF

AUTO RACING

Mario Andretti

Michael Andretti

Ralph DePalma

Peter DePaolo

BASEBALL

Lawrence
"Yogi" Berra

Ping Bodie
(FRANCESCO PEZULLO)

Ralph Branca

Roy Campanella

Rocky Colavito

Tony Conigliaro

Dom DiMaggio

Joe DiMaggio

Vince DiMaggio

Carl Furillo

Tommy Lasorda

Harry "Cookie"
Lavagetto

Tony Lazzeri

Ernie Lombardi

Sal Maglie

Billy Martin
(ALFRED MANUEL PESANO)

Phil "The Scooter"
Rizzuto

BASKETBALL

Louis Carneseca

Hank Luisetti

Rollie Massimino

Jim Valvano

BILLIARDS

Willie Mosconi

BOXING

Fred Apostoli

Tony Canzoneri

Angelo Dundee

Johnny
"The Scotch Wop"
Dundee

Rocky Graziano
(ROCCO BARBELLA)

Pete Herman
(PETER GULOTTA)

Jake LaMotta

Ray "Boom Boom"
Mancini

THE GAME

Joey Maxim
(GIUSEPPE BERARDINELLI)

Rocky Marciano
(ROCCO FRANCIS MARCHEGIANO)

Willie Pep
(GUGLIELMO PAPALEO)

FOOTBALL

Lyle Alzado

Alan "The Horse" Ameche

Angelo Bertelli

Nick Buoniconti

Tony Canadeo

Gino Cappelletti

Franco Harris

Daryl Lamonica

Dante Lavelli

Vince Lombardi

Gino Marchetti

Dan Marino

Joe Montana

Leo Nomellini

Vito "Babe" Parelli

Brian Piccolo

Andy Robustelli

Charlie Trippi

GOLF

Gene Sarazen
(EUGENE SARACENI)

Ken Venturi

Donna Caponi Young

HORSE RACING

Eddie Arcaro

ICE SKATING

Brian Boitano

Linda Fratianne

Joan Zamboni

SWIMMING

Matt Biondi

SIDELINES

Bill Gallo
SPORTS CARTOONS

Paul Gallico
SPORTS WRITING

Pete Llanuza
SPORTS CARTOONS

COOL IN THE EYE OF THE STORM

by Lowell Cohn

To most Italian immigrants, the desire of their children to "play games" learned at American school was a sure sign that education rooted in such frivolity was fatal to survival. Ironically, it is this direct and brutal logic that, after a few generations, produces a Vince Lombardi. "Winning isn't the most important thing; it is the only thing" becomes the battle cry of all American sports. Although he is quieter and classier in his pursuit of it, Joe Montana proves to be no less single-minded about the only thing — winning.

"You don't want anyone else who's ever played on a big drive other than him. He's the biggest winner I've ever been associated with."

— RANDY CROSS

"When we walked out and looked in his eyes, you could almost see the ring on his hand."

— BUBBA PARIS

"Joe Montana is not human. I don't want to call him a god, but he's somewhere in between. I have never seen a guy — and I'm sure he did it in college, high school, pee-wee football — that every single time he's had the chips down and people counting him out, he's come back. He's maybe the greatest player who's ever played the game."

— CRIS COLLINSWORTH

WE HAD SEEN Joe Montana lead the 49ers on that last brilliant Super Bowl drive — eight complete passes in two minutes and thirty-six seconds of pure magic.

Shortly afterward, before Montana had changed out of his wet jersey or shaved or showered, he was talking to the press in the lower reaches of Joe Robbie Stadium. As is his custom at times of his greatest heroism, he was giggling shyly. Someone who had never met Montana would have been amazed that this retiring man had just led the 49ers on the greatest drive in Super Bowl history.

Despite his off-field manner, which is often ordinary, even prosaic, Montana is special. When he faces danger he is at his best — a hunter about to down a charging lion with a poison dart. What we don't know is how he does it.

Reporters asked Montana's teammates what Montana did in the huddle to rally them for the winning drive. The answer was always the same.

Nothing.

No one remembers Joe bursting into the huddle and telling the 49ers to "Win one for Walsh!" just in case the head coach decides to retire. There wasn't one instant when Joe ordered Tom Rathman to block better or told Bubba Paris to be on his toes or said he hated the Bengals. He was removed from all that. In

fact, he was outwardly calm, while his mind worked at attacking the Bengals.

Asked what he said to the team at the beginning of the final drive, Montana searched his memory, and then said apologetically, "I didn't say anything at the beginning of the drive. Someone said that we had enough time, but I don't remember who."

Montana simply went about playing quarterback as if the 49ers were ahead and there were still two quarters to go. Randy Cross, who has heard Montana call plays for the better part of a decade, said Joe's voice was the same as it is in the first drive of the most meaningless exhibition game of preseason.

So what is it that makes Joe special? Just this:

Montana has the ability NOT to get caught up in the emotion of the moment. When other guys feel the sweat on their palms, Montana is totally focused on the next play. No distractions. No sickening fear. He doesn't worry what will happen if a play fails. He doesn't tell himself he'll be a hero if he connects for a touchdown. In fact, he seems to have no concept of personal heroism at all. Although what he does is heroic to us, he experiences himself merely as a man doing a job.

There is something else. Sometimes things happen in slow motion for Joe. At the most crucial times, the world slows down and things get big, and he feels as if he has total control. He was in that world when he

179

THE LAST ROMAN

THE TELEVISION SET flung garish shadows on a glossy white wall. The sounds of the football game were wrong for a hospital where silence is encouraged. The man in the bed was unaccustomed to quiet. The life Vinnie Lombardi cherished was in the TV machine, lurid pictures moving across the window of a cabinet. Death was in Vinnie Lombardi's cancer-wasted body.

He seemed to be dozing. Alienated from football by sickness and pain. The quarterback, Sonny Jurgensen, drifted back to throw a pass to Charley Taylor. The music of Lombardi's life came into the room where he lay dying as the multitude in the distant stadium screamed and shouted. The football went up and out and Taylor was there. It hit his hands, and bounced out and fell on the ground and rolled away. The buffs groaned and Lombardi somehow stirred beneath the sheets.

"Did you see that?" asked his wife, Marie, though she thought his eyes had been closed.

"I saw it," he said in that bark of a voice, hoarse from yelling across the years.

The sideline moved. It was as though the roof went off the hospital and the walls melted. He didn't speak like a dying man. He was Vinnie Lombardi, the football coach. It all came out of him, the beautiful rage that was the poetry of his anger. This was his last football team, the Washington Redskins. He was their coach, and he was still trying to reach them with death in the bed with him.

HE WENT OUT with his philosophy unchanged. It was his unshakable theory that man was entitled to nothing free. You worked for what you got, and paid the full price. There were never any sales and Vinnie Lombardi didn't believe you could make any deals for the important things. He was a hard man, and cancer couldn't break him.

The man who had shaped his coaching style was Earl Blaik, whom he had served as an assistant at West Point. Once Blaik, whom Lombardi formally addressed as Colonel, was asked what Lombardi had that turned him into the greatest leader in sports.

"He is intelligent and loud and violent," Blaik said. "Kids love him once they get to know him."

There was a pole on the lawn of his house, and he raised the flag every morning before going to seven o'clock Mass. He was a kind of evangelist, and he preached at you during a normal conversation. He was an apostle of racial equality, and would not stand for prejudice on his squad. The racists, white or black, were traded. It was why his teams had such ferocious unity. He believed that a football team should be a brotherhood, and he used the word *love* when he described how they regarded each other.

ONE OF THE most savage men in football, Jim Taylor, who was Lombardi's heavy ball-carrier at Green Bay, came to the hospital from New Orleans. But he stayed out in the corridor. He was too shaken to enter the room. But Frank Gifford and Alex Webster, the current Giant coach, were among the infrequent visitors.

"What are you doing here?" he said, maintaining that gruffness which he used so eloquently.

They were there because they loved him. I imagine Vinnie Lombardi knew it. After all he had taught them so much about how to love.

— *Jimmy Cannon*

threw the winning pass to John Taylor.

"It happened sort of in slow motion," Montana admitted. He had dropped back to pass, and suddenly, everything slowed down and became totally clear. Joe saw two defenders go after Roger Craig, and he saw Taylor break into the clear, and he threw his pass as if only he and Taylor inhabited the field. Then he lost sight of the ball, heard the screams of triumph, and the world returned to normal speed.

Roger Craig, another 49er with otherworldly concentration, had the same experience. After he had diverted the two defenders, he looked into the end zone for Taylor. "I saw the ball going," he said. "It was like slow motion. I thought I heard music in my ears."

When the game was over, Bengals cornerback Lewis Billups, still stunned, was trying to understand what had happened. "We wanted to be in that situation," he said sadly. "We talked about it all week. We wanted to come down to the last two minutes and the best team wins."

It did. It had Joe Montana. ❧

A Great Story

by W. C. Heinz

Boxing being the brutal sport that it is, very few of its practitioners deserve to be called artists. Willie Pep was one. Where other boxers, even the best, too often lunged or missed with a punch, Pep could always glide in close, land several percussive jabs, and float away before his opponent knew a dance had begun. That he was also small, Italian American, and from Connecticut raised him as close to my ideal in sport as anyone got, before or since.

Willie Pep scores against Sandy Saddler in their first bout.

▼

"HOW DID YOU get my number?" he said on the phone. I had called him one evening late in January at his home in Wethersfield, Connecticut.

"Come on, Willie," I said. "You're not unheard of."

"I'm a has-been," he said. "Nobody remembers me."

He was the greatest creative artist I ever saw in a ring. When I watched him box, it used to occur to me that, if I could just listen carefully enough, I would hear the music. He turned boxing contests into ballets, performances by a virtuoso in which his opponent, trying to punch him out, became an unwilling partner in a dance, the details of which were so exquisite that they evoked joy, and sometimes even laughter.

In 1940 when Guglielmo Papaleo — Willie Pep — turned professional after winning the Connecticut amateur flyweight and bantamweight championships, he was seventeen, still an adolescent. He won fifty-three fights in a row, and then at age twenty, beat Chalky Wright for the featherweight championship of the world. He won another eight before Sammy Angott, the former lightweight champion, a grabber and smotherer and too big for him, outpointed him. Then he won another seventy-three before Sandy Saddler knocked him out in the first of their four fights. In other words, of his first 135 fights, he won all but the one in which he was out-muscled and out-wrestled. In our time we never saw another like him.

"I'm on the Boxing Commission," he said. "It's in the State Building, so see me there. I'm there every day from 8 until 4:30."

He gave me directions, rapidly, for he always talked the way he boxed, the words spurting out. He told me what exit to take from the interstate and what streets and how to get around the park and how to recognize the building. Hartford is a city I once knew and walked, but when I drove down the ramp of the elevated interstate and got into the noontime traffic, I turned into the parking space of the high-rise motel, and checked in. I had lunch, and I took a cab. At my age I had to have something left for Willie Pep.

HE CAME THROUGH the doorway quickly, sticking out his hand. He is five feet five, and he never had any trouble making the 126 pounds, but he was a little heavier now, his fifty-four years in his face, and he was wearing a glen plaid suit and a striped sports shirt open at the neck. He let me down, walking rapidly with those small, quick steps, thrusting the door open, talking.

"It's a good job," he said. "Last year we had about thirty-five wrestling shows, twenty-three boxing shows. We supervise. We check to see a guy hasn't been knocked out in thirty days. If one guy's got forty fights and another's got ten, we don't allow. We go in before the fight and see that they bandage properly. Hugh Devlin is the director. A good guy. I'm under him with Sal Giacobbe."

He led me into the office and introduced me to Devlin, a rather short, gray-haired, smiling man behind one of the gray metal desks. There were three desks, filing cabinets, a metal locker, a weigh-in scale, a sofa and armchair, and a coat rack.

"Hughie was the bantamweight champion of Massachusetts," he said, and then to Devlin, "How many fights you have?"

"I had 121," Devlin said, "and I won 113."

"He was a good fighter," Willie said.

"You weren't bad yourself," I said.

"Thank you," Willie said.

"The greatest I ever saw," Devlin said. "I can still see Willie's fights. I'll never forget them."

"He was a creative genius," I said to Devlin, "and he could do those things because he had the reflexes of a housefly."

"Thank you very much," Willie said, sitting down behind his desk. "That's very kind of you."

"TELL HUGHIE," I said now, "about the time you fought the local boy in the town where the sheriff weighed you in."

"That's right," he said, and then to Devlin, "They didn't have no boxing commission, so the sheriff weighs you in with a gun on his hip. The fight's in the ballpark, so when he calls us to the center of the ring . . ."

"Wait a minute, Willie," I said. "Tell him about the kid at the weigh-in."

"Oh yeah," he said. "So at the weigh-in, the kid I'm gonna box comes up to me and says, 'Mr. Pep, can I have your autograph?' I looked at him, and I said,

'Get away from me, kid. There's people watchin' here. We're boxing tonight, and what are they gonna think?'"

"You were his hero," I said.

"Yeah," he said. "So at the ballpark they got a pretty good crowd, and the referee calls us to the center of the ring to give us the instructions. I look at the kid, and he's white. He's scared stiff. I'm thinking, 'Oh, boy, what kind of fight can this be?' So the bell rings and we move around, and a lot of guys turn white, but this guy is startin' to turn purple. I figure I have to do something, so I threw a right hand over his shoulder, that would look good to the crowd but that would miss, and I stepped inside and grabbed him under the arms, and I said: 'Look, kid. Just relax. These people here paid their money, and we'll give them a show. We'll just box, and you won't get hurt. We'll have a nice evening, and everybody will like it.' That's exactly what I told him."

"And wait until you hear the ending," I said to Devlin.

"So I take my arms out from under his and let him go," Willie said, "and he falls right on his face and the referee counts him out."

"I love that," Devlin said, laughing. "That's a great story."

"WILLIE'S GREATEST WAS the second Saddler fight," Devlin said.

"Great."

Willie's record in *The Ring Record Book and Encyclopedia* is a gallery of great art, from the meticulous miniatures that went only a few rounds to the masterpieces that went the distance. Of the latter, the second Saddler fight in the Garden was the greatest boxing exhibition I ever saw, for Saddler had knocked him out in their first fight and had the height and reach and punch on him. He hurt him the second time, too, cut him under both eyes and over the right, and rocked him time and again, but it was Willie's fight from the first round on when he jabbed Saddler thirty-seven times in succession without a return. There were times when he had Saddler so befuddled that he could stop the dancing and stand right there and rock him back, and, though battered and cut and bruised, he won it big on everybody's card to send the sell-out crowd out into the streets still buzzing, still carrying the electrical charge of it.

"Willie sold a lot of TV sets that night," I was saying now. "In those days, you remember, boxing and Milton Berle sold TVs. Guys who didn't have sets gathered in bars or in the homes of others who had sets to watch the fights, and I'll bet Willie sold a lot that night."

"I bet you're right," Devlin said.

THE REAL ROCKY

STANLEY KETCHEL, THE middleweight champion whom they called the Michigan Assassin, was shot and killed in Coway, Missouri, sixty years ago. When Wilson Mizner, the writer, heard about it, he said, "Start counting over him. Ketchel will get up before the bell."

Mizner's words come back now because of an anniversary that has just passed. It was a year ago that Rocky Marciano went down with a private plane in Iowa. It is still hard to believe that he didn't get up in that field.

Rocky was by no means the most skillful of boxers and may, indeed, have been the crudest operator ever to win the heavyweight championship. Primo Carnera would crowd him for that distinction, though, and it would be difficult for anybody who saw Joe Louis to regard Rocky as the greatest fighter of our time, no matter what the records say.

The records make Rocky the best. In forty-nine fights, nobody ever held him to a draw and only six opponents finished on their feet. Only one other heavyweight champion could show comparable figures: Gene Tunney, the most grievously underrated fighter of them all, lost once in seventy-six bouts.

Rocky Marciano couldn't box like Tunney and probably couldn't hit like Louis, but in one respect he had no challenger. He was the toughest, strongest, most completely dedicated fighter who ever wore gloves.

Fear wasn't in his vocabulary and pain had no meaning. Sixteen years ago this month he defended his title against the former champion, Ezzard Charles, for the second time. In their first match Charles had stood up to a frightful beating for fifteen rounds and walked out of the ring, unrecognizable but upright.

In the seventh round of their second bout a punch split Rocky's nose like a walnut. In the eighth blood poured from this wound and a cut opened above the left eye. One good punch would have spread the nose all over his face and the doctor would have been forced to order a halt, but Rocky wouldn't let Ezzard throw one punch.

Boring in through a crimson haze, he clubbed Ezzard to the floor twice. In five years, only Ezzard Charles was good enough to walk into the ring against Rocky and walk out. Now here he was just one stiff jab away from the title and the jab wasn't there. He took the count on his knees.

Any decent boxer could outpoint Rocky for a few rounds. A marksman could cut him up. Gladiators like Jersey Joe Walcott and Archie Moore could and did knock him flat. But whenever a man started counting over him, Rocky got up.

On his word, no punch ever stunned or dazed him, though some wounded him and some knocked him down. He said that when he went down he was perfectly aware of going down, could see and recognize faces at ringside, could follow the referee's count.

"What did you think," Bill Heinz asked him, "when Walcott dropped you?"

Walcott was the champion and favorite, Rocky the crude young challenger, and this was only the first round.

"Funny thing," Rock said. "I didn't think anything when I was on the floor, but going to my corner after the bell I thought, 'Hey, this old man knocked you down. He might knock you down three, four more times tonight. This could be a tough fight.'"

He wouldn't stay down and he wouldn't lose. That was unthinkable.

But it might be a tough fight.

His extraordinary fortitude was part courage and part physical condition. "Marciano," Frank Graham wrote, "is addicted to exercise as some men are addicted to the bottle."

Even in the months when he had no fight in sight, Rocky would train, living in the airport cottage above Grossinger's in the Catskills, jogging, hiking, sparring, punching the bag, skipping rope, doing calisthenics.

He even had an eye exerciser, a doo-dad he would set in motion and then follow with his eyes as he lay motionless. It used to make his trainer, little Charley Goldman, snicker.

"He wants stronger muscles in his eyeballs," Charley would say, shaking his head.

Once Rocky was asked when he had discovered that his physical equipment was out of the ordinary. He told about playing "king of the hill" one winter day when he was just a nipper in Brockton, Massachusetts. For hours he struggled to gain and hold a snowy summit against bigger boys. Making his way home at supper time, he passed two of the larger kids in the early dark. "Gee," one was saying, "that Rocky's tough, isn't he?"

"I knew then that everything was going to be all right." And it was, until a year ago in a field in Iowa.

— *Red Smith*

"Who knows?" Willie said.

WHEN IT WAS coming up 4:30, I asked him to call a cab for me, but he said he would drive me to where I could cross the street to the motel. We walked out to the parking space, and the TV set was on the passenger's side of the front seat. I got in the back, and Willie seemed small, peering out over the wheel. City-soiled snow, sand mixing into it, was banked along the curb where a half-dozen cars were backed up at the stoplight.

"Now don't cross here," he said to me, as I started to get out, "Cross at the corner. I don't want to see you get hurt."

"I never wanted to see you get hurt, either," I said.

"Thank you," he said. "Good luck."

As I approached the corner, the light changed and the cars began to move. When he passed me he waved quickly, just once, and then turned back to the wheel, and that was the last I saw of the great artist, the likes of whom I'm sure I shall never see again. ❧

Musician's Tales

SAINT FRANCIS OF HOBOKEN

by Daniel Okrent

WHAT HE HAD, what he has, what made and makes him different and greater than any singer who has stalked a stage, is sex.

For fifty years now, Frank Sinatra has been coming on to us. Along the way — maybe all the way — he has treated some people badly; a highly erotic nature tends to expose the nerve ends. It has also led too many to think too much about too little — about whether Sinatra's a *nice man.* But does it really matter if Mozart was an infantile boor, or Picasso a libertine?

Forgiveness isn't the issue here. Nor is the silly exercise of trying to reconcile the private life that has played across our mind-screens with the performing life that has sounded only in our ears and hearts. You could read all 633 lurid pages committed by Kitty Kelley and not know that Frank Sinatra ever sang a note. You don't need to live next door to an artist, or invite him for dinner. You only need to listen to him sing.

I SOMETIMES THINK great singers are nature's freaks, born with an unexpected gift which they are able, when accompanied by some dedication and discrimination, to parlay into a career: Mel Torme, say, and his uncanny pitch; Sarah Vaughan and her multioctave range. But listening to the first recordings Sinatra made nearly half a century ago with Harry James, and then with Tommy Dorsey, one hears only a nice voice.

Then in the early forties he left home, and in leaving released the power of his own singular, unexpected gift. He abandoned Papa Dorsey, and all the strictures on acceptable postadolescent behavior brought to bear in any family. He went out on his own, soon to the Paramount Theatre in Times Square on Columbus Day in 1944, and Frank Sinatra started riots.

It was no cheap and easy trick. Only three times in memory has the advent of a particular performing act led to riots — Sinatra in the forties, Elvis in the fifties, the Beatles in the sixties. Certainly the nascent talent each demonstrated gave little hint of what they would develop later. Sinatra at the Paramount was a very, very good singer, but the voice — this was before it became known as The Voice — was two-dimensional. The shadings and complexities he would develop in the years ahead were only barely present.

The hormone irritants, though — they were fully developed. Back in the forties you could feel the seductive power on songs such as "You Go to My Head" and "The Nearness of You." It was the vulnerable, wounded sound of the boy every woman wants to comfort, to hold to her breast and make whole. Sinatra knew this: The male of the species has never developed a more effective seduction line than the display of frailty.

When those fifteen-year-olds sat through ten-a-day performances at the Paramount, they stayed because they were being seduced, made love to, psychic orgasms multiplying as "Violets for Your Furs" followed "Ghost of a Chance," and "These Foolish Things" followed that. Every boy in America but one was off to war, and this one (exempted from the service because of a punctured eardrum) was onstage, available, singing to you.

FRANK SINATRA INVENTED nothing. From Bing Crosby, he learned how to use the microphone, how to make the sighing implied, the crack in the voice only a hint.

One thing Italian Americans have never been denied is their preeminence in music. The Italian music teacher, the virtuoso, and the opera singer have from the beginning been virtual American archetypes. What Frank Sinatra added to the archetype was sex, and the threat that goes with it — which plays into another American archetype, the threatening Italian. Sinatra's conscious play with both, including the idea that the threat might be real, is an act that still, after all these years, plays well in Peoria.

▶
Frank Sinatra, heartthrob of the 1940s and the first crooner whose singing started riots

From Tommy Dorsey, he learned the virtue of the legato line, the smooth, seamless manner of phrasing that approximated speech. He would swim underwater laps in a Hoboken pool, building up the lung power that would enable him to wrap his voice around a song. He would absorb the content of a lyric by writing it out longhand, concentrating on the words in the absence of music. On paper, the lyrics were hardly Robert Browning. But then he would sing them, and they took life not from the lyricist's efforts at meter and meaning, but from the ardency of the singer's voice, his astonishing belief.

And from Billie Holliday, he learned to lay back on the beat, to let the rhythm of his accompaniment tug him along, opening up the line of the song before him, making a lyric into a story. In the mid- to late forties, he liked to go listen to Holliday at the Three Deuces, and during her breaks she would take both Sinatra and their friend Sylvia Sims across the street to hear the great Mabel Mercer.

"We were attracted to words," Syms remembers. Words, to each of them, were not just sounds to be manipulated, but meanings, substance, to be elaborated.

Most distinctive popular singers — Lena Horne and Judy Garland come immediately to mind — stay ahead of the beat, a trick that imparts a wild, feral quality. Horne, for one, seems some form of cat, ready to pounce; by staying ahead of the beat, she keeps her eyes open, her claws bared. For Sinatra, no claws. In his ballad singing, the infinitesimal lagging accents his ache, his hurt. All but imperceptibly, the listener moves to the edge of his chair, soon to the edge of his emotions, longing for the rhythmic resolution that only comes at the end of a telling phrase.

"So, that's how it goes," he sings, "and Joe, I know you're getting . . . [pause] . . . anxious to close."

Always, what Sinatra knew, what no singer who has ever electronically dubbed his voice onto recording tape could possibly know, was that singing is inevitably a reflection of humanness. Though one can dance to much of his music, Sinatra doesn't sing for dancing; he sings for listening, for communication to another being.

"It's not the pale moon that excites me," he whispers, his voice barely trembling, "that thrills and delights me," and if you are listening, you know that nothing is more real than that moon. Nothing, that is, but the thrill and the delight — the quivering sex — that is now coursing between singer and listener.

OVER AND OVER, Sinatra has made and remade himself — not merely as a public personality, veering from soft to tough, or as a political amateur, from Left to Right. He has done so as a singer as well.

With Dorsey he was a pleasing voice on top of an improbably floppy bow tie and a pair of coat-hanger shoulders. On his own at Columbia in the forties, he was callow, a heartthrob. He grew up at Capitol in the fifties, acquiring the rueful irony of the worldly wise. It was a period of accomplishment greater than any popular singer has ever achieved. With arrangers Nelson Riddle and Billy May, he was able to record the lion's share of those American classics that all at once became known not as the works of their composers, but as "Sinatra songs": "Angel Eyes," "I'm a Fool to Want You," "You Go to My Head" — songs not the property of Gershwin or Rogers or Porter or Berlin, but songs made by the singer, eternally Sinatra's.

When he began the sixties with his own company, Reprise, he was the Ring-a-Ding-Ding swinger, and when that disruptive decade came to its end he bore its scars. "Nobody's writing songs for me anymore," Sinatra said toward the end of this period, "and I don't know what to do about it." What he did was run to the only audience that would have him, and after too much of that, in 1971, he announced his retirement. He was fifty-six.

Today, Sinatra is no single thing he ever was before (he calls his brief retirement "my leave of absence"), but an amalgam of everything he has been. Experience adheres to those who will pay attention to it, and always he has paid attention to how, and what, he sings.

As his best work in the last fifteen years has shown, he found a way to summon the resources that expand with age — not the physical ones, but those that are emotional and intellectual. On *Trilogy*, he did his knockout version of George Harrison's "Something" by turning its lyric into a dramatic soliloquy. And on the Quincy Jones–produced *L.A. Is My Lady*, he turned technical losses into emotional virtue. The very tentativeness of his attack on "Stormy Weather" makes the torch in that song dim to an ember. So different from the wide-eyed yearning he brought to it in 1944 — it is the song of an aging man; every bruise shows on his skin.

What will be next? The breath will grow shorter, the voice less strong, the astonishing stamina will start to erode. But to imagine him not singing is impossible.

My guess is that when his voice can finally no longer traverse an octave, he will passionately perform songs that require less than an octave; when he can no longer sustain the energy required by four choruses, he will confine himself to two; when he can no longer dominate a stage, or hold a note, he will follow Mabel Mercer to a chair at stage center, and speak the lyrics he knows so well.

And when he does, he will not be so far removed from the vulnerable boy at all. Yearning will have given way to cherishing; the promise of sex will have been replaced by the memory of sex. And what, finally, is the memory of sex, but love? ❧

THE GHOSTLY PRESENCE OF RUSS COLUMBO

IN THREE YEARS, 1931–1934, he had become a top radio singer, Bing Crosby's only serious challenger, a major recording star who wrote three of his own hits — "You Call It Madness But I Call It Love" (his theme song), "Too Beautiful for Words," and "Prisoner of Love." He was also an emerging film actor, and a bandleader who at one point had such jazz talents in his ranks as Gene Krupa, Joe Sullivan, and Benny Goodman.

The last of twelve children, he bore the full Christian name Ruggiero Eugenio de Rudolpho Columbo and early in his life he showed great talent for Italian opera as well as popular love songs. As a violinist in Gus Arnheim's band, he was influenced by its boy singer, Bing Crosby, and he succeeded him in that spot after Bing left. Within a year, Columbo had also started his solo career, and the two became embroiled in a mythical "Battle of the Baritones," Bing on CBS and Russ on NBC. Whereas Crosby was sometimes lighthearted, at other times romantic, Columbo concentrated entirely on romance. Every song he recorded was a love ballad, sung as a violinist would play it, with tender feeling and an easy flow of sound.

In early 1932 he described his singing to a Detroit reporter: "I'm not a crooner or a blues singer or a straight baritone. I've tried to make my phrasing different, and I take a lot of liberty with the music. One of the things they seem to like best is the voice obbligato on repeat choruses — very much as I used to do them on the violin."

Others described the romantic-voiced performer as "the crooning troubadour of the screen and radio," "the Romeo of song," "tall, broad-shouldered, shining black hair, fierce Latin eyes," and "having more than a faint resemblance to Valentino."

In spite of the fact that one director told him he was "too Latin" to get beyond movie bit parts, Russ Columbo made three films, *Broadway Through a Keyhole*, *Moulin Rouge*, and *Wake Up and Dream*, and was the star of the last. Actresses Carole Lombard and Sally Blane reportedly were in love with him. Fan letters from other adoring but unknown women poured in every week.

But a gun ended it all — an antique dueling pistol used as a paperweight and believed to be unloaded. While his close friend, a leading Hollywood photographer, was striking a match against the pistol, the gun accidentally fired, and the bullet ricocheted off a desk and struck Russ in the head. He was twenty-six years old. For his funeral thousands filled the church and sidewalks outside. Bing Crosby was one of the pallbearers.

▲ Russ Columbo, the Romeo of song

Though the pistol accident ended Columbo's real career, it started a mythical one that lasted another ten years. Seriously ill at the time of the shooting and later blind, Columbo's mother was never told of her son's death. The family — including Carole Lombard — read "letters" from Russ in London, Paris, and other cities, where an ever more demanding career kept him from coming home to visit her. Every month a check arrived — actually payment from his insurance policy.

Mrs. Columbo died in 1944, happy for her son's "success."

— *George T. Simon*

THE TEACHINGS OF LENNIE TRISTANO

by Robert Palmer

"WOMEN ARE MORE open, they're looser," the late pianist Lennie Tristano once said when asked why so many of his budding jazz students were women. "They're more intuitive and original; they're never out to prove how fast or how loud or how high they can play. And they don't have the same opportunities. Everyone gives them a hard time because they're women."

Lynn Anderson, a jazz singer and former student of Tristano's, quoted those words in an unpublished tribute she wrote shortly before the Lennie Tristano Memorial Concert, held at New York's Town Hall in late January. The six-hour concert was a remarkable confirmation of Tristano's thesis. Women sang — their traditional role in jazz — but they also played intense, two-fisted piano, and at least two of them, Connie Crothers and Liz Gorrill, were brilliant.

There were men, too, most notably tenor saxophonist Warne Marsh, a student of Tristano's in the forties and early fifties, and Eddie Gomez, favorite young bassist of the late Charles Mingus.

Still, the strongest, most vibrant presence was Tristano himself, who died of a heart attack on November 18, 1978, but who seemed to live on in every note played.

TRISTANO WAS THE mystery man of modern jazz — a blind pianist with a reputation as a pedagogue who rarely performed in public during the last twenty years of his career. His influence has been felt most strongly through the work of his students, among them the

Lennie Tristano was serious about jazz. His attempt to distinguish between emotion and feeling came out of his sense that "hysteria and hostility" emoting from musicians were not jazz but expressions of ego. He wanted jazz to come out of the id. As he said, "Real jazz is what you can play before you're screwed up; the other is what happens after you're screwed up."

great alto saxophonist Lee Konitz; pianists Ronnie Ball, Joanne Brackeen, and Sal Mosca; and vocalist Sheila Jordan. In the late forties and early fifties, Tristano was one of the more celebrated and controversial jazz musicians in America.

Born in Chicago in 1919 at the height of a flu epidemic that damaged his eyes, Tristano had his sight further weakened by a serious attack of measles at age six. He went to a school for handicapped children, and then to Chicago's American Conservatory of Music. He moved to New York in 1946 and immediately established himself as a formidable player: "In 1944, I had reached a point where I could rifle off anything of Tatum's," he once said, "and with scandalous efficiency."

Among the souvenirs of that period is a remarkable 1947 radio broadcast that united Tristano with Charlie Parker, Dizzy Gillespie, and Max Roach. His dense, jagged chording was probably the most challenging accompaniment Parker and Gillespie had ever experienced, and they responded with exceptional playing.

During the next few years, Tristano became the guru of a small, select circle of jazzmen, with saxophonists Konitz and Marsh and guitarist Billy Bauer as his most impressive disciples.

Instead of playing within the demanding bebop idiom that had been devised by Parker and Gillespie, Tristano and his cohorts struck out into new territory. While improvising, they would completely reharmonize standard tunes until the original melody and chord progressions were almost unrecognizable.

In 1949, with bassist Arnold Fishkin and drummer Denzil Best, they recorded the first free-form jazz improvisations, "Intuition" and "Digression." The sides had no fixed meter or structure, and all the musicians improvised at once.

Critic Barry Ulanov called this "the most audacious experiment yet attempted in jazz — an experiment to create a spontaneous music, out of skill and intuition, which should be at once atonal, contrapuntal and improvised on a jazz base." So bewildered was Capitol Records by what it heard that "two of the sides were erased from the tape, and the other two were put aside, with their date indefinitely postponed."

I MET TRISTANO a year ago at Carnegie Recital Hall, where he was sponsoring a recital for one of his prize pupils, Liz Gorrill. Tristano was smiling broadly and talking a mile a minute to Gorrill, who plays with a steamroller left hand.

Unlike many blind people, who are careful and fastidious with their personal appearance, Tristano let it all hang out. He had on wrinkled slacks, and a short, lived-in dressing gown, tied carelessly at the waist. He wasn't wearing dark glasses and I remember those sightless eyes as if I'd seen them yesterday.

The main thing I recall is the man's great warmth and humor. Through the years, Tristano was criticized for being unemotional, for playing intellectual games. Yet every time one of his protégés performed and his fans, friends, and families of students gathered, the assembly simply radiated good cheer. I wondered, as Tristano talked volubly about Gorrill and some of his other favorites, whether he had dropped out of live performing, as he did during the middle and late fifties, because he found the jazz scene cold. Certainly he must have created a more comfortable world of his own.

One wishes he had at least recorded more. Tristano hadn't made an album since 1962s *Descent into the Maelstrom*, released first in Japan and later, just before his death, by Inner City, an American label. It is a challenging record, by turns pretty, astringent, open, dense, constricted, and anarchic. One hopes that more tapes have been salted away and will be released some day.

Tristano was a private man, and he evidently gained a great deal from his teaching. But his long silence is everyone's loss. ❧

191

VENUTI ACTED LIKE THE DEVIL AND PLAYED LIKE AN ANGEL

"**H**OW COULD ANYONE act like the devil and play like an angel?"

Joe Venuti's mother is said to have made that remark about the youth who would grow up to become the world's first great jazz violinist. She was not far off the mark. For the whole of his career, which spanned more than sixty years, Joe Venuti was a mass of contradictions.

He was a serious musician with all the classical credentials who turned to jazz, adapting the idiom to an instrument so difficult that very few others in jazz ever mastered it. The sound of his violin was smooth and even, but the guttural tones of his speaking voice were such that Marlon Brando could play the lead in a movie based on Venuti's life.

What a movie that would be. Venuti's achievements in the area of recordings alone were monumental. It is difficult to decide which is more amazing — the exquisite swinging musicianship of *Stringing the Blues,* a duo performance he made in 1926 with the guitarist Eddie Lang, or the fact that he was in prime form on records made almost fifty-two years later. Nobody else in the history of recorded music could match that track record.

Everything about Venuti was either admirable or astonishing. When he wasn't playing the violin for applause, he was playing life for laughs. He took delight in going along with the legend that he was born on a ship that was bringing his parents to the United States from Italy, and gave various ages for himself according to the mood of the moment, until someone allegedly unearthed a 1903 birth certificate from Lecco, Italy. His first wife, however, assured me that he was born in Philadelphia.

NOTHING SEEMED TO faze Venuti as long as he could play, maintain his sense of humor and pull the practical jokes for which he soon became legendary.

The best-known story concerns Wingy Manone, the one-armed trumpet player. For a Christmas present, Venuti sent him one cuff link.

Another tale, which Venuti told with wild variations, dealt with the occasion

▲
Joe Venuti: stringing the blues for over 60 years

when he found the names of thirty-seven bass fiddle players in the Musicians' Union directory, called them all up and told them to meet him for a gig Saturday at 8 p.m. at the corner of Fifty-second Street and Broadway. The men showed up, lugging their basses, making the sidewalk impassable, while Venuti drove around the block several times, roaring with laughter at the scene he had created. "But the union called me in, and made me pay everybody scale," he said.

In 1936 Venuti's band and the Paul Whiteman orchestra played at the Texas Centennial in Dallas. Every night Whiteman would start the program with the entire stadium darkened except for

a small spotlight on him while he conducted the "Star Spangled Banner" with a lighted baton.

One evening, Venuti bribed an electrician to throw the spot on him instead. What the audience saw was Venuti, dressed only in long underwear, conducting the orchestra with a fishing pole, at the end of which was an electric light bulb.

THERE WILL BE an empty chair Labor Day when Dick Gibson's musicians assemble for their annual jam session. Joe Venuti's violin will be resting on it, perhaps as a reminder that the man who acted like the devil, and played so much like an angel, can never be replaced.

— Leonard Feather

ITALIAN DOOWOP GROUPS OF THE FIFTIES

Dino & the Diplomats

Vito & the Salutations

Vito Picone & the Elegants

The Passions

THE DEL-SATINS

Dion and the Belmonts

Mario DeAndreade & the Five Discs

THE IMAGINATIONS

Gusy Villari & the Elegants

Tony Canzano & the DuPrees

NINO & THE EBBTIDES

Phil Cracolici & the Mystics

The Royal Teens

JOEY DEE & THE STARLIGHTERS

The Aquatones

Rosie & the Originals

Frankie Valli & the Four Seasons

THE CRESTS

The Chimes

IN THE MATERIAL WORLD

by Joel D. Schwartz

THE PREDOMINANTLY FEMALE thirteen- and fourteen-year-olds who flocked to Madonna's 1985 "Virgin Tour" concerts went home loaded down with overpriced T-shirts, posters, and promo magazines, all, of course, featuring their enigmatic, punked-out heroine.

The most striking photograph in the eighteen-page, seven-dollar magazine shows the star lying on her stomach and looking back over her shoulder at the camera with a mysterious, sultry sneer. Her bleached hair is moussed to the max, and her red lips are painted to match the skimpy lace dress that might have been purchased at a remainder sale in the underwear department at K Mart. A rosary bearing an enormous, gaudy crucifix is draped over her shoulder.

And she is lying in the dirt.

In fact, her face and back are covered with dirt. All in all, a fetching pose — a kind of cross between a tacky pinup for a fertilizer company calendar and a photo for a *True Detective* magazine article about a nun who was mugged by a motorcycle gang while gardening one morning in her Frederick's of Hollywood nightgown.

Madonna, as everyone who hasn't spent the last decade in a coma knows, is a true rock phenomenon. Her popularity transcends the labels and factions that currently partition the adolescent rock scene, and it is just conceivable that she is on her way to becoming a latter-day Elvis — the central icon of mid-1980s teen popular culture.

PSYCHOLOGICAL OR CULTURAL significance aside, Madonna is a talented, sexy performer. Her concerts are at once scrupu-lously professional, Vegas-style shows and a spontaneous explosion of high-energy abandon. To say much more than this risks translating her appeal from the vernacular to the arcane, from the level of her fans' felt experience to the sterile platitudes of the academic social critic.

Still, a considerable amount of Madonna's appeal, captured beautifully in the ironic "dirty Madonna" photo, is that she (or her managers) has carefully constructed an intriguing, enigmatic image. Her blond hair and porcelain-white skin are contrasted with black dirt, her rosary juxtaposed to her red lips and matching cat-house dress. In fact, one of her accomplishments is that, at least until recently, she has nearly reversed the typical pattern of rock idol analysis. The *Rolling Stone*–type critics have dismissed her as top-forty schlock. This time it is the kids — whether in record stores or waiting in line to get into her concerts — who are engaged in a running debate over what she and her music stand for — what they mean.

A fair measure of the seriousness of this debate is that it goes well beyond mere words to the very appearance and demeanor of her fans. For instance, the girls who have turned Madonna's concerts into Madonna look-alike costume parties wear their theories, as it were, on their backs. Some look like innocent bobby-soxers, some look like underage streetwalkers, but most look like an uneasy combination of the two.

Most of the rock stars who have captured the public's imagination since the 1950s have been social critics. While the most conspicuous of this criticism came in the political protest songs of the 1960s and early 1970s, by far the bulk of it has been much more personal in character. This personal or spiritual critique, in turn, has taken at least two forms.

To one camp, a competitive, impersonal

Side by side: Rock star and opera singer. Bargirl and virgin. Madonna and La Biscaccianti. Side by side they taunt us with such a mingling of roles, musical histories, and time periods that we begin looking for Pirandello. So even though Madonna dreams that she is Marilyn Monroe reincarnate, we suggest the possibility that — updated and telescoped, to be sure — she may owe as much to the Biscaccianti.

America is contrasted to a utopia of pastoral innocence characterized by puppy love and a triumph of virtue over crass materialism; of simple honesty over hypocrisy and deception. This theme was introduced by countless male and female balladeers in the 1950s, and continued by many folk groups in the 1960s and 1970s.

To the other camp, the same America — the same enemy — is contrasted to what can only be called a utopia of the libido. There, boys can be boys and girls can be girls, and hormones can be hormones. From Little Richard (who had to censor his lyrics for popular consumption) to the Beastie Boys, the theme has been not lost innocence, but sex, drugs, and rock 'n' roll.

The choice many felt compelled to make a generation ago between the Beatles ("I Wanna Hold Your Hand") and the Rolling Stones ("I Can't Get No Satisfaction") was drawn largely along these lines.

Madonna's talent is to join this debate without tipping her hand.

Some of her songs sound like remakes of sweet-sixteen Connie Francis tunes dripping with old-fashioned, hand-holding romance. "It's so brand new; I'm crazy for you." This is the "Madonna" side of Madonna. The name fits the image so well that if she hadn't actually been christened with it (Madonna Louise Veronica Ciccone) she'd have had to adopt it as her stage name anyway.

But she's also well known for hard-driving dance music, the kind with the senseless lyrics and stirring rhythms that has proved to be so popular with the disco audience. It is this music that fits well with the image of almost vulgar sexuality that she often cultivates, and her penchant for blurring the distinction between clothes and underwear.

Madonna wears commitments like costumes, to be taken off and on at whim. Everything is a pose. Everything is carefully

THE BISCACCIANTI

EARLY IN THE spring of 1852, culture arrived in San Francisco without fanfare and in a single night lifted the city from the rank of a vulgar boomtown to a center of artistic endeavor.

In February a steamer docked — or, rather, it was a sailing ship. It was at the height of the rainy season. The streets were rivers of mud. From the gangplank of the sailing ship a young girl stepped ashore — and sank to her dainty knees in mud. She stood there, with mud all about, and threw kisses to the assembled multitude of miners and businessmen and gamblers. They cheered, and she smiled, and they threw their hats in the air, and she threw more kisses. Then one of the biggest of the rugged men strode through the mud, lifted the girl in his arms and, holding her high above his head, marched with her through the mud and mire to the St. Francis Hotel.

She was a Boston girl, delicate as a bit of French porcelain, pretty as a miniature painted in ivory. Every man in San Francisco was in love with her before the procession had splashed its way into the St. Francis.

A Boston girl, her mother a cultured woman, her father a musician of some distinction, she had received a refined education in New England's more exclusive schools. She had traveled around the world; she was lovely, she was exquisite, she was adored — and she was cultured. Her name was Elisa Biscaccianti.

Biscaccianti! There are San Franciscans still living whose fathers grew mellow-eyed when they spoke of La Biscaccianti — The Biscaccianti. She was the most popular coloratura soprano

▲
Elisa Biscaccianti, the most popular coloratura soprano of her day.

of her day. She had sung leading roles in London, in Paris, in Milan and Vienna and Florence and St. Petersburg. And San Francisco took Biscaccianti to its warm heart just as, a half century later, it would take Tetrazzini. One noble citizen with a prophetic soul proclaimed, "San Francisco shall be the musical soul of the West, and Biscaccianti is the soul's Columbus."

Yet so much would change in a period of just seven years.

After leaving for a world tour, Biscaccianti returned to the city she loved in 1859. San Francisco was no more than a muddy village when she left, but she returned to find a cosmopolitan port. San Francisco had heard many great artists

— pianists, violinists, singers — since her departure. Sadly, by 1859, Biscaccianti had become just another name.

Oh, the crowds still came to hear her sing, but they no longer had to pay bags of gold dust to hear her sing. Indeed, you could now arrive fashionably late at her concerts, and still have your choice of seats.

At first Biscaccianti was dazed, then chagrined, then infuriated by the response. Overnight she forgot her polite training and the traditions of her Boston home. Very well! If they would not pay to hear her sing the great operas, she would sing the bawdy ballads they wanted to hear, not in the Opera House, but in the already disreputable Bella Union.

If you were one of the hundreds who went to this legendary music hall, you would have seen Biscaccianti, night after night, seated at a small table. She was called "Biscaccianti of the Bella Union" now. She had grown stout; her features had grown coarse. She would sit there night after night with the young man for whom she had deserted her husband. She was habitually drunk. Some said she was most amusing and sang best only when she was totally drunk.

For three years, night after night, she sat at her table in the Bella Union, singing for her drinks. And through the fog of those awful hours there would come at times a hopeful glint in her eyes, a proud toss of her head when she thought she saw some recognition of her earlier glories in the eyes of an old-timer passing her table. But no; it was just another sightseer. For three years she sat there, and then, one day she went away and was never heard of in San Francisco again.

— *Samuel Dickson*

scripted and choreographed. To this extent, Madonna stands in satirical aloofness from both traditional camps, proclaiming them both naive to the core.

There was a time when it was a serious criticism to say of someone that he or she is "just role-playing." But Madonna's fans are learning that maturity *is* superficiality, that to be grown-up is to have perfected one's repertoire of roles and the ability to manipulate

them on call. Like a virtuoso actress. Like Madonna.

In this way, the walls of the concert hall are pushed out to include the world — a world, perhaps, soon to be populated with a whole chorus line of Madonnas who see their personalities as scaffoldings of affectation built on paper foundations of seeming "like a virgin," or "like" anything else they please. ❧

Toscanini at Eighty-six

by Milton Katims

His face — the classic shape, detailed in white, that seems to have been made to order for a podium — even without the name signifies music as instantly as Einstein's does science. As to how Toscanini might have got on with Zappa, perhaps he would have found some common musical ground, just as Nicolas Slonimsky did.

I T WAS SHORTLY before 10 a.m. in Carnegie Hall one day last season.

The justly famous NBC Symphony Orchestra was seated onstage, ready for rehearsal. The din of tuning and last-minute practicing subsided as a loud call of "Stand by, Maestro coming down" came from the control booth.

There was silence — the silence that every conductor hopes for.

Seconds later, a slight figure with a black, high-throated tunic setting off the magnificent head walked briskly onstage, hopped dexterously onto the podium, tapped his baton and said, *"Dunque* — now Brahms."

The opening chords of the symphony rang through Carnegie Hall. One sensed that every man was alerted — each strove to reach an artistic peak in his own playing, for this was Toscanini, the greatest of them all. He rehearsed it quietly, going through the first movement from beginning to end, almost as if to set it in his own fabulous memory and to give the men in the orchestra an opportunity to refresh it in theirs before going back to rehearse it in detail.

DURING MY YEARS as a member of the NBC Symphony, I usually had my pockets and viola case filled with the scores that we were rehearsing. On the way home I would jot down a memo here and there, change a bowing or dynamic marking or study a phrase that Maestro had discussed. I was struck over and over, as with a new revelation, by the way everything Toscanini asked for, every minute detail, always added up to a performance that had a clarity making the most involved scores seem absolutely transparent.

The master's keen sense of aural balance, keeping

▲
**Arturo Toscanini: working toward an
ideal, jewel-like clarity**

each instrumental choir in its proper tonal perspective, gives his readings a diaphanous quality difficult to emulate. His loving attention to the inner voices of a symphonic work which support the obvious melodic line helps toward clarity and adds vivid life to a reading.

And no matter how much attention he lavishes on details, he never loses sight of the long line of the composition. He rehearses a work until it has a jewel-like clarity — this, combined with his Latin warmth and great feeling for the drama inherent in the music, makes a Toscanini performance.

PEOPLE ARE ALWAYS asking me about the temperamental outbursts of Toscanini. For my part, these reports have always been overemphasized. Naturally he becomes impatient and stormy if he feels any player is "letting down" — he constantly gives the utmost of himself, and expects the same from every man. Whenever he has "blown up" he has always had good reason — and it is always a musical reason.

After all, this man has, in his mind's ear, an ideal conception of what he has seen in his ever freshly studied score. To bring that aural image to actuality in the living instrument — his orchestra — he will use every device in the book, and many which are not to be found there: praise, sarcasm, cajolery, patient explanation — perhaps even an eloquent visual demonstration of what he wants.

I'll never forget the day he was rehearsing Debussy's *La Mer*. He wanted to achieve a highly evanescent effect in one spot, and at a loss for words to describe what he wanted, he took from his breast pocket a large, white silk handkerchief. He threw it high in the air and every man in the orchestra was hypnotized as it floated softly, sensuously to the ground.

"There," Maestro smiled happily. "Play it like that."

He is a wonderful psychologist. To work in an orchestra under his guidance is to learn the subtle art of rehearsing. I have seen him keep the orchestra working on two or three measures for what seemed an eternity. It looked as if he were straining the nerves of the players to a point where something would snap. Then, with everyone alert and intent, he would go right through the rest of the work without a pause, getting a performance that crackled with vitality.

THERE IS A compelling urgency about his music-making — a constant search for the truth of the composer's intentions. Many have felt that Toscanini literally follows to the dot a composer's score. This is only part of the story. Naturally, he takes it for granted that his musicians play what appears on the printed page. But there is far more — so many inflections that are only inferred in the music.

MEETING ZAPPA

ONE LATE SATURDAY evening in the spring of 1981, I received a telephone call. "Nicolas Slonimsky?" the caller inquired. "This is Frank Zappa. I never realized you were in Los Angeles, and I want so much to get in touch with you about your book of scales."

I was startled. Frank Zappa was the last person who, to my mind, could be interested in my theoretico-musical inventions. His name was familiar to me from a promotional album jacket showing him seated on the john with his denuded left thigh in view, and the legend in large letters: PHI KRAPPA ZAPPA.

We arranged to meet on the following Monday at 2:30 in the afternoon, and at the appointed time his assistant knocked at my door. I stepped out of my apartment and beheld something that looked like a space shuttle — a black Mercedes taking up almost half a block of Wilshire Boulevard. I could not refrain from asking the driver how much such a machine cost. "Sixty," he replied.

It took us an hour to get to Zappa's place in the Hollywood Hills. Zappa met me at the door. He looked like a leading man in the movies — tall, slender, sporting a small Italian mustache. For starters, I asked him the origin of his last name; he replied it meant "the plough" in Italian.

Zappa's wife came in, and served coffee and tea. Zappa told me he did not drink alcoholic beverages; contrary to the legendary habits of most rock-and-roll musicians, he never partook of drugs. But he smoked cigarettes incessantly, tobacco being his only, and quite venial, sin. Zappa led me to his studio, which housed a huge Bosendorfer piano. I asked him how much he paid for this keyboard monster. "Seventy," he replied.

Zappa declared himself an admirer of Varèse and said he had been composing orchestral works according to Varèse's principles of composition, with unrelated themes following in free succession. To substantiate this claim, he brought out three scores, in manuscript and each measuring thirteen by twenty inches,

He asks for a constant singing quality — "canta, canta" — a rhythmic precision — "preciso, preciso." Far from being absolutely metronomic, his freedom (rubato) is so subtle and natural and in such exquisite taste that the listener is not even aware of it. "Follow me — watch me" — he will say — "no two measures are alike."

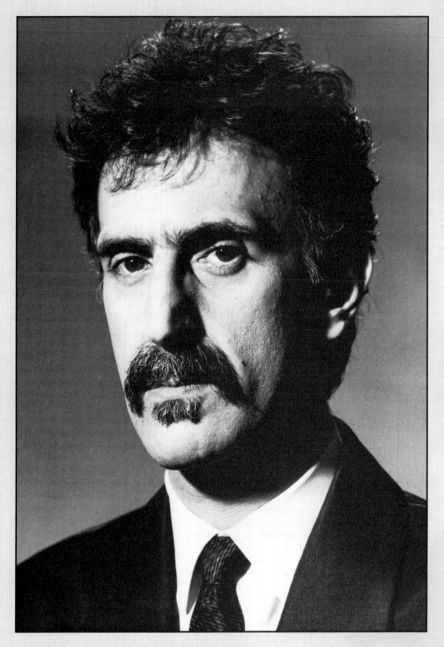

beautifully copied and handsomely bound. Indeed the configurations of notes and contrapuntal combinations looked remarkably Varèsian. Yet he never went to music school, and had learned the technique of composition from the study of actual editions.

Zappa invited me to try out his Bosendorfer. I sat down at the keyboard and played the coronation scene from *Boris Godunov*. Zappa was impressed by these Russian harmonies. He asked me to play some of my own compositions, and I launched into the last piece in my *Minitudes*.

"Why don't you play this piece at my next concert?" Zappa asked.

"When will that be?" I replied.

"Tomorrow. We can rehearse in the afternoon."

I was somewhat taken aback at the offer, but after all, I had nothing to lose. So I decided to take my chance as a soloist at a rock concert.

On stage next day during rehearsal, I sat at the electric piano and played my piece. For better effect I added sixteen bars to the coda. Zappa dictated to his players the principal tonalities of my piece, and they picked up the modulations with extraordinary assurance.

The hall began to fill rapidly. Zappa's bodyguard gave me earplugs, for, when Zappa's band went into action, the decibels were extremely high. Zappa sang and danced while conducting with a professional verve that astounded me. A soprano soloist came out and sang a ballad about being a hooker, using a variety of obscenities.

Then came my turn. Balancing a cigarette between his lips, Zappa introduced me to the audience as "our national treasure." I pulled out the earplugs and sat down at the electric piano. With demoniac energy Zappa launched us into my piece. To my surprise I sensed a growing consanguinity with my youthful audience as I played. My fortissimo ending brought screams and whistles the likes of which I had never imagined possible.

Dancing Zappa, wild audience, and befuddled me — I felt like an intruder in a mad scene from *Alice in Wonderland*. I had entered my own Age of Absurdity.

— *Nicolas Slonimsky*

One day, a few years ago, after one of his rehearsals, we were in his dressing room, discussing the character of a certain passage, and the Maestro, reaching for his metronome, said, "Here, this must be absolutely rhythmically precise — as with a metronome."

He set the instrument in motion and started to play the piano along with it. After a few beats, he was suddenly and impetuously ahead of it. He shut it off with disgust.

"Bah," he exclaimed, "one is not a machine — music must breathe!" ❧

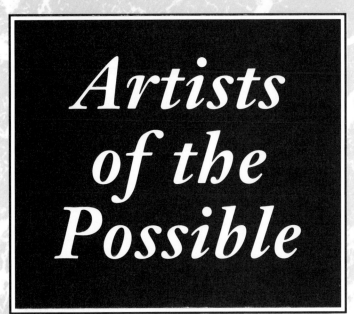

Artists of the Possible

THE LITTLE FLOWER

by Lawrence Elliot

Aside from all he may have accomplished, Fiorello La Guardia brought one unique element to the task of governing the world's most ungovernable city: a spirit of play. He read the Sunday funnies to New York's children over the radio. He chased after city fire engines. He whaled away at confiscated slot machines aboard a barge about to dump them. It all made for great theater for he had an innate sense of drama, the skill to use it politically, and the unshakable conviction that he was the man of the hour. Which he was.

Fiorello La Guardia: a marvelously mobile face that couldn't hold secrets

▼

LATE ONE EVENING between Christmas and New Year's Eve, 1945, New York's Commissioner of Investigation, Louis E. Yavner, drove up to a darkened City Hall. The three-term administration of Fiorello La Guardia was to end December 31, and Yavner, who had served it from the beginning, had some final matters to attend to.

But he wasn't alone. Down the echoing marble corridors came the erratic clacking sound of unskilled typing. It was nearly 8:00 p.m. Yavner followed the sound to the office of the mayor's secretary, and there sat La Guardia, pecking away with one finger and glaring at the keyboard as if it were a political adversary.

"What are you doing, Major?" Yavner asked, addressing La Guardia by his World War I military rank.

The mayor looked up, shoving his glasses back to the top of his head in a characteristic gesture. He was a round little man with a marvelously mobile face that couldn't hold secrets.

"Oh, hello, Lou," he said. "I've got these letters to get out and there was nobody else around. Say, can you type?"

"As well as that. But can't it wait until tomorrow?"

"Tomorrow there'll be something else to do. Come on, sit down."

So Yavner sat at the other typewriter and together he and La Guardia began clearing up the last loose ends of an era. For this was it: It was all over, the zeal, the melodramatics — and twelve years of the best reform government in American municipal history. And it was going out in the antic La Guardia style: The mayor was squeezing one last effort out of himself and whoever else he could lay hands on.

202

THE WONDER IS that he was ever elected in the first place. New York had never had a mayor of Italian descent. Moreover, he was a Republican in a city so overwhelmingly Democratic that not for twenty years had the Republicans won anything more nourishing than a few patronage crumbs and an occasional petty office.

In 1921, the Republican leader of Manhattan warned him, "Fiorello, this town isn't ready for an Italian mayor." In 1929, when he pried the nomination away from the bosses anyway, they sat on their hands while Jimmy Walker, then in his glory as the Beau James of Broadway, gave "the crazy little wop" the worst beating of his political career. When at last a Fusion party was organized to reclaim City Hall from Democratic corruption and fell to arguing about a nominee, one leader slammed a fist on the table and said, "If it's La Guardia or bust, I say bust!"

There was good reason for the regulars to fear the contentious little maverick. He fitted no political category. He was barely more tolerant of his own party than of the Democrats. "Some men who claim to be exponents of Republican principles," he said, "know as much about the teachings of Abraham Lincoln as Henry Ford knows about the Talmud."

He was a lawyer who castigated his profession, a champion of honest garment-center labor unions who was not a Socialist, a reformer who could play ward politics with the most devious Tammany aldermen, a campaigner with a dazzling gift for languages who walked out into the melting pot and talked to each of the city's ethnic groups in its own tongue — Italian, Yiddish, German, Spanish.

He was called the Little Flower but fought like a nettled wildcat. Forever bristling with indignation, he lashed out at every corrupt act, from ticket fixing to judge buying, uncovered by his furious energy. On the very day of his election, hearing that his people were not being allowed to vote in some polling places, he rushed out and found one being "watched" by twenty Tammany thugs.

"Get out! Get out, you bums," he yelled in that falsetto screech of his, "or I'll mop the floor with you!" When two policemen intervened, he threatened to throw them off the force the day he took office.

The day he did take office, he had a one-sentence answer for the shouted questions of reporters massed for his arrival at City Hall: "È finita la cuccagna."

"What the hell does that mean?" someone asked.

"It means," said Fiorello's barber and longtime friend, "Chich" Giordano, "no more free lunch."

HIS FRIEND GEORGE N. SHUSTER, president of Hunter College, thought the mayor's incessant intrusions into nonmayoral realms — he was forever going to fires, answering police calls, and lecturing housewives on cooking and good grocery buys — could be attributed to La Guardia's sense of New York as one big family. He, of course, was the father.

"He ought to have had fourteen children," concluded Shuster.

He would have had a hard time supporting them. He was broke nearly all the time. He had nothing but contempt for the acquisition of money as a personal goal. Be that as it may, the fact no one argues is that in an office whose temptations had overwhelmed many a predecessor, La Guardia was incorruptible.

But though it was in his nature to fly into a rage at even a hint of chicanery, there wasn't a trace of sanctimony or self-righteousness about him; he could never long fend off the essential humanity that animated his better self.

La Guardia had twenty months to live when he left office; those who knew him best say they were the loneliest months of his life. Once, there had been talk of his having a place on the Democratic presidential ticket. But it never happened, and when he came to the end of his third term as mayor, he had reached the end of his political life — the only one that mattered to him.

Two decades later, Robert Moses rose to make a few remarks at the dedication of a La Guardia bust at the New York airport named for the late mayor. They had not had the easiest relationship. An aide remembers at least one stormy meeting after which La Guardia, livid with anger, said, "Someday I'm going to knock that son of a bitch through the door."

But that day in 1964, Moses did not speak of their

THE ITALIAN SIDE OF AL SMITH

I HAVE ALWAYS WONDERED why my father loved Al Smith.

Where Smith was a Tammany Democrat, my father was a lifelong Republican. Smith was the quintessential Irish politician; my father nursed an undying hatred for the Irish. And yet, when he talked of Smith's loss to Franklin Roosevelt for the 1932 Democratic nomination, he spoke of it with the same holy sorrow that James Joyce reserved for the death of the betrayed Irish patriot, Parnell.

While that may be all there was to it — Smith being the despised Roosevelt's opposite, a kind of city-bred Lincoln who rose from the Bowery to challenge a New York Brahmin for the presidency — my guess is there was more.

Could it be that my father sensed, either from Al Smith's looks or from some gestural language that he used, that the New York governor harbored an Italian in his background?

A few years ago, such speculations elicited strong rejoinders from the Irish of Tammany Hall. During Smith's election campaign in 1926, in fact, a report was circulated by opponents that Smith's father had really been a German named Schmidt. The charge was met with outrage and proof to the contrary.

But in Matthew Josephson's biography of Al Smith, several converging lines of evidence are marshaled to support the claim that Smith's background, on his father's side, was Italian. His grandfather, as recorded in the New York Census of 1855, was a mariner named Emanuel Smith, birthplace Genoa. Though the

▲
Al Smith at age seven with his father — Alfredo Emanuelo Smith.

actual Italian surname does not appear, Josephson suggests that Emanuel Smith may well have been a Genoese cabin boy who landed in this country at the age of twelve or thirteen, and that his name was changed by a non-Italian-speaking immigration officer.

Al Smith's father, a teamster of strikingly Italian looks, gave several clues to this background. As remembered by his daughter, Mary Glynn, his key ring, initialed A.E.S., was said by him to stand for Alfredo Emanuelo Smith. Another detail she remembered was her father's boast that "I have an uncle who is Bishop of Naples." And on his death certificate, dated 1886, is found the name: Alfred Emanuel Smith; place of birth: New York City; father's birthplace: Italy; mother's name: Magdalena; mother's birthplace: Germany. It was this Alfredo Smith who married Catherine Mulvehill and fathered the governor and almost president, Al Smith.

Josephson concludes: "So the third generation Alfred Emanuel Smith, who was to be regarded for long years as this country's most famous Irish-American, was after all not a 'pure' Irishman at all, but a fine mixture of Italian, German, English, and Irish strains. . . . But for the whimsical intervention of an immigration officer, his surname might never have been Smith."

I have to wonder if Al, or my father, ever really knew.

— *Lawrence DiStasi*

---

confrontation. With elegance and his legendary wit, he evoked La Guardia, the surging social power plant that had illumined New York for twelve unforgettable years: "His motto was 'patience and fortitude.' He was not equipped with patience by inheritance, temperament, or experience, and perhaps he had a premonition that he would not be around long enough to finish everything. As to intestinal fortitude, known in the vernacular as 'guts,' he had far more than his share.

"The Little Flower invited caricature but never ridicule. . . . He was a gallant man, fiercely proud of our town and of our common humanity. Under La Guardia, reform, which had been merely respectable, became popular.

"Pause at this bust, traveler. Pause and reflect on the Little Flower. Give him a thought. He deserves well of the city. He was quite a man." ❧

After the Fall

by Barbara Grizzuti Harrison

After I got the nomination, if God had shown me pictures of the next six months of my life, I'd have said: "God, do me a favor — give it to Dianne Feinstein." But if God had then said to me: "Oh, Ger, Dianne can't have it; if you don't want it, it's gonna go to a man; I'm not gonna put a woman in that spot till the year 2000," I'd have said, "God, give me five minutes, just let me check this out with John" — and we would have gone for it.

GERALDINE FERRARO MUST have had quite an assortment of fairy godmothers presiding over her birth — good ones dispensing presents, and malicious ones doling out curses. She has had, as much as any woman of her time, her share of triumph and defeat.

She became the heroine of an immigrant saga and a feminist crusader. At the same time she was called a patsy of the mob, a flop who didn't know how to cut her losses. And very few people outside her family are prepared to say with certainty which if any of these things she really was.

More than a year after her disastrous defeat at the polls, when I spoke with her

and her mother, Antonetta Ferraro, a lot of muddy water had gone under a lot of shaky bridges. At that moment, Geraldine Ferraro was in a kind of limbo, reduced to making speeches — weak tea compared with the strong meat of power she'd enjoyed as a respected U.S. representative and the first woman to be nominated for the vice presidency by a major party.

SITTING IN HER mother's cozy apartment in Queens, Geraldine Ferraro didn't show the effects of her ordeal. In the flesh she still reminds us of the thrill many of us felt when she secured the nomination.

There was that familiar staccato voice, words tumbling over words, some of them irretrievably lost in the rush. She looked so familiar — that blond and breezy hair; the enormous green eyes; the somewhat off-puttingly thin lips (the eyes dance; the mouth lends itself to a controlled bitterness). She could have been

It seemed ironic: Italian American women had occupied the shadows forever, yet when the moment arrived for an Italian American to share the presidential ticket, the prize had gone to a woman. So Geraldine Ferraro remains memorable, even while losing. Ella Grasso, on the other hand, always won. When she died in office as Connecticut's and the nation's first woman governor, she had never lost an election.

a suburban matron, any woman dressed for success in cashmere and tweed, any dutiful daughter. But we both knew what the agenda was: Geraldine Ferraro After the Fall.

"I don't know who's the mother and who's the daughter any more," Antonetta Ferraro says. "She's got a heart bigger than the whole world, my daughter. She pays for everything. I wish to God every mother could say this . . . 'cause, see, we were together a lot; she was eight when her father died."

Ferraro is bitter when her father's name comes up in articles alleging family connections to the Mafia. "He was a very big man," she says, "about six foot three, always hugging and kissing and always carrying me . . . My mother had a one-and-ten-cent store, and he had a bar, so during the day he'd sneak off and take me to see Shirley Temple movies."

She says she gets "the most godawful hate mail — devastating." One particularly vile piece was a bloody picture of a slain gang leader. "Here's one of your own," the poison-pen writer had scrawled. Ferraro has stopped reading all mail without an identifiable address.

WE GET BACK to some of the issues for which Mrs. Ferraro was attacked during the campaign. "Do you and your mother have differences of opinion on abortion?" she was asked.

Antonetta Ferraro stubbornly champions her daughter. "I was against abortion," she says, "but I was against what they were doing to you."

"My mother said, 'You've gotta change about abortion, Gerri; they're crucifying you.' I told my mother I honestly couldn't change. I honestly do believe that it is up to the woman . . ."

"But you don't believe they should have abortions, do you?" her mother asks.

"Ma, there are a lot of people who don't believe as we do. It's up to them to make their own decisions. I wouldn't even make that decision for my daughters . . ."

"Look," Geraldine Ferraro says to me, "my mother is a Catholic woman who was brought up on the teachings of the church — just like my mother-in-law — but, whether or not they support my view, they understand why I believe as I do. They're not in a position to affect other people's lives. Until I ran for office, I wasn't either."

"Why, every time they write something about my daughter, they have to put in abortion?" Antonetta says.

Geraldine Ferraro is as protective of her mother as her mother is of her: "I can't ask my mother about any of the awful stuff they're printing about my father. She'd go crazy."

Antonetta Ferraro once happened to tune in to a radio talk show — "savage," Geraldine calls it — and heard a "brutal attack on my father and my husband. They tore me to pieces. My mother called me up in tears. She said, 'I should have died and this wouldn't have happened to you.' For some reason she thought I was attacked because of her, because she was alive. . . She got sick right after the show. I'm not about to subject her to any more garbage."

And yet — what did Geraldine Ferraro mean when she said, "You people who are married to Italian men, you know what it's like"?

"That was not a put-down of Italian men," she says. "Nobody loves Italian men more than I do — my father had a thick Italian accent; my husband is Italian. What I was referring to is that my husband is very *private*."

Donna Zaccaro then says that her mother is private too: "Mom is a firm believer in not trusting anybody but your family," she says. "There are things you share only with your family. You don't go outside."

It's a study in contradictions — an intensely private woman who was the most visible woman in the United States for much of 1984.

WHAT'S NEXT FOR Geraldine Ferraro?

"There's always something else out there. I don't worry. I figure if it's not today, it's gonna be tomorrow. And, if it's not in politics, it'll be something else. The rest of my life I'll have to be so careful. I'll have to be like Caesar's wife; it's like becoming a virgin all over again.

"I was a good trial lawyer; I love the law. Would anybody offer me a job in a law firm now? I don't know.

"But I have no complaints. Thank God, I live well; my mother's well; I have three healthy kids; I've been blessed with love, blessed with John, blessed with resources to do the things I want. I harbor no complaints — or very few. I kind of feel, as a result of that, that I have an obligation."

All of a sudden she is back on the campaign trail, talking about civic obligations, social-justice programs. And I think, this is the first person of my gender ever to have been nominated for the second-highest office in our land.

I am sitting with a historical personage . . .

A historical personage who, in the middle of her campaign speech, as it were, goes to examine her new computer.

I understand — although she doesn't say good-bye — that the interview is over. ❧

ELLA GRASSO PLAYS HOOKY

EARLY LAST MAY, on the eve of her fifty-sixth birthday and four months after her inauguration as governor of Connecticut, Ella T. Grasso rose early, went to pray at a 6:30 a.m. Mass, prayed again at 8 at the governor's annual prayer breakfast, again at 9 at a Memorial Mass for John M. Bailey, her political mentor, and finally arrived at the state capitol at 10.

Flanked by a state policeman in civvies and her husband, a retired school administrator whom she calls "my very best friend, Tommy," the governor, clad in a beige pants suit, strode serenely, shoulders back, aware of being observed, up the central stairs to her second-floor office. People who know her say her walk began changing when a poll showed, about this time last year, that she was destined to rule her state. Her daughter, Susan, once gave Mrs. Grasso a toy duck to remind her not to waddle. Other changes, too: "Suddenly," remarks an old acquaintance, "she's Italian. She never used to mention it, but now she's free at last to be an ethnic."

Ella Grasso likes her new job. She put in twenty-two years of public life to get it and relishes its long, hard days. But this was to be a particularly strife-ridden day at the capitol, which, she decided, might best be served by her playing hooky.

Before the day was over — as she'd sensed — state workers would drown out General Assembly debate with a hallway chant: "Defeat the budget!" Worse still, welfare lobbyists would swarm outside her office door, shouting — and this was no adoring campaign slogan — "We want Ella! Where's Ella?"

Where Ella Rosa Giovanna Oliva Tambussi Grasso was, was on a journey to her childhood, a ceremonial visit to Chaffee School, a half hour's drive from Hartford.

Nostalgically, she directed her driver around the picture-book campus. Her ticket, as a youngster, through this elegant place was provided by a Rockefeller scholarship endowment and her high grades at St. Mary's Parochial School, just as her high grades here opened the way to a scholarship at Mt. Holyoke College.

Her academic energy apparently came from her mother who was "a great reader"; Ella's father, a

▲ Gov. Ella Grasso delivers her State of the State address.

baker, "pretended he could read and write." She commuted daily from her Windsor Locks home to Chaffee by railroad.

"Turn right, turn left," she told the driver, and the car crossed the town line into Windsor Locks, past an ancient, long, red-brick factory.

"That used to be a cotton mill and my mother worked there. My father had his bakery shop right where that orange car is. This is the street where my father was hit by a rock, because he was an Italian looking for work. My mother came here from Italy when she was fourteen and lived with her brother, and made five dollars a week — go right, please — and married my father and moved into his house with all my father's brothers and their mother, who was a tyrant. My mother had to be subservient, and she was not the type.

"And this is Olive Street, my street. That's where I was born, right there, and married Tom and we lived there, until we moved across the street there, 13 Olive Street. My uncle lives right there, we shared a common driveway, and he's still got my mother's cat."

"In my senior year at Chaffee," the governor mused as we headed out of town, "they said in the yearbook I would be the first woman mayor of Windsor Locks. I was horrified — politics!

"I mean, I aspired to something eminently greater."

— Bernard Asbell

POPULIST MANIFESTO

Poets, come out of your closets,
Open your windows, open your doors,
You have been holed-up too long
in your closed worlds.
Come down, come down
from your Russian Hills and Telegraph Hills,
your Beacon Hills and your Chapel Hills,
your Mount Analogues and Montparnasses,
down from your foot hills and mountains,
out of your tepees and domes.
The trees are still falling
and we'll to the woods no more.
No time now for sitting in them
As man burns down his own house
to roast his pig.
No more chanting Hare Krishna
while Rome burns.
San Francisco's burning,
Mayakovsky's Moscow's burning
the fossil-fuels of life.
Night & the Horse approaches
eating light, heat & power,
and the clouds have trousers.

No time now for the artist to hide
above, beyond, behind the scenes,
indifferent, paring his fingernails,
refining himself out of existence.
No time now for our little literary games,
no time now for our paranoias &
    hypochondrias,
no time now for fear & loathing,
time now only for light & love.
We have seen the best minds of our generation
destroyed by boredom at poetry readings.
Poetry isn't a secret society,
It isn't a temple either.
Secret words & chants won't do any longer.
The hour of *om*ing is over,
the time for keening come,
time for keening & rejoicing
over the coming end
of industrial civilization
which is bad for earth & Man.
Time now to face outward
in the full lotus position
with eyes wide open,

208

Time now to open your mouths
with a new open speech,
time now to communicate with all sentient
    beings,
All you 'Poets of the Cities'
hung in museums, including myself,
All you poet's poets writing poetry
about poetry,
All you poetry workshop poets
in the boondock heart of America,
All you house-broken Ezra Pounds,
All you far-out freaked-out cut-up poets,
All you pre-stressed Concrete poets,
All you cunnilingual poets,
All you pay-toilet poets groaning with graffiti,
All you A-train swingers who never swing on
    birches,
All you masters of the sawmill haiku
in the Siberias of America,
All you eyeless unrealists,
All you self-occulting supersurrealists,
All you bedroom visionaries
and closet agitpropagators,
All you Groucho Marxist poets
And leisure-class Comrades
who lie around all day
and talk about the workingclass proletariat,
All you Catholic anarchists of poetry,
All you Black Mountaineers of poetry,
All you Boston Brahmins and Bolinas bucolics,
All you den mothers of poetry,
All you zen brothers of poetry,
All you hairy professors of poesie,
All you poetry reviewers
drinking the blood of the poet,
All you Poetry Police —
Where are Whitman's wild children,
where the great voices speaking out
with a sense of sweetness and sublimity,
where the great new vision,

the great world-view,
the high prophetic song
of the immense earth
and all that sings in it
And our relation to it —
Poets, descend
to the street of the world once more
And open your minds & eyes
with the old visual delight,
Clear your throat and speak up,
Poetry is dead, long live poetry
with terrible eyes and buffalo strength.
Don't wait for the Revolution
or it'll happen without you,
Stop mumbling and speak out
with a new wide-open poetry
with a new commonsensual 'public surface'
with other subjective levels
or other subversive levels,
a tuning fork in the inner ear
to strike below the surface.
Of your own sweet Self still sing
yet utter 'the word en-masse' —
Poetry the common carrier
for the transportation of the public
to higher places
than other wheels can carry it.
Poetry still falls from the skies
into our streets still open.
They haven't put up the barricades yet,
the streets still alive with faces,
lovely men & women still walking there,
still lovely creatures everywhere,
in the eyes of all the secret of all
still buried there,
Whitman's wild children still sleeping there,
Awake and walk in the open air.

— *Lawrence Ferlinghetti*

THE MAN FOR THE TIMES

by Neil MacNeil

The political disaster known as Watergate had the unlikely side effect of thrusting two Italian Americans into pivotal roles. One was the Watergate judge John J. Sirica, whose pugnacious handling of the Watergate burglars led to the breaking of the case. The other was Congressman Peter Rodino, the man who led the Judiciary Committee to the second impeachment vote of a sitting president in U.S. history. It is not known if President Nixon had either in mind when he said, as revealed on the Watergate tapes, "We mustn't forget the Italians. . . . The trouble is . . . you can't find one that's honest."

"YOU NOT ONLY have to be fair — you have to give the appearance of fairness," Chairman Peter Rodino has said of his job, and it often seemed to be an impossible task during the long and wearisome months in which he led his unwieldy thirty-eight-member Judiciary Committee down the path toward impeachment articles.

But even as his committee inched toward its bipartisan vote of 27-11 against the president, the silver-haired chairman with the husky voice was praised for his fairness by House GOP Leader John Rhodes as well as by House Democratic Leader Thomas P. Tip O'Neill, Jr.

"It's magnificent how he rose to the challenge," said O'Neill.

When the Nixon impeachment proceedings first began, Rodino was a little-known congressman from Newark, New Jersey, an established figure who had learned during his twenty-five years on the Hill how the House operates but whose own personal leadership had never been tested. Says "Tip" O'Neill: "He was a flame under a bushel basket."

The son of an Italian immigrant worker, Rodino was raised in the fiercely ethnic Little Italy section of Newark, in a neighborhood so tough that he recalls shootings in the streets. Rodino wrote an unpublished novel about his upbringing entitled *Drift Street*. At one time he had hopes of becoming a poet — he still loves to recite Shakespeare, Byron, Shelley and Keats — but he diligently worked his way through the University of Newark Law School.

After serving as an Army captain during World War II, Rodino was first elected to Congress in 1948. As a congressman, he concentrated on ethnic issues. When the inexorable elevator of seniority made him chairman of the Judiciary Committee in 1973, Rodino was perhaps best known as the man who had made Columbus Day a national holiday.

With a background of modest legislative accomplishment, Rodino failed to inspire the confidence of the House's Democratic leaders when impeachment first became a possibility, a scant seven months after he had become judiciary chairman. Speaker Carl Albert pointedly suggested to Rodino that, instead of giving the matter to the Judiciary Committee, the House should perhaps set up a special select body to conduct the inquiry. Rodino flatly refused to go along, and Albert gave way.

Rodino did not relish the job of conducting the impeachment inquiry. He has had a friendly relationship with Nixon over the years and, he says, "I'd rather find the good in people than the bad." But to get ready, he quietly assigned Jerome Ziefman, chief of the judiciary staff, and two of his assistants to study the process and precedents. Rodino himself began boning up on how the delegates to the Constitutional Convention had viewed impeachment.

Rodino also studied the seminal writings of Edmund Burke, who argued that impeachment should rest "not upon the niceties of a narrow jurisprudence, but upon the enlarged and solid principles of state morality." Three times the chairman read historian Michael Les Benedict's 1973 book, *The Impeachment and Trial of Andrew Johnson*. Rodino was frank enough to admit his awe at his onrushing responsibilities. "I lie awake nights," he once admitted. "I just hope I'll be able to live up to them."

210

Promised an unlimited budget by Speaker Albert, Rodino assembled a staff and started looking for a chief counsel. To avoid any charge of partisanship, Rodino wanted an outsider and a Republican. For two months, while the Democratic leadership squirmed at the delay, Rodino consulted deans of law schools, judges, bar-association officials, and leading attorneys before chooosing John Doar in December.

They made an odd couple — the voluble politician from the streets of Newark and the taciturn Princeton man who worked on civil rights in the Justice Department under Presidents Dwight Eisenhower and John Kennedy. But the two men worked closely with growing mutual respect.

From the start, Rodino recognized the danger that the inquiry could blow up in the hands of the Democrats if the nation perceived it to be a partisan vendetta against the president. Against the advice of Doar, Rodino decided in fairness to allow Presidential Counsel James St. Clair not only to attend the sessions but to question witnesses and to call all the witnesses he wanted. And all the while, the chairman was urging the Democratic firebrands to stop calling for impeachment.

The members went along with Rodino, although not always happily. Snapped De-

troit's John Conyers: "I just want to make sure he's not too damn fair."

Rodino's work load was horrendous. Week after week, the committee met in closed session from 9:30 to 5 every Tuesday, Wednesday and Thursday. But those were only the formal sessions. Rodino was at his desk every morning at 8 and often was still there after midnight, sometimes conferring with his staff as late as 3 a.m. When he got a chance, he relaxed by playing paddleball on the congressional courts or by listening to opera records — *Tosca* is his favorite — in the apartment he maintains near the Capitol.

The pace was too fast. In February, Rodino landed in Bethesda Naval Medical Center for a few days. He feared heart trouble, but the diagnosis was simple exhaustion.

"If I had it to do over," Rodino quipped, "maybe I'd have worked harder to be a poet."

As the inquiry went on, Rodino found himself confronted by an insoluble dilemma: the need to be fast as well as thorough. In closed sessions, Doar droned on and on, presenting the evidence that eventually filled thirty-six black loose-leaf binders — seventy-two hundred pages in all. The whole inquiry was in danger of falling apart. The country was nodding off. "The committee is drowning in a sea of material," complained one

THE RETURN OF FRANK RIZZO

FRANK RIZZO MADE his entrance as usual. A long, black city car pulled up to the pavement outside the church at Sixteenth and Jefferson in North Philadelphia and the once and would-be future mayor stepped out, looked around, adjusted his coat, quickly twisted his neck against the tight, white collar of his shirt, and marched toward the church, shoulder to shoulder with his bodyguards. Instinctively one of them, the giant Tony Fulwood, leaned forward to drive a wedge through the small crowd.

As soon as the people realized that Frank Rizzo was there, they filled the street to get a glimpse of him — reporters, politicians, mourners and neighborhood people, black and white. If Ulysses Shelton could have, he would have risen from his casket there in the church to greet Frank Rizzo, too.

Tonight was just like the old days — only better. Rizzo was thinner, trimmer, more relaxed — and satisfied. Very, very satisfied. You could see it in his face, in the way he beamed at them.

Frank Rizzo, the ex-mayor who had left office in defeat after his suicidal effort to change the city charter to allow him to run for a third consecutive term, was making a rare public appearance, and the people were going berserk. Only this time, it was better. This time Rizzo could taste the vindication.

He was returning from Elba and they knew it. The long march toward the interior, the final anabasis of his political career, was about to begin, and the omens couldn't have been better.

Inside the church, the excited bereaved started paying their respects to Rizzo before they even remembered to say good-bye to old Senator Shelton. Most of the people were black. If any of them had ever trembled before Rizzo's "racist" rhetoric, they weren't showing it now.

He'd been out of office for a year and

a half, but it was, "Good to see you, Mr. Mayor" and "Thanks for coming, Mayor Rizzo."

And Frank Rizzo was luxuriating in it as he settled himself into a pew. He greeted everyone, even the ones he didn't know by name, with that Kodiak warmth that had always been so irresistible. "Thank you," he said. "Call me, don't forget."

Then, Rizzo would nod and smile and squeeze another hand with that huge, soft paw of his.

Frank Rizzo, he seemed to be saying, *is still Frank Rizzo. Just touch him and see for yourself.*

And touch him they did. For some, it was like caressing a relic.

ON THE THIRD day Jesus Christ rose from the dead.

It took Frank Rizzo a little longer, but in the end, he pulled off the same kind of miracle.

The Occasion for Rizzo's Reappearance was the final offensive in the bitterly fought Joe Smith–David Glancey special congressional war for the vacated seat of convicted Abscamer Ray Lederer.

In the end, the handsome Glancey and his progressive campaign of electronic gimmickry, superstar endorsements and enlightened liberal philosophy would lose soundly to the powers of political darkness as personified by the grumpy, inarticulate Joe Smith.

Downtown would lose, and lose badly, to Whitetown.

Frank Rizzo had done it again. He had risen from the ashes once more and this time, the body that he would walk over would be David Glancey's.

Frank Rizzo had actually done next to nothing in the Smith-Glancey race. He'd made a few phone calls, talked to a handful of committeemen and said some kind words about Joe Smith. But he hadn't really campaigned even for one day. The insiders knew that if Smith went down, Rizzo wouldn't have wanted to appear too close to a loser.

But in victory, Joe Smith would become Frank Rizzo's man. All Frank Rizzo had done, in fact, to ensure Smith's victory, had been just to be Frank Rizzo.

But, as they found out, that was more than enough.

— Mike Mallowe

ranking Republican congressman, who was ready to vote for impeachment. The Democratic leaders in the House pressured Rodino to get on with it.

Doar drove himself until his face was gray to prepare his final brief, and Rodino steered his faction-torn committee to its climactic and bipartisan vote to impeach — the goal he had been striving for all along.

Through it all — the proddings from his own leaders and the cries from the White House that he was conducting a "kangaroo court" — Rodino had kept his cool. As his colleagues acknowledged, by and large Chairman Rodino could say with justification, "We have deliberated, we have been patient, we have been fair." ❧

THE ORATIONS
OF
MARIO CUOMO

by Jeffrey Schmalz

MARIO CUOMO LIKES to play games, and on this day in April the game is baseball, the opening of Pilot Field in Buffalo. Thirty-five years ago, as a player in the minor leagues, his position was outfielder. But today he is on the pitcher's mound. No matter that it is politics, not athletic ability, that has put him there; he is in his glory. Uniform No. 5 — his lucky number — is on his back.

Twenty thousand Buffalo Bison fans chant, "Mario! Mario! Mario!"

The governor of New York winds up to throw the opening pitch.

By afternoon's end, Cuomo seems caught up in a rush of emotion — back home on the baseball diamond after all these years. But with his emotions, as with his pitching, little is what it appears to be. "They called me Mario," he says after leaving the field. "That's a good sign politically."

TO MANY SUPPORTERS and political strategists, 1988 was supposed to be the year of Mario Cuomo. Never mind that he announced on February 19, 1987, that he was not running for president. Surely the governor — who won reelection in 1986 by the widest margin in the state's history, and whose speeches stir such emotion — would be drafted at the Democratic National Convention.

But by early April, even before Cuomo said he would not accept a draft, the chances for one appeared dead. Gov. Michael S. Dukakis would be the Democratic candidate. Mario Cuomo, although still certain to exert a strong influence in the debate over issues, had lost his chance, this time out, to be president.

Yet the fascination with Cuomo continues, perhaps even grows. Even Nancy Reagan, taken by the governor's humor, by his dazzling speaking ability and by his compassion toward her husband, is pressing friends to tell her more about him.

Like perhaps only Fiorello La Guardia before him, Mario Cuomo has been able to turn his Italian American story into one that has national resonance. Whether this is due to his oratorical gifts or to a historical moment that favors Italian American values, this ability puts him in possession of one of the most potent political endowments in the country. The mystery is what he plans to do with it.

How did this man, who many thought could be president, come not to run? What was the game he seemed to be playing? And what is he up to now? Four years of covering Cuomo as a reporter have put me at his side day after day, week after week.

The four years are a roller coaster of images:

Cuomo pacing in his office: "Lincoln. Lincoln had bad press too. He wasn't appreciated until after he was gone."

Cuomo backstage in seclusion after one of his major speeches, bent over, breathless and spent, like an athlete who has just finished a race.

Cuomo, the Roman Catholic and quick wit, remaining calm as some around him panicked when one of the two engines on his state plane failed: "What's the matter? Aren't you in a state of grace?"

If there is one lesson from those four years, it is that what you see with Cuomo is not necessarily what you get. Concentrate on what he does, not what he says. The two are often different.

In part, the contradiction seems to flow from Cuomo's struggle to reconcile his upbringing in South Jamaica, Queens, as the son of nearly illiterate immigrants, with his current life as the powerful governor of New York and a potential president. In fact, Cuomo sometimes seems caught not just between two worlds but three — that impoverished past, the powerful present, and the idealized rendering of how he leaped from one to the other, the starting point of the American Dream of his speeches.

He moves audiences with loving stories, many of them now famous, about his upbringing: spending tough days of after-school work in the family grocery store imagining a better life; his father, Andrea, working so hard that his feet bled.

But they are painful stories too. Clearly, the poor days in South Jamaica that he glorifies in his speeches had their cruel moments as well.

"A lot of my stories about the old days, they're delicious and funny," Cuomo says, "but every time I recall the early days, it's painful — painful because you're summoning up the terribly, terribly difficult life of my parents. And it's painful because I didn't realize at the time how hard it was for them."

If there is any solace in public office for Cuomo, it seems to lie in his speeches. They are his hobby, his diversion. The man who spoke only Italian until he entered grade school has a deep appreciation of the English language. He writes the bulk of each speech himself, laboring for hours over language and meter.

They are, in fact, not speeches, really, but something closer to sermons — inspirational messages about a place where the American Dream can still come true, and where those who share in it help those who do not. As such, these addresses have sometimes drawn criticism for merely stating the obvious — that prosperity is better than poverty, that compassion is better than selfishness.

But they are the strongest source of Cuomo's popularity. And like all good sermons, they chastise the audience for the sins of greed and selfishness. They are an appeal to the heart, not the intellect.

Ultimately, that may also be the appeal of Mario Cuomo himself. People seem to react emotionally, not intellectually, to his message of compassion and brotherhood. His major contribution, many political analysts believe, is his ability to bind people together, rather than drive them apart. If Mayor Koch was a voice of divisiveness in the New York primary, pitting Jew against black, Cuomo at his most eloquent is a voice of unity.

"Don't you understand?" he asked me one day when an article on his speech reported that he had spoken in general terms, avoiding the details, "Leadership isn't a multiple-choice test on the issues. Any idiot can study and pass that. Leadership is making the people feel confident in you. Leadership is setting the tone of compassion and working together and respect for the rule of law."

And has Mario Cuomo done that? I asked.

"Mario Cuomo sleeps very well at night," he said. ❧

CUOMO AT THE DEMOCRATIC CONVENTION, 1984

"There is despair, Mr. President, in the faces that you don't see, in the places that you don't visit in your shining city. . .This nation is more a tale of two cities than it is just a shining city on a hill."

"We must make the American people hear our 'tale of two cities.' We must convince them that we don't have to settle for two cities, that we can have one city, indivisible, shining for all of its people."

"And we can do it again. If we do not forget that this entire nation has profited by these progressive principles. That they helped lift up generations to the middle class and higher; that they gave us a chance to work, to go to college, to raise a family, to own a house, to be secure in our old age and, before that, to reach heights that our own parents would not have dared dream of."

THE PIONEER

WHEN JOHN ORLANDO Pastore was growing up on Federal Hill in Providence, Rhode Island, his mother's constant advice was: "Make people respect you."

Rispetto. It meant then what it always has to Italians: the central gauge of a person's worth.

But this was America, and for John Pastore, as for other Italian Americans, it meant also "respectability." It meant achieving a position where never again would a neighbor send a Christmas basket to the Pastore house; never again would his mother be mortified for appearing destitute.

To get respect *and* respectability in those days took luck and determination, and Pastore had both. Born on St. Patrick's Day in 1907, he early decided that the avenue to respectability lay first in a career in law — he went to night school — and then in the Democratic political organization, controlled by the Irish, but just opening up to Italian Americans like Tommy Testa. Pastore went to Testa in 1933 and said, "I'd like to go into politics." Impressed, Testa helped Pastore get the nomination for state assembly. John Pastore won that election in 1934, and again in 1936. It began a familiar pattern: Pastore never lost an election in almost fifty years of politics.

After a stint as a prosecutor, he was the beneficiary of the first of the resignations that would propel him to power. The lieutenant governor, Louis Cappelli, resigned to take a judgeship. Pastore was talked into running for the lieutenant governor's post, then a part-time, decidedly minor post paying $2,500.

But the Pastore luck was running true. Only months after he and the governor, John McGrath, had won, McGrath resigned to accept a post as President Truman's solicitor general. Pastore, a "nobody" in his own estimation, became the first Italian American governor in 1945.

Pastore lost no time in becoming a somebody. Always a riveting speaker, he spoke for any group that asked for him. And he compiled a record for rectitude that paid off. Where in 1946, with no record to run on, he won by a scant twenty-two thousand votes, by the next election he won by a record seventy-three thousand

▲
John Pastore of the littlest state with someone from the biggest state

votes. As Pastore said: "I'm the only governor who ever went from the smallest to the largest plurality in one election."

That blending of little and big is vintage Pastore. Calling himself the smallest governor (he stands five feet, four inches) of the smallest state, he is also known for the stentorian power of his speaking voice. A champion of the little man who still lived in a forty-five dollar a month apartment when he became governor, he spends a good fifteen minutes each morning getting his tie fixed in just the right knot. It even shows up in his political maneuvering: When Democrats in Rhode Island refused to consider anything but a corporate tax on the "bigs" and Republicans demanded a sales tax aimed at the "littles," Pastore found a way to impose both — a one-cent sales tax and a 4 percent tax on corporate income.

Then in 1950 the Pastore luck repeated itself: John McGrath resigned the Senate seat he then held to become attorney general. Pastore ran for McGrath's unexpired term and won big. He has been winning big ever since.

The journey was complete. The little man had moved from Federal Hill to Capitol Hill, and in so doing, added the Senate first to the Governor's first he already had.

It is a measure of the man that he made it seem easy.

— *Thomas DiMauro*

215

The House of Valentino

ADAGIO DANCER

by John Dos Passos

THE NINETEENYEAROLD son of a veterinary in Castellaneta in the south of Italy was shipped off to America like a lot of other unmanageable young Italians when his parents gave up trying to handle him, to sink or swim and maybe send a few lire home by international postal moneyorder. The family was through with him. But Rodolfo Guglielmi wanted to make good.

He got a job as assistant gardener in Central Park, but that kind of work was the last thing he wanted to do; he wanted to make good in the brightlights; money burned his pockets.

He hung around cabarets doing odd jobs, sweeping out for the waiters, washing cars; he was lazy handsome wellbuilt slender goodtempered and vain; he was a born tangodancer.

Lovehungry women thought he was a darling. He began to get engagements dancing the tango in ballrooms and cabarets; he teamed up with a girl named Jean Acker on a vaudeville tour and took the name of Rudolph Valentino.

Stranded on the Coast he headed for Hollywood, worked for a long time as an extra for five dollars a day; directors began to notice he photographed well.

He got his chance in *The Four Horsemen*
and became the gigolo of every woman's dreams.

VALENTINO SPENT HIS life in the colorless glare of klieg lights, in stucco villas obstructed with bricabrac, Oriental rugs, tigerskins, in the bridalsuites of hotels, in silk bathrobes in private cars.

He was always getting into limousines or getting out of limousines,
or patting the necks of fine horses.

Wherever he went the sirens of the motorcyclecops screeched ahead of him,
flashlights flared,

At a time when millions of his countrymen struggled to be seen simply as human, he, a celluloid Italian, became the first screen idol. Women dreamed of him. Men dreamed of being like him, hoping at the same time that the stories of his effeminacy, of his being a love-slave to Rambova, were true. In every Italian American family there was nurtured in dark halls at least one, the handsome one, to keep alive the hope, as vivid as hitting the numbers, that the Valentino syndrome could strike again.

the streets were jumbled with hysterical faces, waving hands, crazy eyes; they stuck out their autographbooks, yanked his buttons off, cut a tail off his admirablytailored dress-suit; they stole his hat and pulled at his necktie; his valets removed young women from under his bed; all night in nightclubs and cabarets actresses leching for stardom made sheepseyes at him under their mascaraed lashes.

He wanted to make good under the glare of the million-dollar searchlights
of El Dorado:
the Sheik, the Son of the Sheik;
personal appearances.

HE MARRIED HIS old vaudeville partner, divorced her, married the adopted daughter of a millionaire, went into lawsuits with the producers who were debasing the art of the screen, spent a million dollars on one European trip;
he wanted to make good in the brightlights.

When the Chicago *Tribune* called him a pink powderpuff
and everybody started wagging their heads over a slave-bracelet he wore that he said his wife had given him and his taste for mushy verse of which he published a small volume called *Daydreams* and the whispers grew about the testimony in his divorce case that he and his first wife had never slept together,
it broke his heart.

He tried to challenge the Chicago *Tribune* to a duel;
he wanted to make good
in heman twofisted broncobusting pokerplaying stockjuggling America. (He was a fair boxer and had a good seat on a horse; he loved the desert like the sheik and was tanned from the sun of Palm Springs.) He broke down in his suite in the Hotel Ambassador in

New York: gastric ulcer.

WHEN THE DOCTORS cut into his elegantlymolded body, they found that peritonitis had begun; the abdominal cavity contained a large amount of fluid and food particles; the viscera were coated with a greenishgray film; a round hole a centimeter in diameter was seen in the anterior wall of the stomach; the tissue of the stomach for one and onehalf centimeters immedi-ately surrounding the perforation was necrotic. The appendix was inflamed and twisted against the small intestine.

When he came to from the ether, the first thing he said was, "Well, did I behave like a pink powderpuff?"

HIS EXPENSIVELYMASSAGED actor's body fought peritonitis for six days.

The switchboard at the hospital was swamped with calls, all the corridors were piled with flowers, crowds filled the street outside, filmstars who claimed they were his betrothed entrained for New York.

Late in the afternoon a limousine drew up at the hospital (where the grimyfingered newspapermen and photographers stood around bored tired hoteyed smoking too many cigarettes making trips to the nearest speak exchanging wise-cracks and deep dope waiting for him to die in time to make the evening papers), and a woman, who said she was a maid employed by a dancer who was Valentino's first wife, alighted. She delivered to an attendant an envelope addressed to the filmstar and inscribed "From Jean," and a package. The package contained a white counterpane with lace ruffles and the word 'Rudy' embroidered on the four corners. This was accompanied by a pillowcover to match over a blue silk scented cushion.

Rudolph Valentino was only thirtyone when he died.

HIS MANAGERS PLANNED to make a big thing of his highly-publicized funeral, but the people in the streets were too crazy.

While he lay in state in a casket covered with a cloth of gold, tens of thousands of men, women, and children packed the streets outside. Hundreds were trampled, had their feet hurt by policehorses. In the muggy rain the cops lost control. Jammed masses stampeded under the clubs and the rearing hoofs of the horses. The funeral chapel was gutted, men and women fought over a flower, a piece of wallpaper, a piece of the broken plateglass windows. Showwindows were burst in. Parked cars were overturned and smashed. When finally the mounted police after

---

SONS OF VALENTINO

By Ed Rachles

repeated charges beat the crowd off Broadway, where traffic was tied up for two hours, they picked up twentyeight separate shoes, a truckload of umbrellas, papers, hats, tornoff sleeves. All the ambulances in that part of the city were busy carting off women who'd fainted, girls who'd been stepped on. Epileptics threw fits. Cops collected little groups of abandoned children.

The fascisti sent a guard of honor and the antifascists drove them off. More rioting, cracked skulls, trampled feet. When the public was barred from the undertaking parlors, hundreds of women groggy with headlines got in to view the poor body,

claiming to be exdancingpartners, old playmates, relatives from the old country, filmstars; every few minutes a girl fainted in front of the bier and was revived by the newspapermen who put down her name and address and claim to notice in the public prints. Frank E. Campbell's undertakers and pallbearers, dignified wearers of black broadcloth and tackersup of crape, were on the verge of a nervous breakdown. Even the boss had his fill of publicity that time.

It was two days before the cops could clear the streets enough to let the flowerpieces from Hollywood be brought in and described in the evening papers.

THE CHURCH SERVICE was more of a success. The police commissioner barred the public for four blocks around.

Many notables attended.

America's Sweetheart, sobbing bitterly in a small black straw with a black band and a black bow behind, in black georgette over black with a white lace collar and white lace cuffs, followed the coffin that was covered by a blanket of pink roses sent by a filmstar who appeared at the funeral heavily veiled, and swooned and had to be taken back to her suite at the Hotel Ambassador after she had shown the reporters a message allegedly written by one of the doctors alleging that Rudolph Valentino had spoken of her at the end
as his bridetobe.

A YOUNG WOMAN committed suicide in London.

Relatives arriving from Europe were met by police reserves and Italian flags draped with crape. Exchamp Jim Jeffries said, "Well, he made good." The champion allowed himself to be quoted that the boy was fond of boxing and a great admirer of the champion.

The funeral train left for Hollywood.

In Chicago a few more people were hurt trying to see the coffin, but only made the inside pages.

The funeral train arrived in Hollywood on page 23 of the New York *Times*. ❧

THE REAL ANNE BANCROFT

by Michele Linfante

A S THE STORY goes, a budding TV actress named Anne Marno screen-tested and signed a contract with 20th Century Fox in 1951, while leaning against the plate glass window of a swank department store on New York's Fifth Avenue. When she arrived in Hollywood, Darryl Zanuck, sure that her moniker and her face would type her, gave her a list of possible names. They all sounded like the names of strippers, with "Bancroft" being the only one that had any dignity, so she took it. Thus one of the living legends of American drama was, in name, born.

It must have been easy enough to change her name by then since she had done it herself a few times. Before Marno she was Anne St. Raymond, having tried out the stage name of Anne Tulane in high school, when in fact she was born Anna Maria Louisa Italiano to Mildred (DiNapoli) and Michael Italiano. That was in 1931, on St. Raymond Street in the Bronx.

Everyone knows by now about the Hollywood system that, until the likes of Pacino and DeNiro made a breakthrough, only created products in an Anglo-American image. It's a system that shaped my longing. I too experimented with several names. I too wanted to be an actress. But even more than that I wanted not to be Italian. Could this have been true of Anne-Italiano-St. Raymond-Tulane-Marno-Bancroft? Does it matter?

In any case the accidental name certainly fit this actress who brought to the American screen that rare combination which she personifies — both class and soul. But underneath that name and the image it conjures, is there a real Anne Bancroft?

In public what we see is an

Anne Bancroft appears as a prototypical Italian American actress. Initially possessed of neither the "look" nor a name Hollywood could merchandise easily, she has made, and remade, herself memorable by virtue of fire and intelligence. One wonders if Ida Lupino's films — films about characters who, cast out of their familiar environments, do not know how to act — reveal the flip side of this alienated terrain.

▶
**Anne Bancroft:
As Anna Maria
Louisa Italiano,
she sang to a
guy named
Whitey.**

elegant woman, apparently well adjusted to an unlikely marriage, who believes it's men who really need careers. Who still, after twenty-four years, finds her husband, the zany Mel Brooks, fascinating. Who loves to grow and to learn, whether it's about plant pruning or filmmaking — she made a writing/directing debut with *Fatso* in 1979. Who loves to work in her garden, raise her sixteen-year-old son, and cook tamale pie for her family.

I'll buy that.

But it's the Bancroft beneath this public portrait that fascinates me. The actor/person is able to create characters that always offer more than we see, that conceal twice as much as they reveal. It takes a lot of living to do that, acting being one-third technique, one-third magic and one-third the person of the actor. So who is this person?

Even if we were to take the trip back to the Bronx to find this big-eyed Italian girl-child who ran out to sing for the WPA workers digging up the street, we would only find a small piece of the puzzle. She once joked with embarrassment that she was singing in those days to a blond guy named Whitey. She was in love with Whitey.

Prophetically, there would be blond princes to follow, all of whom fell by the wayside. As did the guy who asked her to screen-test with him — and she got the contract. As did the boy-interest in high school who said he was going to the American Academy of Dramatic Arts, prompting her to enroll. As it turns out he never went and she did — a move that led eventually to an Academy Award (for her portrayal of Annie Sullivan in *The Miracle Worker)*, several Academy nominations, a couple of Tony Awards, and numerous other accolades.

We might get the idea from these vignettes that she somehow stumbled into her career. Nothing could be further from the truth. She herself has modestly claimed that her sisters had as much talent as she had, but they didn't have her need.

"Acting — it's this early need," she has said.

Maybe it's that need that helped her to see through her early life in Los Angeles when she would drive home so drunk she didn't know how she got there.

Maybe it's that need — the true measure of an artist — that got her to shake her dead-end apprenticeship as a starlet, and return to New York to study first with Herbert Berghoff and then at the Actor's Studio.

She has admitted it was that need that gave her the inspiration to take off her shoe and be found scratching her toe, in character, when the producer walked out to audition her for Gittel, the Jewish eccentric in *Two for the Seesaw*. Her 1958 debut in that part took Broadway by storm. This was to be overshadowed by her shattering performance as Annie Sullivan in *The Miracle*

MOTHER DIRECTRESS

WE OFTEN HEAR the term *Renaissance man.* Seldom is the term applied to a woman, but if anyone in our time deserves to be called a "Renaissance woman," it is Ida Lupino.

Known primarily as an actress — "the poor man's Bette Davis" she once called herself — Lupino has also been playwright, screenwriter, author, dancer, singer, artist, designer, musician, songwriter, composer (her *Aladdin Suite* was played by the Los Angeles Philharmonic), and television and movie producer–director.

And she did all this at a time when Hollywood had made it virtually impossible for a woman to do more than serve, in *front* of the camera, the male-dominated studio system.

LUPINO, IT IS TRUE, arrived in Hollywood with a heritage. Born in London in 1918 (under a dining table during a zeppelin raid, it is said), she came from one of England's oldest theatrical families. Her mother, Connie Emerald, was an actress; her father, actor-author Stanley Lupino, descended from a line of actors, singers, mimes, jugglers, acrobats, and puppeteers dating back to the Italian Renaissance clown, Grimaldi.

With such a heritage, it is not surprising that Lupino wrote and produced, at age seven, a play for her schoolmates called *Mademoiselle*, at age twelve enrolled in the Royal Academy of Dramatic Art, and had her first role in an American film at age fifteen. That same year, 1933, she came to Hollywood and began her career playing "bleached blond ingenues," until, using all her power and influence, she landed the breakthrough role of Bessie Broke in *The Light That Failed*.

Still she was dissatisfied, and in 1949 she got her chance to take more control. She had written the screenplay for *Not Wanted,* and was also producing it, when three days into filming director Elmer Clifton had a heart attack. Lupino took over and completed the film.

With her then husband, Collier Young, she founded her second production company, Filmakers, dedicated, she said, to "high-quality, low-budget independent films on provocative

Worker. She had left Hollywood a disillusioned starlet and returned a star.

Perhaps it's that very need that breaks through into her acting, often revealing a delicate vulnerability beneath an earthy, unyielding strength. Sometimes the qualities are finely interwoven. Sometimes you have to look closely to catch a rare glimpse of this soft side.

I recently caught such a jewel while reviewing her pivotal role as Mrs. Robinson in *The Graduate*. Dustin Hoffman, her young lover, has been trying to engage her in conversation. He finds out she has majored in art in college and says, "I guess you kind of lost interest in it over the years."

Lying on her side in bed, facing us, we see the tough, neurotic alcoholic suddenly crack when she says: "Kind of."

That "Kind of." It's an exquisite moment of humanity that catalyzes her entire portrayal and helps

◀ **Ida Lupino directing an early film**

subject matter." (Her third production company, Four Star Productions, was to produce more than a hundred features for television.)

Five more films followed — most written, produced, and directed by Ida Lupino. They have recently received close attention from film critics and feminists alike. While feminists deplore the "passivity" they find in Lupino's women (though her men are equally passive), others have seen a deeper, more universal sensibility at work. Critic Ronnie Scheib, for example, sees Lupino's films as "small scale rite-of-passage films — passage into womanhood, into nightmare, into lack of control."

"Lupino's characters do not know how to act," Scheib continues. "Their 'problems' — rape, polio, illegitimate children, bigamy — have put them beyond the pale, beyond the patterned security of their foreseeable futures. The 'problem' is not how to reintegrate them into the mainstream; the 'problem' is the shallowness of the mainstream and the void it projects around them — the essential passivity of ready-made lives . . . Lupino's films denaturalize passivity. Her characters are sleepwalkers."

Ida Lupino has, in short, gone her own unique way. As she has said, her efforts, all along, were designed to "justify my ancestors' faith in the ultimate destiny of the theater." She has done at least that.

— *Lawrence DiStasi*

make the film a generational classic.

As Estelle Rolf in *Garbo Talks*, made almost twenty years later, we can see this same fragile humanity threaded into the character of an outspoken New York radical. We know Estelle. She's a dying breed. She refused to attend her own son's wedding because she wouldn't cross a picket line. She gets the audience to cheer when she tells off a bunch of construction workers harassing attractive women in the street.

Then on her deathbed, Estelle/Bancroft finally meets her idol, Greta Garbo. It's another of those brilliant Bancroft moments. Without an ounce of sentimentality, she pries your heart wide as she spins out her own eulogy, a reprise of each of Garbo's films and how they touched her life. She relishes what comparisons she can draw from the details of their respective lives — even to their shoe sizes.

I feel like Estelle in my search for Bancroft. As a performer and writer I read her performances the way I read poetry — for continued inspiration. It's well known she is elusive to the public, but even if that weren't true, these moments of performance are all we really need to understand Anne Bancroft.

Actors of her caliber are born, not made. The combination of timing and will that leads them to the craft is just our luck. She may be willing to reveal her tamale pie recipe, but there are worlds about her personal recipe we'll never be able to decode. In her wisdom she herself has reminded us of that. Sometime in 1962 she was quoted as saying: "In life nobody really understands you. The only thing you can wish for is somebody to accept you and love you for what you are."

Millions already have. ❧

THE MAN OF A THOUSAND FACES

by Umberto Tosi

THE FIRST TIME I saw Arturo Toscanini was on a sixteen-inch state-of-the-art Philco television set at Frank Puglia's house in Beverly Hills.

It was in the early 1950s and Toscanini was conducting his NBC Symphony (now the New York Philharmonic) in *Aïda* live from New York. Although in his eighties, the Maestro was still electrifying, even in fuzzy black-and-white. I was only ten, but I knew I was watching history — a hero who had conducted premieres for Verdi and Puccini, who had spat in Mussolini's eye by refusing to desecrate La Scala with the Fascist anthem, choosing exile in America instead. I knew this mainly because of Puglia, a Dutch uncle and mentor, who never failed to weave tales of what went on behind the screen — be it the silver screen of the movie dream palaces in which I grew up, or the new, tiny electronic screen which soon was to bring that era to an end.

Puglia, it seemed to me, knew just about everything that mattered, for he himself was a figure who had stepped off that silver screen — dashing, witty, urbane, then a slim, balding figure in his early sixties who embodied the gracious playfulness of a Rossini overture.

I'd seen him in a dozen films portraying a variety of types, some of whom recited their lines in semi-comic broken English, even though Puglia himself spoke the language with only a slight accent and as adroitly as he did Italian, Sicilian or French.

My mother, who sang under the name of Alba Floria, was a soprano who performed in operas, concerts and Italian-language theater in Los Angeles at the time. Her circle of friends included musicians and actors who made their daily bread from the Hollywood studios, which, in those days, reeled out films by the score. Puglia was the grand duke of this Italian performers' circle, which included talented, Italian-stage-tutored character actors like Renata Vanni and Vito Scotti.

Puglia had class and film lineage. He and his wife Irene had played major roles in the Italian-language theater that flourished in San Francisco in the 1920s and later in Los Angeles. In 1921, at age thirty, he landed his first significant film role in *Orphans of the Storm* directed by the legendary D. W. Griffith. He made two more movies with Griffith. By his death at age eighty-five in 1965, Puglia had played in more than eighty movies, plus roles in television, stage and opera.

He played comical sidekicks, kindly fathers, bothersome uncles, gabby waiters, simple priests, wise men, drunks, fools and troublemakers. And he played with the best — Lillian Gish, Ronald Coleman, Wallace Beery, Myrna Loy, Cary Grant, Mickey Rooney, James Cagney, Bob Hope, Dorothy Lamour, Errol Flynn, Ingrid Bergman, Humphrey Bogart, Bette Davis, Gary Cooper, Burt Lancaster. His credits include dozens of classics from Hollywood's Golden Age — *Romula, Viva Villa, The Mark of Zorro, Now Voyager, Casablanca, For Whom the Bell Tolls, A Song to Remember, Blood on the Sun, Road to Rio.*

Some of the portrayals were brilliant scene-stealers — the orchestra conductor plagued by Claude Rains in *Phantom of the Opera*, or a poignant convict hoping for parole in Jules Dassin's breakthrough prison film noir, *Brute Force.* A few roles

Frank Puglia in the 1937 Columbia production, "The Boogie Man Will Get You."
▼

Frank Puglia: "the comedy is *never* over."

pastas and other Italian viands, wines, followed by espresso, grappa, biscotti, music and — always — punctuated throughout by lively conversation.

Puglia invariably held court as master storyteller in the grand theatrical tradition of his native Sicily, which, he was fond of reminding me — contrary to stereotypes — produced many of Italy's greatest playwrights, poets and novelists, including Nobelists Luigi Pirandello, Giuseppe di Lampedusa and Salvatore Quasimodo.

He'd tell story after story, few of them about the famous film stars with whom he played, most instead about his experiences in Italian theater in New York (where he met his actress wife Irene Veneroni), San Francisco and Los Angeles. They were tales about stage mishaps and the misadventures of theatrical eccentrics that actors love to relate.

One of Puglia's tales remains particularly vivid to me even now for its Pirandello-like surrealism. He and his wife, Irene, were acting in a play. They had been having an argument the entire day before the performance. In the play they were supposed to be a couple having a spat in the bedroom.

As the argument escalated, they began to interject ad-libs from their personal quarrel. Soon they were in a shouting match. It was stunning, said Puglia. He could sense the people in the audience sitting on the edges of their seats. He could hear them begin to murmur. He pushed the quarrel further, until Irene, having had enough, stormed out through the bedroom door and off the stage.

Fortunately, her exit was called for in the script. What was not called for was that she slammed the door so hard behind her that the entire canvas wall of the bedroom began wobbling wildly and finally collapsed — at which Frank Puglia turned to the audience and, quoting the famous last line from the opera *I Pagliacci*, said, "La commedia è finita." The line was apropos, he said, but not really true. Puglia winked at me.

"You will learn, my boy, that the comedy is *never* over."

That was Frank Puglia. He quoted Dante and Shakespeare with equal ease, and always taught me something, especially to look beyond conventional wisdom.

A showman on and off screen, he had a thousand faces, and not one was false. ❧

were strictly for laughs. Nevertheless, like Gregory Peck, he had the ability to give any part, no matter how trivial, a certain grace and dignity.

Neither did Puglia play the lowest of Italian screen stereotypes that made him and his contemporaries grimace — the pushcart peddlers and the mobsters. Those roles often fell to non-Italian actors. Puglia and other of his Italian character actor colleagues disdained them as abetting the prejudice that still was a fresh memory to their generation, though a few were not above taking such a role when the need for work outweighed their reservations. Not Puglia.

Frank Puglia, my mother always said, *sa da fare* — the untranslatable Italian term for a sense of balance and appropriateness that can be likened to the Tao. This was apparent to the dozen or so friends and relatives who gathered at his house about once a month for musicales that featured recitals by my mother and other artists in the circle — unless preempted by the rare appearance of Toscanini on TV. Each of these musicales would be a full evening of delicately prepared

AN INTERVIEW WITH FRANK CAPRA

by John F. Mariani

THE ISSUE OF Frank Capra's admitted sentimentality ("Capra-corn") is not quite so obvious as it seemed even five years ago. Anyone now reexamining his most important films — *It Happened One Night, Mr. Deeds Goes to Town, Mr. Smith Goes to Washington, Meet John Doe, It's a Wonderful Life* — must realize that a Frank Capra picture is not a gushing paean to an idealized America, but a satiric critique of the insidious evils implicit in a free enterprise system where control of the media is the first step toward demagoguery.

More important, Capra's films have held up as films, for as one of the original advocates of the "one-man-one-film" idea, he was able to fashion a body of work perhaps more personal than that of any other Hollywood director of his era.

His technique — unobtrusive camerawork, colloquial and picturesque composition, headlong pacing — was part of an individual style others so often copied that it became the model of "screwball comedy" in the thirties, even though Capra's films were darker and more troublesome than their happy endings at first indicated.

Capra is a slippery filmmaker and, merely because he is so comedic and so alert to his audience's expectations, we have failed to notice the impeccable orchestration of his comic tragedies in which a lovable hero is brought to ruin by the very forces that utilize that lovableness for sinister purposes. In *Meet John Doe* Capra suggested that folk heroes are manufactured, not born, and that they too should be suspect. But the ideas behind such heroes are a constant inspiration nevertheless.

The following interview was held when Capra gave a lecture at Sarah Lawrence College following a screening of his film *It Happened One Night*.

How does it feel to have a class of college students today respond to a movie you made in 1934 as uproariously as they did?

If Frank Capra did not exist, he would have to be invented. With an engineering degree and no artistic pretensions, he stumbled into moviemaking and became a Hollywood institution. His films may well be the best expression yet of that major stream of Italian Americans who, deprivation aside, took the American dream — the "Rocky" dream — absolutely seriously.

It surprises me. It's just really a phenomenon that they would be so moved. I can't understand it, except in some way perhaps they've got some kind of hungers we don't know about.

Did you tend to diverge from your original scripts much, for instance, in It Happened One Night?

Oh, that's very difficult to say. You tend to find things to use as you're shooting, and you ad-lib a lot. For instance, remember that piggyback scene where Gable and Colbert are crossing the river? Well, we were shooting down by the side of that river, it was late at night, and the sun shone down there and made this beautiful reflection. And I said, "Jeez, we gotta use this." So we made up the crossing of the river. That was completely ad-lib. You see what happens when you shoot without too much attention to script, that's when it seems to turn out best.

We always had a great deal of improvisation. Because you see, I came from the improvisation school. We never wrote anything with Sennett, our gags were all visuals. We didn't have jokes. We had scenes that could develop into a routine. We'd tell a director, "How about if a cat drinks some beer and gets drunk?" The director would say, "Yea, he'll jump in the milk." And from there on cat chases dogs, cat sings "Three O'Clock in the Morning," and so on. We didn't have a word gag. And these sight gags carried over into my sound films.

My favorite scene in all your films is the one in which James Gleason talks about patriotism with Gary Cooper in a barroom in Meet John Doe. *How did you direct that?*

That's one of my favorites, too. I wrote that scene. I wanted to get a patriotic thing in this part but, you know, you can't shout patriotism, you can't have a guy spout it. If I start to tell you about it sober, you won't listen. But if I'm drunk, well, that's a different story. I

can say, "You know, I *love* this country — " and I pester you and you say, OK you love this country. When you get into that hairy stuff, you've got to do it a certain way, you laugh at it — but you listen. It's touching that way. Being drunk, having trouble with that cigarette, that's the only way this hard-boiled guy would talk that way and expose himself.

What about Gary Cooper? Was he easy to work with?

Oh, I had enormous respect for that guy. He's a very underestimated actor. His great power is in his presence. You can't make him look bad. That's why the audience wouldn't accept him jumping off the building in *John Doe*. You can't kill Gary Cooper. That guy just represents America to me. He's strong, he's able, he's kind, he wouldn't steal a penny from you, but if you cross his path, he'll kill you. Or at least give you a punch in the mouth. This is what America is, I think.

There is certainly a view in your films that nothing in the democratic or judicial system will save your heroes. Is that a criticism of the American system of government?

Sure, but it's a criticism of the American misuse of government. Not of the American way. In America the orphan of freedom can be a bastard, but you have other ways to cure that.

Is a concept like the "John Doe Clubs" closer to what America should be like?

No, that was an outcome of times of stress, times of depression, when people help each other out. They have to in order to survive. And you know, I think that when times are tough the people that survive are these ordinary people who are not afraid to show their feelings. They will survive. All the intellectuals will be knocked off or starve. The strength of America is in the kind of people who can plant a seed, sow the grass.

Do you think it's true for the present generation what John Cassavetes said about you: That it's not America we've been believing in all these years, it's Frank Capra? How much does Frank Capra's America have to do with the real America? Is yours an ideal?

I wanted to glorify the average man, not the guy at the top, not the politician, not the banker, just the ordinary guy whose strength I admire, whose survivability I admire. Guys like Gary Cooper. ❧

227

ROCKY, THE RENAISSANCE PRINCE

SYLVESTER STALLONE IS moving through his art collection in the late afternoon, head down, cigar in hand. He takes short blocky steps that have a curious grace — the movie star as club fighter? — when a secretary calls out.

Stallone stops.

"What?" he says.

The stop is all grace, and that's the other side of Sylvester Stallone, the picture of an imperious, if lesser, Florentine prince. Hands on hips, neck craned back, he gets more into one word than almost anyone can — the "what" is question, statement and angry exclamation, the "whaddaya" of the urban East, and more.

▲ Sylvester Stallone as his alter ego

"Look at me: You know what people see?" he says. "I'll tell you — they see dark, brooding, a primitive character. At best, they see the noble savage." Well, they don't see Cary Grant.

"Sure," Stallone says. "But those are the characters I play on the screen. They don't see the art, the poetry I hear in life — I hear it. Even Rambo hears it — nobody could survive doing what he does for so long without a real thirst, a real love of life. Art. Poetry. So," waving the cigar, grinning sadly, "that's what people see."

"I'm no thespian," Stallone says after a pause. "But I'm more complex than I appear to be."

Most things are. Stallone's offices, for instance, which include a warehouse — a warehouse of art. Rodin's *Eve*, sculptures by Remington, paintings by the names of art in the 1980s. If he had all the money in the world, what would he buy?

"Picasso's *Guernica*," he says. Then it changes, quickly. "Cellini's *Perseus* —you know the sculpture? It's Cellini's masterpiece, and he ran out of bronze in the middle of casting. So he's throwing masterpieces into the furnace, to get bronze, for his masterpiece." He shivers. "I love that story."

As for Rambo: "There's no end to the need for that hero, the ethical man in an unethical society, achieving against the odds," Stallone says. "Besides, I like people who go against insurmountable odds."

Stallone leans back, regally, and smiles. "I say, 'How did I get to be here?' It's the pen and the paper," he says. He had $106 in the bank when he wrote *Rocky*.

The first *Rambo* drafts, he says, are all talk — comebacks. Every scene ends with a Rambo comeback, which gradually gets whittled away until the end — he has to be at a loss, his creator says. The audience has to push him forward. You're twelve minutes into *Rambo III* before you hear Stallone say a line.

He laughs. "Rambo is pantomime. For me, it's the ultimate test of writing — just pictures. You've got to keep the character humble: He'll go off when his button is pushed, I cut and cut, dialogue goes and goes — it's the movies, what Chaplin did, what Keaton did. No words. It works." He grins, rolls his shoulders back to the streetwise kid at forty-one. "Even if it doesn't, they paid me good money."

His fanatically loyal audience pays too. It doesn't matter what critics say; Stallone in his two characters has tapped into a young and disenfranchised American culture that finds itself ignored by New York and Los Angeles.

Still, it's not challenging any more, he says; Rambo has gone about as far as he can go. So what's next?

"I've come full circle," says the Florentine prince. The next film could be about the legendary Hell's Kitchen gang, the Westies; as a son of New York's West Side, born in Hell's Kitchen, it could be.

"Orbicular," he says. "There's the word for you. It's orbicular."

— *Joseph Dalton*

Promises to Keep

by Robert Lindsey

For Italian Americans, their portrayal in the movies can easily be divided into two segments: Before Coppola and After Coppola. BC was the era of marginality, disguise, and condescension. AC is, well, the present. The question for Coppola now becomes: Is there a millennial period yet to come?

Francis Ford Coppola and his father, Carmine Coppola, after winning four Academy Awards between them for their work on "The Godfather, Part II."

▼

O UTSIDE, NEW YORK City is sweltering in a heat wave. In an apartment on the Upper West Side of Manhattan, an eleven-year-old girl mixes a strawberry daiquiri in a blender, pours a glass for her mother, then sips from her own tall glass of foamy pink fluid.

Just a few feet away, in a high-backed canvas chair, a large, middle-aged man with receding black hair watches the scene on a television monitor that's perched on his right knee like an affectionate pet. With his high forehead, a thick body bordering on plumpness, a heavy dark beard streaked with gray and thoughtful eyes behind thick eyeglasses, he has the look of a kind and learned rabbi.

"This is going to be as bad as the horse's head," Francis Ford Coppola says. "I know it; people are going to be outraged that I show a little girl who knows how to drink." Then, as if he feels it necessary to defend himself to his cast, he adds: "I think kids who learn about booze are more likely to respect it."

"All I heard after *The Godfather* was 'cruelty to animals,'" he says a few moments later, referring to the 1972 movie that elevated him to stardom as a film director. "Thirty people were shot in the movie," Coppola says, seemingly confounded by human nature, "but people only talked about 'cruelty to animals.'"

On this morning in June, however, Coppola doesn't seem deeply concerned about the public's reaction to the scene he's filming. (It will be included in his segment of *New York Stories*, three short films by New Yorkers — Coppola, Woody Allen and Martin Scorsese.) He is thinking instead about his imminent liberation from Hollywood and what he considers his final Hollywood movie, *Tucker:*

The Man and His Dream. On the eve of its release, he says he is ready to embark on a period of "amateurism and experimentation" as a Hollywood dropout.

Coppola has traveled this road before. Once part of the Hollywood establishment, he broke ranks to create his own studio, but failed. Now, approaching fifty, he is an outsider at once angry with industry moguls who stifle "creative people" and unsure of himself in the world they dominate.

Clearly Coppola's interest in the character of Preston Tucker is in part autobiographical. His interest began, he claims, when he was an eight year old bedridden with polio and fascinated with machinery and inventors. As he grew older, he never forgot the story of the automaker's David-and-Goliath struggle with the auto industry's giants. In 1976, he acquired the rights to film Tucker's life story from the industrialist's family (he also owns two of the forty-six surviving Tucker automobiles), and conceived an ambitious motion-picture musical based on his life and the process of innovation in America.

"It was a dark kind of piece . . . a sort of Brechtian musical in which Tucker would be the main story, but it would also involve Edison and Henry Ford and Firestone and Carnegie," he says.

Leonard Bernstein agreed to write the music, and Betty Comden and Adolph Green were approached about writing the lyrics. They all spent a week planning the musical. But before the project could get off the ground, the economic tailspin at Zoetrope began.

"People no longer felt what I had to offer was of value," he says. "They thought my projects were too grandiose. With the collapse of my studio, everything fell into a black hole — *Tucker*, plus a lot of other things I wanted to do." He says he never called Bernstein or Comden and Green to inform them that the project was dead. "I was too embarrassed."

Then, two years ago, George Lucas, one of Coppola's original wunderkinder, encouraged him to revive his dream of filming the life of Preston Tucker.

"I thought it was the best project Francis had ever been involved with," Lucas recalls. In a poignant role reversal, Lucas offered to produce *Tucker* for the father figure who had helped finance *American Graffiti*, the movie that made Lucas famous. Both producer and director say they are pleased with the product of their collaboration: "I think it's a good movie — eccentric, a little wacky, like the Tucker car — but it's not," says Coppola, "the movie I would have made at the height of my power."

SITTING ON A sofa, watching the filming of a minor scene from *New York Stories* on a television screen and occasionally directing it via a telephone link to the set, Coppola talks about filmmaking and his future. Soft-

MARTY

ALERT, WITH A bird of prey's darting eyes and the tautness of an overwound watch, Martin Scorsese delivers a mock-pedantic lecture on the four stages of movie-making. His intense, bearded face belongs in a Renaissance altarpiece by Masaccio, but his staccato diction and flailing-arm body language are strictly from Jimmy Cagney: "The first part of a film is preproduction, preparation. Then you shoot it. Part three's the postproduction, the editing."

"Then," he adds, with a diabolical giggle, "comes the depression."

Like David Bowie's alien in *The Man Who Fell to Earth*, Scorsese lives and works surrounded by video monitors and audio equipment. His stereo speakers stand as tall as he does. Videocassettes line his bookshelves, making for a cozy, polyresin wallpaper. In the lacunae unfilled by movie books, cassettes, or hardware are movie posters, stills, and awards yet to be hung.

There's virtually no decorative difference between Scorsese's editing room and his living quarters: These are the surroundings of a professional who lives, breathes, and dreams movies. Love and work are one.

The way this workaholic lives, totally absorbed in movieland, is in a sense identical to that of Rupert Pupkin, the protagonist of his film, *The King of Comedy*. Rupert (Robert DeNiro), an aspiring stand-up comedian, surrounds himself with stacks of comedy lore in his Union City basement.

Rupert fantasizes celebrity by identifying with talk show host Jerry Langford (Jerry Lewis) and dreams of hosting Jerry's talk show, of *becoming* Jerry.

When Scorsese first read Paul Zimmerman's script for *The King of Comedy* in 1974, he recalls, "I didn't go for it. Didn't understand it."

It was only after he passed the script on to DeNiro that "I realized Rupert's an extension of me inasmuch as he'd do *anything* to get what he wanted. When I realized he was to comics as I was to the movies, I understood. Rupert reminds me of the hunger I had in the sixties."

Scorsese sees Rupert as the outsider-huckster angling to get on the inside, eager to bask in the limelight. This is a

spoken, at once pensive and candid, he is a man, like Preston Tucker, convinced that he knows a better way of doing things, but frustrated by his inability to convince others to accept it. *Tucker*, he says, will mark his official exit from commercial Hollywood filmmaking.

"My feeling is that cinema is an art form that can have a tremendous amount of variety," he says. "You can do all kinds of styles, like literature, painting or music. But today they want only one type. There used to be room for innovation, but there isn't anymore; I find it hard to work in a regulated industry."

He points to his string of "hired-gun" movies as evidence that he can, if necessary, give Hollywood what it wants. But it is not what Francis Ford Coppola wants: "I'm almost fifty years old; I have to focus more on what I want to say."

characteristic shared by virtually every Scorsese protagonist: Johnny Boy in *Mean Streets,* Travis Bickle in *Taxi Driver,* Jake LaMotta in *Raging Bull.*

Hunger for celebrity is the dominant motivation for their cocky, cockeyed professionalism, and a self-screwing mechanism — usually the feeling of inadequacy — is the key to their fluky success or disastrous downfall.

Scorsese himself is afflicted with the dilemma of celebrity. An outsider whose reputation has made him an insider, he feels hamstrung by success. On the one hand, he presents himself as a recluse, a movie monk sequestered in a cinema cloister. The other Scorsese is the Hollywood director, hassling with unions, meeting deadlines, the adult businessman dealing with the real world.

He wants it both ways, but is frustrated that his fame has made it impossible for him to make movies cheaply and simply. A quote from *Sweet Smell of Success,* handprinted on a three-by-five-inch card, is tacked to a column in his loft, reminding him of the contradiction: "Are we kids, or what?"

— *Carrie Rickey*

He discusses the specifics of his future projects reluctantly. One prospect is a screenplay he has been working on for four years, a story set in contemporary New York that draws parallels with the decadence and decline of ancient Rome and would be "much more ambitious than *Apocalypse Now.* I think there is a whole other way we can do cinema. It will be like a big, dramatic novel."

To reduce production costs, he plans on future films to employ the electronic systems he has been working on for a decade; some are already being used by his twenty-two-year-old son, Roman, to make low-budget features, the first of which will soon be released. "Although they're shot on film, everything else is done electronically; it's as different from the old way as night and day."

He will finance his projects himself, he says, noting that largely because of recent real-estate inflation, "I'm really quite wealthy and can afford to do what I want." Asked if his net worth exceeds $20 million, he says, "That would be conservative."

Coppola expects this second exit from Hollywood to be permanent. "The industry needs guys who are willing to make pictures like *Rambo VII* or *Rambo VIII,*" he says. "I don't say that with bitterness. I'm just not going to participate any more. I'm going to experiment with my own ideas — experiment without the fear that failure will finish me off." ❧

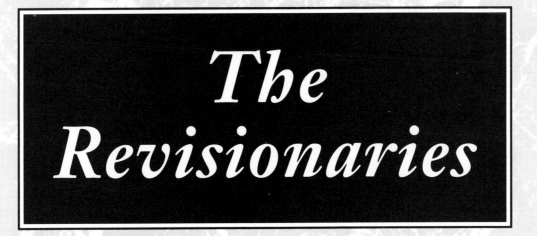

The Revisionaries

REBUILDING THE COMMUNITY

by Mary Sansone

Among the patterns that distinguish Italians in America, none has been more marked than their persistence in city neighborhoods — in effect, urban variations of the Italian village. Yet along with this persistence of place has gone a persistence — often a rigidity — of attitudes. "Italians take care of their own" has been the most sacred of these, and one that Mary Sansone decided to examine. What she found led her to a new version of a very old vision.

I WAS BORN in 1916 on Henry Street in South Brooklyn. At that time we were very, very poor. We were living with my mother's mother. Grandma lived in the basement and we lived upstairs. And my father was busy doing his thing with the International Workers of the World.

In those days most of them did volunteer work. This is why we were so poor. He used to work in a factory sometimes, doing some operating work on men's clothing, but it never lasted too long. He'd pull the shop out on strike and that was the end of his job. From the day I remember my father, that was the only thing he ever did. His aim in life was to get everybody organized and get everybody to live together.

My father left Italy when he was twenty-seven. He was ready to be ordained. He had only six months to go, but something happened that made him give up the priesthood. Nobody knows what. Before he died, he was in a coma for three days and friends of his stayed with him in the hope that he would divulge why he left the Church. He never did. All he talked about was Dante and *The Divine Comedy*.

I GRADUATED HIGH SCHOOL at eighteen. That was in 1934 and my father took quite sick so I went to work in a factory doing sewing. I hated the routine and the surroundings and I just hated sewing, but I wanted to go into a factory because I liked what my father was doing, organizing. I didn't go with the intention of staying there. The way the employers abused the girls was awful. The only way a girl could get a promotion was to go to bed with the employer. It was really disgusting. These were nonunion shops and that's what the union was for, to protect the girls.

When the war broke out, I applied for a job at the Social Service Department of the Brooklyn Red Cross. I used to go to work during the day and go to school at night. I did that for six years. Kids today, I think they have it easy.

Most of my friends never joined me in what I was doing. A lot of their parents thought I was nuts anyway. Going to night school and campaigning and striking and demonstrating. A lot of people would say, "Oh, she's crazy like her father," you know? Crazy like my father. When my father died, he had so many people visit him that the funeral parlor was mobbed for three days. So that means there were an awful lot of people that respected what he did.

WE STARTED CIAO in 1964 from my basement. My husband Zack kept saying he thought it was about time the Italians got together. I had been working for everybody else, so he said, "How about doing something for the Italians?" A number of people felt this way too. And, of course, I knew there were plenty of poor Italians because of the work I had been doing prior to my marriage.

It took us a while to get a name together, but then when we figured out the Congress of Italian American Organizations, which spells CIAO, well, we liked that name a lot. No politicians were involved, just people that had their own organizations and were interested. We had Angela Carlozzi of the Italian Welfare League, and we had the professional and businessmen's association. Then we had the real estate association, and the U.S. Customs Association, and the War Veterans.

For a long time, I couldn't talk about the Italians having problems. We had the same problems as any other group. The only thing is, the Italians didn't want to recognize it. They were ashamed. We opened our first day-care center, and 95 percent of the kids that registered were from Italian families — some broken families, children born out of wedlock. So how different are we from other groups?

Things were changing all over the place. There was the Civil Rights Movement. My brother Joey went down south to help the blacks come up north and my cousin did too. So we knew that the whole world was

Well, we're doing such an excellent job of it that we have the second highest school dropout rate in the city. And we have a very high drug addiction rate. So for a group that's doing such a fine job of taking care of ourselves, we're failing somewhere down the line.

Well, we started in South Brooklyn. We knew that in South Brooklyn there was a very bad narcotic problem. What do we do? We fight to develop a rehabilitation center. It almost took our lives, but we did that and now we have a program, a storefront center.

Finally, we began to get some help from the city, contrary to what the Italians have always said. See the Italians have a beautiful way of gossiping and speaking unkind of the city and the state, not realizing that they never asked for anything or fought for anything. So how the hell does anyone know that they need anything? So I wanted to change that too.

First they kept saying that the Jews get everything. Then it was the blacks get everything. So I said, "How about the Italians getting something? How the hell do you expect to get anything if all you do is organize and play cards? Why don't you get out there and fight?"

My ultimate ambition is to see the development of programs in every Italian community. Because when I develop programs in an Italian community, we're getting Italians to work with other ethnic groups too. That would be something my father always wished for and if I could succeed in doing just that I would be happy. ❧

changing and unless we changed with it, we weren't going to get anywhere.

See the Jewish people would help their people but the Italian people never did. The Italians will only give provided people know and they can play Mr. Bigshot. If they were contributors, we could run groups such as CIAO and we could build our own centers without government money, with all the wealthy people we have. Some of the richest people in this country are Italians, but many of them are still of the old theory that every Italian has it made, so they don't give.

I started with the city because I just felt the city had an obligation to work with us. So what happens, I start going to the city and even to the state and it was the same thing all over the place. Even the Italians in government would say, "Oh come on, you must be crazy. The Italians don't need anything. They take care of their own families."

The Art of Freedom

SOMETIME SHORTLY AFTER the First World War my father, accompanied by his anarchist friend Konrad Bercovici, walked into Brentano's Bookstore on Fifth Avenue. A young and attractive clerk, later to become my mother, recalled her supervisor's warning to stay away from the "notorious" artist, recently apprehended while trying to pull down the statue of Garibaldi in Washington Square. She didn't, perhaps when she learned that it was not Garibaldi's politics, but the banality of the sculptor's conception that had moved young Onorio Ruotolo to such rash action.

By this time, and for other reasons, my father was famous uptown as well as in Greenwich Village, where a pizza was named for him. A headline of the 1919 *Evening Telegraph* asks: "HAS WAR'S GREATEST SCULPTOR BEEN FOUND IN A FOURTH FLOOR STUDIO OF GREENWICH VILLAGE?" while a fullpage of the *Chicago Tribune* displays his statue *The Doomed* protesting capital punishment, and made after a visit to death's row at Sing Sing prison. A year later his bust of Caruso, now in Lincoln Center, was placed in the lobby of the old Metropolitan Opera House.

Over the next decade I remember that such famous Americans as Edison, Dreiser, Helen Keller, Steinmetz, and Toscanini posed for him. The heads of Dreiser and Keller are in the Smithsonian, the bust of Toscanini in New York's High School of Music and Art.

In 1945 his bas-relief *The Four Freedoms* was presented to President Franklin D. Roosevelt by the Italian American Labor Council of New York. I accompanied my father to the White House where the award was given. My father, I recall, pushed his teenage son just behind the president — and so I appear in the *New York Times* photograph, standing next to Attorney General Biddle, as "an unidentified member of the Council."

But above all my father is remembered for founding in 1923, and directing for two decades, the Leonardo DaVinci Art School, established for young working men and women — all classes were at night — who could not afford instruction. Initiated before the days of public support for art, it has

▲
Onorio Ruotolo and Rudolph Valentino with a famous radiator cap.

been called the first free art school in the country.

During much of my childhood, at night after classes had ended, swarms of teachers and students, mainly Italian, returned with my father to our apartment. Among the most striking was the white-haired Attilio Piccirilli, once likened by Mayor Fiorello La Guardia to a "well-cultivated, perfect, sweet California orange . . . so typically American — only the seed came from Italy." La Guardia was an ardent supporter of the school. He had married my parents and remained one of my father's closest friends. Not surprisingly, Onorio designed La Guardia's inaugural medal.

A cartoon in the 1913 *Evening Sun* reveals five of my father's earlier drinking companions and one of his favorite chefs in the restaurant at 115th Street.

Fiorello and Caruso were often part of this group as well as Giovanni Fabrizio, later a flutist in Toscanini's NBC Symphony Orchestra.

Equally popular places to eat, drink, and talk were La Guardia's apartment and, of course, my father's studio on East Fourteenth Street. A newspaper woman once described the latter as the most authentically Bohemian studio in the city.

Among the enticements of this building was an early film studio of film pioneer D. W. Griffith on the ground floor. There were, evidently, an abundance of attractive women auditioning for parts, and on more than one occasion they were invited to join the festivities.

About this time Rudolph Valentino asked my father to design a radiator cap for his car. I am unsure if my father made the sale, but the flying centaur, displayed in the photo of the two men, is now in the Tate Gallery collection in London.

— *Lucio Ruotolo*

NEIGHBORHOOD POWER

by Don Crinklaw

Of the many Italian American neighborhoods known as "the Hill," one of the most renowned is the one in St. Louis. Both Yogi Berra and Joe Garagiola grew up there, across the street from each other in fact. Father Salvatore Polizzi has also made a name there — as the neighborhood activist who stopped a freeway and saved this hill from the cultural flattening suffered by so many others. Would that "a thousand Polizzis" might bloom.

Father Salvatore Polizzi: "I'm not here to be liked."

▼

BY TEN IN the morning, the autumn sun still hadn't cleared the bell tower of St. Ambrose's Catholic Church on the Hill, the Italian community in southwest St. Louis. The black metal statues called *The Italian Immigrants*, set on a postage stamp of land just north of the church door, were in deep shadow and looked cold.

"Striking, isn't it?"

The old lady standing next to me had lots of white curls and a sweet smile.

"I'm here to do a magazine piece on Father Polizzi. You know him?"

"Oh, yes."

"Controversial isn't he, this Polizzi? People either love him or hate him."

"I can't imagine anyone hating Father Polizzi," the lady said. "Everyone adores him. Especially the younger people; he's so good with them."

FATHER SALVATORE POLIZZI is a small man, under five feet, ten inches, and heading into his forty-ninth year. His age sits lightly on him. His dark hair is still full, though he wears it shorter than he did in 1974 when *Time* magazine made so much of him, and the clear brown eyes gaze out at the world from an unlined face. Since 1964 he's been associate pastor of St. Ambrose's Catholic Church in St. Louis's Twenty-Fourth Ward, or that part of it known as Dago Hill until someone decided that Ethnic is just fine, but Ethnic Slurs aren't. So, it's just the Hill now.

I asked him about those statues. Didn't the immigrants want to forget that beaten look, get away from being the wretched refuse of the teeming shore?

"No, not here. Not us," Father Polizzi answered in his light tenor voice. He speaks rapidly, articulating precisely as he goes. "The statues aren't as old as they look; they were cast in Florence around 1973. Before that, we took models into the local taverns where the men gathered. The men put that tag on the man, the name tag immigrants had to wear. They added the straps on the suitcase. The idea was to remind people where they came from; that they — we — came to an immigrant land and that we banded together because people looked down their noses at us. That we have much to be proud of."

The priest's manner is friendly enough, but there is a growliness somewhere in the tone, a reminder that, yes, this is the Father Polizzi who carries around with him a banner reading:

I WOULD NOT LIKE TO HAVE LIVED WITHOUT HAVING BOTHERED SOMEONE

IN 1974, *TIME* wondered where all the leaders had gone, and after looking around decided that maybe things weren't too awful as long as the U.S.A. still contained people like Ted Kennedy and Ralph Nader and . . . Father Salvatore Polizzi. He was, *Time* said, "no mere parish priest". Not only had he halted the decline of the old Italian neighborhood, he had in fact turned it around and molded it into a real power in the city.

Three years ago Father Polizzi was awarded the Order of Merit of the Italian Republic, bestowed on him by the President of the Republic, no less, for "work in helping people from the motherland," as the priest puts it. But when the Italian government attempted to bestow the Order of Merit upon the priest for his good work, they clearly had to wrestle him to the ground. Like Caesar and the kingly crown, Father Polizzi refused it thrice.

"I wouldn't accept it for so long," he explained, "because they had been giving it to people who didn't deserve it. A number of people in the community got it simply because they knew the consuls. I told the consulate I wouldn't take the award unless they began honoring the right people. They did."

Shortly afterward the Italian government closed its consular office in St. Louis.

"They didn't particularly like me," Polizzi said, no trace of wistfulness in his voice. "I really didn't care whether they liked me or not. I'm not here to be liked."

Father Polizzi's rumbustious behavior on the Hill does raise some questions. One is the matter of priestly involvement in worldly matters. Does anyone in the church heirarchy ever tell him to pipe down?

"No. My outspokenness is also prudent. When I'm speaking out I never involve the church. It's me who is speaking. It's Father Polizzi who works day-to-day with his fellow Italians. Nobody else. I'm careful about that."

And isn't there another organization that is supposed to help Italians, the one there was a movie about and a north county restaurant named after the movie, an organization that begins with an M . . . ?

"The Mafia. It seems people in this town identify Mafia with Italian and Italian with Saint Ambrose, therefore . . ."

But it does exist, doesn't it?

"Yes. It does exist in the city — that's their problem. It does not exist in this neighborhood. But call it *organized crime* and stay away from *Mafia* — that word takes away my human rights. And I don't want to be indicted."

And that should be that, except for that restaurant. "I told the owner that I would never step in a restaurant named The Godfather as long as I live; I am against anyone who continues this slander. His answer was that *padrino* simply means a godparent at a baptism. That's all well and good, except when he sent out the invitation to the opening, it read: 'An Offer You Can't Refuse.'"

And what about *ethnic*. It isn't the same word it was twenty years ago. Ethnic is in now, now that it seems to mean an outpost of savoriness in a world gone bland. I wondered how Father Polizzi felt about the shift?

"You're talking to an ethnic," he said, his voice lower now. "A while back I spoke in Newark. When I started my talk, I said: 'Some of us are ethnics. Some of us have lived as ethnics. And there are others who write about ethnics.'"

Oh.

"But yes, all of a sudden 'ethnic' is fashionable," he said. "But remember that most of the people on the Hill have always lived here and they've never pushed this 'ethnic' bit — that's a word that's been tacked on by outsiders. To the Italians, it's just a way of life. They're not reading about it in a book; they're not living somewhere and saying, 'Isn't this a wonderful ethnic place to live?' They're just doing what they always did: living in their small houses on their narrow streets, and now it turns out they were ahead of their time: lots of people want to do just that . . ." ❧

SON OF ANGELA

▲
Joe Garagiola still calls the Hill home.

ELDERLY WOMEN ON the Hill in St. Louis call him "son of Angela."

National TV audiences know him as Joe Garagiola.

He's one and the same, a walking, talking, gesticulating commercial for the Italian Hill section of St. Louis where he was raised.

Garagiola was returning to the old neighborhood on an official visit but official visits on the Hill tend to look very unofficial, downright familial even, when they involve the return of favorite sons. Especially favorite sons like Garagiola who give every impression of having been away for perhaps an hour to run an errand downtown rather than for fifteen years.

"When people ask me where I'm from I tell them St. Louis," Garagiola said during an interview in the rectory of St. Ambrose Parish. "I tell them that I live in New York. That's where I make my money. But I'm from St. Louis and proud of it."

Garagiola was on a return visit of three days to film and narrate a piece for the NBC "Today" show. A writer came in from New York, soaking up Hill lore and writing the script. Not that Garagiola needed much of a script. He was brought to the house at 5446 Elizabeth Street as a baby and lived on the Hill until he was married in 1949. Even after he moved off the Hill he lived in nearby South St. Louis until he went to New York with NBC in 1960.

"The point of the segment that we did on the Hill was that here is a neighborhood where I was born fifty-one years ago come February and where I was raised and I come back to it today and it hasn't changed. I can still recognize it. People don't believe that. They think of their own old neighborhood which might have been bulldozed for a housing development or a highway and they can't believe that anyone can go back to their old neighborhood and find things the same.

"So that's what we filmed — that I can go to the old streets, to my old house, to the old Missouri Bakery, to the old parish church and it hasn't changed. And fifty years ago the center of the neighborhood was the church and it's still the center of the neighborhood."

Father Polizzi, associate pastor at St. Ambrose, nodded.

"We had a sewing group at the school yesterday when Joe was doing some of the filming at the school. These were older ladies and I think Joe must have known by name at least three-fourths of them. And, of course, they knew him but they didn't call him 'Joe.' They called him what all the old ladies on the Hill in the neighborhood would call him — *fiur d'Angela* —

the Lombard language phrase that means 'son of Angela,' which is his mother's first name."

"YOU HAVEN'T ASKED me my finest moment on television," Garagiola said at the end of our interview. "I'm going to tell you. My finest moment came in 1960 when I was working a dinner in honor of John Kennedy who was running for President. I was the master of ceremonies and I was filling in time because Kennedy's plane was late. So I got an idea. I was at the head table with former President Truman and Senator Symington and Governor Dalton and Mayor Tucker and I asked them all to stand up and the television was live so I knew they couldn't cut me off and I stood in the middle with my arms around them and looked into the camera and said, "Hey Pop, look who I'm hanging around with these days."

He howled laughing at his own story — the irony of the kid from the Hill introducing his friend the former president to his Pop. But the irony is even richer than that because when he's really enjoying himself, Joe Garagiola is with people to whom his Pop never needed an introduction, people who still know him as the "son of Angela."

— *Stephen Darst*

F E S

Sacralizing the Streets

I HAVE OFTEN wondered why I have such mixed feelings about the Italian American street *feste* we have these days.

That I am still drawn to them is undeniable. Therein may lie part of the problem. Though I was born in "the Hollow," the Little Italy of Bridgeport, Connecticut, we early began circling outward to other, less fragrant neighborhoods. Going to the *festa* centered around the old neighborhood Church of St. Raphael, therefore, always meant going somewhere else — going back, if not consciously backward.

It was always a kind of psychodrama. There were the sights and the smells that seemed a part of my very insides: colored lights strung from every available tree, pole, or booth; ferris wheels and blaring music and game booths festooned with stuffed animals begging to be won; row after row of food stands swirling their smells of sausage and peppers and *torrone* and *calzoni* with the competing smells of sugar-powdered *zeppoli* and garlic and hair oil; and crowds, dark crowds, boisterous crowds, threatening crowds, cynical joyous familiar slick-haired-teen black-garbed straight-backed crone crowds. But it was all too close, too evocative of something packed away, too recently left.

Even thirty years later, and apparently secure, I was still drawn. I was still susceptible to the hope that going to one of these *feste* — in San Francisco, or New Haven, or San Gennaro in the Village — would somehow do for me what I have always wanted done: settle me in that inner memory of the dreamed-for street where all is dense and flavorful as only one's very own childhood street could be.

It never works out. In San Francisco, the annual Festa Italiana is held in a gigantic barn of an abandoned pier. Booths are set up to mimic a neighborhood; one walks through them as on a street; but there is no sky overhead, and no real stores or houses elbowing in. It is a stage set.

In New Haven it's better. The old Italian quarter, reduced now to a few restaurant blocks of one street, is lined with booths, stages for singers, and sausage stands. But the crush is overwhelming, the vendors surly, the food often contemptuously done, the whole a not very convincing pantomime of what once was.

As for San Gennaro in New York's Greenwich Village, an experience in the sixties there soured it for good. At the height of my repression of my Italian-ness, I went only because my wife and some college friends thought it would be a lark. It was, as long as I was able to pretend I was an outsider come to see the natives play street theater. But then I bought a sausage sandwich, paid with a twenty, and in the crush simply palmed my change and walked. A few steps and I realized the cashier had given me change for a five. I went back, explained her mistake. She said, politely, "Oh sure, just go see the guy in back of the tent, he'll take care of you." I did. Explained I was Italian too. The guy was a three-hundred-pounder, bald, sneering. He took me by the nape of the neck, snarled a few obscenities about college shits trying to rip him off, at which four equally snarling *paesani* came threatening, and threw me into the crowd; if I ever came back I'd be dead. I never did.

IN SPITE OF all this, street festivals, Italian street festivals that is, still attract me like a magnet.

For a while I concluded that either I was just dumb or helplessly in the grip of terminal nostalgia.

Then I read Robert Orsi's brilliant study of the grandaddy of all street festivals, that held in

T A !

Italian Harlem in honor of The Madonna of 115th Street.

It began to make sense. The street *festa* is not simply an occasion to eat sausage or *scungilli* among a crush of similarly hungry tourists. It is, in its origins, religion in the streets. Religion *of* the streets. As Orsi says, the urban agriculturalists who migrated to American cities had learned, in the Italian towns from which they hailed, to "claim the streets by blessing them."

So in Italian Harlem. The procession of the Madonna's surrogate statue (the real one, imported from Italy in the 1890s, and officially crowned in 1904 by order of Pius XIII, remained in the official sanctuary — one of only three such sanctuaries in the New World), carried through every street of Italian Harlem, preceded by bands and official societies, followed by barefoot penitents bleeding and wailing to demonstrate their devotion, did not amount to a simple public display of wealth or clothes or angst, though it did that.

It was meant to *sacralize* the streets.

And they needed sacralizing desperately. The immigrants knew the Harlem streets were filthy, knew they were heartless and crime-filled. But they also knew they needed them, had to live much of their lives in them. And so once a year, they scrubbed the streets as they scrubbed their own homes; and then set up stands to eat in them and buy in them and play in them and walk barefoot behind the most sacred of their icons in them to claim and reclaim them for another year.

What made this possible was la Madonna. Southern Italian to her core — she was a lifelike representation of a young Mediterranean woman holding a child, both of whom have *real hair*, the Madonna's long, thick and to her shoulders, the Christ Child's also long and thick the way many Italian women kept their infant sons' until age four or five — she was more than the virginal Mary known to American Catholics. She was closer to a full-hipped Mediterranean deity.

Penitents came to her not simply for intercession with a male God; they came to *her* to be healed. Vendors sold wax body parts on the streets — limbs, internal organs — to be deposited at the Madonna's feet. The ailing part would then be healed. Some, women all, crawled on hands and knees with tongues dragging along the church pavement, to deposit themselves at her feet. Most importantly, la Madonna too was an immigrant. She too had migrated from Italy to begin life in the New World. She too had begun her life in America in a tenement apartment, her first shrine. And even when she had been allowed to take her rightful place in the church, she too had been relegated, as Italian parishes everywhere had at first been relegated, to the basement.

When Italian Americans journeyed from Brooklyn, the Bronx, Connecticut, New Jersey to the *festa* of la Madonna of Harlem, therefore, they were, in their heart of hearts, coming home. They were recapitulating their experience as migrants, as wanderers. They were asking that the moral and physical and psychological degradation they feared they had suffered upon leaving their villages, or later upon leaving their archetypal, sacralized neighborhood in Harlem, would be healed.

I'M NOT SURE how all this will affect my response the next time I go to an Italian street *festa*. Maybe it will sharpen my taste buds, and the food will taste better. Maybe it will soften my disapproval of the cheap commercialization of the whole thing. Maybe it will increase my longing for the *festa* as it once was.

Or maybe it will reinforce what I already know: That I cannot help going to *feste*, however Disneyfied they may become, because the dream is in my cells. And though it is a dream that moves counter to my father's, in some curious sense it is the same — the dream not so much of streets paved with gold, but streets that are, once a year, alive, peopled, sacred.

— *Lawrence DiStasi*

A SIMPLE GAME OF GOLF

by Elizabeth Mullener

J OE MASELLI IS a small, dapper man, just the other side of trim, with the timing of a vaudevillian and a penchant for telling stories. His prop is a fat brown cigar that he chomps and flicks and waves through the air, although he hasn't lit it up for years. His tough-guy Hollywood Italian accent provides an intriguing foil for his expressive style and the fancy fifty-cent words that ripple through it. He speaks in anecdotes, in a one-thing-leads-to-another kind of way.

"In my neighborhood," says Maselli, who was born sixty-one years ago in Newark, New Jersey, "you were either Italian or you were American. American meant you were anything *but* Italian. You had to be one or the other."

Maselli never had any doubt about which one he was. His parents were Italian immigrants and his first language was Italian, as were his friends and his school and his neighborhood. Even his lunch was Italian, which meant that it was oily and aromatic, as opposed to peanut butter and jelly on Wonder bread, which he found downright exotic.

"I never *suffered* from discrimination as a child," he says, "but it was there. You know how I found out it was there? I found out in the book, *Growing Up* by Russell Baker.

"I went to school with Russell Baker and I was the Joe in that book. We were the ones who taught him how to fight. And we were the ones who showed him how to kiss a girl. He said it tasted like chewing gum.

"Well, he hipped me up in that book to the fact that his mother didn't like him associating with us. His

The revitalization of urban centers never follows a single pattern. In New Orleans it was the creation of a cultural monument that succeeded in carving out, artificially or not, an open, festal space. Like most other things Italian American in New Orleans, the Piazza d'Italia got much of its energy from Joe Maselli. Future plans include an archive to preserve the contribution of such Italian Americans as jazz pioneer Nick LaRocca.

mother told him not to fool around with Italians. I had never realized that."

Long before he saw the handwriting on the wall, Joe Maselli left Newark under the auspices of the U.S. Army and got himself stationed at Camp Plauche outside New Orleans.

"I thought I had died and went to heaven," he says. "I couldn't believe how nice people were here. In my part of the world, you can't ask anybody about anything. They always think you're trying to get a bite on them." Shortly after he hit town, Maselli met Antoinette Cammarata at a USO club on Canal and Carondelet. When he was discharged from the Army, he married her and they soon started a family. Maselli worked full-time as a bookkeeper and also attended Tulane on the GI bill. When he graduated — in a record three and a half years as a night student — he launched the City Wholesale Liquor Company and went into business for himself.

Making money came easy to him, and for years he worked hard, played golf and lived the good life.

Maselli says the incident that galvanized him and launched him as an Italian activist was when he applied for membership in the Metairie Country Club in 1967.

"That's when I found out the whole world isn't peaches and ice cream and apple pie," he says. "I had played golf there for maybe ten, twelve years as a guest. I had been there hundreds of times — I'd play tournaments, go to parties, dances. And these two guys, my friends, they kept badgering me, when am I going to become a member? So finally I said OK, and I put my application in. I thought it was just a formality."

Maselli says he waited several weeks to hear about his membership and was finally advised by his two buddies to withdraw his application. Maselli took that to mean that he was going to be blackballed and he concluded it was because he was Italian.

"I didn't like that," he says, shaking his head slowly and lashing his cigar through the air with a swagger. "It threw cold water on me. *Ice water.* That's when the fuse was lit in me."

Today, Maselli treasures the experience. He considers it a turning point in his life. And he thinks it's important to keep the memory of it alive.

Aside from his real-estate interests and his duties as owner of a wholesale liquor company, Joe Maselli today is the president, founder and guiding spirit of the American-Italian Renaissance Foundation, a museum and research library that documents the history of the Italian community in New Orleans. He has also founded an Italian American newsletter. He was a leading force in the establishment of the Piazza d'Italia — the centerpiece of a two-square-block downtown revitalization project. He was the proprietor of the Italian Village at the World's Fair. He got the Renaissance Foundation off the ground. And at least once a year, he flies off on the Concorde for a visit to Italy.

He has also made it his business to learn. With the passion of a scholar and the enthusiasm of a convert, Maselli has immersed himself in the history of Italians in the South. When asked for the ten most important Italians in New Orleans' history, he rattles off a list of sixteen.

A self-appointed watchdog, Maselli also keeps tabs on the portrayal of Italians in the popular culture. He reads novels, watches television, goes to movies. And he winces when Italians are portrayed only as Mafia members. He thinks *The Godfather* set the Italian movement back by years.

"I'll be the first to admit that there are Italians who are criminals," he says. "What I don't like is when the bad guy is *always* Italian."

If Joe Maselli sounds like a zealot, he isn't. He knows when to stop. And he knows how to have a good time. Which he also thinks is Italian.

"I used to resent that a little — to be considered fun-loving. Because I didn't want to always be shown doing the tarantella or eating a big pizza.

"But now I have to think that we're good at it. I've paid my dues as far as working. I knew nobody was going to leave me any money.

"My children aren't waiting around for me to kick the bucket either. In fact, they tell me to spend my money. Well, I'm trying!" he says, elevating his voice an octave or two. "I don't know if I'm going to live long enough. But if I do, I'll spend it all." ⁊

Nick LaRocca and the Original Dixieland Jazz Band

A FEW YEARS BEFORE his death on February 22, 1961, Nick LaRocca, the mainspring leader and cornetist of the Original Dixieland Jazz Band, was my host at his home in New Orleans. For two days we discussed the formation, history and success of the band that had revolutionized the world of popular music.

Nick LaRocca was born in New Orleans on April 11, 1889, the son of an Italian immigrant shoemaker, who wanted his youngest boy to be a doctor. Though Girolamo LaRocca was himself a good amateur cornet player, he steadfastly refused to allow Nick to learn music (smashing the first two cornets he acquired). But the boy persisted in teaching himself.

After his father's death in 1904, young Nick went to work as an electrician in the Opera House, where he heard all the great performances by the elite of the opera world. He also loved to watch the parades by the marching bands that played for prizefights, circuses and funerals.

He noticed the interplay of the voices on the opera stage, and that of the horns, brasses and reeds of the marching bands. He invented little tunes of his own, based sometimes on existing harmonic structures, and after meeting trombonist Edwin Bransford

Edwards in 1912, he began to think in terms of having a band of his own.

It was while LaRocca, with Edwards, was working for "Papa" Jack Laine that a Chicago nightclub owner heard him and invited him to form a band and bring it to Chicago as a novelty.

For three months, starting at Schiller's Café on March 3, 1916, LaRocca's "jass" band set Chicago on fire with their new music. By October, with Tony Sbarbaro on drums and Larry Shields on clarinet, the band took its real shape. Shields on clarinet, particularly, fitted LaRocca's conception of what he wanted his band to do.

"I cut the cloth," said LaRocca later, "Shields put the lace on it, and Edwards sewed it up."

Most of us have no recollection of a world without jazz of some kind. It is thus difficult to imagine the colossal impact that an improvising quintet of cornet, trombone, clarinet, piano and drums made on a public completely unaware of what was coming. But into an atmosphere of small string orchestras,

playing arrangements of the outstanding tunes of musical comedies and love-lorn ballads, the blazing heat of jazz burst like a bomb.

The late Al Jolson, on tour in Chicago, heard the band one night and was spellbound. He gave them an introduction to the management at Resienweber's on Columbus Circle, New York, where they opened on January 26, 1917.

Within a week they had made their first records (two popular songs, for Columbia) and a month later, with considerably greater success musically, they made two of Nick's numbers for Victor.

No other band has ever quite managed to sound as they did. As James H. S. Moynahan said in an article in 1937, "It is my contention — and I am not wanting as high authorities as the late Bix Beiderbecke to concur with me in this — that the Original Dixieland Jazz Band was the greatest jazz band of all time."

— *Brian Rust*

THE BOHEMIAN SPIRIT

by Umberto Tosi

Italian neighborhoods, the so-called Latin quarters, have often been attractive to artists drawn, no doubt, by the vibrant street life, tolerance for diversity, and cheap rents. San Francisco's North Beach has gone through several phases of this symbiosis, none richer than the one following World War II. If it had a "squire" in this "beat" phase, Enrico Banducci deserves the title. Of its poets, none has had a more enduring connection than Philip Lamantia.

IN THE FALL of 1945, San Francisco's North Beach seemed the same as it had been for decades — a vital center of Italian settlement. Yet changes were blowing in the velvety autumn-evening breeze. Soon the GI Bill and postwar prosperity would enable many Italians to migrate to the suburbs. The McCarren Act would slap a Nordic bias on immigration and severely limit new arrivals from Italy. Though North Beach would retain its Italian character for some time to come, it would soon become something more — a catalyst of counter-cultural revolution.

Two unlikely-looking prophets of this coming transformation — a violin student from Bakersfield named Enrico Banducci and a radical sculptor named Benny Bufano — would walk into the Half Moon Café most evenings that fall. The café offered one of the best family-style meals in town for under three dollars.

"Ah! My distinguished artists, the violinist and the sculptor," the matronly proprietress would greet them, "How many meals tonight, one or two?"

Enrico would grin sheepishly and hold up one finger, indicating that the pair had managed to scrape up the price of only one meal between them. But as always there would be plenty to go round. Typically, a three-dollar dinner consisted of all-you-can-eat bowls of minestrone, pasta, risotto, or polenta, salad, platters of veal, squid, broccoli braised in olive oil, pastry — and the duo would get a split of Chianti on the house. It was that kind of place.

In fact, in those days, all of North Beach was that kind of place — brimming with Italianate warmth, love of the arts and artists, conversation, and nurturance of individual expression. As such it soon became Mecca for a new kind of immigrant — not from overseas, but from within the country — moving against the flight to the suburbs, rebelling against postwar materialism and acutely aware of being the first generation to live under the shadow of the mushroom cloud.

In 1949, seeking a hangout these new migrants could truly call their own, Ed ("Big Daddy") Nord opened the *hungry i* ("i" for "id" — Freud was chic then) in a basement at Broadway and Kearny. A marble staircase descended into what had once been a dining room. Banducci was a regular, occasionally serenading fellow bohemians with a violin solo. It was clear to him by then, however, that he was not destined to be another Paganini.

He had talents in other areas. Like his Tuscan ancestors, Banducci had both feet firmly planted on the ground when it came to business. Nord, on the other hand, proved better at habituating than at managing a bistro.

It wasn't long before Banducci borrowed and begged eight hundred dollars and bought the foundering "i" from Nord. He put another eight thousand dollars into the place to cover Nord's debts and with the help of bartender-waiter Walter Wong, soon began to make a go of it.

Enrico proved vastly more talented than Nord at being an impresario. He began making his mark with daring bills of entertainment, featuring esoteric and exotic performers from classical pianists, to jazz-blues experimenters, to outraged and outrageous comics holding forth in a bare-bones setting.

"It was all very Jean-Paul Sartre," says Banducci.

The press, including columnist Herb Caen — who coined the term *beatnik* — began frequenting the place. Banducci, quick to give promising unknowns a tryout, soon

SPIDERS

THERE WAS NO mistaking Philip Lamantia in the downstairs room of North Beach's City Lights Bookstore. Surrounded by floor-to-ceiling bookshelves, his arms loaded with books, his almost courtly voice suggesting we go to the Caffè Roma, he seemed as natural to this place as the birds he watches are to theirs. This is not only because Lamantia was one of the original poets who made North Beach the center of an artistic renaissance in the l940s and 1950s. It's also because his family were among the first settlers in the Italian colony established in North Beach around 1900.

They had come — his father and grandmother — from Palermo. "I was there once for a few hours . . . on my way to Greece . . . and it was spectacular . . . and I remembered that quote from Goethe . . . the most amazing Bay he'd ever seen . . . and it was."

After the 1906 earthquake leveled North Beach, the family moved to what seemed the safer environs of the Excelsior District. It was there that Donna Mattea Lamantia, Philip's grandmother, became a seminal influence on his early life.

She was a jovial, powerful woman who essentially ruled the household. "Here was a woman who danced the tarantella and won a prize at one of these . . . they held them in the woods, great Italian picnics. And she won, and she was about seventy then!"

Donna Mattea's power extended

▲ **Philip Lamantia: in "the Marco Polo zone"**

outside the family as well. "She was a noted storyteller. I remember a group of twenty or so women would come to our house . . . and she held them spellbound. And her *conti,* I later found out, were not just the famous tales of Orlando, but also tales she had heard from *her* mother about . . . hanging Death up . . . outwitting Death, you see. And I used to love to sit on her lap, to listen to this, every afternoon while she was cooking."

Mornings she tended her garden, "and if one were awake, you could see she would be speaking to the flowers and . . . the garden was luxuriant." To cap it off, she was "an aficionado snuffer . . . I still have the little silver case, lovely thing she had . . . so I picked up, well, the background habit by, um, osmosis . . ." I understand the import of his reference later: A lifetime of smoking has eventuated in mouth cancer and its theater of cruel cures — surgery, cobalt treatments.

A SNUFF-TAKING, STORY-TELLING Sicilian grandmother who spoke with her plants. With this endowment it is perhaps not as astonishing to hear that at the age of

sixteen, Philip Lamantia was published in the surrealist journal *View,* hailed as "a voice that rises once in a hundred years," and hanging out in New York with the legendary exiles of surrealist France, André Breton, Yves Tanguy and Max Ernst.

Still, he says, it was finally a bit disappointing — the constant infighting that went on among these supreme egos — and not a little overwhelming for even as "old a soul" as Lamantia must have been. He returned to San Francisco, finished high school in a small academy — "a nest of unstable youths," Philip laughs — and looked for bohemia nearer home.

It was not long in coming. Kenneth Rexroth was sponsoring poetry readings, Dizzy Gillespie and others were pushing jazz into bebop in the Fillmore District clubs, and in Berkeley George Liete was publishing Lamantia, Henry Miller and Anaïs Nin in his *Circle Magazine.*

"Suddenly," says Philip, "droves of people from all over the country were arriving in North Beach" — conscientious objectors, anarchists, poet-orientalist-surrealist-magic-jazzed-out-alchemy heads. "We did a poetry reading at the museum in 1946. Someone came up and asked if I knew where to get some marijuana." The rest, as they say, is history.

WE GATHER OUR things, our spent cappuccino cups by now stuck to the tiny round table. Outside, the Sunday crush of tourists is unabated. In the dark, Lamantia's head, leonine in the light, seems more fragile. So does he. "I don't know if we got anything — we both like to talk so much. Maybe we can do it again," he says. I say sure.

A slightly awkward "ciao," and he heads down Columbus Avenue.

His back fading into the North Beach evening makes me want to call out to him.

I do not.

— *Lawrence DiStasi*

earned a reputation for discovering far-out talent.

Mort Sahl was only one of a constellation of bright new and often controversial performers to break into the limelight at the *hungry i.* Among others who debuted or got an early boost there were Barbra Streisand, Bill Cosby, Bob Newhart, Woody Allen, Richard Pryor, Dick Gregory, Mike Nichols and Elaine May, Flip Wilson, the Kingston Trio, and the Limelighters.

The club seated only 265 customers, but a run there was a ticket to stardom. The place made national

TV and the cover of *Time.*

Banducci was no angel. He could be difficult at times. A large, flamboyant, mustachioed man in his beret — another trademark — he would argue politics, haggle with suppliers, fight with his wife. He and Sahl had a number of running feuds, which they later patched up. "He had two sides, and one was always counting the money," said Sahl bitterly at one point.

IN 1958, ENRICO BANDUCCI blazed a new trail — opening his sidewalk café, the first in San Francisco. For the

next thirty years, *Enrico's* was the favored spot of artists, celebrities, media-makers, and gawkers, who could sit in the heated front patio, sip cappuccino or dine on fettuccine while watching the parade of the straight and the strange visiting Broadway's carnival mixture of theaters, jazz clubs, topless bars, porn shops and restaurants lit by the garish kaleidoscope of Vegas-style signs.

Every day for those thirty years, Enrico Banducci could be found, beret in place, holding court at his table just inside the door, talking with politicians, publicists, or poets. Poet Richard Brautigan was a regular, as was North Beach's quintessential boulevardier, Henri Lenoir. Mayors stopped by, as did cops, lawyers, and topless dancers on their breaks.

The "Squire of North Beach," as Banducci came to be called, held forth on food, music, the business of show business, and, increasingly, the deteriorating scene closing in on him. As he told an interviewer once: "We are an oasis in a desert of dreck."

When Francis Coppola, new owner of the nearby Flatiron Building, became a regular in the 1970s, the topic took on new urgency. Coppola was flush with millions from his *Godfather* films. So he and Banducci mounted a plan to buy up most of the buildings around Broadway and Columbus, close the strip joints, and restore much of North Beach's vintage Italian character. They would transform Broadway into a stylish, creative multiarts theater row. Coppola, however, eventually poured most of his cash into his enormously costly production of *Apocalypse Now*. The plan to revive North Beach never came to fruition.

IN 1988, MOUNTING losses finally forced Enrico Banducci to sell his landmark café. He didn't see an end to North Beach, though — just continued transformation.

"North Beach is going through big changes once again," he said just after closing his doors. "Most of this is good. We have all races and nationalities now and they get along very well. There was always a mixture here and there always will be. Some Italians will stay. It's like the rest of America. It's going through some growing pains. Sure, there are some old Italians who complain about the Chinese moving in, but what the hell do they have to complain about anyway? *We* all did all right, didn't we?" ❧

THE SOURCE BOOK

1. CITIES ON THE HILL

The Abbot of Arcosanti (6-7) by J. Tevere McFadyen first appeared in Horizon Magazine, reprinted with permission of Horizon Publishers, Inc., March 1980. Ivan Pintar's Soleri portrait and Tomiaki Tamura's model reprinted courtesy of the Cosanti Foundation. **Minnesota Morning Ode** (8-9) by Diane di Prima first appeared in *Selected Poems: 1956-1975*, published by North Atlantic Press, copyright © 1976 by Diane di Prima. Soleri drawings reprinted courtesy of M.I.T. Press and the Cosanti Foundation. **Earthly Paradise** (10) by Eduardo Galeano excerpted from *Memory of Fire:Genesis*, translation by Cedric Belfrage, translation copyright © 1985 by Cedric Belfrage, reprinted by permission of Pantheon Books, a Division of Random House, Inc. Woodblock illustrations reprinted from the public domain. **Fasanella Remembers Marcantonio** (11-12) by Patrick Watson excerpted from *Fasanella's City*, by Ralph Fasanella and Patrick Watson, text copyright © 1973 by Patrick Watson, reprinted by permission of Alfred A. Knopf, Inc. The Marcantonio photographs reprinted courtesy of the New York Historical Society. **Mazzei in America** (13) by Charles Guzzetta excerpted from "Jefferson & Mazzei," in the Italian Journal, reprinted courtesy of the Italian Academy Foundation, Inc. Woodcut reprinted from the public domain. **Andrea Sbarbaro's Vision** (14) by Lawrence DiStasi printed courtesy of the author. The Sbarbaro portrait reprinted courtesy of Alessandro Baccari. **Giannini** (15-16) by Matthew Josephson excerpted from "Big Bull of West," reprinted from the Saturday Evening Post © 1947, the Curtis Publishing Co. The Giannini portrait reprinted courtesy of the Bank of America. **The End of the Line** (17-20) by Rob Haeseler excerpted from "An Old Man Waits, and Says Little of His Towers," reprinted courtesy of the Contra Costa Times, Walnut Creek, CA. The Rodia and Watts Towers photographs reprinted courtesy of the Special Collections Department, University of California Los Angeles. **The Human Mole** (21) by Charles Hillinger excerpted from "Human Mole's Maze," copyright © 1975 Los Angeles Times, reprinted by permission. The Forestiere photo reprinted courtesy of the Fresno Bee.

2. CORNUCOPIA

Life On A Mushroom Farm (24-25) by Tullio Francesco DeSantis printed courtesy of the author. The DeSantis photograph reprinted courtesy of Tullio Francesco DeSantis. **The Summer Kitchen** (26) by Sandra Gilbert, copyright © 1988 by Sandra Gilbert, reprinted courtesy of the author. **A Visit To Tontitown** (27-28) by John L. Mathews excerpted from "Tontitown," reprinted from the public domain. The Bandini photograph reprinted courtesy of the Washington County Historical Society. **Secchi DeCasale and The Italians of Vineland** (29) by Lawrence DiStasi printed courtesy of the author. Woodcut from the public domain. **Rooted in the Earth** (30-31) by Angelo Pellegrini excerpted from *The Unprejudiced Palate*, copyright © 1984 by Angelo Pellegrini, published by North Point Press and reprinted by permission. The Nick Gunderson photograph of Pellegrini reprinted courtesy of North Point Press. **The Kublai Khan of Kern County** (32-33) excerpted from "Joseph DiGiorgio," copyright © 1946 Time Inc., reprinted courtesy of Fortune, Inc. The DiGiorgio photograph reprinted courtesy of the Kern County Museum. **The Father of Farmer's Market** (34) by Dwight Chapin excerpted from "Father of Farmer's Market," © 1989 The San Francisco Examiner, reprinted with permission. The Brucato photograph reprinted courtesy of Alessandro Baccari & Associates. **The Fish King** (35-36) by Pauline Jacobson excerpted from "How I Began Life," reprinted from the public domain. The Ken Rinciari illustration reprinted courtesy of the artist. The accompanying photograph reprinted courtesy of Kiki Paladini. **Frank Pomilia: Still Hooked On Fishing** (37) by Howard Taylor, Jr. excerpted from "Still Hooked on Fishing," © 1989 The San Francisco Examiner, reprinted with permission. The Ken Rinciari illustration reprinted courtesy of the artist.

3. WORKERS & ANARCHISTS

Carlo Tresca, Troublemaker (40-42) by Max Eastman excerpted from "Troublemaker," reprinted by permission, © 1934, 1962 Max Eastman, originally in The New Yorker. The Tresca photograph reprinted courtesy of UPI/Bettman Newsphotos. **The King of Little Italy** (43) by Lawrence DiStasi printed courtesy of the author. The Ken Rinciari illustration reprinted courtesy of the artist. **English Lessons** (44-45) by Pascal D'Angelo excerpted from *Son of Italy* by Pascal D'Angelo, reprinted from the public domain. The illustration is by Gian Banchero, reprinted courtesy of the artist. **The Light of**

Insurrection (46-47) by Bartolomeo Vanzetti excerpted from *The Letters of Sacco and Vanzetti*, edited by Maron D. Frankfurter and Gardner Jackson, reprinted from the public domain. The Vanzetti photograph reprinted courtesy of the New York Daily News. **Portrait of A Boardinghouse Woman** (48-49) by Angelo Pellegrini excerpted from *Americans by Choice*, copyright © 1956 by Angelo Pellegrini, renewed 1984, reprinted with permission of MacMillan. The Rosa Mondavi photograph reprinted courtesy of C. Mondavi & Sons, St. Helena, CA. The Boarding House illustration is by Lourdes Livingston, reprinted courtesy of the artist. **Angela Bambace of the ILGWU** (50) by Laura Segretti printed courtesy of the author. The Bambace Silhouette reprinted courtesy Labor-Management Documentation Center, Cornell University. **The Unpredictable Petrillo** (51-52) by Jack Gould first appeared in The New York Times Magazine, copyright © 1947 by The New York Times Company, excerpt reprinted by permission of The New York Times Company. The accompanying original illustrations courtesy Visual Strategies. **The Real Antonini** (53) by Arturo Giovannitti excerpted from "About the Author," the introduction to *Dynamic Democracy* by Luigi Antonini, reprinted from the public domain. The Antonini photograph courtesy Labor-Management Documentation Center, Cornell University.

4. THE PEOPLE'S EYE

The Color of Humanity (56-58) by Patrick Watson excerpted from *Fasanella's City* by Ralph Fasanella and Patrick Watson, text copyright © 1973 by Patrick Watson, reprinted by permission of Alfred A. Knopf, Inc. The Fasanella painting reproduced courtesy of Ralph Fasanella. **The Return of Hercules** (59-60) by Charles Gaines excerpted from *Yours in Perfect Manhood: Charles Atlas*, reprinted from the public domain. The Atlas photograph courtesy of Charles Roman. **A Conan Grows in Brooklyn** (61-62) by Lawrence DiStasi printed courtesy of the author. The Frazetta drawing reprinted courtesy of Frank Frazetta. For full catalog of Frazetta art, send $3.50 to Frank Frazetta, PO Box 919, Marshalls Creek, PA 18335. **Eulogy for Jimmy Grucci** (63) excerpted from *Fireworks* by George Plimpton, copyright © 1981 by George Plimpton, used by permission of Doubleday, a division of Bantam, Doubleday, Dell Publishing Group. The Grucci photograph reprinted courtesy of the Grucci family. **Bufano's Peace** (64-65) by Randolph Falk excerpted from *Bufano* by Randolph Falk, Celestial Arts:1975, reprinted courtesy of Randolph Falk, © 1975. The Bufano photograph also reprinted courtesy of Randolph Falk. **A Lost Art** (66) by Rick Dower excerpted from "A Lifetime of Stone Memorials," reprinted from the public domain. The accompanying artwork courtesy of Visual Strategies. **Manteo's Marionettes** (67-68) by Mark Singer excerpted from "Opera dei Pupi," reprinted by permission, © 1979 The New Yorker Magazine, Inc. The Marionette photograph courtesy of the Manteo family. **Romano Gabriel's Wooden Garden** (69) by Patricia Elsen excerpted from "Where Will Gabriel's Garden Go?" and reprinted courtesy of Patricia Morgan Elsen, © 1979. The Gabriel photograph courtesy of Dolores Vellutini.

5. AN EMPIRE OF FOOD

The Face That Made Spaghetti Famous (72-73) by Lawrence DiStasi printed courtesy of the author. The Boiardi photograph courtesy of American Home Foods. **Balducci's Theater of Food** (74) by Lawrence DiStasi printed courtesy of the author. **The Real Mr. Peanut** (75-76) by Dominick Lamonica excerpted from "Obici: America's Peanut King," reprinted from the public domain. The Mr. Peanut logo and trademark reprinted courtesy of Planters LifeSavers Company. **A House Made of Chocolate** (77) by Robert O'Brien excerpted from "The Story of Domenico Ghirardelli," reprinted from the public domain. The Ghirardelli photo courtesy of the Ghirardelli Chocolate Company. **The Transfiguration of Benno Blimpie** (78-79) by Albert Innaurato excerpted from *The Transfiguration of Benno Blimpie*, © 1977 by Albert Innaurato, reprinted by permission of the author. The Ken Rinciari illustration reprinted courtesy of the artist. **Little Big Man** (80-81) by Ellen Wojahn excerpted from "Little Big Man," reprinted with permission, Inc. magazine, June 1986, copyright © 1986 by Godlhirsh Groups, Inc., 38 Commerical Wharf, Boston, MA 02110. The Paulucci photograph courtesy of Michael Douglas. **An Aria, A Game of Cards, and an Expresso** (82) by Anthony Telesino printed courtesy of the author. Illustration courtesy of Visual Strategies. **Gallo Crushes the Competition** (83-84) by Jaclyn Fierman excerpted from "How Gallo Crushes Competition," reprinted by permission of Fortune

6. THE MUSICAL THEATER

7. DA VINCI'S CHILDREN

8. SAINTS

9. SINNERS

10. THE ELECTRONIC PUPPET SHOW